Regional
Conflict Management

Regional Conflict Management

Edited by
Paul F. Diehl and Joseph Lepgold

ROWMAN & LITTLEFIELD PUBLISHERS, INC.
Lanham • Boulder • New York • Oxford

50773477

ROWMAN & LITTLEFIELD PUBLISHERS, INC.

Published in the United States of America
by Rowman & Littlefield Publishers, Inc.
A Member of the Rowman & Littlefield Publishing Group
4501 Forbes Blvd., Suite 200, Lanham, Maryland 20706
www.rowmanlittlefield.com

PO Box 317, Oxford, OX2 9RU, UK

British Library Cataloguing in Publication Information Available

Library of Congress Cataloging-in-Publication Data

Regional conflict management / edited by Paul F. Diehl and Joseph
Lepgold
    p. cm.
Includes bibliographical references and index.
    ISBN 0-7425-1901-5 (cloth : alk. paper)—ISBN 0-7425-1902-3 (pbk. :
alk. paper)
  1. Regionalism. 2. Conflict management. 3. Security, International.
I. Diehl, Paul F. (Paul Francis) II. Lepgold, Joseph.
   JZ5330 .R437 2003
   327.1'7—dc21

                                       2002151737

Printed in the United States of America

∞™ The paper used in this publication meets the minimum requirements of
American National Standard for Information Sciences—Permanence of Paper
for Printed Library Materials, ANSI/NISO Z39.48-1992.

To Joe Lepgold (1954–2001),
scholar, collaborator, and friend.

We only wish that you
had lived to see the final product.

Contents

Tables and Figures

TABLES

FIGURES

Acknowledgments

This volume is the product of a multiyear project dedicated to understanding and evaluating regional conflict management efforts. Several of the ideas for this project and preliminary drafts of the some of the chapters were first presented at an annual meeting of the American Political Science Association. We would like to thank William Durch, who acted as discussant on that panel, for his insights and the direction that he gave the project. A full set of papers was presented at the "Workshop on Regional Conflict Management" at the University of Illinois. This workshop was made possible by the generous support of the Mackie Trust of the Department of Political Science at University of Illinois. Workshop support and arrangements were provided by the Program in Arms Control, Disarmament, and International Security (ACDIS) at the University of Illinois. We owe special gratitude to Sheila Roberts and Srini Sitaraman for their dedicated work in making the conference a success. A number of people served as discussants at the workshop and we are grateful to them for their comments: Badredine Arfi, Michael Greig, Clifford Singer, Srini Sitaraman, Robert Pahre, Change Su, and Dexter Boniface.

The unexpected and tragic death of one of the project directors, Joseph Lepgold, created some roadblocks for our completion. Delinda Swanson, Becky Osgood, and Matt Rosenstein came to the rescue and were responsible for helping put the final manuscript in order.

Acronyms

ACDIS	Program in Arms Control, Disarmament, and International Security
ACRI	African Crisis Response Initiative
ACRS	Arms Control Regional Security
AIDS	acquired immunodeficiency syndrome
AL	Arab League
ANZUS	Australia–New Zealand–U.S. Pact
APEC	Asian-Pacific Economic Cooperation
ARF	ASEAN Regional Forum
ASEAN	Association of Southeast Asian Nations
ASEM	Asia-Europe Meeting
ASPAC	Asia and Pacific Council
AU	African Union
BJP	Bharatiya Janata Party
CBM	confidence-building measure
CBW	chemical biological weapon
CCM	collective conflict management
CEEAC	Economic Community of Central African States
CFC	Combined Forces Command
CIA	Central Intelligence Agency
CICAD	Inter-American Drug Abuse Control Commission
CiO	Chairman-in-Office
CIS	Commonwealth of Independent States
CJTF	Combined Joint Task Forces
CMC	Conflict Management Center
CMCA	Commission for Mediation, Arbitration, and Conciliation
CPC	Conflict Prevention Centre
CSBM	confidence- and security-building measure

CSCAP	Council for Security Cooperation in the Asia-Pacific
CSCE	Commission on Security and Cooperation in Europe
CSSDCA	Conference on Security, Stability, Development, and Cooperation in Africa
CTBT	Comprehensive Test Ban Treaty
DOP	Declaration of Principles
DPRK	Democratic People's Republic of Korea
EAC	East African Community
EAEC	East Asian Economic Caucus
ECHO	European Community Humanitarian Office
ECMM	European Community Monitor Mission
ECOMOG	ECOWAS Cease-Fire Monitoring Group
ECOWAS	Economic Community of West African States
EPLF	Eritrean People's Liberation Front
EPRDF	Ethiopian People's Revolutionary Democratic Force
EU	European Union
FARC	*Fuerzas Armada Revolucionarias de Colombia,* or the Revolutionary Armed Forces of Colombia
FLS	Front Line States
FPDA	Five Power Defense Arrangement
FSC	Forum for Security Cooperation
FSU	former Soviet Union
FTAA	Free Trade Area of the Americas
GCC	Gulf Cooperation Council
GDP	gross domestic product
GUNT	Transitional Government of National Unity
HCNM	High Commissioner on National Minorities
IADB	Inter-American Development Bank
IAEA	International Atomic Energy Agency
ICJ	International Court of Justice
IDB	Inter-American Development Bank
IFOR	implementation force
IGAD	Inter-Governmental Agency on Development
IGO	intergovernmental organization
IMF	International Monetary Fund
IMS	integrated military structure
ISI	import-substitution industrialization
JVP	Janatha Vimukthi Peramuna
KEDO	Korea Energy Development Organization
LOC	Line of Control
MC	Military Committee
ME	Middle East
MINUGUA	United Nations Verification Mission in Guatemala
MIPONUH	Civilian Police Mission

MITI	Ministry of International Trade and Industry
MONUC	UN Organization Mission in the Democratic Republic of the Congo
MSD	multilateral security dialogue
MTCR	Missile Technology Control Regime
NAFTA	North American Free Trade Agreement
NATO	North Atlantic Treaty Organization
NEACD	Northeast Asia Cooperation Dialogue
NGO	nongovernmental organization
NIC	National Intelligence Council
NMOG	Neutral Military Observer Group
NPT	Non-Proliferation Treaty
OAS	Organization of American States
OAU	Organization of African Unity
ODIHR	Office of Democratic Institutions and Human Rights
OECS	Organization of East Caribbean States
OMIB	Burundi Observer Mission
OMIC	Comores Observer Mission
ONUC	United Nations Operation in the Congo
ONUCA	United Nations Observer Group
ONUSAL	United Nations Observer Mission in El Salvador
OSCE	Organization for Security and Cooperation in Europe
PFP	Partnership for Peace
PKK	Kurdish Workers' Party
PLO	Palestine Liberation Organization
PMC	postministerial conference
PML	Pakistan Muslim League
PNA	Palestinian National Authority
PPP	Pakistan People's Party
PPP	Purchasing Power Parity
PRIO	Peace Research Institute Oslo
PSC	Political and Security Committee
RCD	Rally for a Democratic Congo
RCMO	regional conflict management organization
RENAMO	Mozambican National Resistance
RIMPAC	Rim of the Pacific
ROK	Republic of Korea
RSS	Rashtriya Swayamsevak Sangh
RUF	Revolutionary United Front
SAARC	South Asian Association for Regional Cooperation
SADC	Southern African Development Community
SADCC	Southern African Development Coordinating Conference
SAPTA	South Asian Preferential Tariff Agreement
SEATO	Southeast Asian Treaty Organization
SFOR	stabilization force

SLFP	Sri Lanka Freedom Party
SOFA	Status of Forces Agreement
SOM	senior officials meeting
SRSG	special representative of the secretary-general
SWAPO	South West African Peoples Organization
TCOG	trilateral coordination and oversight group
TEU	Treaty on European Union
UAE	United Arab Emirates
ULIMO	United Liberian Movement
UMA	Arab Magrib Union
UN	United Nations
UNOMSIL	UN Observer Mission in Sierra Leone
UNHCR	United Nations High Commissioner for Refugees
UNITA	National Union for the Total Independence of Angola
UNMEE	UN Mission in Ethiopia and Eritrea
UNP	United National Party
USFK	U.S. Forces–Korea
WEU	Western European Union
WMD	weapons of mass destruction
WTO	World Trade Organization

Introduction

PAUL F. DIEHL

When U.S. President George Bush proclaimed a "new world order" governed by the rule of law in 1990, there was an expectation that many of the security problems of the past forty years would dissipate and those that persisted could be handled by collective global efforts. There were surely dissenters to this position[1] but the general assumption was that violent conflict would decline in the world and that global institutions, especially the United Nations (UN), would play increasingly prominent roles. The outbreak of various wars in the Balkans and Africa quickly dispelled the first notion.[2] The shift away from global efforts at conflict management and resolution to more regionally centered efforts has been more gradual and stems from a number of different influences.

Kolodziej argues that most of the security problems confronting the contemporary world will be found and addressed at the regional level.[3] There are a number of reasons for a de-emphasis on the global level. Most obvious is the end of the Cold War. The Cold War period defined much regional conflict in terms of superpower interests. In individual spheres of influences or "shatterbelt" regions of competition, the superpowers often assumed primary roles in regional conflicts. Within their respective spheres of influence, the United States and the Soviet Union were able to suppress most violent conflict, either through direct military intervention or at least the threat of it. To the extent that regional organizations and efforts existed, they were largely subordinate to the interests and directions of the leading states. Beyond the Western Hemisphere and Eastern Europe, in areas of competition, the superpowers were as frequently involved in exacerbating conflict as they were in mitigating it. Most notably in Africa and the Middle East, the superpowers supplied arms and political support to client groups and states. When the superpowers did "cooperate"[4] to manage conflict, it was frequently to prevent escalation of those conflicts that might have drawn themselves into the fray. Rare were the instances in which the two leading states sought to resolve a conflict fully with joint action. Even during the Cold War there were areas outside the interests of either leading state, and in those instances regional conflicts were left to fester. Only occasionally would the UN Security Council supply a bandage, in the form of a peacekeeping operation, to those conflicts. The end of the Cold War created a vacuum in some regions, with new opportunities for regional efforts to fill the gaps.

The end of the Cold War also led to a change in the international security environment and the interests of the leading states. With a few exceptions, such as the Iraqi invasion of Kuwait or internal conflicts in Afghanistan after the 11 September terrorist attack, regional conflicts no longer directly affected the economic and security interests of Western states. Furthermore, domestic political support in those same states for intervention into regional conflicts has also declined (and strategic doctrines have been adjusted accordingly).[5] The net effect is that the leading states in the world no longer desire to play as great a role in such conflicts, and actively seek alternatives to unilateral action.

The movement toward regional conflict management, however, is not solely a function of the Cold War's demise. Some of the recent regional efforts follow on the heels of failed global efforts, especially by the UN. In the early 1990s, there was optimism that the United Nations would play a major role in addressing threats to international peace and security. These hopes were only enhanced by the global cooperation in redressing Iraq's invasion of Kuwait. Yet the limits of a new world order were quickly apparent as failed peacekeeping in Somalia, genocide in Rwanda, and war in Bosnia exposed flaws in global efforts. As optimism faded by the middle of that decade, regional alternatives to UN sponsored efforts began to emerge.

The search for alternatives to UN efforts paralleled the development of regional institutions poised to adopt conflict management roles. Some organizations, such as the European Union (EU) and the Economic Community of West African States (ECOWAS) had been in existence for a number of years, but had primarily economic missions. These institutions and others have adapted to assume roles in the security realm[6]—for example, the EU's efforts at mediation in the Bosnian conflict and ECOWAS's peacekeeping operation in Liberia. Other organizations, such as the Organization of American States (OAS), exhibited renewed vigor to deal with regional security issues.

This collection is one of the first to address the implications and the efficacy of regional conflict management in the new world order. It is tempting to paint regional conflict management in broad terms. Certainly one of our goals is to develop generalizations that transcend regions and offer insights on international security as a whole in the coming decades. At the same time, we are sobered by the diversity in conflict management across different geographic areas and along several dimensions. As will be evident by the chapters that follow, the kinds of security threats faced by actors in different regions of the world may be dramatically different. Drug cartels and terrorism rampant in one region may be completely absent in another. Furthermore, the incentives for conflict management and the available structural mechanisms for action may also vary widely. Kolodziej notes that there may be multiple kinds of regional security complexes, with dramatic variations across regions.[7] Thus, we need to strike a balance between generalizations, to the extent that they are possible, broadly applicable across different geographic regions on the one hand and region specific conclusions on the other.

We begin with a focus on the general, and the opening two chapters seek to provide frameworks for analyzing regional conflict management efforts. In chapter 1, Joseph Lepgold adopts a strategic choice perspective with respect to regional conflict. He first outlines the general advantages and disadvantages attendant to regional mechanisms for managing conflict. Lepgold also posits several types of conflict management outcomes. For him, the key dimensions of this taxonomy are (1) the degree of negative security externalities in the region (how much a given conflict spills over or affects others) and (2) the extent to which there are states or other institutions capable of managing conflict in the region. These dimensions define the outcome types, but the strategic choice perspective helps us understand why one regional conflict ends up as one type versus another. Lepgold illustrates his typology by reference to case illustrations for each prototype.

In chapter 2, I shift the emphasis from conflict types to the mechanisms or strategies available to manage such regional conflicts. I concentrate on three major categories (and their variations) of response to regional conflict: enforcement, peacekeeping, and peacemaking. For each of these approaches, I lay out the basic rationale and actions designed to promoted conflict management. Specifically, I also identify the conditions necessary for, or associated with, success in each of the approaches. I also include a preliminary assessment of the extent to which those conditions or requirements are present in different regions of the world. Perhaps more critically, I look at the comparative effectiveness of conflict management approaches conducted at the regional versus the global level. This serves two purposes. First it offers insights into the implications of the shift from global to regional approaches to conflict management. Second, it provides information about wisdom of adopting one approach versus the other in the situations where regional and global alternatives still exist side by side on the menus of international decision makers.

If Part I focuses on general analyses of regional conflict management approaches, Part II is dedicated to understanding the application of those strategies in specific regional contexts. Security complexes are still largely defined in geographic terms. Most important, there is tremendous variation across regions on the key dimensions noted in chapters 1 and 2. For example, formal security structures are highly developed in Europe, but nonexistent or largely inapplicable in the Middle East. Accordingly, with individual case study chapters, we explore regional conflict management in six different areas of the world: Latin America, Sub-Saharan Africa, South Asia, North Asia, the Middle East, and Europe.

Each case-study author was asked to address broadly the following sets of concerns:

1. *What security problems are on the regional agenda?* The efficacy of conflict management in a given region depends centrally on the kinds of challenges addressed. An integrated system of military alliances may be quite effective in deterring traditional acts of aggression, but largely inappropriate to deal with heavily armed drug lords who operate across international borders. We are especially concerned with the sources, types, and severity of contemporary conflicts within the region. We also pay attention to how security threats have changed over time, specifically changes since the end of the Cold War (e.g., failed states). Special attention is given to which of these conflicts have negative externalities or potential for spillover effects to nonparticipants.

2. *What incentives do regional actors have to act upon, or ignore, the problems in the region?* Our strategic choice perspective indicates that actors, be they individual states or regional organizations, must have incentives to attempt conflict management. The focus here is on the material and nonmaterial motivations for regional actors to work toward a regional conflict-management regime. These might include traditional security concerns (e.g., deterrence, prevent the spread of conflict) or less traditional (e.g., humanitarian, refugees, promote democracy) ones.

3. *What regional actors are involved in collective conflict management activities?* A critical element in the success of regional conflict management is the identity and capabilities of the actors undertaking such efforts. Potential actors include regional hegemons, ad hoc regional coalitions, regional intergovernmental organizations (IGOs), or other states particularly affected by spillover effects from local conflicts. In discussing these actors, our authors look to their incentives to be involved in collective conflict management. Specific attention is directed at whether appropriate and effective regional institutions exist that can be used for regional conflict management. Capabilities, or lack thereof, of those actors are also critical for assessing prospects for regional conflict management.

4. *What nonregional actors might have the incentives and capabilities needed for involvement in regional conflict management?* Regional conflict management may not always be conducted primarily or exclusively by actors in the region of the conflict. Other actors may be relevant as well. For example, it is inconceivable to imagine regional conflict management in the Middle East without some involvement of the United States. Relevant actors include specific great or middle powers, ad hoc coalitions, or global IGOs (perhaps in partnership with regional organizations).

Each case study provides an overview and analysis of conflict management in a particular region. The conclusion, however, attempts to integrate patterns and findings across regions. The goal is to provide generalizations and lessons for conflict management over the globe, albeit through region specific mechanisms.

NOTES

1. John Mearsheimer, "Back to the Future: Instability in Europe after the Cold War," *International Security* 15 (1990): 5–56.

2. See Peter Wallensteen and Margareta Sollenberg, "Armed Conflict, 1989–2000," *Journal of Peace Research* 38 (2001): 629–48, for an overview of post–Cold War conflict.

3. Edward Kolodziej, "Modeling International Security," in *Resolving Regional Conflicts*, ed. Roger Kanet (Urbana: University of Illinois Press, 1998), 11–40.

4. Edward Kolodziej and Roger Kanet, eds., *The Cold War as Cooperation: Superpower Cooperation in Regional Conflict Management* (Baltimore: Johns Hopkins University Press, 1991).

5. Kolodziej, "Modeling International Security."

6. Katherine Powers, "International Institutions, Trade and Conflict: African Regional Trade Agreements from 1950–1992," (Ph.D. diss., Ohio State University, 2001).

7. Kolodziej, "Modeling International Security."

I

REGIONAL APPROACHES TO CONFLICT MANAGEMENT
Incentives and Approaches

1

Regionalism in the Post–Cold War Era

Incentives for Conflict Management

JOSEPH LEPGOLD

> I think there's an important principle [in the Kosovo operation] that I hope will be upheld in the future . . . and that is that while there may be a great deal of ethnic and religious conflict in the world—some of it may break out into wars—that whether within or beyond the borders of a country, if the world community has the power to stop it, we ought to stop genocide and ethnic cleansing.

> I didn't like what went on in Rwanda . . . but I don't think we should commit troops to Rwanda, nor do I think we ought to be the peacekeepers all around the world.

These two views—the first from President Clinton,[1] the second from President George W. Bush[2] during his campaign for the White House—reflect a dilemma in the management of post–Cold War conflicts. It is easy to be horrified by the humanitarian tragedies they bring. Deliberate attacks on civilian populations have become common; amazingly, genocide reappeared in Europe and Africa just a few decades after the Holocaust and little was done to stop it. But it is hard for leaders in other states to make credible promises deal with these problems, especially when they do not affect specific national goals. Even though President Clinton made a moving apology to the survivors of the Rwandan genocide—acknowledging that in failing to stop it, outsiders bore some responsibility for it—neither he nor any other leader could guarantee it would not be allowed to happen again. Having emerged from the bloodiest century in history, the world still lacks reliable mechanisms to prevent, interrupt, or forcibly resolve inter- and intrastate conflict.

Over the last decade, efforts have been made to address these issues at two distinct levels of activity. One has involved various United Nations (UN) military operations in places such as Bosnia and Somalia. Another has involved the development of regional security coalitions and institutions. Some of these efforts are associated with long-standing formal intergovernmental organizations (IGOs) such as the North Atlantic Treaty Organization (NATO), while others, such as the Desert Storm coalition that fought the Gulf War, have been ad hoc. During the Cold War, regional security mechanisms were typically suppressed unless they served Soviet or U.S. purposes. That pattern has been broken, but policy makers still have little experience with effective regional arrangements and, except for NATO and the Organization for Security and Cooperation in Europe (OSCE), little available institutional infrastructure. We thus see noteworthy variation in the presence and effectiveness of regional security mechanisms. In Europe, NATO has the material means to carry out difficult enforcement operations outside its treaty area, but its members' appetite for those missions is uncertain. Russia is an active conflict manager around its periphery, but its chosen tool, the Commonwealth of Independent States (CIS), is essentially a hegemonic instrument. Africans are struggling to develop more broadly based military means to manage local conflicts and may be making incremental progress. This chapter suggests a theoretical framework by which patterns of regional security cooperation can be explained.

By "conflict management," I mean participation in at least one of three broad groups of activities: prevention (through diplomacy or prophylactic military deployments), peacekeeping, or enforcement of some collective mandate to the belligerents. The issue of whether such activity should be organized globally or regionally is an old one. Tension between these two concepts reflects that each carries advantages and disadvantages. Backed by a diverse enough group of states, global mechanisms such as the UN may provide a certain broad legitimacy for action. What they often lack is a sensitivity to the regional context at hand (including a feeling that global efforts led by the major powers often smack of imperialism) and the incentives to act that often accompany nearby problems. All else equal, the closer a problem is to home the more there is at stake in solving it. These advantages may be available within regional coalitions and institutions. But regional groups may find themselves paralyzed by *too close* an identification with a local problem. One or more states may be a party to a conflict, or simply determined to impose a solution. When the first President Bush called for a "new world order" at the time of the Gulf War, the geographic scale at which security would be organized was left open. A decade later, that omission seems prudent. There is no single formula for allocating security responsibilities either to global or regional forums. Conflict-management incentives vary according to the issues at stake, the actors involved, and the regional context in which a problem originates. The fact that regional politics now tends to be more strategically autonomous from the major states than it was during the Cold War simply restores the possibility that incentives to use regional mechanisms may be stronger than the disincentives.

To sort out these incentives, I begin by assuming that actors make strategic choices: they behave purposively, recognizing that outcomes reflect interdependent choices. Assuming that policy makers want to create or maintain a safe and stable international environment, choices about where to allocate conflict-management responsibilities reflect two broad factors: the extent to which regional security problems create ongoing negative externalities with which regional actors believe they need to deal, and the degree to which formal and informal institutions exist that actors believe can be legitimately and effectively used to deal with regional conflict issues. From this perspective, effective conflict management at the regional level requires compatible strategic and political incentives within and across the relevant regional states, as well as any extraregional actors with a desire and ability to affect choices within a region. More specifically, for collective conflict management (CCM) to work, ways must be found to make the benefits (typically a public-goods–like condition of relative regional order, often appearing in the form of problems that don't occur or get worse) at least as attractive as the costs (typically onerous, up-front diplomatic or military efforts borne by a few states). Identifying the particular incentives involved is central to the substantive analysis that must be done for each region. In sketching out how this might be done, I assume that some of the Cold War's legacy lingers on. To varying degrees, each region is on a path-dependent trajectory in which multilateral security cooperation must be built largely from scratch. At the same time, because the major states have relatively less reason than before to intervene in regional disputes, the local strategic situation will often be more important in driving choices about whether to create and use local security mechanisms.

This argument is developed in three main sections. The first section examines the generic advantages and disadvantages of regional mechanisms for managing conflicts, the prevalent expectation that the locus of conflict *and* its management will more often than before be regional, and briefly summarizes some of the evidence to date that bears on the latter prediction. It then posits, based on regional conditions, four types of conflict-management outcomes. The second section presents a strategic-incentives argument as one alternative way to explain why specific regional cases belong to the various types, and the third section sketches out illustrative examples of each type using this argument. These "case sketches" are not designed to replace full-blown case studies; they are intended to illustrate the plausibility and utility of the theoretical approach. The conclusion suggests avenues for further research based on the argument.

COLLECTIVE CONFLICT MANAGEMENT IN THE POST–COLD WAR WORLD: REGIONAL VARIATIONS AND A TYPOLOGY OF OUTCOMES

During the Cold War, most regional conflicts were subsumed under a wide-ranging U.S.–Soviet rivalry. With that era gone, it is common to infer that "regional conflicts are more likely to stay regional, responding to their individual circumstances and developments."[3] This hypothesis is a good place to begin, but it underspecifies whether and how conflict will be *managed*. Conflict management reflects three sets of incentives: the type and severity of regional security problems, the availability of regional actors or mechanisms with the desire and ability to handle them, and the presence of any extraregional actors that can affect choices at the regional level.

Collective Conflict Management: Global and Regional Organizing Principles

As used in this chapter, collective conflict management (CCM) is a pattern of group action, usually but not necessarily sanctioned by a global or regional body, in anticipation of or in response to the outbreak of intra- or interstate armed conflict. It includes any systematic effort to prevent, suppress, or reverse breaches of the peace in cases where states are acting beyond the scope of specific alliance commitments, which have been the traditional means of international security cooperation.[4] CCM takes three broad forms: multilateral diplomacy, peacekeeping, and multilateral enforcement. Diplomacy includes any effort to prevent a conflict from becoming violent or resolve an ongoing conflict peacefully. Peacekeeping involves monitoring a pause in an ongoing conflict by positioning military forces or observers between the belligerents. By interrupting the fighting, it is hoped that political space can be created for diplomacy to resolve or dampen down the underlying conflict. Multilateral enforcement involves using coercion to suppress armed violence. Its purposes include facilitating negotiations among the belligerents, imposing a particular settlement on them, and protecting noncombatants.[5]

CCM can occur at the global or regional level. At the global level, the UN authorizes many of these missions, though in practice the Security Council manages them to varying degrees. The broad international coalition that fought the Gulf War (with a UN imprimatur but only loose oversight) is one model for securing global legitimacy without close operational control. At the regional level, conflict management can occur under the auspices of a formal IGO—typically a regional alliance, socioeconomic institution, or a multipurpose organization[6]—or through an ad hoc coalition. There is more formal regional collaboration than ever, in relative as well as absolute terms. In 1989, there were 223 regional IGOs, constituting 74.3 percent of the total IGOs (global and regional combined); this proportion has increased steadily over the last century, from 28 percent of the total in 1914.[7]

It is useful to recall the long-standing tension between the costs and benefits of regional as opposed to global or "universal" paths to peace. The former recognizes that particular regions might have distinctive practices or institutions for dealing with conflict. The latter recognizes only global norms as appropriate in dealing with the threat or use of force. For example, Woodrow Wilson's vision of collective security was inherently universal. But its impracticality led to a major reappraisal during the 1930s and 1940s of how security responsibilities should be structured. In thinking about the post–World War II security system and a blueprint for the United Nations, Franklin Roosevelt and especially Winston Churchill emphasized the importance of a regional approach to conflict management—in Churchill's case, as a vehicle for continued British leadership of a large empire. Under the influence of Cordell Hull, Roosevelt's long-serving secretary of state, U.S. policy was briefly altered. Hull worried that too regionalist an orientation within the UN might recreate a competitive balance-of-power system—an outcome he abhorred—or give U.S. isolationists an excuse to disengage from Europe and the Pacific after the war. Then, under pressure from a group of Latin American states that wanted to preserve elements of a distinct inter-American system, U.S. policy veered again toward more freedom of action for regional groups within the framework of UN Charter obligations.[8]

Articles 33, 51, 52, and 53 of the UN Charter reflect these tensions. Article 51 recognizes the "inherent right of individual or collective self-defense *until* [emphasis added] the Security Council has taken the measures necessary to maintain international peace and security." Article 52 recognizes the validity of regional arrangements, especially for peaceful settlement of disputes, provided that they are compatible with the Charter. Article 33 requires member states to use regional arrangements "first of all" in peacefully resolving their conflicts. Article 53 suggests that the Security Council might itself use regional mechanisms, albeit "under its authority." Although the Charter does not define the term "regional arrangements"—perhaps because its meaning was seen as self-evident among diplomats—the Charter language implies that geographical proximity among states often creates common interests.[9] The intention seems to have been that regional institutions would take major responsibility for local problems, especially if no enforcement action were taken, although the Security Council would have overall authority and the prerogative to deal with any case at any time. The result was an ambiguous compromise, giving both regionalists and universalists reason to claim victory.[10]

Such compromises typically reflect real benefits and liabilities in both directions. On the one hand, regional security mechanisms have many advantages.[11] Local states may be more immediately affected than others by conflict, giving them more incentive to get involved. It may be logistically easier and less expensive to sustain peacekeeping, humanitarian, or enforcement operations nearby than from a more distant place. Regional mechanisms may also allow policy makers to operate in ways suited to regional practices—for example, either by hammering out details of a CCM operation through a formal institution or achieving such results in more ad hoc ways. Action can be tailored more flexibly to local conditions when there is no need to satisfy a cross-regional coalition or act on the basis of global precedents. Moreover, regional procedures are likelier to give the "have nots" of the UN a voice they are denied by the alleged elitist orientation of Security Council decision making.

On the other hand, region-based actors may be either too inhibited *or* too eager to get involved. Many regional organizations are reluctant to act in any way that compromises state sovereignty, often considered the weapon of the weak in world politics. There may, moreover, be so few resources within some regions that effective CCM action is impossible. Other than NATO, few regional military institutions have the resources to plan, coordinate, and sustain a complex military operation. During the Rwandan massacre, calls for troops by the Organization of African Unity (OAU) were ignored; when Belgium withdrew logistical support, even the Ghanian troops that were in Rwanda under a UN mandate were cut to the bone. And if a region is dominated by one state, as is Western Africa and the region of the former Soviet Union, that state may be able to flout or manipulate broader norms.

Regional and global arrangements are not, of course, mutually exclusive. Over the last decade, permanent members of the UN Security Council have worked more often with regional coalitions and organizations in cases of mutual interest. President Clinton's African Crisis Response Initiative (ACRI) is consistent with a regional-global partnership. The United States helps pay for and train African peacekeeping forces, which then assume some local CCM responsibilities. In the Haiti crisis, the Organization of American States (OAS) recommended sanctions and applied much of the initial multilateral pressure; when this failed, the UN entered the dispute, approving economic sanctions against the Cedras regime and using a single negotiator to represent it and the OAS.[12] Such partnerships, anticipated in Article 53 of the UN Charter, are useful when a controversial or difficult operation threatens unanimity among the permanent Security Council members.[13] In those cases, involvement by a regional body or coalition can spread the costs of CCM operations and help enhance their local legitimacy.

The Empirical Puzzle

Although policy makers in principle can select some mix of regional or global CCM strategies, recent developments would seem to be pushing them toward the creation and greater use of regional security arrangements. After forty years, Russia and the United States have exhausted their ideological rivalry and are less inclined to intervene militarily in third areas. This means that regional states can no longer count on high levels of support from one of them. In Lawrence Freedman's words, "the big players have not ruled out fighting each other again, but at the moment it is hard to see why they should. Those among the smaller players, even the smallest, who still have things to fight about must therefore set their own standards."[14] In short, the local strategic situation—the facts on the ground—tend to affect regional stability more now than the incentives of extraregional states.[15] Some analysts go a step further, predicting that the locus of conflict *and* its management will become largely region-based. David Lake and Patrick Morgan expect that "efforts to cope with violent conflicts, as well as to achieve order and security, will primarily involve arrangements and actions devised and implemented at the regional level."[16]

It is clear that the United Nations cannot fill a large portion of such needs. Considering how often the Security Council was paralyzed during the Cold War, a striking turnaround in the scale of the UN's CCM activities began as the superpower rivalry eased in the late 1980s. Many new CCM operations were authorized, some of them very ambitious. Yet public pressure often pushed member governments to bring the UN into difficult situations without adequate commitments for follow-up support. Consequently, "in the first years of the 1990s, the Security Council explored, reached, and exceeded the United Nations' capacity to undertake UN-run military and military-related field operations."[17] The Kosovo operation suggests that militarily demanding CCM missions, if they are carried out at all, will most likely be undertaken by regional organizations or ad hoc coalitions. With no civil police force of its own, the UN even has trouble carrying out less demanding operations. At one point nine thousand police officers were needed for four peacekeeping operations on three continents. Alarms began to sound when just over half that many were recruited.[18] In *An Agenda for Peace*, Secretary-General Boutros Ghali took note of such problems, pointedly observing that regional security organizations could be used to "lighten the burden" of the Security Council.[19] His comments heralded a significant institutional retreat by the UN in undertaking CCM operations.

Thirty years ago, Ernst Haas observed that regional security arrangements "grow in direct proportion to disappointment with the efficacy of the UN collective security system."[20] Despite such disappointment and other seemingly compelling incentives toward regionalization, post–Cold War regional CCM capabilities have developed so far along quite distinct trajectories. Consider briefly three illustrative stories.

In Europe, NATO's unified command has fostered ingrained patterns of multilateralism in military planning and operations. The result is a well-equipped, highly professional, and increasingly flexible intervention instrument. So long as the United States remains an active part of a West-Central European strategic "region," the Bosnian and Kosovo operations suggest that NATO has adapted effectively to a new military role. But the United States may not remain involved in European CCM indefinitely, and Europeans may not be ready to cope with serious armed conflict on their own. Even though UN Secretary-General Perez de Cuellar and the first President Bush considered the breakup of Yugoslavia to be a European matter, an effective response turned out to require U.S. participation. Partly in response to that episode, European leaders are planning to form a rapid-reaction force to be used when the United States opts out of military missions. Yet such talk has been heard before, with few results to show for it. It remains to be seen whether an autonomous European security force will actually be created and, if it is, how effective it becomes.

African leaders face far more serious conflicts and have very few multilateral traditions or institutions on which to draw. Achieving the consensus on which concerted regional action would be based has been very problematic. In the Congo, the local states fought one another. As noted above, the United States has helped to train a ten-thousand-man local force of light infantry units that could be used for traditional peacekeeping tasks. But such troops are ill-equipped for enforcement missions, which one U.S. official estimated comprise 90 percent of the African intervention scenarios. African governments even had to ask the UN to disarm the combatants when war widened in the Congo in the late 1990s.[21] And when ninety-two UN officials were captured by a militia in Sierra Leone, a further pall was cast on UN-led CCM operations in Africa. UN Secretary-General Kofi Annan said, "We know that the international community and the Western countries were not ready to go to Rwanda . . . after Sierra Leone, I think there's going to be very little encouragement for any of them to get involved in operations in Africa."[22]

By contrast, there is a mechanism of sorts in place to help police the periphery of the former Soviet Union. When the USSR disintegrated in 1991, Russia instigated formation of the Commonwealth of Independent States (CIS) as a loose confederation designed to coordinate or legitimate joint policies. Acting largely under CIS auspices, Russia has carried out conflict-management operations in the Caucasus and Central Asian areas. Yet Russia clearly has the means and the incentives to act on its own, and it has essentially acted as a regional hegemon in imposing its version of peace operations on its neighbors.

The puzzle here is to make sense of these varied trajectories. Why do we see the outcome predicted by Lake and Morgan—"security arrangements and actions devised and implemented at the regional level"—appear unambiguously in only one case? Only in the Russia/CIS case is conflict management being pursued at the regional level in a way that effectively insulates it from outside participation or scrutiny. The situation in West-Central Europe is ambiguous in this respect (because the United States is neither historically nor geographically an unambiguous part of the region), and Africa remains vitally dependent on outside actors to secure itself.

A first step in interpreting these cases is to arrange them along some central dimensions of variation. Two are suggested in this chapter. First, to what extent are there serious recognized negative security externalities in a region? The answer to this question should help in identifying the type and severity of security problems likely to appear on regional policy agendas, as well as policy makers' incentives to deal with them. Second, to what extent are there states or institutional mechanisms in the region capable of managing conflict? The result is a two-by-three matrix (see figure 1.1).

Beginning with dimension # (1) on negative externalities, externalities are costs or benefits that do not accrue only to the actors that produce them; they "spill over" onto bystanders as an unintended by-product of other activity. For example, pollution that permeates a bystander's air or water is a negative externality. Negative security externalities include the following: movement of refugees from a conflict into the territory of bystander states; use of bystanders'

Serious Recognized Negative Security Externalities in the Region	Community Actor or Coalition	Solo Actor	Neither a Community Nor a Solo Actor Available
Yes	[I] Rough neighborhood, episodic community policing (e.g., Southeast Europe)	[II] Regional trouble, vigilante regional response (e.g., Russia/CIS)	[III] Regional trouble, no response (e.g., Africa)
No	[IV] Calm neighborhood, reliable community policing (e.g., West-Central Europe)	[V] Calm neighborhood, vigilante in waiting	[VI] Little immediate need for CCM (e.g. South America)

Figure 1.1.   Regional Actor/Mechanism Prepared to Manage Conflict?

territories as a base for attacking a combatant; disruption of the regional (or global) economy from a conflict; the spread of a conflict to bystander allied states. Both classical notions of collective security and Realist arguments underspecify actors' incentives to respond to negative security externalities. According to Wilsonian doctrine, states must resist any aggression because security is indivisible. This assumes that all states invariably suffer large and comparable negative externalities from armed attacks, no matter where they occur—a claim that is clearly false. Realists typically make the opposite, equally restrictive assumption: that policy makers care only about their own state's security and will at most cooperate conditionally with others to achieve it if that is instrumentally necessary. We might begin with the proposition that, all else equal, the greater the costs that conflict imposes on bystanders and the larger the number of security externalities, the likelier it is that states will create collective arrangements to deal with conflict.[23]

Turning to dimension # (2), the number of actors, three possibilities are evident. Regional conflict management might be undertaken by a community actor or coalition, or by a solo actor; alternatively, neither a community nor a solo actor may be available. It is not surprising that, aside from contemporary NATO and Russia, regional CCM mechanisms tend to be weak. During the Cold War, both superpowers acted in ways that had the effect of suppressing autonomous capacity in those mechanisms. This can occur in several ways. First, in cases that Barry Buzan calls "overlay," a powerful state imposes order on a region, subduing indigenous relationships.[24] Overlay can lead to more or less voluntary (and thus legitimate) submission; imagine a continuum of cases running from pure submission (e.g., Stalinist Russia in East-Central Europe) to more benign forms of influence (e.g., contemporary U.S. ties to Europe or

Japan). In situations of imposed overlay, conflict-management procedures and outcomes reflect the dominant state's preferences. In terms of contemporary norms, imposed overlay may not be "collective" at all. If so, only in situations captured by cell IV of figure 1.1 does one find a reasonably regular pattern of *collective* conflict management. Second, when regional hegemony is exercised less coercively, local mechanisms are allowed more autonomy, but they may not develop in ways that allow them to be exercised. Third, when strong outside states compete within a region, as was the case in Cold-War Africa, local conflicts tend to be amplified rather than suppressed.[25] The effect may be to tax further the capacity of any regional CCM mechanism to deal with the underlying security problems.

The result of any of these trajectories tends to be a certain degree of regional path dependence. That is, the costs of reversing a previous conflict-management strategy—one that in most cases kept regional institutions weak or overwhelmed relative to the demands on them—tend to be high.[26] Even though policy makers understand that both global and regional CCM arrangements have advantages, more or less autonomous choices are made at particular points to invest resources in one, often at the expense of the other. So even when the context shifts and the other organizing principle becomes more useful, it may be hard to shift course. This does not rule out the possibility of effective regional CCM arrangements in places (e.g., outside of European NATO) where they are currently underdeveloped. It does, however, lead one to expect substantial inertia in building them.

What we are likely to see, then, is cross-regional variation not in whether the local strategic situation matters more than it did during the Cold War—this seems to be the pattern so far—but in what the "local facts" are. To help in diagnosing key aspects of particular cases and explaining major patterns of policy choices, the dimensions that constitute this typology should highlight noteworthy features of each group of cases. For example, European NATO's reliable in-house protection differentiates it from another area with fairly few serious negative security externalities—today's largely democratic South America—that has no community police force. That kind of knowledge can be useful in developing midrange propositions about each type.[27] One might hypothesize, for example, that regional CCM will be especially problematic where local negative security externalities are high, there are strong local disincentives to manage those problems, and outside incentives to intervene on the side of order are also low.

So far, I have argued that the two dimensions comprising figure 1.1 capture the major substantive incentives that affect choices about where and when one would try to manage conflicts. To explain such choices—that is, to explain how policy makers can be expected to *react* to the strategic environment created by such incentives, given their underlying preferences—one needs an argument that connects situational incentives to strategic choices. I sketch out this argument in the next section.

EXPLAINING PATTERNS OF COLLECTIVE
CONFLICT MANAGEMENT OUTCOMES

Foreign-policy choices are necessarily strategic choices—choices about ways to pursue interdependent outcomes. Because international outcomes depend on the goals, perceptions, and relative power of at least two actors, all of world politics (if not all politics) involves strategic choices. Strategic interaction occurs when two or more actors, recognizing that the options available for achieving their goals depend on the preferences and choices of others, evaluate their options according to what they expect the others to do. In other words, the situational incentives actors face in domestic and international arenas affect the consequences of their choices; realizing that, they presumably order their preferences, search for options, evaluate the expected consequences of each option, and make choices with those consequences in mind. Such an argument does *not* carry assumptions about how actors will carry out these tasks; it assumes only that people act purposively—as if they have goals and care about achieving them.[28] The processes of interdependent choice are thus a key part (though not the only part) of politics.

I assume that choices about when and where to manage conflicts are best seen as a distinctive kind of strategic choice problem. In foreign policy, choices reflect the compatibility of actors' objectives, their relative power positions, their degree of attachment to relevant norms, their time horizons, and the care with which they monitor the situational cues around them. Political incentives reflect actors' desire to maintain their influence within a policy coalition and among their constituents, regardless of their desire to achieve certain international outcomes. Choices reflect trade-offs between desires to maximize policy and political benefits, or to minimize the two types of associated risks. With these points in mind, one might begin by noting that decision makers take on conflict-management responsibilities only when the perceived international incentives are high enough to overcome the substantial international and domestic costs and risks that accompany them. In this section, I use a general understanding of the politics of strategic choice to explain how policy makers are likely to react to various sets of domestic and international incentives.

Responses to Negative Regional Security Externalities

Negative security externalities arise in several ways. In unstable neighborhoods, conflicts spread across states when war or internal turmoil pushes refugees from danger and toward safety, or when soldiers use adjacent territory as sanctuaries. Conflict can also diffuse across boundaries through a process of social learning. A group that sees itself as mistreated at home might develop a stronger sense of its identity, and thereby its dissatisfaction, by observing a comparable struggle in other states. Groups that already are dissatisfied might learn from conflicts elsewhere how they can become less vulnerable or more autonomous.[29] Either way, conflict is likely if political leaders in these other states resist the demands. A different kind of spillover effect occurs when genocide or other humanitarian emergencies tugs at ethnic kinsmen or morally outraged citizens elsewhere. However such externalities arise, their negative impact on neighbors' goals and values might induce action to remove or ameliorate the problem.[30]

Of course, in any given situation of spillover, trouble must begin somewhere. Local conflict is likely if actors have serious grievances against others, low value is placed on noncoercive relationships, and the status quo is seen as unacceptable in the short run. Regional actors who want to upset the status quo no longer can get major-power help fairly easily, as was often true during the Cold War. On the other hand, those who don't need the resources of an outside ally may see fewer external constraints to acting on their own. Because Western military involvement in the Third World is now seen as more strategically discretionary than before, those who see profit in starting a conflict will logically want to keep the violence, and their own role in it, below the threshold that would presumably spur outside intervention. Moving swiftly across contested terrain will minimize resistance in populated areas, containing the large damage to life and property that might bring in outsiders.[31] Most worrying, then, are regional leaders who have international or domestic reasons to fight and the resources to win in a fait accompli.

Whether undertaken globally or regionally, CCM typically entails some distinct disincentives for dealing with the sorts of problems just identified. First, it tends to require high, up-front costs if *any* benefits are to be achieved. In cases where two or more parties are sharply at odds, truly impartial intervention is generally impossible. Conflict management then entails coercion which, depending on the level of resistance encountered, can be burdensome.[32] For example, military responses to emergencies involving refugees more often demand compellence than deterrence, since the source of the problem and the actual displacement of refugees will likely be under way before anyone decides to address the problem.[33] Compellence (making an adversary change his behavior) is typically considered more militarily demanding than deterrence (which does not require a target to visibly change his behavior). Second, the benefits CCM provides tend to be public or semipublic—available to all who value peace and stability, whether they contribute toward their realization or not. Yet the costs are borne privately, by specific states, and often only a few. Third, the benefits of successful CCM often arrive only in the future (as when peacekeeping buys time for adversaries to resolve a conflict) or present themselves as counterfactual results (problems, such as renewed war among longtime rivals, that allegedly either do not arise or do not worsen because someone is engaged in prevention or peacekeeping). Wilsonian collective security is a polar type of CCM regime precisely because its requirements magnify all of these disincentives.

These disincentives imply that CCM operations are more likely to be undertaken (1) when the benefits appear closer to the costs in time, (2) when the benefits are less rather than more public in nature, and (3) when the benefits come less in the form of counterfactuals and more in the form of tangible results. Each of these conditions merits elaboration.

Policy makers typically discount costs and benefits of alternative options over time, and strategic-choice theorists have examined the behavior patterns that typically result. The less control actors have over policy choice and implementation within the coalitions of which they are part, the more they will prefer future costs over current costs and the more they will discount future benefits relative to current benefits. Moreover, the higher the immediate political risks of preferred policy options (the risk that their relative political standing will suffer from taking some action), the more willing they will be to defer policy benefits in exchange for a reduction in current political risks. On the other hand, the higher the expected value actors attach to achieving a specific policy outcome, the less actors' choices will be affected by discounting future benefits.[34] These propositions explain why CCM operations that pay quick benefits—such as safe zones or havens in which threatened populations are protected militarily—are more attractive to potential providers than long-term peacekeeping operations, especially those involving a risk of military casualties. Related to this, conflicts closer to home are likely to induce greater commitment than those far away. Not only will the costs of inaction be felt sooner; it is easier to project force over small distances than large ones. How "regions" are defined can thus become a strategic choice with key ramifications for CCM responsibilities.

Even if regional states perceive security externalities in similar ways, or otherwise come to share a common view of what the regional security order should be, local collective-action problems constitute another constraint on joint action. The troops, equipment, and political will needed to make local security arrangements work may be seriously underprovided. NATO's problems in this regard have, for example, worsened significantly with the end of the Cold War. Now that nuclear forces cannot credibly be used to deal with local security problems, NATO states need to cover the terrain they pledge to police with enough quick-reaction units and specially trained forces to do the specific jobs at hand. One solution may be to partially privatize the security goods involved by delegating primary responsibility for protecting certain areas to small subgroups of like-minded states.[35] That would make more obvious the connection between the sources of externalities and the private utility of specific states. But this solution will not work for every kind of security problem, nor is it likely to stop free-riding entirely.

Finally, the disincentives identified above will operate less powerfully when the benefits of CCM operations come less in the form of counterfactuals and more in the form of results that can be tangibly observed or experienced. The reasoning here is similar to that involving the discounting problem. Policy makers and their constituents are typically reluctant to pay major costs when they cannot see the benefits. Unfortunately, these incentives mean that CCM help is often withheld until the need for external intervention is beyond doubt, a condition that typically requires a crisis.

Arguments in favor of CCM have, of course, been made not just in the name of dealing with particular security problems. Historically, CCM has also been justified in terms of progress toward building regional or global communities characterized by shared notions of interstate and domestic justice. Such shared commitments to norms are often weak. This generalization suggests an important paradox that surrounds the politics of CCM. In the absence of a shared sense of community, the higher the costs and risks of CCM operations, or the more the costs must in practice be borne by a small subset of states, the more likely it is that policy makers and their constituents will need distinctive private benefits to justify the costs.

This syndrome undercuts the community-building and community-maintaining aspects of CCM. In cases where the disincentives noted above are strong, what is needed to make CCM work at either the regional or global level undercuts the very notion of CCM itself—that it is *collective*, that is, not based entirely on private incentives. Historically, the collective nature of the benefits promised by CCM operations have been seen as a key normative justification for their costs. Only in West-Central Europe, where a fairly strong sense of community has been built over the last five decades, have the effects of this paradox been softened.

Are Regional Actors or Mechanisms Prepared to Manage Conflict?

People can agree that conflict is costly, yet be unprepared to work together to prevent or stop it. Soon after it was clear that the South had lost the Civil War, a Virginia woman wrote that while she wanted peace, she opposed the idea of rejoining the Union: "I could not consent to go back with a people that has been bent on exterminating us."[36] Conversely, political actors can more easily cooperate on security where a sense of regional or global community exists, or where, perhaps for other reasons, institutionalized mechanisms of cooperation already exist and function in ways that reduce the distinctive costs that must be borne by individual actors. In these ways, formal or informal institutions help address an accountability dilemma that accompanies CCM. For CCM to work, help must be reliable and prompt. But an international obligation to respond reliably and promptly cuts against a domestic obligation to consult about external commitments, an obligation that is especially strong in contemporary democracies.

Even in a nascent form, an international community that includes shared notions of domestic and interstate legitimacy can help soften this dilemma. If people value the creation and maintenance of legitimate relationships and if they think a political process and the outcomes it produces are legitimate, they are more likely to accept that outcome, even if they would have preferred something else. If they think either the outcome or the process is illegitimate, they are far likelier to oppose it.[37] West-Central Europe increasingly approximates such a community. Some of the NATO and EU enlargement debates have focused on just this question: do these prospective members share our values, including our sense of justice? At either the global or (more likely) a regional level, such a community softens the accountability dilemma, since it necessarily includes notions of domestic legitimacy that help in justifying CCM activity to domestic audiences. Especially in contemporary democracies, the accountability dilemma must be resolved in ways that appear legitimate to domestic audiences.

Any detailed examination of global or regional CCM patterns should pay attention to such communicative action and its effects. Much of what goes on in the process of CCM involves talk—appeals to norms, efforts at persuasion, and attempts to frame costs and benefits in particular ways. One of the main purposes of formal and informal regional organizations is to facilitate such talk. As Inis Claude put this point in referring to the UN: "Collective legitimization is an answer not to the question of what the United Nations can *do* but to the question of how it can be *used*."[38] Where joint action is important for normative as well as practical reasons, such forums are places where consensus is shaped, and national positions can change in an effort to find a collectively legitimate consensus. For all these reasons, incentives rise to manage conflicts in places where such communities exist or are being built (which is not to say that any particular CCM efforts will succeed).

By ameliorating collective action problems, regional institutions can also cut the risks and costs of CCM activity in ways that soften the accountability dilemma. Institutionalization increases as actors' expectations in an issue-area converge, as those expectations become more precise, and as an institution has greater autonomy to adapt its own rules and procedures.[39] As figure 1.1 illustrates, states can coalesce for purposes of CCM through a formal institution (such as NATO or the OAS), through a long-standing coalition (such as the anti-Iraq sanctioning group that grew out of the Gulf War), or through an ad hoc coalition. Not every such group needs to be highly institutionalized. But the better developed international institutions become, according to Neoliberal Institutionalist arguments, the likelier it is that states can make and enforce mutually beneficial agreements.[40] Such agreements can be used to define and implement burden-sharing responsibilities. More equitable burden-sharing can soften the accountability dilemma directly, by leading to an outcome seen as more legitimate at home and abroad. It can also produce that effect less directly, by eliciting enough contributions for public goods that fewer private benefits need to be offered. CCM is seen as more legitimate when there is less need to induce action through private benefits, which are resented by those who don't receive them. The less need there is for private side-payments, the less need there will be for extensive consultations about the ends and means of CCM activities: if people feel the outcomes are legitimate, they will not demand the same kinds of elaborate procedural safeguards as they would otherwise.

As noted above, whether effective local CCM mechanisms exist has a lot to do with how regional security was handled during the Cold War. In the West,

competition with the USSR provided a shared sense of international and domestic norms. By allowing Western Europe and Japan to develop free of Soviet
coercion, it also created a reinforcing short-term and long-term benefits that
were *not* counterfactuals. The Cold War also legitimized a distinctive U.S. leadership role, which allowed U.S. leaders to run international and domestic risks
for collective Western goals. Finally, NATO's high level of institutional coordination facilitated a relatively efficient Western response to this situation. While
none of these incentives exist now, political leaders are not entirely prisoners
of that period. Gareth Evans has distinguished between existing security bodies
and "discussion forums and emerging new bodies" that take on such a role
later.[41] Liberal Institutionalists expect that it will be easier to adapt old institutions to new goals than to create effective mechanisms from scratch. This has
been true of NATO: it is hard to imagine that an institution of comparable functions could have been created after 1990. Yet institutions such as the OAU may
be so cumbersome or have such negative legacies that a fresh start may make
more sense. This reasoning suggests that the longer the time horizons of leaders who share security externalities *or* have compatible views of a legitimate regional order, the likelier it is that old mechanisms will be adapted to new security purposes or new ones will be created.

Finally, incentives to seek regional solutions to regional security problems will
also depend on what outside states are expected to do. Depending on the kind
and level of the interdependencies they share with states within another region
and their commitment to applicable humanitarian norms, outsiders may want to
stem refugee flows, protect trade routes, deliver relief help, or facilitate or impose
a settlement of a conflict. They may, in other words, have the same goals as those
within a region. But for reasons already discussed, these inducements to act tend
to be weaker than those within a region, and the disincentives will often weigh
heavily. Western governments typically fear they will become vulnerable to the
savagery with which contemporary conflicts have become associated. Air power
is often seen as an attractive option for avoiding entanglement on the ground. But
because it is most effective when used along with ground forces, Western states
that do not want to insert their own land forces often must work closely with one
of the belligerents, even if they do not entirely support its aims.[42] In such situations, it is important to map the strategic incentives from the standpoint of the potential intervening state, taking into account the policy and political risks of intervening quickly and delaying in the hope a better option will appear. In general,
since these are strategic-choice situations, each actor's perception of the situational
incentives will depend on how it believes others are reading the comparable cues.

ILLUSTRATIVE SKETCHES OF THE OUTCOME TYPES

A principal claim of this chapter is that a focus on the processes of strategic
choice can capture the international and domestic incentives underlying conflict-

management choices. This section complements that claim by providing "case sketches" that illustrate an example of each outcome type arrayed in figure 1.1. Careful process-tracing would be needed to match predicted and actual outcomes closely. As before, these sketches are not intended to replace full case studies; they function here to illustrate the plausibility and utility of the suggested theoretical approach.

Russia and the Commonwealth of Independent States: Regional Trouble, Vigilante Regional Response

Even though the Cold War ended peacefully, much of the former Soviet Union has broken up violently. Out of this process has come a patchwork of new states, many of them mired in discord and headed by leaders of uncertain internal legitimacy. Although Russia has weakened considerably over the last decade, its leaders have remained determined to police the troubled area around their country's periphery, a zone known euphemistically as "the near abroad." Because they have done this essentially alone, their efforts cannot meaningfully be called "collective" conflict management.

All of the situational incentives have moved them in this direction. Internationally, Russia's long land borders make it vulnerable to spillover effects at many points, and many existing conflicts in fact have this effect. Separatist violence in the Georgian regions of South Ossetia and Abkhazia blocks important Russian trade and transportation routes; in Central Asia, Russian leaders fear that the Islamic movements threatening the governments of Tajikstan and Kirgistan could, if left unchecked, spill over into the multiethnic Russian Federation and produce a wave of refugees. According to a statement issued by the Russian Foreign Ministry in 1992, "The most important foreign policy tasks in the near abroad [consist of] curtailing and regulating armed conflicts around Russia, preventing their spread to our territory and guaranteeing strict observation in the near abroad of human and minority rights, particularly of Russians and of the Russian-speaking population."[43]

An assertive policy in these areas is also popular domestically. According to one analyst, Russia's foreign-policy constituencies have explicitly embraced "missions and interests that demand the restoration of a powerful and influential Russia."[44] Although the presence of Russian troops throughout the near abroad gives the military a major organizational stake in regional security policy, that policy has not been dominated by the military; the foreign-policy debate among civilians has evolved over time toward the position previously held by the military. The result is strong internal elite consensus.[45] And in an era of political and social upheaval, one of the few goals on which most ordinary Russians agree is maintaining a vigorous presence in the near abroad, including an ability to control the external borders of the former Soviet Union.[46]

Quickly after the Soviet Union collapsed in 1991, a framework for a system of regional conflict management was developed for much of the post-Soviet area. The Commonwealth of Independent States (CIS) consisted of Russia and most of the former Soviet republics except the Baltics and, initially, Georgia. Russian leaders envisioned the CIS as a way to promote economic, political, and security integration among the former Soviet republics. In March 1992, CIS members established terms for creating multinational armed forces and the procedures that were to be followed before the initiation of CIS CCM operations. Many of the non-Russian members were eager for economic ties, though they resisted security ties. Consequently, no regional forces were created, though a CIS Joint Command was established.

The first regional CCM operation in the former USSR took place in mid-1992, when a largely Russian force was sent to South Ossetia to combat separatist forces. The presidents of Russia and Georgia rather than the CIS made the deployment decision. Russian-dominated units subsequently also went to deal with separatist conflicts in Moldova and Tajikistan.[47] Soon after active hostilities concluded in South Ossetia, unrest flared up in Abkhazia and Russia intervened in mid-1993. In return for Russian help in addressing the deteriorating situation, Georgian President Eduard Shevardnadze had to join the CIS and allow continued basing rights for Russian troops in his country. At the same time, Russian military commanders were apparently providing Abkhaz separatist forces with supplies and even bombing Georgian troops.[48]

The CIS and the post-Soviet security system more generally have been organized to give Russia a dominant voice. Most leadership positions within the CIS, including all key defense posts, are held by the Russian president or his appointees. Philip Roeder concludes that "[the] CIS has served more as a vehicle to reinforce Russian hegemony than as a multilateral constraint on Russia."[49] Path dependence works in Russia's favor because all the post-Soviet national military officers were trained and equipped by Russians. Russian leaders have also ensured that their country is either the major antagonist of every belligerent, the primary ally of both sides in a dispute, or the principal mediator in every dispute within the four major theaters of the near abroad (Western, Baltics, Transcaucasian, and Central Asian).[50] These actions reflect sentiments frankly articulated by former Russian Foreign Minister Andrei Kozyrev: "It would be a mistake to ignore the role of the United Nations and the CSCE, but it would be another extreme to abandon this sphere completely to the hands of these organizations. This is a zone of Russian interests and this is understood by all sides."[51] Consistent with these views, when Russian leaders have sought UN and OSCE approval for CIS actions in the Caucasus and Central Asia, they have insisted on no external oversight, no limits on unilateral actions, and no provisions for timely withdrawal of Russian forces stationed on the territory of other regional states.[52]

A long-term view of the strategic situation is at work here. Russian leaders believe that a multipolar rather than a U.S.-centered world order is desirable and that Russia must be one if its great-power poles. Getting back to that situation may take some time. Russia's gross domestic product (GDP) has dropped at least 40 percent since 1991, at which point it was about 60 percent of the last Soviet GDP.[53] With these constraints in mind, former Russian Foreign Minister Yevgeny Primakov has argued that Russia must be "a great power now"; it must act, he said, "by no means on the basis of current circumstances but on the basis of its colossal potential."[54] These kinds of time horizons, coupled with the belief that Russia cannot allow itself to be dictated to by the West, has hardened the view that what happens in the near abroad is no outsider's business.

Africa: Regional Trouble, No Response

A decade after the end of the Cold War, Africa[55] remains a region torn by conflict. In 1999, more major wars occurred there than on any other continent. Angola, both Congos, Ethiopia, Eritrea, Rwanda, Somalia, and Sudan were involved in wars causing at least one thousand battle deaths a year, while lower-intensity wars plague Burundi, Chad, Djibouti, Senegal, Sierra Leone, and Uganda.[56]

When added to Africa's other social and demographic problems, the spillover effects of these conflicts constitute a crisis. The regional trafficking in arms has increased significantly in recent decades, making it easy for insurgents in one state to acquire arms from those fighting elsewhere. Continued warfare, in turn, has produced a massive refugee problem. Over eight million of the world's twenty-two million cross-border refugees are estimated to live in Africa, aside from the millions more that have become displaced in their own countries. In a global assessment of humanitarian emergencies conducted by the National Intelligence Council, it was noted that the total demand for humanitarian assistance through 2000 in Africa will likely exceed donor countries' willingness to respond.[57] There is no reason to expect that pattern to change soon. Of all the world's regions, Africa is least able to afford such devastation. It is home to thirty-three of the world's forty-eight least developed countries, is the only region to experience a continuous economic downturn since 1980, and is in the midst of an AIDS epidemic. In a May 1998 report, UN Secretary-General Kofi Annan said that "preventing such wars is no longer a matter of defending states or protecting allies [but] a matter of defending humanity itself."[58]

Since the late 1980s, these conflicts have become much more locally contained, meaning that half of the Lake-Morgan prediction has come to pass in Africa. Moscow, for instance, gave the Ethiopian regime as much as $11 billion in military assistance between the mid-1970s and the late 1980s, before that support ended rather abruptly.[59] Zaire's President Mobutu could no longer buy off or repress his opponents once the United States stopped subsidizing him, and the result has been a continuing civil war largely undisturbed by those outside the region. Even though President Clinton paid more attention diplomatically to Africa than any of his recent predecessors, the United States took the position that it had no strategic interest in Africa that would justify military intervention or major economic aid.[60] France, the most militarily involved of the former colonial powers, tended to be most concerned about maintaining political stability in Africa as a way to protect its investments. But the U.S.–Soviet competition in Africa also drew Paris in to some extent. French leaders saw a historic mission for their country as the most involved European state in Africa, especially as a way to counter the superpowers' influence. With that incentive gone, the French presence in Africa has plummeted. And even though sentiment has grown among UN officials and diplomats that African conflicts must somehow be managed, UN involvement has been hesitant and far below the scale needed.[61]

The other half of the Lake-Morgan prediction has not been borne out: at the level of sub-Saharan Africa as a whole, CCM has been weak. Two regional norms have driven the strategic incentives for choice: the inviolability of the borders within which state independence was achieved and noninterference in the internal affairs of other African states. Because African colonial borders were typically drawn without regard for tribal boundaries, there has been a widespread fear that questioning the legitimacy of any state's borders could threaten them all. Because internal authoritarianism has been the rule, leaders have been reluctant to pass judgment on how others in the region govern themselves. African leaders have gone to great lengths to maintain these norms. When Eritrean insurgents won their war of independence against Ethiopia in 1991, the OAU emphasized that its recognition of the new state was a narrow exception to the norm that existing borders were inviolate. When Tanzanian forces joined Ugandan insurgents to overthrow the genocidal ruler Idi Amin, the OAU condemned the action, since many African leaders feared that a precedent permitting intervention might be used against them.[62] These norms privilege a procedural notion of what constitutes a legitimate state while providing no way for substantive grievances to be redressed peacefully. Dissatisfied parties thus have strong incentives to use force to achieve their goals, while others in the region have little leverage to prevent, contain, or resolve those disputes. The African bargain, like the Westphalian one, stipulates that rulers receive their legitimacy from one another, rather than from domestic arrangements.[63] When those arrangements break down, regional norms severely limit the available options to respond.

Not surprisingly, "in Africa weak states have created relatively weak regional organizations that consequently have struggled to be effective in promoting conflict management and more responsible sovereignty."[64] The OAU, created in 1963, illustrates this basic problem. The OAU Charter urges members to settle their disputes peacefully, and a Commission of Mediation, Conciliation, and Arbitration was accordingly established in the OAU's first year. But the Commission's mandate was limited to interstate disputes, its jurisdiction was made optional, and its reports can only be published with the consent of parties.[65] With authority more akin to the League of Nations Council than the UN Security Council, it is small wonder that the Commission has never been used. At a 1993 OAU summit meeting, a Conflict Prevention, Management, and Resolution

Mechanism was established, ostensibly to prevent a recurrence of the failed Somali state elsewhere in the region. But this mechanism suffered the same weakness as the OAU as a whole. According to the final resolution of the summit that produced it, it "will be guided by the objectives and principles of the [OAU] Charter, and in particular, the sovereign equality of states, non-interference in their internal affairs, and respect for the sovereignty and territorial integrity of member states."[66] OAU weaknesses do not end there. Limited finances and logistical capability mean that an OAU presence in a trouble spot typically consists of an understaffed, underequipped team of observers. To conserve costs, diplomats posted in the host state often serve on these missions.[67]

One alternative to a continentwide organization in which everyone has a veto is a more cohesive group whose members have a larger stake in handling particular problems. The most promising African CCM effort to date has come from an offshoot of the Economic Community of West African States (ECOWAS)—the ECOWAS Cease-Fire Monitoring Group (ECOMOG).

Nigeria, the most populous and potentially the wealthiest state in Africa, spearheaded the formation of this force in mid-1990 to restore order in Liberia, then in the midst of a civil war. Although the effort was ultimately unsuccessful—after five years, it had been possible to restore order only briefly before the conflict resumed—it suggested that action at the subregional level, where cross-border problems are more acutely felt, may be Africa's best hope for managing conflict.[68] Nigeria's neighbors were acutely aware of the possibilities for regional dominance in this situation, and such fears inhibited ongoing CCM efforts in Liberia.[69] But the alternative to action organized by a local hegemon may be inaction, the all-too-frequent outcome in Africa.

West-Central Europe: Calm Neighborhood, Reliable Community Policing

For fifty years, West-Central Europe has been a calm neighborhood with a fairly well-equipped community police force—the only region, in fact, that can be characterized this way. There are no security rivalries in the area, much less any active conflicts. How did a region that for centuries was consumed by war become so reliably pacified? Nearly a decade after Germany was defeated in World War II, two-thirds of French respondents to an opinion poll believed that German rearmament for purposes of waging the Cold War was dangerous, and nearly a third of those who responded believed it could be benign only if adequate international safeguards were put in place. Only when the United States and Britain guaranteed Paris that they would not withdraw their forces unilaterally from the continent did French leaders acquiesce to German rearmament. That guarantee, and the way it is reinforced in NATO's integrated military command—within which German forces have been tied operationally to other members' units—began the process of building peace in postwar Europe.[70]

Even though West-Central Europe is now securely at peace, ongoing security externalities outside the immediate neighborhood provide a reason to maintain a robust military capability in Europe even without a Russian threat. As stated in NATO's revised strategic concept, adopted in 1991, NATO members now believe that threats to their security are less likely to come from "calculated aggression" than from "the adverse consequences of instabilities that may arise from the serious economic, social, and political difficulties, including ethnic rivalries and territorial disputes, which are faced by many countries in Central and Eastern Europe."[71] According to the document, such tensions could "involve outside powers or spill over into NATO countries."[72] Accordingly, NATO members believe that they must manage crises originating outside their treaty area to be secure within it. One path-dependent element here is that NATO members spent decades learning how to work as a highly integrated military coalition. That kind of mechanism might not be created from scratch under present conditions. But NATO governments know how to use it, and developing an alternative would entail various start-up costs. One appealing aspect of NATO as it is built today is that these costs have been paid.[73]

The new strategic concept implied a willingness to take military action outside the NATO treaty area in situations other than an attack against a NATO member— something that would have been impossible during the Cold War and was controversial within NATO itself well into the 1990s. That commitment was first implemented in 1995, when NATO took direct military action to force a settlement of the Bosnian conflict, and a year later when an implementation force (IFOR) of sixty thousand troops was sent there to enforce the military aspects of the Dayton Peace Agreement. After IFOR's one-year mandate expired, it was succeeded by a stabilization force (SFOR) with much more ambitious aims: "promot[ing] a climate in which the peace process can continue to move forward" and "provid[ing] selective support to civilian organizations within its capabilities."[74] In effect, CCM in this situation entailed state-building or state-repair tasks such as accelerating the return of displaced people to their homes and providing military support for the construction or revival of democratic institutions.

Insofar as West-Central Europe is a truly peaceful neighborhood, that refuge is based on more than effective policing or a shared fear of destabilization from the East or South. It also reflects a strong stake in a shared liberal identity. As a result, West-Central Europe has moved toward a real community over the last few decades. The OSCE has nurtured this process in many ways: by promoting political consultation and multilateral agreements among members; by setting liberal standards for governance and the treatment of minority groups; through active efforts to prevent or resolve conflicts within the group peacefully; by promoting confidence-building military policies; and by helping to reestablish the rule of law and effective governing institutions after conflicts have occurred. Tying together these pieces are expectations that each state's legitimacy depends on liberal internal governance, accountability for its actions to the group, and a renunciation of force within the group.[75] In some parts of Europe—most clearly within Scandinavia—the value attached to sustaining legitimate relationships is so strong that it seems to dominate national purposes.

Many reinforcing incentives went into producing these results. To reassure its neighbors after World War II, Germany adopted many attributes of a community identity rather than a traditional national identity. Over time, that remarkable shift has given others reason or the confidence to begin following suit. The common struggles to recover economically after 1945, to integrate national economies, to deal with the Soviet Union during the Cold War, and then to reunite culturally with the East after 1989 have all deepened the sense of a shared European project. West-Central Europe's dense pattern of interwoven institutions would be hard to duplicate elsewhere, at least in the short run.[76] But for that very reason, the institutional and normative underpinnings of a calm West-Central European neighborhood look pretty durable.

Southeast Europe, by contrast, is a rough neighborhood that has episodic community policing at best. It was evident soon after the Cold War ended that the Balkans would be unstable and violent, but European and U.S. officials waited three years before any sustained effort was made to define and enforce terms for ending the fighting in Bosnia. NATO members have given themselves the authority to conduct CCM operations out of the Alliance's treaty area, but they do so at their discretion. Even when they decide to take such action, the evidence to date suggests that they may often lack the will to complete the self-assigned tasks. The air campaign in the Kosovo War sufficed to punish the Serbs and degrade their military capability. But it was not sufficient to achieve NATO's political goals: an end to Serbian violence against the Kosovars and Serbian acceptance of some form of self-government for them. U.S. leaders apparently hoped that ground forces would not be needed and did not plan for contingencies that might follow should that assumption prove incorrect.[77] European leaders, perhaps waiting for the United States to lead, showed no more resolve than Washington.

The issue of who will do the lion's share of policing in West-Central Europe—and perhaps someday in Southeast Europe as well—is uncertain over the long run. In December 1999, leaders of the EU countries announced plans to create a rapid-reaction force of sixty thousand troops that would be able to act independently of the United States in a European military contingency. Europeans have been down this road rhetorically before, but many of the incentives suggest a new seriousness this time. Unlike his Tory predecessors, British Prime Minister Tony Blair supports a closer European Union. Precluded by strong opposition at home from participating in the single European currency, he decided to join France and others in an effort to build a military force that would be available for CCM operations in which the United States would not be involved. Like his EU colleagues, Blair was appalled that with two million men under arms, the EU had to rely on Washington to fly two-thirds of the combat sorties in the Kosovo operation, identify virtually every military target, launch nearly every precision-guided weapon, and provide essential logistical and communications services. In this operation especially, European leaders felt marginalized by Washington's ability to dictate the military strategy involved—

leverage backed up by the disproportionate size of the U.S. military contribution.[78] Europeans also realized how tentative Washington was about the operation, and they could not miss the fact that even while it was going on there was
substantial criticism in Congress of their paltry military contribution. Such criticism may reflect an emerging U.S. consensus that unbalanced burden-sharing
has become politically unacceptable.[79]

The real question is whether European leaders will take the political risks entailed in creating an autonomous strike force with teeth. Europeans are experienced and skilled at peacekeeping, but decades of dependence on the United
States mean that they lack the military forces to take on more coercive operations. All three of the major missions in which they have participated in the last
decade—the Gulf War, Bosnia, and Kosovo—required significant coercion.
They are particularly lacking in airlift, sealift, reconnaissance aircraft, precision-
guided munitions, all-weather and night-strike capabilities, and highly sophisticated communications capabilities. They lack, in short, much of what allowed
the United States to prevail quickly in the Gulf War and Kosovo with few casualties. The United States spends about 3.2 percent of its GDP on defense; EU
members collectively spend only about 2.1 percent of GDP, and their military
budgets are falling. With unemployment rates of about 10 percent—over twice
the U.S. rate—and public support for tax cuts, the requisite investments seem
risky at home. No leader seems prepared to spend political capital in creating a
domestic policy coalition that could reverse this long-standing trend.[80]

South America: Little Immediate Need for CCM

There are reasons for examining South America as a distinct conflict-
management region, though doing so is unusual. Latin America has long
been seen as relatively cohesive culturally. Building on the traditions of a
common Iberian civilization and a Pan-American diplomatic system, its
diplomats were staunch advocates of a distinct role for regional organizations in the planning for the United Nations. Yet South America can be seen
as a region in its own right and not just as a piece of Latin America. Not only
it is literally of continental size; it has a history of its own indigenous security dynamics, in the form of several substantial wars among states on the
continent from the early days of their independence in the nineteenth century through the 1930s.

By historic standards, regional inducements toward conflict have dropped
considerably since the late 1980s. Chile and Argentina almost fought in 1978
over control of islands off Tierra del Fuego, but have since settled more than
twenty specific disputes along their lengthy border. In 1999, Chile agreed to implement a commitment made after a nineteenth-century war with Peru and Bolivia to award Peru facilities off Arica, a Chilean port. Argentina's dispute with
Britain over the Falklands remains unsettled, but the two governments have
tried to insulate it from their economic relationship.[81] Converging territorial ob-

jectives have been reflected in progress toward regional arms control. In 1990, Argentina and Brazil agreed to renounce the military use of nuclear technology. This was a considerable step; neither had fully adhered to the 1967 Treaty of Tlatleloco, the purpose of which was to create a nuclear-free zone in all of Latin America. Chile joined them the following year in an accord to prohibit chemical and nuclear weapons in the region. In 1991, Bolivia, Colombia, Ecuador, and Peru agreed to renounce all weapons of mass destruction.

The wave of democratization that passed through South America in the 1980s also fostered regional pacification. During the 1960s and 1970s, for example, military regimes in Argentina and Brazil had espoused inflammatory geopolitical doctrines. Brazilian officials talked of their country's historic mission to regional dominance, "moving frontiers," and "platforms for expansion." A different dynamic was begun during the early stages of democratization. A group of politicians and government officials became convinced that democracy in their countries was fragile and that it required regional peace. Otherwise, it was feared that nationalist and militarist factions would have continued causes around which to mobilize public opinion, demand a greater political role, or press for heightened arms spending.[82] Democratization also fostered an unprecedented kind of transparency that was conducive to arms control. As the Brazilian press and public began to discuss the government's nuclear program, the domestic and international risks of military confidence-building dropped.[83]

The region's identity now seems centered around democratic governance. This was implied symbolically in the so-called Santiago Declaration, adopted by the OAS in June 1991. Titled "The Santiago Commitment to Democracy and the Renewal of the Inter-American System," it explicitly connected a new chapter in regional cooperation to popular rule. A rather startling shift in public attitudes has accompanied—or pushed—such diplomatic developments. Democracy now draws support in the region not just from constituencies such as intellectuals and labor organizers, but also from military officers, religious leaders, and corporate executives. After decades in which democracy was seen as a luxury, if not an impediment to economic development, democratic and human rights are increasingly seen as necessary for development as well as peace.[84]

The OAS role in these developments has at most been weakly facilitative. Founded between 1889 and 1890 as the International Conference of American Presidents, it is the oldest regional IGO. The Cold War was getting under way just as the OAS Charter was signed in 1948, and Washington thereafter saw the organization chiefly as a tool for its regional diplomacy. It remains institutionally underdeveloped for strenuous CCM tasks. For example, it does little preventive diplomacy and has no specific mechanism for that purpose. Its three primary forums that deal with peace and security issues—the General Assembly, the Permanent Council (ambassadorial level), and the Ministers of Foreign Affairs group—focus on verbal sanctions. Occasionally, economic sanctions may be imposed. For the most part, however, the OAS is a socialization mechanism. Norms are shaped and applied to specific cases, and those assembled content themselves with either approving or disapproving of members' behavior.[85]

On balance, such institutional complacency seems justifiable. Even though regional territorial disputes still exist, there seem to be few plausible scenarios that might provoke a major conflict. Ironically, economic development could conceivably work in the other direction. Historically, nearly all of the region's territorial boundaries have run through mountainous terrain or have been covered with dense jungles. As the rainforests disappear and roads are built throughout the region, these boundaries will less often be covered or far away from populated areas.[86] They could thus become more salient and, in a crisis, more of a focal point for military confrontation. There may, finally, be a safety valve if this were to change. When armed conflict is imminent, regional states traditionally try to work out peaceful solutions, typically through ad hoc, flexible mechanisms.[87]

CONCLUSION

A decade after the end of the Cold War, it is useful to reexamine the incentives driving the organization of international security problems. The appropriate scale at which to tackle such issues is a perennial concern. It got settled during the Cold War largely as a by-product of major-power competition and penetration of regional subsystems. There is reason now to believe that conflicts will be more locally contained for the foreseeable future. It need not follow that effective regional management will take place. The legacy of the Cold War remains strong in various regions; conflict-management arrangements have institutional histories that are difficult to reprogram. Even in the presence of strong, recognized negative security externalities, the disincentives to pursuing CCM may be disabling. For these reasons, the prediction that conflict *and* its management will become locally contained is confirmed unambiguously in only one of the cases sketched out in this chapter.

A situational-incentives framework can illuminate the variety of outcomes that can be observed. Doing so helps us see how and why regional security problems *may* come to be viewed as common concerns that demand action. It also helps us see how path-dependent institutional trajectories *may* be shaped to meet changing incentives. For CCM to work, ways must be found to make the benefits (often a public-goods–like situation of regional order that comes in the form of a counterfactual) at least as attractive as the costs (typically up-front, onerous, diplomatic, and military efforts). For example, John Ikenberry has shown that in the aftermath of World War II, Washington created a set of regimes that allowed the United States to effectively write a preferred "constitution" for large areas of international governance. In the key economic and security regimes, substantive outcomes preferred by the United States were legitimated in the eyes of others when Washington allowed itself to be bound by institutional rules that constrained the discretionary use of American power on a case-by-case basis.[88] Comparable arrangements might be put in place in other regions, in which case the principal local powers would trade some policy discretion for regional-conflict institutions that, in a broad sense, codify its influence while binding it to multilateral procedures and norms. There is, of course, no guarantee that such mechanisms would work in regions where rivalry is still rife and the local hegemon does not have a benign reputation. But some such mechanism could provide a set of reinforcing incentives for localizing responses to serious negative security externalities.

A broader theoretical point is also clear from the discussion in this chapter. To create a viable CCM system at any scale of organization, decision makers must find a fit between the international incentives at work and their internal political needs. All of politics involves trade-offs among those two fundamental sets of pressures. Mapping them successfully offers the prospect of a shared lens by which to examine an important set of analytic and policy issues—one likely to be on the agenda of decision makers long into the future.

NOTES

1. Quoted in Ivo H. Daalder and Michael E. O'Hanlon, "Unlearning the Lessons of Kosovo," *Foreign Policy* no. 116 (Fall 1999): 128.

2. David E. Sanger, "Two Paths on Foreign Policy: Advice and Instinct," *The New York Times,* 5 March 2000, A24.

3. David A. Lake and Patrick M. Morgan, "The New Regionalism in Security Affairs," in *Regional Orders: Building Security in a New World,* ed. David A. Lake and Patrick M. Morgan (University Park: The Pennsylvania State University Press, 1997), 6.

4. This definition is taken from Joseph Lepgold and Thomas G. Weiss, "Collective Conflict Management and Changing World Politics: An Overview," in *Collective Conflict Management and Changing World Politics,* ed. Joseph Lepgold and Thomas G. Weiss (Albany: State University of New York Press, 1998), 5.

5. Many classification schemes and lists of multilateral peace operations have appeared in recent years. This one draws on William J. Durch, "Keeping the Peace: Politics and the Lessons of the 1990s," in *UN Peacekeeping, American Politics, and the Uncivil Wars of the 1990s,* ed. William J. Durch (New York: St. Martin's Press, 1996), 3–8, and Lepgold and Weiss, "Collective Conflict Management and Changing World Politics," 15–21. The key dimension along which these operations vary is the degree of consent among the parties (highest in the use of traditional diplomacy, lowest in cases of collective enforcement). One can also imagine several intermediate categories: preventive military deployments, which envision less consent than peacekeeping but more than traditional diplomacy, and what Durch calls "multidimensional operations," which are typically designed both to interrupt the fighting and to help implement a solution that addresses the root causes of conflict. The latter might be exemplified by an operation that separates the belligerents in an internal war and then helps to prepare and supervise elections. See Durch, "Keeping the Peace," 3–4.

6. These categories are taken from A. LeRoy Bennett, *International Organization: Principles and Issues,* 4th ed. (Englewood Cliffs, N.J.: Prentice-Hall, 1988), 357.

7. Samuel S. Kim, "Regional Political Associations: Political," in *Encyclopedia of Government and Politics*, ed. Mary Hawkesworth and Maurice Kogan, vol. 2 (London: Routledge, 1992), 982.

8. Inis L. Claude, Jr., "The OAS, the UN, and the United States," in *Regional Politics and World Order*, ed. Richard A. Falk and Saul H. Mendlovitz (San Francisco: W. H. Freeman and Co., 1973), 270–72.

9. Tom J. Farer, "The Role of Regional Collective Security Arrangements," in *Collective Security in a Changing World*, ed. Thomas G. Weiss (Boulder: Lynne Rienner, 1993), 161–62.

10. Claude, "The OAS, the UN, and the United States," 273. See also D. W. Bowett, *The Law of International Institutions*, 3d ed. (London: Stevens and Sons, 1975), 143–48.

11. This paragraph draws on Ruth Wedgewood, "Regional and Subregional Organizations in International Conflict Management," in *Managing Global Chaos*, ed. Chester A. Crocker, Fen Osler Hampson, and Pamela Aall (Washington, D.C.: United States Institute of Peace Press, 1996), 276–80.

12. Wedgewood, "Regional and Subregional Organizations in International Conflict Management," 281.

13. Christopher Daase, "Spontaneous Institutions: Peacekeeping as an International Convention," in *Imperfect Unions: Security Institutions Over Time and Space*, ed. Helga Haftendorn, Robert O. Keohane, and Celeste Wallander (Oxford: Oxford University Press, 1999), 257.

14. Lawrence Freedman, "The Changing Forms of Military Conflict," *Survival* 40, no. 4 (Winter 1998–99): 39.

15. Aside from Freedman, quoted above, this argument has been made by many observers. See Barry Buzan, "New Patterns of Global Security in the Twenty-First Century," *International Affairs* 67, no. 3 (1991): 435; Lake and Morgan, "The New Regionalism in Security Affairs," 3–7; Edward A. Kolodziej, "Modeling International Security," in *Resolving Regional Conflicts*, ed. Roger E. Kanet (Urbana and Chicago: University of Illinois Press, 1998), 11–13.

16. Lake and Morgan, "The New Regionalization in Security Affairs," 5.

17. Durch, "Keeping the Peace," 28. See also Brian Urquhart, "Who Can Police the World?" *New York Review of Books*, 12 May 1994, 29.

18. Barbara Crossette, "The U.N.'s Unhappy Lot: Perilous Police Duties Multiplying," *The New York Times*, 22 February 2000, A3.

19. Boutros Boutros-Ghali, "An Agenda for Peace," reprinted as appendix A in Adam Roberts and Benedict Kingsbury, eds., *United Nations, Divided World: the UN's Role in International Relations*, 2d ed. (Oxford: Clarendon Press, 1993), 491.

20. Ernst B. Haas, *Tangle of Hopes: American Commitments and World Order* (Englewood Cliffs, N.J.: Prentice-Hall, 1969), 93.

21. James Rupert, "U.S. Troops Teach Peacekeeping to Africans," *The Washington Post*, 26 September 1997, A16; Barbara Crossette, "Africans Want U.N. to Play a Stronger Role in Congo," *The New York Times*, 13 February 2000, A12.

22. Quoted in Norimitsu Onishi, "A Shadow on Africa," *The New York Times*, 5 May 2000, A1.

23. See a similar discussion in David A. Lake, "Regional Security Complexes: A Systems Approach," in *Regional Orders*, ed. Lake and Morgan, 48–55. Unlike Lake, I do not define regions as groups of states that share security externalities. Regions can also be constituted on a nonmaterial basis, such as a shared identity. Nevertheless, on whatever

basis members of a region define it, it is reasonable to infer that they are likelier to manage security problems collectively if they share important security externalities.

24. Barry Buzan, *People, States, and Fear: An Agenda for International Security Studies in the Post–Cold War Era* (Boulder, Colo.: Lynne Rienner, 1991), 219–20.

25. Buzan, *People, States, and Fear*, 208.

26. A variety of definitions of path dependence exist in the literature. This one comes from Margaret Levi, "A Model, a Method, and a Map: Rational Choice in Comparative and Historical Analysis," in *Comparative Politics: Rationality, Culture, and Structure*, ed. Mark I. Lichbach and Alan S. Zuckerman (Cambridge: Cambridge University Press, 1997), 28. It might be compared with the much more stringent definition used by Bruce Bueno de Mesquita: "the extent to which a particular outcome could only have arisen through one unique combination of historical circumstances" (see "The End of the Cold War: Predicting an Emergent Property," *Journal of Conflict Resolution* 42, no. 2 (April 1998): 132, footnote 1).

27. Paul Diesing, *Patterns of Discovery in the Social Sciences* (Chicago: Aldine-Atherton, 1971), 189.

28. Alan C. Lamborn and Joseph Lepgold, "Purpose and Politics: Using Purposive Choice as Reference Point to Frame More Productive Theoretical Conversations," unpublished manuscript, July 1998; Thomas C. Schelling, "Micromotives and Macrobehavior," in *Micromotives and Macrobehavior,* ed. Thomas C. Schelling (New York: Norton, 1978), 17.

29. Michael E. Brown, "The Causes and Regional Dimensions of Internal Conflict," in *The International Dimensions of Internal Conflict,* ed. Michael E. Brown (Cambridge: The MIT Press, 1996), 579–80; Stuart Hill and Donald Rothchild, "The Contagion of Political Conflict in Africa and the World," *The Journal of Conflict Resolution* 30, no. 4 (December 1986): 719–20.

30. Andrew Moravcsik, "Taking Preferences Seriously: A Liberal Theory of International Politics," *International Organization* 51, no. 4 (Autumn 1997): 520–21.

31. Freedman, "The Changing Forms of Military Conflict," 49.

32. Richard K. Betts, "The Delusion of Impartial Intervention," *Foreign Affairs* 73, no. 6 (November/December 1994): 20–33.

33. Barry R. Posen, "Military Responses to Refugee Disasters," *International Security* 21, no. 1 (Summer 1996): 80–81.

34. Alan C. Lamborn, "Theory and the Politics in World Politics," *International Studies Quarterly* 41, no. 2 (June 1997): 196.

35. For a more detailed discussion of these issues, see Joseph Lepgold, "NATO's Post–Cold War Collective Action Problem," *International Security* 23, no. 1 (Summer 1998): pp. 78–106.

36. Quoted in Richard Bernstein, "The Month That Lincoln Was Shot," *The New York Times,* 25 April 2001, B9.

37. Lamborn, "Theory and the Politics in World Politics," 193–94.

38. Inis L. Claude, Jr., "Collective Legitimization as a Political Function of the United Nations," in *International Organization: A Reader,* ed. Friedrich Kratochwil and Edward D. Mansfield (New York: HarperCollins, 1994), 197, emphasis in original. I thank John Duffield for a very helpful set of comments on this point.

39. Robert O. Keohane, "Neoliberal Institutionalism: A Perspective on World Politics," in *International Institutions and State Power: Essays in International Relations Theory* (Boulder, Colo.: Westview, 1989), pp. 4–5.

40. Robert O. Keohane, *After Hegemony: Cooperation and Discord in the World Political Economy* (Princeton, N.J.: Princeton University Press), chapter 6, 85–109.

41. Gareth Evans, *Cooperating for Peace: The Global Agenda for the 1990s and Beyond* (St. Leonards, Australia: Allen and Unwin, 1993), 29–33.

42. Freedman, "The Changing Forms of Military Conflict," 46, 49.

43. Quoted in Philip G. Roeder, "From Hierarchy to Hegemony: The Post-Soviet Security Complex," in *Regional Orders,* ed. Lake and Morgan, 227.

44. Sherman W. Garnett, "A Nation in Search of Its Place," *Current History* (October 1999): 330.

45. John W. R. Leppingwell, "The Russian Military and Security Policy in the 'Near Abroad,'" *Survival* 36, no. 3 (Autumn 1994): 70.

46. Roeder, "From Hierachy to Hegemony," 228–229; Jeff Checkel, "Russian Foreign Policy: Back to the Future?" *RFE/RL Research Report* 1, no. 41 (16 October 1992): 15–29.

47. Maxim Shashenkov, "Russian Peacekeeping in the 'Near Abroad,'" *Survival* 36, no. 3 (Autumn 1984): 52, 54; S. Neil MacFarlane, "On the Front Lines in the Near Abroad: The CIS and the OSCE in Russia's Civil Wars," *Third World Quarterly* 18, no. 3 (1997): 512–13; Roeder, "From Hierachy to Hegemony," 225; "Tajikistan Under Pressure," *The Economist,* 3 February 1996, www.economist.com.

48. Karen Dawisha and Bruce Parrott, *Russia and the New States of Eurasia* (New York: Cambridge University Press, 1994), 239–40; "How to Make Friends and Influence People," *The Economist,* 19 August 1995, www.economist.com; "Where Worlds Collide," *The Economist,* 19 August 2000, www.economist.com; MacFarlane, "On the Front Lines in the Near Abroad," 522.

49. Roeder, "From Hierarchy to Hegemony," 224.

50. Roeder, "From Hierarchy to Hegemony," 224–25.

51. Quoted in Shashenkov, "Russian Peacekeeping in the 'Near Abroad,'" 65. Kozyrev was considered among the top Russian officials friendliest to the West—and was dismissed when that became a liability—so these sentiments can be interpreted as reflecting a broad elite consensus.

52. Roeder, "From Hierarchy to Hegemony," 223; Wedgewood, "Regional and Subregional Organizations in International Conflict Management," 281.

53. Garnett, "A Nation in Search of Its Place," 328.

54. Garnett, "A Nation In Search of Its Place," 329.

55. Africa" refers here politically to the Sub-Saharan Africa and the Horn region, but not the northern states of the Maghreb. Although all states on the continent except Morocco are members of the OAU, the Maghreb is politically part of a Middle Eastern/Arab region.

56. John Stremlau, "Ending Africa's Wars," *Foreign Affairs* 79, no. 4 (July/August 2000): 119.

57. Stremlau, "Ending Africa's Wars," 119.

58. The quote is from Stremlau, "Ending Africa's Wars," 119. See also Connie Peck, *Sustainable Peace: The Role of the UN and Regional Organizations in Preventing Conflict* (Lanham, Md.: Rowman and Littlefield, 1998), 158.

59. Edmond Keller, "Rethinking African Security," in *Regional Orders,* ed. Lake and Morgan, 303–5.

60. Frank Bruni, "Bush Vows to Put Greater U.S. Focus on Latin America," *New York Times,* 26 August 2000, A9.

61. Keller, "Rethinking African Security," 308, 310.

62. Terrence Lyons, "Can Neighbors Help? Regional Actors and African Conflict Management," in *African Reckoning: A Quest for Good Governance*, ed. Francis M. Deng and Terrence Lyons (Washington, D.C.: Brookings Institution Press, 1998), 74–75.

63. See Alan C. Lamborn, "Theoretical and Historical Perspectives on Collective Security," in *Collective Conflict Management*, ed. Lepgold and Weiss, 38–39, for a discussion of these issues. In the classical balance-of-power era it was assumed that domestic legitimacy ultimately sprang from royal and aristocratic rights. The Concert of Europe began to come apart when the less liberal members (Austria, Russia, and Prussia) sought to use it as an instrument for domestic intervention to maintain traditional rule. That made more liberal members—France, and especially Britain—uncomfortable.

64. Lyons, "Can Neighbors Help?" 69.

65. Peck, *Sustainable Peace*, 161.

66. Quoted in Amadu Sesay, "Regional and Sub-Regional Conflict Management Efforts," in *Africa in the Post–Cold War International System*, ed. Sola Akinrinade and Amadu Sesay (London: Pinter, 1998), 52.

67. Sesay, "Regional and Sub-Regional Conflict Management Efforts," 53.

68. Keller, "Rethinking African Security," 311. For a detailed case study of this episode, see Herbert Howe, "Lessons of Liberia: ECOMOG and Regional Peackeeping," *International Security* 21, no. 3 (Winter 1996/97): 145–76.

69. Sesay, "Regional and Sub-Regional Conflict Management Efforts," 57.

70. Norrin M. Ripsman, "The Causes of Peace in Western Europe After World War II," unpublished manuscript, no date, 8–9.

71. "The Alliance's Strategic Concept," Agreed by the Heads of State and Government Participating in the Meeting of the North Atlantic Council, Rome, November 7–8, 1991, reprinted in NATO Handbook (Brussels: NATO Office of Information and Press, 1994), 237, paragraph 10.

72. "The Alliance's Strategic Concept," 237, paragraph 10.

73. Robert B. McCalla, "NATO's Persistence After the Cold War," *International Organization* 50, no. 3 (Summer 1996): 464.

74. North Atlantic Treaty Organization, "History of the NATO-Led Stabilization Force in Bosnia and Herzegovnia," 18 August 2000, www.nato.int.

75. Emanuel Adler, "Seeds of Peaceful Change: The OSCE's Security Community-Building Model," in *Security Communities*, ed. Emanuel Adler and Michael Barnett (Cambridge: Cambridge University Press, 1998), 132–38.

76. Wedgewood, "Regional and Subregional Organizations in International Conflict Management," 275.

77. Ivo H. Daalder and Michael E. O'Hanlon, *Winning Ugly: NATO's War to Save Kosovo* (Washington, D.C.: Brookings, 2000), 210–11.

78. Philip H. Gordon, "Their Own Army? Making European Defense Work," *Foreign Affairs* 79, no. 4 (July/August 2000): 14; Daalder and O'Hanlon, "Unlearning the Lessons of Kosovo," 136.

79. Charles A. Kupchan, "In Defense of European Defense: An American Perspective," *Survival* 42, no. 2 (Summer 2000): 24–25; Gordon, "Their Own Army?" 14.

80. Gordon, "Their Own Army?" 16.

81. "Border Disputes: The Costs of Petty Nationalism," *The Economist*, 19 August 2000, 32.

82. Andrew Hurrell, "An Emerging Security Community in South America?" in *Security Communities*, ed. Adler and Barnett, 233–34, 243–44.

83. Hurrell, "An Emerging Security Community in South America?" 244.

84. Jean-Philippe Therien, Michel Fortmann, and Guy Gosselin, "The Organization of American States: Restructuring Inter-American Multilateralism," *Global Governance* 2, no. 2 (May–August 1996): 219.

85. Peck, *Sustainable Peace*, 142–43.

86. Buzan, *People, States, and Fear*, 207.

87. Monica Serrano, "Latin America," in *The New Security Agenda: A Global Survey*, ed. Paul B. Stares (Tokyo: The Japan Center for International Exchange, 1998), 153.

88. G. John Ikenberry, *After Victory* (Princeton, N.J.: Princeton University Press, 2001).

2

Regional Conflict Management

Strategies, Necessary Conditions, and Comparative Effectiveness

PAUL F. DIEHL

Although there is little doubt that regional conflict management efforts are on the rise, often to the exclusion of global efforts, there remains the question of whether such efforts will be effective, and whether they will be superior to the alternatives. To gain insights into these questions, this chapter analyzes three broad categories of conflict management and resolution strategies: enforcement, peacekeeping, and peacemaking. For each of these strategies, I describe the processes by which the strategies are supposed to promote regional conflict management. Then, I explore the requirements for their success as delineated in scholarly and policymaking analyses. I then discuss whether regional groupings and efforts, both broadly and more specifically, can satisfy those requirements. Emphasis is placed on their comparative (dis)advantage vis-à-vis global efforts at conflict management; the choice is not usually between regional conflict management efforts and nothing, but between regional and global approaches (or some combination thereof). The intent is to identify the potential and limitations of regional conflict management efforts as a precursor to the case studies that follow in this collection.

Before proceeding to the analysis, there are three caveats or qualifications that should be made. First, in focusing on three particular conflict management processes (enforcement, peacekeeping, and peacemaking), I have necessarily ignored other possible approaches. These include balance of power, most forms of national deterrence, and the like. This is not to indicate that these are unimportant. Rather, the three chosen are those that are most commonly discussed or used in response to regional conflicts. In addition, the emphasis in this chapter is on multilateral[1] or collective actions toward conflict management rather than unilateral efforts, such as arms buildups, nuclear weapons acquisitions, or unilateral military interventions. This is not to say that such efforts cannot produce conflict management (although they may be as likely to precipitate escalation), merely that they are best left to analyses of individual state behavior. Accordingly, the three general strategies chosen for examination represent a continuum of coercion, allowing us to assess a range of options for conflict management and their relative success.

Second, the focus in this analysis is necessarily on the ability of the different approaches to produce conflict management, although they may have other purposes as well. For example, humanitarian assistance may be achieved through several different actions (e.g., enforcement, peacekeeping). This is not to ignore the importance of those other specific purposes, but only to note that they are secondary to the concern of this volume. Furthermore, one might argue that the achievement of conflict management may be a prerequisite, at least in the long run, for several of those other purposes, including human rights protection, political stability, and the like.

Third, it is necessary to make a distinction between conflict management and conflict resolution. Conflict resolution signifies that fundamental issues in dispute between parties are settled such that violent confrontations, crises, and wars no longer occur. Conflict management, on the other hand, may mean continued militarized conflict even if hostility levels are reduced. Even following successful conflict management, states may still view their relationship in militarized terms if no conflict resolution occurred. Conflict management may set the stage for conflict resolution to occur, but may not result in conflict resolution. For example, traditional peacekeeping operations have had some notable successes in managing conflicts in the sense of mitigating armed conflict, but they have been much less effective in promoting the final resolution of those conflicts.[2] As with other chapters in this collection, the main concern is with the management side of the fence, although elements of conflict resolution are addressed as relevant to given strategies and outcomes. The next section focuses on the most prominent form of regional conflict management: enforcement.

ENFORCEMENT

Traditionally, enforcement refers to large-scale military operations designed to defend the victims of aggression and restore peace and security by the defeat of aggressor forces; enforcement may also be designed to impose a particular solution in a given conflict.[3] More broadly, enforcement can be used to refer to any coercive, military action in response to a violation of international or regional norms. This strategy relies on the deterrent value of collective military action; if deterrence fails, however, states need to carry out the threatened military action and restore peace and security in the region. Recent examples of this include NATO actions against the former Yugoslavia. It may appear paradoxical to describe a large-scale use of military force as a strategy to manage conflict. Yet typically, the coercive use of military force is designed to stop armed conflict and prevent outcomes that the states or organizations taking the action regard as unjust and likely to produce more violence in the future. In this way, military force is used to produce outcomes that have the effect of managing conflict.

Enforcement actions can be roughly subdivided into two types. First is *collective security* in which a coalition of states, generally acting through an international organization, seek to deter or defeat (if necessary) any coalition member(s) that uses military force to alter the status quo. Most obviously, the provisions contained in Chapter VII of the UN Charter exemplify this type of arrangement. A second variation is what has been referred to as *collective defense*. This also involves deterrence or military action against an aggressor, but is more often the product of a traditional military alliance rather than an international governmental organization. A major difference is that collective defense is usually directed against a specific enemy *outside* of the grouping, whereas in collective security arrangements all members are potential aggressors, victims of aggression, or coalition partners. The original role of the NATO alliance in Europe is the prototypical example. A variation of collective defense, multilateral intervention, occurs outside the rubric of formal alliances. The size of the coalition of states is variable and may only number slightly more than two or three; their cooperation also may be ad hoc and thereby temporary. Such actions may also not be done for the public good, but rather for private interests. The Gulf War against Iraq is an example, although it did have UN approval.

Collective Security

Although collective security ideas have been around for centuries, they did not take institutional form until the League of Nations. Globally, collective security arrangements have not met the expectations on their founders.[4] The Korean War and the Gulf War are often cited as examples of UN collective security action, although technically neither conformed to Charter provisions for an operation directed by the UN Military Staff Committee, conducted under the direct auspices of the Security Council, and with military forces contributed by a broad set of member states. Part of the reason for the infrequency of collective security operations may be the difficult conditions necessary for such arrangements to be successful. Those requirements have been outlined in a classic study by Inis Claude.[5] This raises the question of whether those conditions might be fulfilled at the regional level, even as they remain unlikely at the global level.

Collective security arrangements may promote peace through greater transparency, promoting cooperation among members, and in socializing states to peaceful norms.[6] Yet fundamentally collective security relies on the threat or actual use of military force. Collective security is predicated on deterring any potential aggressor within a given set of states, and most critically on being able to identify the aggressor once an armed conflict breaks out. The former is largely a function of a credible threat by the coalition to respond any time and anywhere to military aggression; this credibility is determined by a series of other conditions below. The latter assumption is a difficulty in and of itself. First, there is the presumption that an aggressor can be objectively determined. Unfortunately, we know that some cases involve ambiguity; for example, preemptive strikes muddle the distinction between aggressor and victim. We also know that during the course of a violent conflict, the aggressor may sometimes shift (e.g., Iran-Iraq War), complicating decision making on when to take military action and against whom. The UN has adopted a Definition of Aggression,[7] but some leading states reject key provisions and the document does not fully solve the problems associated with aggression identification—a political judgment applying the criteria to a given situation is still required. Second, and most critically, identifying the aggressor is most often not an objective process, but a subjective one concluded as a part of decision making in politicized bodies. For collective security to work effectively, however, there must be consensus among member states on the identity of the aggressor in a given conflict. A split among the membership in that decision will lead to inaction or perhaps conflict escalation if competing coalitions support opposite sides in the conflict.

Certainly, many of the problems associated with identifying an aggressor are similar on the regional and global levels. During the Cold War, bipolar politics often made it difficult for the UN Security Council to agree on courses of action in response to peace and security threats. One might initially expect regional organizations to have an advantage over the United Nations because their membership is more homogeneous. In theory, states in a regional organization are more likely to be at the same development level; share historical, ethnic, or tribal roots; and have similar political outlooks from facing common regional problems. Although to some extent, one removes global concerns (e.g., outside economic interests) from the regional calculation, and proxy wars have greatly diminished, there still may be problems with consensus in regional settings. Within most regions, there may be considerable divergence on who an aggressor is and whether to take action against that actor in the event of a war. For example, a conflict involving North and South Korea might lead to stalemate in Asia as China and Japan could line up on opposite sides. Similarly, an inter-Arab conflict could split the League of Arab States apart and paralyze any efforts to deal with such a conflict. Ongoing regional rivalries (e.g., India-Pakistan) are the most likely threats to peace, and most regions of the world would have a difficult time reaching consensus on which side or the other to support in the event of war, especially in light of past support given to rivals by different states in the region.

Traditional global collective security, as elucidated in the UN Charter, is largely predicated on responding to an interstate war. This is not necessarily the case for a regional collective security effort, and indeed conflicts with a civil war component are the most likely threats to regional order. Assuming that collective security is even an applicable strategy for such conflicts, it is difficult to identify an aggressor. Does collective security mean that a coalition of states will always come to the aid of a challenged government? In many regions of the

world, organizations may be reluctant to involve themselves in what are regarded as internal or sovereign matters. The OAU and OAS have had long-
standing policies against external intervention in domestic matters. Leading
states, such as Russia and China, have also voiced opposition to international
intervention in domestic conflicts (e.g., Chechnya and Tibet, respectively).

Related to these concerns is the collective security requirement that states be
willing to fight for the status quo.[8] Generally collective security actions are designed to protect or restore the status quo in the event of an outbreak of violent
conflict. This presumes some consensus that the status quo is just, or at the very
least it presumes the availability of peaceful mechanisms for change in the status quo as alternatives to war. This condition may vary widely across regions.
Among Latin American states, there are settled borders and in recent years a
strong norm of democracy. It is quite conceivable that states in the region
would support the status quo, and indeed have done so in the recent past with
respect to domestic crises in Peru and Ecuador respectively. Elsewhere, that assumption is less tenable. For many years, enshrined in the OAU Charter, was
the principle that borders would not be altered through military force. Yet as the
Congo War demonstrates, consensus among some African states has broken
down and neighboring countries have shown a propensity to use military force
unilaterally in support of change. In West-Central Europe, the status quo also
seems desirable to most members. Yet it is unclear in Southeastern Europe (e.g.,
the case of Kosovo) whether the status quo (and this has been a moving target)
is acceptable and worth fighting for by the member states.

Even with support of the status quo and consensus on who the aggressor
might be, actors must still be willing to make a positive commitment to take action against that aggressor.[9] This means taking a number of risks and possibly
incurring significant costs; of course, costs vary across different contexts, and
thresholds for tolerance of costs can vary substantially across states. Supplying
troops and financing military efforts are the most obvious costs. In any collective action, there is the tendency for actors to "free ride" on other coalition
members, especially if there is a hegemon or other states who benefit disproportionately from the action and will provide much of the public good (deterrence and defense in this case) anyway. At the global level, this is a significant
problem as some UN members see little direct benefit to themselves in redressing conflicts on different continents; they also find mainly domestic political disincentives to supply military forces in support of such action. Some regions
would be more prone than others to the problems that attend to hegemony. In
Latin America, the United States stands out well above other OAS members in
terms of military capacity and political influence. In other regions, such as Europe, the playing field is considerably more level, and that region may not need
to depend on, or be as prone to, free ride on any given state. Still, regional conflict management would seem to produce less free-riding and more potential
for contributions to collective action; there are fewer actors in regions, and
hence each contribution is more essential, as well as that free-riding is more

transparent at the regional level. Presumably states will find themselves more affected by regional disorders than they would from conflicts that occur on the other side of the globe. As noted below, this can have some deleterious effects, but apathy is not the likely outcome.

Another element of political will is taking action no matter who the aggressor might be. This goes well beyond labeling one side or the other as the aggressor, but authorizing and using military force against that state. Some of the concerns about fighting for the status quo were elucidated above. Beyond those, however, some states play the role of villain better than others. To that extent that collective security actions might crosscut existing alliance patterns, it will be difficult to mobilize members to take action against a friendly state. Collective security requires that the principle (peaceful resolution) outweigh traditional loyalty in security decisions. In reality, we know that many states will be reluctant to take action against their allies and potentially in favor of their enemies. Regional efforts are not immune from this problem. One can imagine Chinese reluctance to aid South Korea in the event of an attack from the North. The Iran-Iraq war badly split the Arab League. In the Cold War world, bipolarity often made regional conflict management difficult because many states were aligned with one bloc or the other. This impediment is largely removed, but many regions still seem split by regional rivalries. For example, the India-Pakistani rivalry in Southeast Asia is a fault line along which some of the region's politics lie. Any attempt at collective security with respect to that or similar rivalries would almost assuredly fail.

The willingness to carry out military actions in the pursuit of collective security is really only half of the equation. Organizations or groups of states must have the military capability to take such action.[10] In the absence of this, deterrent threats will not be credible and defense actions unsuccessful. The capability component of collective security has several subelements. First, the collective security effort must have military power to deter or defeat any potential aggressor. A related second element is that there must be the proper structural or coordination mechanisms to direct and implement necessary actions. Assuming that all member states cooperate, most scenarios involving "all against one," the heart of collective security, find sufficient military capability for the group to defeat the individual aggressor. Collective security is deemed to work best when there is a diffusion of power.[11] At the global level, except perhaps with respect to a superpower, this seems assured. At the regional level, the conclusion is less clear. In opposing most small state aggressors, regional collectivities should, in theory, have little difficulty in mustering military superiority. This is true even whether one adopts various 3:1 or 5:1 attacker-to-defender force ratios necessary for victory. Yet several regions may have to face aggression by a hegemon, and it is unclear whether collective security is viable against such states. Hegemons may be strong enough to resist any collective efforts and at the same time impose significant military and economic costs on its neighbors. In the Western Hemisphere, the United States assumes this role and it is inconceivable that OAS members could take any action against that country. Similarly, Asian states could probably not take effective action against China, although one does recall Vietnam's successful resistance to the Chinese invasion of the border region of Vietnam in 1979. Russia exercises a hegemonic role in the Commonwealth of Independent States (CIS), and that organization was not created to deal with any potential Russian aggression in its former territories. The other members are not capable of defeating Russia in any conventional military engagement.

Major power states are not the only ones capable of resisting regional collective security efforts. States that are weak in the global arena may be hegemonic in a smaller regional context. For example, Nigeria is the leading power in West Africa and ECOWAS, and regional cooperative efforts are heavily dependent on its support. It is unlikely that any regional collectivity could take effective military action against Nigeria. Similarly, South Africa enjoys a dominant position in the southern portion of that continent. Thus, substituting regional collective security for global has the effect of limiting the potential aggressors against whom military action would be taken.

The second elements of effective military action are the presence of the rules, procedures, and structural apparatus to carry out collective security actions. These should include provisions in the charter of an organization and the appropriate bureaucratic structures to carry out military action. For virtually every nation-state, this comes in the form of a standing army, a defense ministry, and legal provisions relating to the military action. At the global level, these components are absent or moribund. The United Nations has provisions for collective security beginning with Article 39 in Chapter VII of the UN Charter. The Security Council is empowered to authorize such military action, and the Military Staff Committee is designed to direct such action. In theory, the UN has the infrastructure necessary to conduct collective security operations. Unfortunately, this veneer of preparedness is only a shell hiding inadequacy. The agreements needed to provide national military forces to UN service have never been negotiated. Thus, any operation must be ad hoc, clearly undermining any deterrent effect and jeopardizing any defensive action that might be needed. The Military Staff Committee is a toothless tiger largely ignored by the Security Council and UN member states. Russian proposals in the late 1980s to revive it only met with rejection by other leading states.

The structural components at the regional level for collective security are even less developed than those at the global level. At best, only NATO has the necessary components, and as noted below that organization is really carrying out a collective defense rather than a collective security mission. Within Europe otherwise, neither the European Union (EU) nor the Organization for Security and Cooperation in Europe (OSCE) have the mandate to conduct collective security operations.[12] Within Africa, perhaps a legacy of the Congo War in the early 1960s, the OAU has been resistant to any kind of international intervention. Its organizational structures were kept deliberately weak, and as such it does not have the structures to carry out any collective security operation, even if it were to have available military resources. Perhaps only with respect to the OAS are there the legal mechanisms in place to facilitate collective security. The Rio Treaty is essentially a collective security agreement in which an armed attack or threat of aggression against a signatory nation, whether by a member nation or by some other power, is considered an attack against all. Nevertheless, beyond that document, North, South, and Central American states do not have the joint forces, procedures, or experience necessary for collective security. In general then, global problems with collective security mandate and infrastructure are mirrored, if not exacerbated, at the regional level.

Collective security at the global level has been problematic because rarely, if ever, have the conditions for its success been present. The end of the Cold War has made consensus within the UN Security Council more likely, but far from certain. At the regional level, it appears that collective security operations are equally unlikely, or perhaps even more so. Because regional conflicts involve negative externalities[13] more than distant conflicts, it appears that regional entities will have incentives to take military action. Still, they may not be able to agree on what action to take against what target state. Furthermore, the problem of responding to aggression by a hegemon is magnified at the regional level. Finally, regional organizations have yet to be granted the mandate to perform collective security actions, much less have the processes and infrastructure in place to carry one out.

Collective Defense

Collective defense is similar to collective security on a number of dimensions. Both seek to manage conflict through effective deterrence, and failing that through the judicious use of military force against an aggressor. Many of the same requirements (and attendant problems) for collective security are also present for collective defense, including fighting for the status quo and having an effective military capability. Yet the major difference is that the former is generally directed against an external aggressor rather than one that comes from within the membership.[14] Collective defense is most often the purpose of formal alliances. For example, the NATO alliance was not designed to deal with a war between Greece and Turkey (two of its members) but was originally formed to meet the challenge of an invasion from the east by the Soviet Union and its allies. Problems with aggressor identification and common interests found with collective security are obviated with collective defense. In effect, the aggressor is identified by the alliance partners before the act of aggression. Many alliances are created with particular external threats in mind. Furthermore, the fact that states join an alliance is often an indication of common interests and policies that they are willing to fight to protect. States would not join a particular defense pact directed against a given enemy state if they had close relations with that state. Joining a collective defense effort also forces states to make an explicit commitment to come to the aid of a member who is attacked, whereas the commitment in the form of collective security is usually more imprecise and uncertain. There are many reasons for joining an alliance,[15] but for purposes of collective defense, states seek to combine their military capabilities in order to be superior to an enemy.

In theory then, collective defense arrangements may be superior to collective security for regional conflict management. Nevertheless, there are several pitfalls. Consensus may be less evident in actual practice in a given situation than it is with respect to principle. In addition, very few regions actually have such alliances to perform collective defense actions; this may indicate the aforementioned presumption of common interests among proximate states may not be accurate. The United States attempted to construct regional alliances in the early days of the Cold War in order to stem the tide of communism. Accordingly, NATO, the Southeast Asian Treaty Organization (SEATO), and the Australia–New Zealand–U.S. Pact (ANZUS) were created. Yet most of those, save NATO, withered away. There is now little in their place, and formal alliances are at a low ebb in the post–World War II era. NATO, however, still has the mandate and the military strength to carry out collective defense actions, but of course it may have lost its enemy with the breakup of the Soviet Union and the end of the Warsaw Pact.

Even when alliance structures exist in a region, they may cause more conflict than they solve. The security dilemma suggests that targets of those alliances may view any alleged defensive preparations as hostile and begin countermeasures. Actions that may have been intended to deter opponents run the risk of provoking them. In other cases, alliance coverage may not be complete for a region, creating "out-of-area" problems. That is, collective defense is predicated on certain scenarios and protecting alliance members. What happens when conflict occurs outside of those boundaries? The challenge for NATO in Kosovo or Macedonia highlights the problems of holes in defense coverage for the region. NATO's military capacity for collective defense is unquestioned, but burden-sharing and other problems arise when it is confronted with out-of-area challenges.[16] Yet it is exactly these kinds of problems, rather than a Russian invasion, that are the most likely threats to peace in Europe over the coming decades.

In summary, collective defense stemming from formal alliances appears to be a more viable regional strategy than collective security, but at present few regions have the arrangements in place to do an effective job. The alternative is ad hoc multilateral interventions by states in the region. Because such actions are only in response to outbreaks of violence, however, deterrence is limited. Most states in the world have a standing military with the ability to carry out enforcement actions outside their borders (although to varying degrees). Thus, capability will not often be a constraining factor; rather, it will be a question of how often and in what numbers will states band together to intervene in extant conflicts.

Most obviously, state intervention into ongoing conflicts is not common. We cannot expect that every conflict will generate interventions from the more than 190 other states in the international system; indeed, most interstate militarized conflicts remain dyadic[17] and civil wars do not always prompt intervention. Yet when interventions do occur, they are predominantly unilateral, as multilateral military interventions, outside of international organizations, are even more rare. Even when multiple states intervene in a conflict, they may support opposing sides and those on the same side may not coordinate actions, belying the term "multilateral."

What generally motivates states to take military action is that the conflict in question significantly affects some national interest. States that are in closer geographic proximity are more likely to take part in interventions,[18] largely because negative externalities are greater in such cases. This is because such states are more likely to be affected by a nearby conflict than states further away. Major powers are unlikely to commit military force unless their strategic interests or those of an ally are jeopardized. Thus, the United States, Britain, and France were willing to commit military forces to redress the Iraqi invasion of Kuwait because allies (Israel, Saudi Arabia) were threatened and oil price spikes might have jeopardized the global economy. In contrast, those same states have been reluctant to commit troops to deal with the war in the Congo. Yet humanitarian motives have become more prominent[19] in interstate interventions over the last twenty years, and indeed are associated with the increased likelihood of intervention in civil wars as well.[20] Accordingly, there are some interventions that are not easily explained by conventional realpolitik or national interest reasons.

The purpose, although not exclusively, of most multilateral interventions is more limited: to stop the fighting.[21] Yet military intervention is as likely to produce conflict escalation than it is conflict management or resolution. I have treated collective enforcement as designed to promote conflict management and resolution, both of which are public goods. Yet there is a greater risk with military intervention that the states that intervene do so in pursuit of private, rather than public, goods. After all, as noted above, national interest is a strong motivating factor for intervention. Thus, states may take enforcement actions that directly serve their own narrowly defined interests. This may lead a conflict to be bloodier or last longer than if intervention did not occur. It may also lead to outcomes that are perceived as unjust, or do not contribute to long-term peace and stability.[22] Thus, military enforcement by ad hoc coalitions of states may be more likely than other forms of collective enforcement, but it is also less likely to achieve the kinds of ends envisioned in a regional conflict management strategy.

Regan identifies a number of conditions associated with intervention success in civil wars, but these are applicable as well to some interstate contexts.[23] First, he finds that for relatively low-level conflicts, intervention may actually be counterproductive. In these cases, regional management efforts might better be delayed lest actors intervene in conflicts that might otherwise resolve themselves. Fortunately, states do not usually intervene in a conflict until it has reached a critical point, often after the conflict has escalated and a significant number of casualties have occurred.[24] Yet, Regan also notes that waiting too long can be just as damaging to success. When intervention occurs during a civil war that has already experienced high casualties, it becomes quite difficult to stop the fighting. At that point, positions on both sides have been hardened and hatred has been intensified because of the fighting. This effect is perhaps why the Israeli-Palestinian conflict becomes more difficult to solve with each death. Second, intervention is less successful in ethnic or ideological civil wars. The latter are less prominent than they were during the Cold War, but regional conflict, especially in Africa and the Balkans, has been increasingly characterized by ethnic disputes.

Multilateral military interventions do not appear a likely solution to the problems of collective security and defense. Relative to global or extraregional interventions, they seem to have mixed attributes. On the one hand, restricting interventions to those by coalitions of states from the region eliminates the influence of outside states, especially major powers. For those concerned with limiting imperialism and the like, this is an advantage. At the same time, however, major power interventions are among the most likely to succeed in stopping the fighting.[25] Multilateral military interventions in the past (e.g., the Korean and Gulf Wars) have traditionally been broad coalitions in membership, but narrow in leadership. It is not clear that regional collectivities would always have a given state to lead the way or that other states would tolerate a leadership role by one of their own. Certain regions, such as South Asia, are unlikely candidates for such an arrangement. Extraregional efforts widen the scope of the potential participants as they narrow the incentives for those participants to join the coalition. Overall, multilateral military interventions and collective defense in particular are not good candidates for regional conflict management in the near future.

Enforcement and Civil Conflict

In the discussion of conflict enforcement, the emphasis has been on the conditions necessary to take such action, and whether they would be present or not on a regional level. Largely ignored in this section has been whether collective military action would be *effective* in promoting conflict management in the kinds of conflict that challenge regional order. On this count, there is reason for doubt, even were the prerequisites for collective enforcement action present. In the past decade (and this is likely to be true for the immediate future as well), the challenges to regional order have come from conflicts that have an exclusive or primary internal war component. Unfortunately, many collective security arrangements and to a lesser extent collective defense ones seem to presuppose an *inter*state conflict, most conventionally where one state crosses international borders to attack and occupy a portion of another state. Such conflicts still exist; witness the Iraqi invasion of Kuwait and more recently the border war between Ethiopia and Eritrea. Still, most recent analyses[26] regard such wars as the minority of conflicts in the world today. Internal conflicts of various kinds—ethnic conflicts, failed states, and old-fashioned civil wars—have become more common.

In the context of civil conflict, collective security and, to a lesser extent, collective defense may lose some of their meaning. Generally, provisions for those strategies are not triggered by civil conflict, unless it spills over and threatens the peace of surrounding states. Even then, collective actions become difficult. Who is the aggressor against which military action might be taken? This is not always clear. It may be impossible to determine who fired the first shot. It also raises the prospect of making judgments on what is the suitable exercise of force by the extant government in order to maintain order. When is coercive action the standard part of government function and when does it cross the line and become unacceptable, and thereby aggression? These are also questions that other states do not want to address, largely because they deal with issues of sovereignty. Although sovereignty is perhaps more permeable than it was a decade or two ago, there is still strong support for the principle of state sovereignty and its corollary of nonintervention in the internal affairs of states; indeed, this is a hallmark of OAS relations. Thus, it is unlikely that collectivities will frequently be willing to enter a civil war and fight against the ruling government. Coalitions of neighboring states may be equally reluctant to intervene consistently in support of the local government against internal opponents. Indeed, past interventions in civil wars have been about equally divided in favor of and in opposition to the extant government.[27] No collective security or defense arrangement is conceived of as performing local police or security functions. In the context of failed states, distinctions between government and opposition are superfluous.

Were collective enforcement action undertaken, it is not clear that brute military force would be able to bring peace and stability to these troubled areas of the world. A preponderance of military might is capable of defeating an aggressor state and compelling its forces to withdraw from a disputed territory. Such military force cannot, however, reestablish government authority or legitimacy on its own. Traditional military force may also be less capable of eradicating or defeating informal militias, underground movements, guerrilla bands, and the like. This would seem to require a more holistic and less fully coercive strategy than is suggested by collective enforcement.

In general the prospects for collective enforcement as a strategy for regional conflict management are not promising. Collective security in its traditional form has been all but impossible at the global level, and many of the problems there are similar to those encountered at the regional level. Specifically, problems in securing consensus for military action and the lack of enforcement infrastructure are likely to cripple any collective security efforts at the regional level. Collective defense efforts overcome some of these limitations, but there is still the problem that few alliance structures presently exist to carry out such actions. Furthermore, collective defense efforts carry with them problems of their own, such as responding to out-of-area conflicts and favoring preidentified friends at the expense of preidentified enemies, even when this is counterproductive to conflict management. Finally, multilateral interventions lack whatever deterrent value the other forms of collective enforcement have. It is also the case that interventions may serve the private interests of the intervening parties, rather than global or regional interests of conflict management and resolution.

PEACEKEEPING

A less coercive set of conflict management strategies are encompassed under the peacekeeping rubric. This refers to the deployment of lightly armed troops, most often under the sponsorship of global or regional organizations, to address threats to peace and security. In contrast to collective enforcement, peacekeeping operations involve significantly fewer troops, with the typical peacekeeping operation numbering less than six thousand during the Cold War periods and more than ten thousand thereafter; these figures are still considerably less than collective enforcement operations, which may involve several hundred thousand troops as was the case in the Gulf War. Unlike traditional military operations, peacekeeping operations also include only lightly armed personnel, the typical soldier carrying no more than a rifle. Peacekeeping missions do not generally require the identification of an aggressor, and thereby are more likely to play neutral or impartial roles in the conflict. Peacekeeping may include a variety of functions, including cease-fire monitoring, election supervision, humanitarian assistance, nation building, arms control verification, and others. Recent examples of regional peacekeeping efforts include the ECOMOG operation in Liberia and the Australian-led effort in East Timor.

Although the value of peacekeeping operations depends on the exact missions assigned to them and their match with particular conflict situations, there are several ways in which peacekeeping forces can promote regional conflict management and resolution. Peacekeeping operations generally cannot enforce a peace; therefore it is unlikely that they can mitigate armed conflict through coercive action. Clearly, a lightly armed military force, even at the high end of the size range (at its peak, sixty thousand troops were in NATO's force in Bosnia) will have difficulty defeating many highly motivated opponents and establish stability, except in a small sector. Although peacekeepers might be placed in situations in which armed conflict is active, such as in Bosnia, they are generally deployed after a cease-fire has been achieved. For example, peacekeepers have taken up positions on the Ethiopia-Eritrean border, but only after the war between those states ended. Thus, to some extent, the peacekeeping strategy occurs in contexts in which some conflict management has already been achieved.

Peacekeeping solidifies extant conflict management and facilitates further management in several ways. By acting as an interposition force between combatants or by patrolling given sectors of a country (or both), the peacekeeping force has the effect of separating combatants, thereby preventing "accidental" military engagement. Thus, small incidents, which could escalate and reignite full-scale armed conflict, are avoided. The presence of peacekeeping forces also makes deliberate violations of cease-fires and other hostile acts more transparent. Those willing to use armed force may wish to do so anonymously (e.g., sniper fire around the Green Line in Beirut), so that responsibility for the action cannot be attributed to any actor. Peacekeeping provides a mechanism to detect cease-fire violations and identify parties responsible for the action. Furthermore, in the case of interstate conflict, peacekeepers can detect military movements that suggest a military strike is imminent. If successful, such detection removes some of the advantage to striking first (surprise attack), and lessens the preemptive urge from nervous enemies worried that such an attack might happen. In either case, by denying anonymity and dissipating first-strike incentives, peacekeepers may deter hostile parties from renewing conflict. In promoting conflict management, peacekeeping also relies on the moral power of the organization or coalition conducting the operation. Parties may be reluctant to renew conflict when peacekeeping efforts are supported by the broader regional or global community. Although not the same deterrent effect supposedly present in collective security, an attack against the peacekeepers and violations of the cease-fire still carries with it normative implications and potential loss of political support for the violator.

Peacekeeping has been increasingly called upon to promote conflict resolution as well. This is also accomplished in several ways. Peacekeeping is designed to provide a fruitful environment for negotiations between warring parties. Parties engaged in military conflict are thought to be less likely to talk with their enemy, much less offer meaningful concessions at the bargaining table. An exception may be a "victor's peace" imposed on the losing side; yet these often provide no lasting end to the conflict. Peacekeeping relies on the hope that the absence of military combat will allow enmities to dissipate enough for negotiations to take place. Indeed, peacekeeping is an important first step in cooperation; generally, both sides must agree to accept peacekeeping and, in the case of the host states, accept troops on their soil as a means of limiting the conflict.

Once there is acceptance of the peacekeeping option, each side may be open to conciliation or mediation efforts because of the spillover of cooperation from that initial agreement. The hope is that the initial agreement will lead to an echo effect of mutually reinforcing, reciprocal, and conciliatory actions—cooperation at one point in time will increase the likelihood of cooperation in subsequent interactions between the same parties. A valuable cooling-off period might also follow the introduction of peacekeeping troops and the beginning of conciliatory efforts.

Of course, there is the risk that the opposite may occur.[28] Negotiations appear to be more successful when there are significant time pressures on the parties involved. Concessions are more forthcoming when there is pressure to reach an agreement; it is not surprising that conciliatory actions tend to increase as a deadline for settlement approaches. States will also make concessions when they believe the situation might adversely change in the near future or they tire of the political, economic, or human costs of war. Peacekeeping, according to this line of thought, removes much of the immediacy from the situation, and thereby takes away some of the incentives for negotiations or concessions. With a cease-fire, internal political or moral pressures to end the conflict are dissipated. In the absence of these pressures, states could fear that offers of concessions or conciliatory actions will be viewed as signs of weakness by an opponent and correspondingly not reciprocated. Once peacekeeping forces are in place, bargaining positions may harden, precipitating a stalemate.[29] The status quo becomes an acceptable alternative to serious negotiation or renewed fighting; the status quo entails no bloodshed, as well as no need to offer concessions that affect national interests or are difficult to sell to a domestic political audience. Thus, a patient strategy of doing nothing yields some benefits, and the hope for a more favorable set of circumstances at a later time is preserved. A tolerance (if not preference) for the status quo of a cease-fire by one or both parties can also cause problems.

Other ways that peacekeeping promotes conflict resolution relate to specific functions that peacekeepers are asked to perform. Most of these occur during the latter phases of a conflict, after a cease-fire has been achieved and often following some kind of agreement between the conflicting parties. There are a number of different roles or missions that peacekeepers, beyond simple interposition, might perform to promote conflict resolution. For example, *election supervision* consists of observation and monitoring of a cease-fire, disarmament, and a democratic election following a peace agreement among previously warring internal groups. UN operations in Namibia in the late 1980s and Cambodia in the early 1990s are examples. *State/nation or peace building* includes the restoration of law and order in the absence of government authority, the reconstruction of infrastructure and security forces, and facilitation of the transfer of power from the interim authority to an indigenous government. The United Nations carried out some of these functions in the Congo in the early 1960s, but it was unable to do so in Somalia after the deployment of forces in the early 1990s. In each of these cases, the peacekeeping operation is not the instigator of the conflict resolution process but is an important facilitator and perhaps a necessary condition to keep the process on track.

There are a number of different factors that are associated with peacekeeping success. These can roughly be categorized under consensus/support, resources, and various elements related to the exact peacekeeping mission undertaken. Each of these components are elucidated below and discussed in the context of regional peacekeeping operations (with global operations as a point of comparison).

Consensus and Support

In order for a peacekeeping operation to be successful, an essential ingredient is broad-based support for the operation from a number of sources. First, it has to be authorized. This means that consensus must exist among regional groups to carry out a particular peacekeeping mission. At the same time, there must be acceptance of a regional solution by extraregional parties. Most likely, regional peacekeeping operations will be carried out by a regional organization. Indeed, the limited record of non-UN operations finds regional organizations far more likely than single states or ad hoc groups of states to conduct peacekeeping operations.

Regional homogeneity might promote more consensus than the diverse UN membership would.[30] These commonalities are supposed to provide greater consensus among the members and make authorization of peacekeeping operations easier, as there will be fewer disagreements blocking strong action.[31] That the problem is in their backyard is also supposed to increase state interest and thereby avoid inaction.[32] In practice, however, these expectations have gone unfulfilled. Regional organizations have authorized few peacekeeping operations (and very few operations of any sort) in their histories. One often finds great splits among members of regional organizations when dealing with regional conflicts. Regional animosities also tend to hamper regional organizations' actions. Unity from homogeneity comes in response to threats to security *external* to the organization, such as Arab unity against Israel or African support for decolonization in Angola. The most common threats to regional peace—internal threats—are exactly those least likely to generate consensus.

Consensus as an ingredient for peacekeeping success extends beyond the initial authorization. Regional conflict management requires continuing cooperation between the states and the organization conducting the operation. A second key element for regional peacekeeping success is the support given them by the disputants and the local population.[33] This is especially critical given that peacekeeping operations will be largely ineffective in disarming local military forces.[34] The people and governments in a region have an inherent suspicion of what they perceive as outside intervention. Thus, there are frequently calls for "Arab" or "African" solutions to regional conflicts before international forces intervene. Disputants may be more accepting of actions by a regional organization, but, just as important, subnational groups and others in the conflicting states may see such actions as more legitimate. Thus, one might expect the operation to run more smoothly and the peacekeeping force to be less subject to controversy and attack. The experience of African states in the UN peacekeeping operation in the Congo (ONUC, 1960–64) soured those countries on global peacekeeping operations. They believed that the UN was not sensitive to their situation, and many withdrew support from ONUC amid claims that it was serving imperialist interests. Similarly, the Arab states tried to find an Arab solution to the

Iraqi invasion of Kuwait, rather than rely on U.S.-led activities in the United Nations. In general, states and their people will prefer to localize conflict rather than expand it to the global arena.

To the extent that regional peacekeeping operations can generate more support than UN missions, they have an important advantage. The regional organization and its peacekeeping forces must be accepted as honest brokers in the conflict. This again may be difficult to achieve. For example, an OAS operation that is led by the United States and that may serve U.S. interests will have less legitimacy than a UN force. A Syrian-led force in Lebanon would encounter similar difficulties. If the conflict at hand causes splits in the region as a whole, then an operation is unlikely to receive authorization and, even if approved, may not be perceived as neutral or fair by all parties. Thus, while the advantage of greater support is true in theory, it is less likely to be manifest in practice.

Another important element for the success of peacekeeping is the behavior of third-party states.[35] These typically are neighboring states to the conflict, although they might also include states that are allied with the combatants or extraregional states who have a vested interest in the outcome of the conflict. Such states are usually better positioned to undermine a peacekeeping mission than they are to facilitate success.[36] Third-party states can directly intervene, but more likely they will supply arms and political support to one or more of the combatants or take other actions detrimental to the cause of peace. Regional peacekeeping forces may be better able to secure the support of the neighboring third-party states. The latter, as members of the authorizing organization, will almost assuredly participate in the debate and approval of a regional peacekeeping operation; this may not be the case with a UN operation authorized by the Security Council. In this way, such third-party states have a better chance of modifying the operation according to their views and are more likely to support it. More important, they are less likely to sabotage the peacekeeping operation, a major cause of the failure of UN operations. One might also presume that active third-party opposition to a peacekeeping force could prevent that force's approval by the regional organization, thus avoiding the embarrassing failures experienced by some UN operations. Extraregional third-party states, especially major powers, may also be important. Yet, with a few exceptions (Middle East, Bosnia, Kosovo), leading states have shunned regional conflicts in the post–Cold War period, quite in contrast to the patron-client relationships that existed in earlier decades.

The support of third-party states is a definite benefit for regional peacekeeping operations and constitutes the primary advantage of those operations over missions run by global organizations or multinational configurations. Yet one must recognize that there may be instances in which a third-party state is not cooperating with the peacekeeping force (e.g., North Korea in any potential operation on the Korean peninsula), and regional groups may still have to contend with opposition from subnational actors, much as the United Nations does. Third-party opposition might also prevent the regional organization from taking any peacekeeping action at the outset.

RESOURCES

Similar to the requirements for collective security, effective peacekeeping necessitates the availability and provision of resources (financial, material, and human capital) to carry out the mission; this is a common theme in many peacekeeping analyses,[37] especially those written by former peacekeeping officials.[38] As the peacekeeping strategy has evolved from simple interposition functions to more complex tasks, those requirements have increased. There is a strong risk that the difficulties the United Nations has experienced in paying for peacekeeping operations and soliciting contributions for equipment and other supplies would be magnified in a regional operation.[39] A regional peacekeeping operation would incur expenses similar to a UN operation, but may have fewer states to draw upon for contributions. Each member would have to pay more than if the costs were borne on a global level; an organization with a small membership could find the burden crushing. Of course, one must be careful not to infer too much of an advantage for the UN on this dimension. The UN may have a broader membership, but it has had significant burden-sharing controversies, and spending on peacekeeping operations has often been at the forefront of those debates.

One may not need to worry as much about funding and supplying a peacekeeping operation if the regional organization is composed of wealthier, developed states, as is the EU—although it also has financial constraints. Yet an organization of less developed countries, such as the OAU, cannot rely solely on its members to pay for the operation. Even setting aside the financial aspects, many of these organizations' members are not sufficiently advanced technologically to provide equipment such as helicopters or personnel carriers to the peacekeeping force. Thus, regional organizations in some cases may have the willingness but not the means to authorize a peacekeeping force. The U.S. sponsorship of the African Crisis Response Initiative (ACRI) in which the United States and western states provide financing and training for African states' peacekeeping troops was designed to address this concern (as well as obviate the need for western troops); it remains to be seen whether this idea will be fully implemented, much less be successful.[40] Resource constraints were most prominent in the OAU operation in Chad. Many states failed to follow through on promises to support the peacekeeping force with troops and financial contributions. Indeed, the OAU had to appeal to the United Nations and external states for assistance in paying for the operation. It is doubtful that the OAU or a similar grouping of poor states could sustain a peacekeeping force for an extended period without outside aid. Other regional groupings might fare better. The League of Arab States may be able to rely on oil-rich members as benefactors of an operation. Similarly, the OAS would not encounter resource difficulties if the United States were to bear a disproportionate share of the burden in providing money and equipment. Nevertheless, resource constraints may determine which organizations can carry out peacekeeping operations and for how long they can do so.

A second problem associated with regional peacekeeping operations is their organization. Regional organizations that are structurally underdeveloped, with a small and weak secretariat, such as the League of Arab States, would have difficulty managing an operation. The OAU, for example, had to rely on an ad hoc monitoring commission headed by the secretary-general to direct its operation in Chad. Most obviously, NATO has the organization and the military personnel to conduct a peacekeeping operation. Nevertheless, the shift from a coercive military mission to a peacekeeping one is not as easy as it first might appear.[41] The structures and training for peacekeeping are dramatically different that for those involving traditional military operations. Accordingly, NATO has sometimes struggled with the "softer" aspects of its missions in Bosnia and in Kosovo. Furthermore, its partnership with the UN in Bosnia was not especially successful, suggesting limits of coordination between different organizations in carrying out regional conflict management.[42]

Even if regional organizations have some structures that could direct peacekeeping operations, most, if not all, lack procedures and precedents for organizing and operating a peacekeeping operation. The United Nations is successful in its ad hoc arrangements in part because of its experience in running previous operations. Regional organizations have little experience, and in some cases the precedents established, such as the OAU operation in Chad, did not provide methods that should be repeated. This reflects on the path-dependent effects from existing institutional arrangements noted in the previous chapter. Until the regional organizations explicitly plan for peacekeeping operations and gain some experience in the task, they will be at a comparative disadvantage vis-à-vis the United Nations.

Missions

In carrying out a peacekeeping mission, there are several concerns that affect its success. These include the ability of the peacekeeping force to act in a neutral fashion, the clarity of its mandate, the geographic configuration of the deployment area, and the suitability of the peacekeeping force to undertake the particular mission specified.

A key requirement for the success of most peacekeeping operations is that the combatants perceive the peacekeeping forces as impartial. Regional peacekeeping forces will have difficulty meeting the standard established by the United Nations. First, with the exception perhaps of the Nordic countries, most regional groupings have few personnel trained in peacekeeping techniques and philosophy. This means that a peacekeeping force would likely be composed of regular soldiers from national armies; indeed, this was the case in previous regional peacekeeping efforts. These personnel are more likely to go beyond the limitations imposed by the peacekeeping strategy and become embroiled in the conflict. Of course, this scenario could change with experience, and regional groupings could draw from those who served in past UN missions. Still, many plans for a regional force designate using the same force in enforcement and peacekeeping duties.[43] Indeed, NATO has experienced problems resulting from this in Bosnia and Kosovo.

Beyond limited training in peacekeeping philosophy and tactics, regional peacekeeping forces may have difficulty in drawing troops from nonaligned countries. UN operations will often draw the bulk of their troops from outside the region of conflict, believing that these states are more disinterested in the conflict than those in the immediate area. Regional organizations do not have that luxury. In this Chad operation, the OAU tried to limit troop contributions to states that did not share a land border with the area of conflict. This practice certainly helps promote the neutrality of the force, but it does not exclude other states that have economic or political ties—or who desire them—to the area involved (e.g., Iraq or Syria in the Middle East). The smaller the area and the fewer the members of the regional organization, the more difficult it will be to put together a neutral force. Even if a regional organization is successful in acquiring properly trained forces from neutral states, it still must deal with the disputants' perceptions of the forces. A force composed of personnel from regional states may be viewed more suspiciously, regardless of its behavior. It is possible to put together a neutral regional force, but the task is much easier on the global level.

The mandate given a peacekeeping mission defines what its mission will be and often sets out goals that are to be achieved, and this can have a significant effect on the outcome of the mission.[44] On some occasions, the mandate also sets out precise plans for deployment and duties to be performed. The key aspects of the mandate are its clarity,[45] specificity,[46] and open-endedness. The first refers to how precisely the purpose and actions of the force are spelled out: that is, is it clear why the forces are there? The second concerns how much detail is provided as to how and where those duties will be carried out. The last element concerns whether there is a meaningful exit point, beyond a perfunctory termination date, for the achievement of the goals.

The mandate is thought to influence the success of peacekeeping operations in several ways. First, a clear and detailed mandate with definable goals sets the expectations of the actors involved; this is especially important in that there is no explicit treaty commitment involved and an ad hoc coalition will usually need to be assembled to undertake the mission. Presumably, the mandate reflects an existing consensus among all parties (the protagonists and the authorizing agency) on what the peacekeeping force will do in the area. Thus, there is less room for disagreement over varying interpretations of the mandate. This helps ensure continued support for the operation among the protagonists and members of the authorizing body. Withdrawal of support or attacks on the peacekeeping force stemming from disagreements over peacekeeping duties or actions is less likely when the force's mission is clear.

Second, a clear mandate helps ensure public support (domestic and regional) for the peacekeeping operation. In order to bring the weight of domestic and international public opinion behind a peacekeeping operation, the force must have clearly identifiable goals and duties. Without those, the public may not understand why the troops are there or may question the validity of the peacekeeping strategy in the situation at hand. Yet sometimes mandate clarity suffers as a condition of authorization. For example, during the UN's first operation in the Congo during the 1960s, the peacekeeping mandate was vague and contradictory.[47] That is, the price of consensus to authorize a mission may be a vague or imprecise mandate on which all states can agree. Another particular concern in analyzing mandates is the specification of exit points. This has become critical for political and logistical support by some countries. The main problem is finding a balance between two risks. One is having the peacekeeping mission leave too early, before the conflict is stabilized and on the road to resolution; UN operations in Somalia (UNOSOM II) is an example. At the other extreme is a peacekeeping operation lingering too long, but unable to withdraw without threatening the peace; the UN operation in Cyprus, about to complete its fourth decade, is illustrative.

Geographic considerations are also an important dimension of peacekeeping operations and their prospects for success. Conventional wisdom and experience in several operations suggest some expectations about the effect of the local geography on peacekeeping success. One expectation is that the larger the area of deployment, the more difficult it will be for the peacekeeping force to achieve its mission.[48] Peacekeeping forces are small in size relative to regular military units, and it is impossible to maintain constant vigilance over thousands of miles. There is clearly more opportunity for cease-fire violations, acts of genocide, and other undesirable behavior to remain undetected, or at least for the perpetrators to remain unidentified. Thus, peacekeeping efforts in the Congo are more likely to encounter problems than those in East Timor. The disadvantage of a large area to patrol is partially offset, however, by other characteristics of the deployment zone.

The terrain of the area can also affect the operation. An open area with little vegetation or few buildings provides an easy line of sight to detect hostile activity. For example, the Sinai is a desert terrain that provided for easy observation. In contrast, natural barriers such as mountains or hills or man-made obstructions, such as factories or houses, decrease the ability of peacekeeping forces to supervise the area of deployment. Peacekeepers had great difficulty deterring attacks on cities in Bosnia, when artillery in the surrounding country-side could attack urban areas and responsibility for attacks could not easily be determined. Indeed, some journalists and others on the ground argued that Bosnian Muslims bombed their own people, hoping the Serbs would be blamed and NATO would retaliate with air strikes.

Problems with a large area are also offset to some extent by low population density there. If there are few people in a desert area, for example, almost any movement is a sign of trouble. In contrast, an urban area means that thousands of people are constantly moving about, and it may be next to impossible to stop all of them at checkpoints to detect those smuggling weapons or explosives. Thus, peacekeeping forces are likely to be most effective when they are the only group in the area, and hostile movements will be most obvious. Thus, a peacekeeping force for the Korean DMZ would likely fare better than one assigned to Chechnya.

The peacekeeping force must also be deployed so as to protect itself. If the force is in an area where it is easily subject to attack or infiltration, fatalities involving the force are likely. Although a peacekeeping force is not a military one in the traditional sense, it still needs to adopt defensive positions that are the most invulnerable to attack—otherwise domestic support in contributing states for the operation can become tenuous. There have been a number of unfortunate incidents in Bosnia and in Sierra Leone in which peacekeeping soldiers have been captured and held hostage.

During the Cold War era, peacekeeping missions could be classified largely by the political context of the disputes they dealt with.[49] Nevertheless, they all roughly shared the same mandate or mission. Peacekeeping operations were dedicated to being interposition forces (i.e., separating combatants) that performed cease-fire monitoring functions. Some peace observation missions were too small in number and were unarmed and therefore did not necessarily function as a buffer between the disputants. Nevertheless, the passive monitoring of a temporary peace agreement was the hallmark of traditional operations.

One of the greatest changes in peacekeeping operations over the past decade has been the dramatic expansion in the number and types of tasks they might now be asked to perform. To sort some of this out, Diehl, Druckman, and Wall[50] developed a taxonomy of actual and potential (those suggested by policymakers and scholars) peacekeeping missions, broadly defined. These are presented in box 2.1.

It is quite likely that different types of missions will be influenced by different factors. For example, neutrality has been identified as a key factor in traditional peacekeeping and might be important in other monitoring functions. Yet one might expect it to be unrelated (or perhaps even negatively related) to peacekeeping success in missions that help restore civil societies. Dandeker and Gow[51] argue that more coercive missions (e.g., pacification), what they label as "strategic peacekeeping," must maintain political support from domestic audiences, some of those in the host state and beyond to achieve success. This legitimation is significantly less important in traditional peacekeeping.

Peacekeeping operations were originally designed (number, rules of engagement, etc.) for monitoring cease-fires. Not surprisingly, then, new peacekeeping missions that fall closer to this traditional standard tend to be more successful.[52] Arms control verification and election supervision are two examples. With respect to the latter, peacekeepers have a good record in facilitating free and fair elections in Cambodia, Mozambique, El Salvador, and elsewhere.[53]

Similarly, those peacekeeping operations most different from traditional operations tend to have, or are likely to have, great difficulties. In large part, this is because the peacekeeping forces are ill-designed to carry out the tasks required of them. For example, nation building is a multifaceted enterprise that cannot be achieved or imposed through the application of military force. Although peacekeeping may provide one of the necessary conditions in the nation-building process (e.g., peace), peacekeepers are not necessarily suitable for developing government infrastructure, although they can be an important component in the process.[54] Highly coercive missions may also be incompatible with peacekeeping philosophy, functions, and design. In those cases, operations may be better conducted along conventional military lines, with the training, equipment, size, and rules of engagement suitable for coercive missions.[55] Thus, although there is a range of different functions that might be performed by peacekeepers, not all of them are conducive to success.

A second consideration is the compatibility of different missions under the umbrella of one peacekeeping operation. Although one can distinguish between different missions, in practice a given peacekeeping operation may attempt to perform more than one mission, either simultaneously or sequentially. The net effect can be extremely problematic. For example, the attempt to combine pacification efforts with humanitarian assistance efforts in Somalia is illustrative of such incompatibility of functions, at least when performed by the same operation. One implication may be that divergent missions are best handled by different sets of personnel or separate operations. In the cases of pacification and humanitarian assistance, a prominent role for traditional military forces in the former and NGOs in the latter, with appropriate coordination between the two, would be preferable to having peacekeepers attempt both roles simultaneously.

Regional conflict management can develop from peacekeeping operations, but it is clear that much depends on the context of the problem faced. Peacekeepers appear best in their traditional functions in facilitating conflict management, rather than being able to impose conflict abatement themselves or in promoting conflict resolution. At present regional mechanisms for peacekeeping are underdeveloped relative to the global counterparts (e.g., UN). Even those regions with adequate institutions and mechanisms (i.e., Europe) have not fully adapted those to the peacekeeping strategy.

BOX 2.1. A TAXONOMY OF PEACEKEEPING MISSIONS

1. Traditional peacekeeping is the stationing of neutral, lightly armed troops with the permission of the host state(s) as an interposition force following a cease-fire to separate combatants and promote an environment suitable for conflict resolution. Traditional UN peacekeeping troops were deployed in Cyprus beginning in 1964 and southern Lebanon starting in 1978.
2. *Observation* consists of the deployment of a small number of unarmed, neutral personnel with the consent of the host state to collect information and monitor activities (cease-fire, human rights, etc.) in the deployment area, sometimes following a cease-fire or other agreement. The UN observer mission in the Middle East (UNTSO), first deployed in 1948, is an example.
3. *Collective enforcement* is a large-scale military operation designed to defend the victims of international aggression and restore peace and security by the defeat of aggressor state forces. The multinational operations in Kuwait in 1991 and Korea in the 1950s fit this profile; so too would a "collective security" operation, as envisioned by the UN Charter, carried out by an international army.
4. *Election supervision* consists of observation and monitoring of a cease-fire, disarmament, and a democratic election following a peace agreement among previously warring internal groups; this function may also include the assistance of local security forces. UN operations in Namibia in the late 1980s and Cambodia in the early 1990s are examples.
5. *Humanitarian assistance during conflict* involves the transportation and distribution of life-sustaining food and medical supplies, in coordination with local and international nongovernmental organizations, to threatened populations during a civil or interstate war. Operations in Somalia and Bosnia during the 1990s are examples.
6. *State/nation building* includes the restoration of law and order in the absence of government authority, the reconstruction of infrastructure and security forces, and facilitation of the transfer of power from the interim authority to an indigenous government. The United Nations carried out some of these functions in the Congo in the early 1960s, but it was unable to do so in Somalia after the deployment of forces in the early 1990s. The U.S. Marine involvement in the Caribbean during 1920–30 is another example of nation building.

. PEACEMAKING

Enforcement and peacekeeping involve the deployment of soldiers to carry out specific missions. Yet regional conflict management is not confined solely to "military" strategies; rather, there are a series of less coercive or noncoercive options available, which may or may not be used in conjunction with the aforementioned enforcement and peacekeeping strategies. We generally group these under the rubric of peacemaking.[56] This refers to a panoply of nonviolent strategies including diplomatic alternatives (mediation, negotiations, good offices), arbitration and adjudication, and economic sanctions. The Mitchell mission to Northern Ireland and the assignment of mediators to conflicts in the Solomon

7. *Pacification* consists of quelling civil disturbances, defeating local armed groups, forcibly separating belligerents, and maintaining law and order in an interstate war, civil war, or domestic riot, especially in the face of significant loss of life, human rights abuses, or destruction of property. The international community was reluctant to take this kind of action after the start of the Bosnian conflict in the early 1990s, despite the high level of casualties and ethnic-cleansing campaigns.

8. *Preventive deployment* consists of stationing troops between two combatants to deter the onset or prevent the spread of war. The UN-sponsored troops in Macedonia, deployed in the early 1990s to deter the spread of war in the former Yugoslavia, is an example of this type of nontraditional use of military force.

9. *Arms control verification* includes the inspection of military facilities, supervision of troop withdrawals, and all activities normally handled by national authorities and technical means as a part of an arms control agreement. Multinational peacekeeping troops performed some of these functions in the Sinai operation that followed the 1979 Egyptian-Israel peace agreements.

10. *Protective services* includes the establishment of safe havens, "no fly" zones, and guaranteed rights of passage for the purpose of protecting or denying hostile access to threatened civilian populations or areas of a state, often without the permission of that state. International actions in the 1990s to protect the Kurds in Iraq (Operation Provide Comfort) and the Muslims in Bosnia are consistent with this purpose.

11. *Intervention in support of democracy* is a military operation intended to overthrow existing leaders and to support freely elected government officials or an operation intended to protect extant and threatened democratic governments; activities may include military action against antidemocratic forces and assistance in law, order, and support services to democratic regimes. The U.S. invasion of Panama in the 1980s and the 1994 intervention in Haiti (at least until General Cedras agreed to relinquish power) are illustrative of such missions.

12. *Sanctions enforcement* is the use of military troops (air, sea, and land) to guard transit points, intercept contraband (e.g., arms, trade), or punish a state for transgressions (e.g., human rights abuses) defined by the international community or national governments in their imposition of sanctions. A blockade of North Korea or other nuclear weapons-seeking states to punish them for violations of the Nuclear Non-Proliferation Treaty would be one example; the U.S. blockade of Cuba in 1962 is another.

Islands and Sierra Leone are indicative of such efforts. We explore each of these categories in turn.

Diplomatic Alternatives

Diplomatic alternatives represent a fundamental shift in strategy away from enforcement options, and, to a significant extent, even away from peacekeeping. Diplomatic efforts presume that conflicts cannot ultimately be managed or resolved except by the disputants themselves. That is, outside forces cannot impose a settlement, or at least one that is likely to hold beyond the near term. Although diplomacy places the primary responsibility for conflict management on the parties, there is the recognition that they are incapable of that management alone. Hence, third-party intervention is essential to assist in the achievement of conflict management and resolution. Unlike enforcement or peacekeeping, there is the expectation that some type of formal agreement or outcome (e.g., withdrawal of forces, agreement to hold elections) will be the result of the diplomatic efforts.

Diplomatic efforts are able to achieve conflict management in a number of different ways. Most notable is that such efforts bring together the parties in dispute, who otherwise might not negotiate with one another. Political pressure, legitimacy, and prestige are elements that allow a third party to bring warring parties to the bargaining table. Third parties may also play an active role in the negotiations themselves. They may clarify the positions of the parties, redefine the issues,[57] serve as conduits for negotiation, pressure each side to make concessions, and formulate alternative proposals. Third parties may also play a role in providing additional incentives for the parties to come to an agreement, such as economic or political aid. Third parties might also offer themselves as guarantors of any conflict management agreement, undertaking an ongoing role in the implementation of the peace agreement.

From extensive analyses of international mediation, we know that although third-party diplomatic attempts are frequent, they are not always successful; indeed, failure is far more common that success. Nevertheless, even when mediation is not able to resolve disputed issues between states, the process itself often results in improved relations, thus producing a different conflict management achievement nonetheless.[58] There are a number of conditions associated with the success and failure of third-party mediation attempts. Below, we outline these briefly and then discuss how these might intersect with regional conflict management efforts.

Most commonly cited in analyses of mediation are the characteristics of the mediator. Generally, the impartiality[59] and legitimacy of the third party are thought to be essential to get disputants to the bargaining table and also to facilitate an agreement.[60] Quite simply, if protagonists do not trust or respect the third party, it is unlikely that an agreement will be forthcoming from a process initiated or facilitated by that party. For regional conflicts, obviously much depends on the actor that plays the role of mediator. The United Nations has frequently intervened diplomatically to try to solve regional conflicts. Most commonly, a mediator has been assigned as a special representative of the UN secretary-general to try and negotiate cease-fires or complete peace agreements. In some conflicts, the UN would be welcome as an impartial third party, at least initially. In others, the UN would be regarded as biased or have no legitimacy based on the prior or concurrent actions of the organization. For example, the United Nations was recently able to broker an agreement to end the war in the Congo, but Uganda subsequently dropped out of the agreement after the UN released a report criticizing that state's actions in the conflict. The UN might also have difficulty playing a mediating role in the Korean conflict, the Middle East, or in Rwanda, given its past involvement in those areas.

Regional organizations or groups may or may not be able to play impartial roles in conflicts, depending on the particular grouping and the conflict at hand. As a special representative of the Organization of African Unity, Nelson Mandela has both the stature and legitimacy to act as an impartial third party in the Burundi conflict—although he has yet to achieve success there. Similarly, the Contadora Group was able to play a valuable third-party role in Central American conflicts during the 1980s. Yet the League of Arab States cannot possibly serve as mediator in any conflict involving Israel. NATO would also have a difficulty playing mediator in the former Yugoslavia, although it has attempted to do so following the Dayton Accords and with respect to Macedonia.

Mediation roles often fall to individual states, internal and external to the region. Most prominent has been the continuing mediation role played by the United States in the Arab-Israeli conflict. In other cases, Australia has attempted to mediate unrest in Fiji and the Solomon Islands. Individual states may be better suited to play a mediating role if they are accepted, or even invited by, the parties. Indeed, impartiality may not be essential in some cases. The United States is widely perceived as favoring Israel, but nevertheless Egypt and the PLO previously preferred the United States as a mediator (as compared to the UN or other states) because the United States could pressure Israel into some concessions and because the United States could act as a guarantor of any accord reached. Thus, full impartiality may not be needed if the parties regard the mediator as legitimate and the biased mediator can deliver the side it is biased toward in a final agreement. Still, there is clearly the risk that many third party states in the region will be regarded as biased. For example, China would not be recognized as a suitable mediator between North and South Korea.

A second element associated with the success of diplomatic interventions is their timing. Scholars agree that conflict management in general, and mediation in particular, can function best if the moment of entry is just right. The importance of proper timing has been highlighted by a number of scholars, though often in a tautological fashion. Conflicts, like any other social process, go through various points or distinguishable phases. Northedge and Donelan note that mediation attempts can be successful "when there exists a concatenation of circumstances already tending toward an improvement of the situation."[61] Zartman has suggested that the parties' assessment of the dynamics of the conflict, its combination of plateaus, precipices, deadlocks, and deadlines, will produce a distinct moment of "ripeness."[62] The assumption here is that in the waxing and waning of the complex social forces that make up an international conflict, there are moments (e.g., a change in power relations) that may affect the perceptions and attitudes of the disputants and thus the likelihood of mediation success. There is some disagreement on when this ripeness may occur, although a "hurting stalemate" is frequently mentioned.[63] This suggests that the dispute must proceed for a period of time until which both parties begin to pay significant costs of continuing the war or confrontation. Kriesberg and Thorson believe that conflicts have to go through some phases, as well as moves and countermoves before a serious attempt to mediate it should be made.[64] Mediation is clearly more likely to be successful when disputants think that they can gain a better settlement through mediation than through unilateral action. The downside of this, of course, is that significant bloodshed may occur before mediation can be successful, and many early conflict management attempts will be failures. The conditions noted above are endemic, and therefore there are no intrinsic advantages or disadvantages to regional versus global efforts at mediation. To the extent that one organization or state can react more quickly to a conflict seems negated by the fact that successful mediation is more a function of the "right" moment rather than the earliest moment.

Mediation success cannot be achieved in every dispute. Much depends on the kind of dispute into which mediators are sent; opportunities and constraints are therefore common to global and regional efforts. Some disputes are essentially intractable, with no overlap in the bargaining positions of the protagonists; thus, there is no solution or agreement that will be acceptable to both sides. In such circumstances, the best that mediators can do is to achieve some measure of short-term conflict management, that is, limiting or preventing violence. Mediation is usually not requested or even necessary in most low-level conflicts, as parties can resolve the problems themselves. Not surprisingly, then, international mediation is more common in the most severe conflicts.[65] Mediation research on a variety of contexts, however, suggests that mediation is more successful in such high-level conflicts,[66] but it is unclear whether this finding is applicable to intra- or interstate conflict.

A key factor is the divisibility of the stakes in the dispute.[67] Divisibility of stakes means that they can be allocated to or divided among the disputants. In contrast, indivisible stakes indicate that there is less basis for compromise in which disputants each get something. For example, a regional dispute over resources might be solved by dividing the resources in half, or by facilitating favorable trade for the revisionist side that claims the resources, but does not presently possess them. Sometimes the opportunity to compete for the stakes is sufficient—thus, an agreement to hold democratic elections may be a mediated solution between groups competing for the control of the state, as in Cambodia, Mozambique, Nicaragua. In contrast, a dispute over territory might easily be indivisible. This may seem odd in that territory is a tangible good that might be easily divided. Yet we know that disputants often attach intangible value (religious, ethnic) to some territories (e.g., Jerusalem, Kashmir) that prevent division from being a resolution of the conflict. For some regional conflicts, it will be difficult for a mediator to construct possible agreements that satisfy both sides; the bargaining spaces of the protagonists may not overlap. With indivisible stakes, the ability to expand the bargaining spaces or bring additional rewards to the negotiations is limited.

Beyond the characteristics of the mediator and the conflict, diplomatic attempts at conflict management are influenced by parties to the conflict and related actors. Most specifically, any agreement to halt or limit conflict must have the support of the disputants. Although this is self-evident in a bilateral conflict, the situation is considerably more complex in multilateral conflicts. For example, conflicts in Lebanon have historically involved multiple Lebanese militias, PLO factions, Israel, and Syria. Similar complexity is evident in the present-day conflict in the Congo, reflecting what some commentators have called Africa's "world war." Having the support of a majority of actors in conflict management attempts is insufficient. If one or more actors oppose a peace agreement or cease-fire, it will be extremely difficult to be successful. Of course, much depends on the kind of opposition encountered. Important concerns are the number of actors working to undermine conflict management efforts and their capacity (military and political) to undermine an agreement. A strong opponent (acting here as a "spoiler") can easily break a cease-fire and unravel an agreement between other parties who had desired peace.[68] This suggests that all relevant parties be brought to the table for negotiations. On the other hand, there is an inherent dilemma. Bringing more parties into the process may increase the potential success of regional conflict management efforts, but decrease the likelihood that an agreement will be reached. Adding another set of preferences to the negotiation process may delay, if not prevent, it from achieving successful completion.

Other than local actors, regional and global major powers may be essential for promoting regional conflict management. There are several ways that they can assist—or undermine—management efforts. Such states can first pressure allies in the regional conflict to de-escalate the violence and perhaps make concessions in their bargaining positions. Russia actually declined to play this role substantially with respect to the Serbian government. Leading states might also act as guarantors of any peace agreement. That is, they may play a substantial role in implementation of the agreement (e.g., a troop withdrawal) and may act as ongoing arbiter for disputes that arise about the agreement. The United States performed this function with respect to the Camp David Accords between Israel and Egypt. Finally, global or regional powers can provide incentives to actors in the region, in effect favorably tipping the cost-benefit of conflict management initiatives. This may come in the form of security guarantees, economic aid, and the like. For many regional conflicts, global actors may be superior for providing these given the power and resources of major power states.

Arbitration and Adjudication

Another form of conflict management and potential resolution is referring disputes to arbitration panels or international courts. In each case, disputants present their claims and supporting arguments to third parties, after which a ruling is made on the substance of the dispute. This promotes conflict management in several ways. First, when parties agree to move the dispute to a legal or quasi-legal forum, they are able to remove, at least temporarily, that dispute for their overall relationship.[69] The net effect is at least a short-term reduction in hostility, and most likely a respite in the violence. Second, the decision to appear before a judicial or arbitration panel indicates a willingness by the parties to resolve the dispute peacefully. The legitimacy of a potential decision may also serve as a constraint on the parties to reopen or escalate the regional conflict. Third, legal forums have the effect of equalizing power between disputants, obviating imposed settlements that may not hold in the long run. Fourth, the decision may actually serve to resolve the conflict. That is, there is the promise that whatever disposition of the stakes occurs, it will be accepted by the parties and end the confrontation.

In order for arbitration or adjudications to be an effective tool in regional conflict management, there need to be several conditions present. Legal solutions generally require legal problems. Not all international disputes are fundamentally over issues that can be adjudicated. Disputes over ideology or regional hegemony are not those by which international or comparative law can offer much resolution. In contrast, some territorial or resource conflicts might be well-suited to legal settlement. Technically, arbitration does not require legal bases for decisions. Yet in practice, claims and other tribunals rely heavily on international legal principles. Thus, some regional conflicts will be excluded from this legal option.

Conflict resolution through legal means requires the presence of appropriate legal forums. These are well developed on the global level. The International Court of Justice (ICJ) and its predecessor date back to the founding of the League of Nations. The Permanent Court of Arbitration pedigree extends back even further. At the regional level, however, the options are more limited. Several regions have legal forums, but these are as likely to focus on human rights as other issues (e.g., Inter-American Commission on Human Rights). Perhaps only the European Court of Justice is the kind of multipurpose forum that could serve as a model of regional conflict management. A limitation of most, but not all, of these courts is that standing is limited to nation-states. Thus, with respect to internal conflicts, subnational groups do not have full access to legal solutions to their disputes. It is possible, however, for states or internal groups to create ad hoc tribunals or arbitration panels to resolve their disputes.

Legal mechanisms for regional conflict management are only effective if disputants are willing to use them, as adjudication and arbitration depend on their consent. Yet even global forums have been historically underutilized. The ICJ has handled little more than two cases per year since its inception. More important, the cases that international legal forums have adjudicated have tended to be between normally friendly states (e.g., Belgium versus Spain) and over issues that pose little risk of violent conflict: investments, fishing, and similar matters. The last decade, however, has seen a change in this trend, with the ICJ increasingly taking on key issues in interstate conflict. For example, the ICJ has adjudicated territorial disputes between Guatemala and Belize and Libya and

Chad respectively; the ICJ has also heard cases involving use of military force and genocide in Bosnia and Kosovo. Regional courts have not yet experienced this change, and accordingly serious disputes are more likely to be handled in regional *political* forums, such as the OSCE. Ad hoc arbitration panels have been numerous, but most often as a consequence of conflict management rather than a precursor to it. It is common for states to negotiate agreements to their main sources of disagreements and then refer remaining issues of dispute to a claims tribunal for disposition. The Iran–U.S. claims tribunal, created in the aftermath of the hostage seizure at the U.S. Embassy in Tehran, is an example.

Parties remain reluctant to refer their most vital concerns to a third party in arbitration and adjudication. Doing so clearly involves significant loss of control and a significant risk of losing (unlike negotiations). This is not to say that change in this direction is not possible. Only twenty or thirty years ago, it would have been inconceivable to envision the adjudication procedures of the World Trade Organization (WTO), and yet they are a reality today, albeit concentrated narrowly on specific trade issues. A similar evolution is possible for security issues.

Finally, there must be a concern with compliance. Arbitration panels and supranational courts rely on the parties to accept and implement any decisions rendered. This presumption is not unfounded given that the parties initially consented to the process. There are also significant reputational costs to flaunting any ruling, costs that are less easily borne by small countries than by major powers. If necessary, decisions can be enforced by the actors themselves (but this can renew violent conflict) or by international or regional organizations. The attendant problems with the latter are evident in our earlier analysis of military enforcement.

Economic Sanctions

A final strategy to be considered here is the use of economic sanctions. These might include, most commonly, restrictions on trading certain goods with a given state as well as arms embargoes to an entire region. One might find it strange to have sanctions classified under peacemaking. This is largely because economic sanctions have a coercive element attached to them, and thus are far less consensual than the diplomatic and other third-party approaches to conflict management discussed in this section. Nevertheless, economic sanctions share with other approaches in this section the characteristic of relying on nonmilitary instruments to promote conflict management. Furthermore, economic sanctions might also be thought of as "coercive" diplomacy, attempting to influence the decisions of disputants through the use of "sticks," whereas other diplomatic initiatives may rely more on "carrots."

Economic sanctions are designed to promote conflict management in several ways; to some extent, this varies by the type of sanctions imposed. Economic sanctions are usually imposed following the outbreak of violent conflict. Generally, one purpose of the sanctions is to change the behavior of one or more parties in the conflict. If successful, and this usually involves moderating or halting the violence, then conflict management is achieved. Most often, economic sanctions are designed to promote behavioral change by altering the cost-benefit ratio of military action for one of the protagonists. Presumably, the use of military force entails some benefits to those actors that pursue that strategy. Sanctions are designed to impose economic costs that outweigh the benefits attained by continued fighting, or indeed any behavior considered undesirable. The expectation is that the target state will cease or reverse the behavior when confronted with sanctions. Sometimes implicit with the promise of lifting sanctions is additional financial aid. This was the case with Western sanctions against the government of the former Yugoslavia. Change in behavior might also be achieved by normative pressure. Sanctions impose not only economic costs, but indicate the disapproval of the regional or international community. States may respond to the disapproval of their neighbors and other states because it may indirectly affect relations in a wide variety of other areas. Nevertheless, we should recognize that economic sanctions are sometimes put in place without the expectation that behavior will be changed, but rather only as a moral statement by the international community or simply as an effort to indicate that something was being done to address an undesirable situation.

Finally, an arms embargo may not stop an aggressor from further military action. Yet restricting arms flow is designed to limit the possible spread of conflict or at least diminish the damage and casualties associated with it. If the protagonists cannot obtain new or more sophisticated weapons, it will limit their ability to press any military actions to new venues or hopefully result in fewer people dying in the ongoing conflict. Clearly, the arms embargo during the Bosnian war was constructed to achieve these aims.

Although economic sanctions are designed to change behavior, their record of success is limited, and oftentimes that success is only achieved after a long period of time; according to one source, sanctions only achieve their goals approximately one-third of the time.[70] Part of the reason for this is the difficult conditions that must be present for the target state to respond to sanctions. First, the target state must be vulnerable to actions by other states. If a state is an exporter of only one or a limited range of products, then sanctions that prohibit the purchase of that product(s) will impose significant costs on the target state.[71] Implicit in this element of vulnerability is the expectation that the government is responsive to the needs of its own people. If a vulnerable state is willing to endure the cost of sanctions for its people or insulate its key supporters (e.g., the military) from the effects of sanctions, then there is unlikely to be a change in behavior.[72] This has been evident most recently with respect to the Hussein government in Iraq. Indeed, the ruling government may use international sanctions as a rallying point to build popular support for the regime. Of course, a state that is relatively invulnerable (not many significant trade or other links) is unlikely to respond to economic sanctions; Myanmar/Burma is an example.

Even with the vulnerability of the target state(s), there still must be continuing cooperation among the sanctioning parties to impose those sanctions. If one or more key states overtly or covertly sells to or buys products from the target state, effectiveness can be undermined. The key elements then are the degree to which the sanctioning coalition includes the relevant states that can impose costs on the target state and the degree to which that coalition holds together over time. The latter is critical in that most sanctions are not designed to produce immediate results, but may takes months or years to produce a change in state behavior.

With that thumbnail sketch of sanctions effectiveness, we turn to whether sanctions are more likely to be successful on the regional or global level. Historically, sanctions have been imposed at the international level, either through ad hoc multilateral coalitions (e.g., sanctions against the Mugabe regime in Zimbabwe) or by concerted United Nations action (e.g., sanctions against Libya for alleged terrorist actions). This may be because purely regional efforts at sanctions have a number of drawbacks. First, it is likely that vulnerability by any given state is likely to be greatest external to the region. In an era of globalization, cutting off trade or arms from only neighboring states may have little impact on a target that operates through global markets. Not many states trade exclusively with their neighbors any more. Any regional effort at sanctions would have to be supplemented by cooperative efforts from the United States, European Union, Japan, and other key economic players external to the region. An international blanket of sanctions would be more likely to create vulnerability on the target state.

Similarly, purely regional sanctions leave the target state to make deals with states outside of the region. That is, even if the target state were vulnerable to its neighbors, it may be able to substitute new markets to sell its products or buy arms, for example. Of course, much hinges on the identity of the target state, its interdependence patterns, and the particular region. One might expect that states in the European Union are more vulnerable to sanctions, for example, than those in Asia. Nevertheless, it is hard to envision scenarios in which global efforts at sanctions are inferior to regional efforts. Sanctions against the apartheid regime in South Africa are often cited as the prototypical sanctions effort. Yet, regional sanctions by African states made little difference. Frontline states were more dependent on South Africa than the reverse, and correspondingly there was a great deal of covert trade and labor migration into South Africa. If sanctions worked at all there, and this is a debatable point, it was the global sanctions that made the difference, and even then the desired result (move to majority rule) did not occur for over twenty years after the imposition of sanctions.

Thus, in summary, sanctions are not a highly effective tool for conflict management. To the extent that they might promote the termination or lessening of armed conflict, those imposed at the global level are more successful than purely regional efforts.

CONCLUSION

This chapter was devoted to surveying the strategies available for regional conflict management and the conditions associated with their success. A second purpose was to assess the comparative advantages of regional and global efforts for each of those strategies. There is a wide range of different strategies available to conflict managers, running the gamut from highly coercive actions to those that rely on traditional diplomacy. Yet the conditions for success are frequently difficult to achieve no matter what strategy is adopted. Still, a number of patterns emerged in the analysis.

Highly coercive measures of conflict management (e.g., collective security and collective defense) were perhaps the least likely of alternatives to achieve conflict reduction and resolution. Although, in theory, groups of states could impose their will on aggressor states, in practice the ideal conditions for such actions are rarely met. More likely to be effective are peacekeeping and peacemaking strategies, although they too have their limitations and may be ill-suited to certain kinds of threats to international peace and security. It is against this backdrop that global and regional conflict management efforts must occur.

Are regional efforts likely to be more effective than global ones? The analysis here suggests that regional efforts may have some limited advantages. Specifically, regional organizations may be more willing to take conflict management action because states in the region have direct interests affected by local conflicts. There may also be some benefits from greater homogeneity of membership, although strong political splits may obviate that advantage. Finally, regional efforts may have greater legitimacy in the eyes of local protagonists. These advantages may be most useful with respect to the diplomatic aspects of peacemaking efforts.

Regional organizations have some notable disadvantages vis-à-vis global efforts, especially by the UN, at conflict management. Regional organizations lack many of the necessary structures and procedures to carry out some conflict management. With perhaps the exception of Europe, regional institutions are ill-designed to conduct enforcement and peacekeeping operations or facilitate judicial solutions to conflicts. Complicating this are the relatively more limited resources, especially in developing areas, available to regional organizations. To some extent, the more extensive the effort, the greater the advantages enjoyed by UN efforts.

The efficacy of regional conflict management efforts clearly varies greatly by the kind of conflict encountered, the strategy employed, and the region of the world where the conflict occurs. Still, it is clear that regional efforts are no panacea for the limitations of global conflict management. Indeed, in many cases, regional efforts will be less effective, even if increasingly common, than global actions to promote international peace and security.

NOTES

1. John Ruggie, "Multilateralism: The Anatomy of an Institution," in *Multilateralism Matters,* ed. John Ruggie (New York: Columbia University Press, 1993).

2. Paul F. Diehl, Daniel Druckman, and James Wall. "International Peacekeeping and Conflict Resolution: A Taxonomic Analysis with Implications," *Journal of Conflict Resolution* 42 (1998): 33–55.

3. Joseph Lepgold and Thomas Weiss, eds., *Collective Conflict Management and Changing World Politics* (Albany: SUNY Press, 1998).

4. For a brief historical review, see Lynn Miller, "The Idea and the Reality of Collective Security," *Global Governance* 5 (1999): 303–32.

5. Inis Claude, *Swords into Plowshares,* 4th ed. (New York: Random House, 1971).

6. Charles Kupchan, "The Case for Collective Security," in *Collective Security Beyond the Cold War,* ed. George Downs (Ann Arbor: University of Michigan Press, 1994), 41–67.

7. A/RES/3314 (XXIX).

8. Miller, "The Idea and the Reality of Collective Security," footnote 10.

9. Claude, *Swords into Plowshares,* 253, footnote 11.

10. Claude, *Swords into Plowshares,* 257–60, footnote 11.

11. Claude, *Swords into Plowshares,* 256, footnote 11. See also George Downs and Keisuke Iida, "Assessing the Theoretical Case Against Collective Security," in *Collective Security Beyond the Cold War,* ed. George Downs (Ann Arbor: University of Michigan Press, 1994), for a discussion.

12. For a different if somewhat dated view, see Charles Kupchan and Clifford Kupchan, "Concerts, Collective Security, and the Future of Europe," *International Security* 16 (1991): 114–61.

13. See Joseph Lepgold, "Regionalism in the Post–Cold War Era," chapter 1 in this collection.

14. Miller, "The Idea and the Reality of Collective Security," footnote 10.

15. See James Morrow, "Alliances and Asymmetry: An Alternative to the Capability Aggregation Model of Alliances," *American Journal of Political Science* 35 (1991): 904–33.

16. Joseph Lepgold, "NATO's Post–Cold War Collective Action Problem," *International Security* 23 (1998): 78–106.

17. Daniel Jones, Stuart Bremer, and J. David Singer, "Militarized Interstate Disputes, 1816–1992: Rationale, Coding Rules, and Empirical Patterns," *Conflict Management and Peace Science* 15 (1996): 163–213.

18. Frederic Pearson, "Foreign Military Intervention and Domestic Disputes," *International Studies Quarterly* 18 (1974): 259–89.

19. Frederic Pearson, Robert Baumann, and Jeffrey Pickering, "Military Intervention and Realpolitik," in *Reconstructing Realpolitik,* ed. Fran Wayman and Paul F. Diehl (Ann Arbor: University of Michigan Press, 1994), 205–25.

20. Patrick Regan, *Civil Wars and Foreign Powers* (Ann Arbor: University of Michigan Press, 2000).

21. Regan, *Civil Wars and Foreign Powers.*

22. See the interventions by Uganda, Rwanda, Angola, and Zimbabwe in the Congo war.

23. Regan, *Civil Wars and Foreign Powers,* 138–44, footnote 26.

24. See Lepgold, "Regionalism in the Post–Cold War Era," chapter 1 in this collection.

25. Regan, *Civil Wars and Foreign Powers.*

26. Peter Wallensteen and Margareta Sollenberg, "Armed Conflict, 1989–2000," *Journal of Peace Research* 38 (2001): 629–48, footnote 2.

27. Regan, *Civil Wars and Foreign Powers,* 29, footnote 26.

28. Paul Diehl, *International Peacekeeping,* revised edition (Baltimore: Johns Hopkins University Press, 1994).

29. Nathan Pelcovits, "UN Peacekeeping and the 1973 Arab–Israeli Conflict," *Orbis* 19 (1975): 146–65.

30. A. Leroy Bennett, *International Organizations: Principles and Issues,* 5th edition (Englewood Cliffs, N.J.: Prentice-Hall, 1991).

31. Of course, if perfect consensus existed, there would be no conflict. Thus, some disagreement within the region is inherent.

32. Neil MacFarlane, "Regional Peacekeeping in the CIS," in *United Nations Peacekeeping: Reflections on the Continuing Challenge,* ed. Ramesh Thakur and Albrecht Schnabel (Tokyo: draft manuscript, 2000).

33. Stephen Ratner, *The New UN Peacekeeping* (New York: St. Martin's Press, 1995).

34. William Durch, "Keeping the Peace: Politics and Lessons of the 1990s," in *UN Peacekeeping, American Politics, and the Uncivil Wars of the 1990s,* ed. William Durch (New York: St. Martin's Press, 1996), 1–34.

35. Diehl, *International Peacekeeping,* chapter 3, footnote 34.

36. Dennis Jett, *Why Peacekeeping Fails* (New York: St. Martin's Press, 2000).

37. For example, Michael Wesley, *Casualties of the New World Order* (London: Macmillan, 1997).

38. For example, Indar Jit Rikhye, *The Theory and Practice of International Peacekeeping* (New York: St. Martin's, 1984).

39. Gino Naldi, *The Organization of African Unity: An Analysis of Its Rule* (London: Mansell, 1989).

40. The George W. Bush administration has given signals that it intends to discontinue this effort.

41. Lepgold, "NATO's Post–Cold War Collective Action Problem."

42. Gordon Wilson, "Arm in Arm After the Cold War? The Uneasy NATO-UN Relationship," *International Peacekeeping* 2 (1995): 74–92.

43. James Jose, *An Inter-American Peace Force Within the Framework of the Organization of American States* (Metuchen, N.J.: Scarecrow Press, 1970).

44. Jett, *Why Peacekeeping Fails,* footnote 22.

45. Naomi Weinberger, "Peacekeeping Options in Lebanon," *Middle East Journal* 37 (1983): 341–69.

46. John MacKinley, "Powerful Peacekeepers," *Survival* 32 (1990): 241–50.

47. Ernst Lefever, *Uncertain Mandate* (Baltimore: Johns Hopkins University Press, 1967).

48. Kjell Skjelsbaek, "UN Peacekeeping: Expectations, Limitations and Results—Forty Years of Mixed Experiences," in *The United Nations and Peacekeeping: Results, Limitations, and Prospects,* ed. Indar Jit Rikhye and Kjell Skjelsbaek (New York: St. Martin's Press, 1991), 52–67.

49. See Alan James, *Peacekeeping in International Politics* (London: Macmillan, 1990), for a typology.

50. Diehl, Druckman, and Wall, "International Peacekeeping and Conflict Resolution," 33–55.

51. Christopher Dandeker and James Gow, "The Future of Peace Support Operations: Strategic Peacekeeping and Success," *Armed Forces and Society* 23 (1997): 327–48.

52. Diehl, *International Peacekeeping,* chapter 5, footnote 34.

53. See Durch, "Keeping the Peace," footnote 40.

54. Michael Doyle and Nicholas Sambanis, "International Peacebuilding: A Theoretical and Quantitative Analysis," *American Political Science Review* 94 (2000): 779–802.

55. James Allan, *Peacekeeping: Outspoken Observations by a Field Officer* (Westport, Conn.: Praeger Publishers, 1996).

56. Boutros Boutros-Ghali, *An Agenda for Peace,* revised edition (New York: United Nations, 1995).

57. P. Terrence Hopmann, *The Negotiation Process and the Resolution of International Conflicts* (Columbia: University of South Carolina Press, 1996).

58. Keith Kressel and Dean Pruitt, eds., *Mediation Research* (San Francisco: Jossey-Bass, 1989).

59. Oran Young, *The Intermediaries: Third Parties in International Crises* (Princeton, N.J.: Princeton University Press, 1967).

60. For other conditions not discussed here, see Dean Pruit and Peter Carnevale, *Negotiation in Social Conflict* (Pacific Grove, Calif.: Brooks/Cole, 1993).

61. F. S. Northedge and M. D. Donelan, *International Disputes: The Political Aspects* (London: Europa, 1971).

62. I. William Zartman, "Ripeness: The Hurting Stalemate and Beyond," in *International Conflict Resolution After the Cold War,* ed. Paul Stern and Daniel Druckman (Washington, D.C.: National Academy of Sciences Press, 2000), 225–50.

63. Saadia Touval and I. William Zartman, "Mediation in International Conflicts," in *Mediation Research,* ed. Keith Kressel and Dean Pruitt (San Francisco: Jossey-Bass, 1989).

64. Louis Kriesberg and Stuart Thorson, *Timing the Deescalation of International Conflicts* (Syracuse, N.Y.: Syracuse University Press, 1991).

65. Jacob Bercovitch and Paul F. Diehl, "Conflict Management of Enduring Rivalries: Frequency, Timing and Short-Term Impact of Mediation," *International Interactions* 22 (1997): 299–320.

66. James Wall and Ann Lynn, "Mediation: A Current Review," *Journal of Conflict Resolution* 37 (1993): 160–94.

67. John Vasquez, "The Tangibility of Issues and Global Conflict: A Test of Rosenau's Issue Area Typology," *Journal of Peace Research* 20 (1983): 179–92; see also Kressel and Pruitt, *Mediation Research.*

68. Stephen Stedman, "Spoiler Problems in Peace Processes," *International Security* 22 (1997).

69. Dana Fischer, "Decisions to Use the International Court of Justice," *International Studies Quarterly* 26 (1982): 251–77.

70. Gary Hufbauer, Jeffrey Schott, and Kimberly Elliott, *Economic Sanctions Reconsidered* (Washington, D.C.: Institute for International Economics, 1991).

71. T. Clifton Morgan and Valerie Schwebach, "Fools Suffer Gladly: The Use of Economic Sanctions in International Crises," *International Studies Quarterly* 41 (1997): 27–50; Robert Pape, "Why International Sanctions Do Not Work," *International Security* 22 (1997): 90–136.

72. T. Clifton Morgan and Valerie Schwebach, "Sanctions as An Instrument of Foreign Policy: The Role of Domestic Politics," *International Interactions* 21, no. 3 (1996): 247–63.

II

CASE STUDIES IN REGIONAL CONFLICT MANAGEMENT

3

Regional Conflict Management in Africa

I. WILLIAM ZARTMAN

Contemporary conflicts in Africa have two characteristics that pose special challenges for collective conflict management (CCM): they arise from state collapse and they come in regional clusters. African conflicts do not take place among or within well-established states in control of their policies, people, and territories, but between and inside states out of control of their actions, with privatized economies and security, and competing rebel groups, as well as multinational forces, vying for control of political space. At the same time, because of the weakness of the state's control over its territory, conflicts spill over to engulf neighbors and become, paradoxically, struggles for regional balance of control, much as if well-formed states were really involved. Conflict and its resolution in these conditions loses its character as a clever contest on a chessboard and becomes a multidimensional interplay of checkers, chess, mah-jongg, and dominoes all played at the same time on top of each other.

Because the Organization of African Unity (OAU) prohibited alliances within its membership as part of its founding compact, the continent's collective efforts at dealing with these conflicts tend to come in organized packages rather than in ad hoc cooperation or in coalitions of the willing. But the OAU, Africa's continental organization, has been ill-oriented to resolve such conflicts; its primary purpose is to protect state independence, and thus it can neither interfere in internal affairs nor take strong measures opposed by any of its members. Recognizing its weakness, the OAU members in July 2001 replaced their organization with a new body, the African Union (AU), still untested but by all appearances even more unsuited to meeting the challenges of conflict management.[1] However, active regional organizations exist in northern, western, southern, and the Horn of Africa, and they take up the challenge in varying degrees in a variety of conflict-related roles. Because the clusters of conflict are also part of the politics of the region, the organizations' conflict management roles are often confused with their conflict involvement. Collective defense coalitions pit one part of the organization against another and weaken its collective security role; collective security is much more difficult to practice toward internal conflicts than toward interstate conflicts. "It is . . . no coincidence," notes Andrew Hurrell, "that the most elaborate examples of regionalism . . . have occurred in regions where the state structures remain relatively strong and where the legitimacy of both frontiers and regimes is not widely called into question. . . . States remain the essential building blocks with which regionalist arrangements are constructed."[2] Effective regional organization depends on effective states, yet Africa's conflicts come from the collapse of state effectiveness, and those members that are able to maintain their state capabilities are more absorbed in filling the vacuums with their own interests than in collective conflict management.

THREATS TO PEACE AND SECURITY

The first characteristic is state collapse, the cause and not the result of conflict. It is not primordial enmity, resource deficiency, or a state-to-nation imbalance, as it has been variously claimed, that causes conflict but the situation that occurs when "the structure, authority (legitimate power), law and political order have fallen apart."[3] State collapse is a process rather than a single well-defined event, and so even when the state does not fully disintegrate, the near-occurrence of collapse has similar effects. Somalia, Liberia, Sierra Leone, and the two Congos continue to be collapsed states into the first years of the new century, and the effects of previous collapse from the 1990s are still being felt in Rwanda, Burundi, and Angola and are threatening in Guinea, Cameroon, Togo, and others. The process of collapse is similar to aspects of revolution as described by Brinton and as characterized by Huntington as the Western pattern, where "the political institutions of the old regime collapse," rather than being overthrown by a revolutionary force.[4] Revolution, however, is marked by "the mobilization of new groups into politics and then by the creation of new political institutions,"[5] whereas in the phenomenon of state collapse, political society is so weakened by the collapsing process that it cannot provide the new groups to restore the new state (even if both civil society and predatory groups are able to operate on the local level).

Usually, the collapsing process produces a vindictive, brutal state with a very narrow social base and limited capacity and control of its territory. Where the state is weak rather than brutal, it is often forced by its weakness to privatize security and neglect welfare.[6] The vacuum of power outside the capital area invites competing forces to take over other parts of the country, often from external sanctuaries and with external support. Their goal, however, is not necessarily to succeed the weak leader in office but merely to control a part of the country and its resources;[7] even if overthrow is their ultimate goal, the competing forces may be too narrow in their own base to rule the whole country or to constitute anything but yet another round of the same sort of incapacitated authority that they have replaced. Somalia, the two Congos, Burundi, and Sierra Leone follow this pattern; in Liberia, Angola, and Sudan the governments remain well entrenched but rule only half a state, but otherwise follow a similar course. In such conflicts, there are no border disputes because borders are irrelevant, and so there are no territorial claims by neighboring states because additional territory is a liability and already-populated territory provides no Lebensraum.

Future threats to peace and security can be expected to follow the same pattern. Already or nearly collapsed states continue to constitute vacuums of power and authority that require long times and focused efforts to fill, and the deep wounds left on the decimated and displaced populations by the conflict make reconstitution of a normal order even more difficult. New candidates can be expected to be added to the list of collapsed states as well, where the penultimate stage of either a weak and exhausted or a narrow and repressive regime in the capital and dissidence in the countryside is already present. In these situations, the basic nature of the conflict lies in the incapacity of the state to provide the supplies and controls expected of it. The reasons for this inability are partly material—the absence of resources for the economy—but they are also human or spiritual—the absence of a civic spirit, the inability to make allocating decisions, the dedication to a narrow client group rather than to public service, the prevalence of a time-at-the-trough ethos.

There is one additional category of conflict, related to the conflicts derived from collapse because it depends on an assumption of collapse by one or more of the parties. This is the border war, a relatively infrequent event considering the number, newness, and uncertainty of African boundaries, occurring four times in the 1960s,[8] thrice in the 1970s (including two repeats),[9] four times in the 1980s (including one repeat),[10] and only twice (with one repeat) thereafter.[11] Border wars tend to occur when one side considers the other internally weak enough to succumb to the challenge, and they are natural aftermaths—immediate or delayed—of situations unresolved at the time of independence. The most costly and long-lasting of these was the latest one, the two-year war between Ethiopia and recently independent Eritrea, where Eritrean leaders believed Ethiopia to still be in an internally weakened condition after its earlier collapse and thus ready for a lesson by the feisty Eritreans. But such "classical" interstate conflicts are rare in Africa, overshadowed by conflicts arising from internal collapse and related external involvement.

Such internal conflicts alone would present their own special characteristics and challenges for conflict management, but these are compounded by the fact that the conflicts come in regional clusters and confrontations.[12] Africa's political interactions are regional rather than continental, and so their conflicts come in regional clusters. Regionalization of conflict is produced by both pull and push factors, from the inside and outside respectively, negative externalities of the original process of state collapse. The mechanism of these externalities begin with the vacuum produced by the collapsing process. The state, already weak, is weakened further by the militant forms of alienation that it produces; the conflict creates zones of no-control, further increasing alienation; and the rebellion looks to outside sanctuary and sources of support.

Complementing these pull forces from the inside are seven push forces from the outside—preemptive, aggressive, exploitative, defensive, hegemonic, ethnic, personal—working individually or in combination. The push may be preemptive, the result of a fixation on relative gains as in the Cold War, to make sure that an opposing regional coalition does not take over the conflicted state, as animated Nigeria and a Francophile coalition working against each other in Liberia. Or it may be aggressive, to support the internal enemy of the neighboring state, as motivated Uganda's support of the Rwandan refugees who became the Rwandan Patriotic Front and overthrew the Rwandan government. Or it can be exploitative, to take advantage of the vacuum to extract some valuable natural resources, as in the case of Zimbabwean and Rwandan officers in Congo. Or it can be defensive, to counter the neighbor's support for a rebellion in the intervening state, as in the case of Sierra Leone's support for the United Liberian Movement (ULIMO) against Liberia supporting the Revolutionary United Front (RUF) in Sierra Leone. Or it may be hegemonic, to assert the dominant regional role of a larger neighbor, as in Nigeria's role in Liberia or Zimbabwe's role in Congo. Or it could be ethnic, to protect ethnic relatives of the intervening state's population, as Rwanda intervened in Congo to protect the Banyarwanda, or as Somalia intervened in Ethiopia to protect ethnic Somalis. Or it could be merely personal, to back a friend or punish an enemy of the president, as Nigerian President Ibrahim Babangida intervened in Liberia to protect his friend Samuel Doe. There are perhaps other effects, alone or in combination.

Regional conflict clusters are characteristic of three conflict arenas, in west, central and the Horn of Africa, with a potential in north Africa, after having once also been dominant in a fourth region, southern Africa. The current and the earlier types are different. In southern Africa in the 1960s–80s, the regional conflict was structured on a clear battle line between white settler regions, centered on South Africa, and the newly independent states.[13] In the contemporary cases, regional instability began with the collapse of one or more states in the region through the predation of a narrowly based autocrat. A successor of the same ilk tries to take advantage of the established patterns of politics; neighbors try to control the collapsed system while also exploiting the resulting vacuum for their own ends. Neighbors respond to subversion from next door by countersubversion of their neighbors, often extending beyond the bilateral level to alliance groups involving both states and rebel movements. The pattern of vacuum and alliance ties together domestic and international elements of the conflict. In these conflicts, all three classical motivations are involved: Socio-political needs of the neglected populations provide a mass base for the eco-political greed of political entrepreneurs, who also mobilize ideo-political creed—based on ethnic, not ideological, identities—in support of their cause.[14]

The original regional confrontation came into shape in the 1960s as the wave of independence swept into the southern part of the continent. National liberation movements caused the collapse of the colonial state in Angola and Mozambique and challenged the neocolonial state in Rhodesia and South West Africa. However, South Africa saw these movements as part of the "total communist onslaught" and so launched repeated attacks into neighbors' territory and supported counterrebellions in Angola and Mozambique after their independence in 1975. The civil war of the National Union for the Total Independence of Angola (UNITA) continued into the next century; but the nationalist rebellion against Rhodesia ended with its independence as Zimbabwe in 1979, the civil war of the Mozambican National Resistance (RENAMO) ended with a negotiated agreement in 1992 and elections in 1994 and 1999, and the national liberation war of the South West African People's Organization (SWAPO) ended with independence in 1989. These outcomes led to the negotiated opening of the South African political system itself to majority rule between 1990 and 1994. The conflict pitted two regional alliances against each other. Facing the combined forces of South Africa, Portugal, and the white regime of Rhodesia was the alliance of the Front Line States (FLS) and then the Southern African Development Coordinating Conference (SADCC), which with the defeat of the apartheid-colonial combination became the regional collective security organization of all states of the region, the Southern African Development Community (SADC) in 1994.[15] SADC has intervened to manage conflict in Lesotho and also as both an ally of the government and a mediator in the internal conflict in Congo.

In west Africa, the collapsing of the state in Liberia at the end of the 1980s at the hands of Samuel Doe invited the rebellion of Charles Taylor and other splinter groups in the early 1990s, which spilled over into the collapsing states of Sierra Leone and Guinea, and then spilled over into Guinea-Bissau and Senegal. These linked internal conflicts took place within a larger rivalry over the security structure of the region between Nigeria and some French-speaking states within the Economic Community of West African States (ECOWAS), the organization of the subregion. The ECOWAS Cease-Fire Monitoring Group (ECOMOG) was sent to Liberia in 1990 as an attempt by Nigeria to save its ally, Doe, and to thwart Taylor, who was backed by Francophile neighbors, Ivory Coast and Burkina Faso, and by Libya. Taylor finally made a deal with Nigerian dictator Sani Abacha, still of unknown content, and the Abuja Agreement of 15 August 1995, revised on 16 August 1996, brought a cease-fire and permitted Taylor's election to the Liberian presidency the following year.

But Taylor's war and its negative externalities continued into Sierra Leone, where Taylor launched and then traded diamonds for the Revolutionary United Front (RUF) of Foday Sankoh and Sam Bokarie, then spilled over into Guinea, and also extended into Guinea-Bissau, where leftover guns and rebels from the

Liberian war fueled internal political confrontations and also the separatist rebellion in neighboring Casamance in Senegal. The sudden step to the brink of collapse in Ivory Coast, a core state of the region, beginning with the 1999 Christmas Eve coup, remained remarkably contained in one state but contained possible ramifications for extended regional conflict.

In the Horn, state collapse in Ethiopia at the end of the 1980s after thirty years of war with Eritrean nationalists led in turn to extended state collapse in Somalia at the same time and contributed to repeated instability in the thirty-five years of war in southern Sudan, spilling over into Uganda as the latter emerged from its own collapse. State structures disintegrated in Ethiopia under the pressure of ethnic rebellions led by the Ethiopian People's Revolutionary Democratic Force (EPRDF) against the repressive ideological regime of Mengistu Haile Meriam and in Somalia under clan factionalism nurtured by the repressive ethnic regime of Mohammed Siad Barre. The Ethiopian state was soon restored by the EPRDF under Meles Zenawi and an independent Eritrean state was set up by the Eritrean Peoples Liberation Front (EPLF) under Isaias Afworki; the Ethiopian-Eritrean war of 1998–2000 completed the split between the two states. The disappearance of the traditional Ethiopian enemy left the Somalis without a uniting cause and so without a restored state after 1990.

The southern Sudanese rebellion raging since 1955 (with a decade's interlude in 1972–83) repeatedly involved Sudan's eastern neighbors and, in response, Sudanese support for rebellions in their territories. These interlocked conflicts occurred within the Inter-Governmental Agency on Development (IGAD), which conducted a conflict management initiative between Ethiopia and Somalia in 1986–88 and then another in the Sudanese conflict after 1993. The first led to a truce in the conflict, and then indirectly to the collapse of the Somalian state; the second arrived at a Declaration of Principles (DOP) in 1994 and then bogged down in the typical problems of involvement and interference.

In central Africa, the War of the Zairean Succession took place throughout the 1990s over the vacuum created by Mobutu Sese Seko's collapsed state and drew in the civil wars in Congo-Brazzaville, Central African Republic, Rwanda, and Burundi during the same decade, as well as the spillover from the longer-running Angolan civil war. Uganda and Zimbabwe then joined in the late 1990s to protect and further their interests, and other countries in the region were pulled in as participants and mediators. The unusual characteristic of the regional confrontation in central Africa is that it is contained within no single regional organization that can work to manage the conflict because central Africa is no clearly defined region. As a result, the conflict is in addition a conflict between regional organizations—Southern African Development Community (SADC), the East African Community (EAC), and Economic Community of Central African States (CEEAC)—which include Congo (SADC and CEEAC) and Rwanda and Burundi (EAC) as members. SADC, the most active of the lot, is thus both the peacemaker and party in the conflict, reflecting a policy conflict among its members.

The War of the Zairean Succession has been termed Africa's first world war, because some of the nine states involved are intervening to protect their own security (a judgment clouded by the persistence of ethnic, personal, and exploitative motives). Although state security reasons for intervention are largely absent in the central conflict in West Africa and elusive in much of the confrontation in the Horn of Africa—that is, the intervening state is not intervening as a result of a threat to its security by the neighboring conflict—they were dominant for some intervenors in southern Africa and are arguably present on the part of the Sudanese government in the confrontation over southern Sudan. Regional involvement in internal conflicts is certain to continue for the same array of motives as has been shown in the past—preemptive, aggressive, defensive, exploitative, hegemonic, ethnic, and personal—whether they also involve state security reasons or not.

In north Africa, a complex mechanism of intraregional tensions and restraints has kept the regional rivalries from reaching the level of war for most of the period since independence in the mid-1950s and has kept the moments of direct confrontation between Morocco and Algeria in 1963 and 1975 from lasting and spreading.[16] However, the tension of relations between the two countries has been played out since 1975 by conflict over the Western Sahara, in open hostilities between Morocco and Algeria's proxy, the Polisario Front, in the late 1970s and early 1980s, and in a wary cease-fire since then. The conflict has stood at the brink of war under the cease-fire, moved a step closer in 2000, and threatens to enter open hostilities under frustration and provocation. The regional organization, the Arab Magrib Union (UMA), along with the OAU, is paralyzed by the conflict, which the UN has been trying to resolve. While state collapse is not the source of an inviting vacuum, the deep debilitation of the Algerian state under internal unrest has increased the issue's symbolic importance to its ruling junta, reinforcing a more straightforward interstate rivalry.

CONFLICT MANAGEMENT ROLES AND INCENTIVES

In addition to acting unilaterally, states can practice collective conflict management (CCM) in one of three ways: through the continental organization (the OAU), through regional organizations (as noted for each region), or through alliances (ad hoc or established). Under Africa's norms, unilateral action and alliances lack legitimacy and so are only infrequently used; Africa has almost no established alliances outside of the security commitments in regional organizations.[17] The rare unilateral actions look more like conflict than conflict management, but they were all carried out for the purpose of bringing an explosive situation of state collapse under control. Tanzania, attacked by Uganda, used the excuse to overthrow the brutal Ugandan regime of Idi Amin in 1979, and was roundly criticized for it in the OAU; Uganda and Rwanda intervened in Congo (without any explicit alliance) in 1996–97 and again in 1998–2001 and were vigorously castigated for it; and Ivory Coast and Burkina Faso (again without any explicit alliance) intervened to overthrow the autocratic regime of Samuel Doe in 1989 and thereafter.

Although they dealt with the immediate problem of the egregious ruler, none of these joint or unilateral actions was very successful in managing the conflict in the longer run. Instead, states have strong incentives—as well as disincentives—to act together with others, and hence to use regional organizations, in Africa as elsewhere. Multilateral action clothes unilateral motives with collective legitimacy. It is far more acceptable to intervene multilaterally than unilaterally. Nigeria understood this in its intervention as ECOMOG into the Liberian conflict, and then into its Sierra Leonean extension; South Africa understood, too, in bringing along Botswana in its intervention into Lesotho under the SADC cloak.[18] As a corollary, multilateral action within a regional organization neutralizes possible opposition by delegitimizing it, as Ivory Coast and Burkino Faso found regretfully in regard to Liberia in 1990–96 and South Africa found in regard to Congo in 1998; in extremis, after temporarily prevailing over South Africa within SADC over whether to support Congo or be neutral, Zimbabwe hastily formed a treaty of alliance with its cointervenors within the regional organization in 1999. Multilateral action can also pool resources, reducing the need for one state's expenditures or augmenting them to the level of necessary significance. Acting alone, Zimbabwe, Angola, and certainly Namibia would not have had the available resources out of their individual military strengths to provide the support that Congo needed in 1998–2001, whereas together they could hold the Rally for a Democratic Congo (RCD) and its Ugandan and Rwandan backers in check.

But there are disincentives as well: acting multilaterally means taking others' interests into account and therefore tempering action that one might have taken alone. Thus states weigh their need for legitimization and resources against the constraints that it might bring in considering whether to act multilaterally, through regional organizations, or alone. At the same time, it is inappropriate to look for regional organizations' incentives and motivations in managing conflicts in their areas. Regional organizations do not have incentives and motivations; indeed, regional organizations do not have anything, since they are not corporate actors. It is their members who have incentives and motivations to act multilaterally, through regional organizations, rather than acting unilaterally—or not acting at all.[19]

There are three ways that a regional organization can be used toward conflict: collective defense, through an alliance against an external enemy; and two types of collective security, through a commitment to constrain a nonpredetermined member of the organization who attacks another member, and through an agreement to act against an internal rebellion, of predetermined nature or not.[20] The first is a measure of one-sided conflict involvement, not evenhanded conflict management, whereas the other two can conceivably serve either purpose under specific conditions and difficulties. These can be graded in terms of their difficulty in organization and implementation. A collective defense alliance is the easiest to mount and its cohesion depends on the common sense of threat from a designated external enemy. Thus its internal success depends on the depth of commitment, and its success in conflict depends on the power relations between the two sides, a measure external to the group. In the OAU, collective defense against colonial rule and colonial return was one of the two major purposes of the organization, subscribed to with zeal and practiced with commitment, although with diffused results.[21]

The two types of collective security commitments are more relevant to conflict management. A collective security organization against interstate aggression is more difficult to create than collective defense since it hangs on a prior commitment by the members of the group to turn against any one of their own number who deviates from group norms. While collective security has traditionally been thought of as rallying to the defense of the aggrieved or aggressed party, it can also take the form of conflict management measures, a more evenhanded exercise. Since aggression is hard to define in principle and harder to assign in fact, and since a firm stand against a fellow member (or, more likely, even against its government of the moment) is usually difficult to achieve, conflict management measures are the more frequently assigned policy. However, even conflict management is not as straightforward as it might appear, since actions can easily tilt or be perceived as tilting toward one side or the other, and in any case even-handed measures are clearly not a tilt in favor of the aggrieved party. The efforts of the OAU in the Ethiopian-Eritrean war of 1998–2000 are an example of an attempt at evenhandedness that eventually worked. Other examples are rare, since interstate aggression is less frequent in Africa and when it does occur, the inhibitions operating on any collective security system operate. Nonetheless, collective security in interstate conflict is the second of the organization's two announced purposes.

Collective security against intrastate conflict requires a very specific policy of support for its conflicted member from a regional organization. It is not only the usual prohibition against interference in internal matters that inhibits a more evenhanded conflict management policy, but also the fact that the conflicted state is one of the constituent members of the organization taking action, unlike the case of interstate collective security where both parties are members. Furthermore, also unlike the interstate situation, mediation means recognition and the major issue of an internal conflict is recognition and hence equal status for the internal rebellion.[22] Finally, intervention is internationalization; interstate conflict is already internationalized, but in internal conflict, the government wants to avoid internationalization or at least to keep it on the state-to-state level in its own defense. As a result, intrastate collective security actions through conflict management are the most difficult to obtain from a regional organization, both per se and because they are overridden by actions of solidarity behind the conflicted government.

On the other hand, collective support for a besieged government—a Holy Alliance—is less difficult to achieve in a club of incumbents. The Biafran War in Nigeria (1966–70) provides a good example: When the OAU tried to manage the conflict, it was rebuffed by Nigeria, causing it to fall back on a policy quite consistent with its purposes, that of proclaiming solidarity with the beleaguered state against the rebellion.[23] When the organization tried to manage the Saharan conflict after 1975, it dropped its attempt at evenhandedness and sided with the rebel movement in 1981, caught between its purposes of state support and liberation. The beleaguered state—Morocco—resigned, leaving the organization powerless to manage anything. These categories are useful in discussing the purposes for which regional organizations are used by their members in a conflict.

In discussing CCM, it is best to use the standard categories of conflict reduction: peace enforcement, peacekeeping, peacemaking, and peacebuilding,[24] remembering that these are conceptual categories that often blur in practice.[25] The last named is the most amorphous and most elusive of the array of possible CCM exercises and will be given less than full treatment here.

Peace Enforcement

Peace enforcement generally refers to the collective security function of bringing collective forces to the defense of an aggressed state, in interstate or intrastate conflicts, but it could also refer to forceful interposition as an adjunct to peacemaking. It has been attempted once by the OAU in Chad in 1981–82 and six times by two regional organizations: by ECOWAS (ECOMOG) in Liberia in 1990–98, in Sierra Leone in 1997–9, and in Guinea-Bissau in 1999; and by SADC in Lesotho in 1994 and 1999 and a rump SADC of Zimbabwe, Namibia, and Angola in Congo in 1998–2002 (and perhaps beyond). The OAU case concerned a mixture of internal and external conflict; the others all concerned intrastate conflicts.

The OAU sent a multinational force of Nigerian, Zairean, and Senegalese troops to Chad for half a year to replace the Libyan protection of the Transitional Government of National Unity (GUNT) of Goukouni Weddei against the forces of one of its members under Hissene Habre.[26] The OAU force's mandate, funding, and command were unclear, and Habre's troops walked around it in their way to take over the capital. The organization has not been able to overcome these problems ever since and, as a result, realistically, has not even tried, leaving the challenge to the regional organizations.

In the SADC and ECOWAS cases, it was the regional hegemon—South Africa and Nigeria, respectively—that initiated and predominated in the organizations' initiatives (except in the instance of Guinea-Bissau, where Senegalese troops were used), with some other members' troops participating to a lesser degree. The SADC cases can be called a success, in that the domestic mutiny and political crises were resolved and new, acceptable elections held, although the military intervention itself caused significant casualties and damage. The "rump SADC" case involved three members (Zimbabwe, Angola, Namibia), organized with Congo on 15 April 1999 after the fact in a defense agreement by Zimbabwe, the rival of South Africa for hegemony within SADC; it was a success in the sense that the intervention saved the government of Congo, held the rebellion in check, and provided the opportunity for SADC mediation (which began to be implemented only two years after signature, following the change in the government in Kinshasa).

The ECOWAS cases in the end were a costly failure, even though the efforts of the West African states to deal with their own conflict were generally applauded. There is a tendency to confuse the two judgments. West African states, abandoned by the United States,[27] applied African solutions to African problems, a laudable effort. But this effort failed to accomplish its goals of either saving Doe, defeating Taylor, or bringing about an intermediate solution. In addition, its failure involved great cost and arguably brought to power a Taylor worse than Doe, surrounded by paranoia, child soldiers, and competing warlords, spreading his ravages into Sierra Leone and Guinea, and necessitating more ECOMOG interventions, which also failed—an entirely deplorable result.

The SADC and ECOWAS peace enforcement efforts were possible only through the engagement of the regional hegemons, who bore the costly burden of the interventions and used the regional organization to legitimize and collectivize their action. Without their motivation and leadership, there would have been no collective security by the regional organizations. The "rump SADC" intervention was decidedly one-sided in support of the government against rebels and external intervention from outside the organization's membership. But it permitted a soft stalemate of fatigue that in turn permitted the peacemaking efforts of the organization to take place, an action that has parallels elsewhere such as in the NATO–U.S. intervention and mediation in Bosnia.[28] The other SADC efforts were more evenhanded conflict management than those of ECOWAS, particularly in their early stage, although in the end Doe was gone (dismembered and assassinated on the ECOWAS compound) and peace was possible only through a mediating effort among the warlords. The Nigerian-led ECOMOG was able to overcome militarily neither the Liberian nor the Sierra Leonean rebellion.[29]

Peacekeeping

Peacekeeping generally refers to an interposition force agreed to by the conflicting parties who call on international efforts to maintain their cease-fire. However, many UN peacekeeping efforts—the so-called Chapter VI 1/2—have slipped toward enforcement by having to take military action against cease-fire infractions. The OAU has engaged in some very small and marginal peacekeeping efforts, such as the Neutral Military Observer Group (NMOG) in Rwanda in 1991–93 in connection with the Arusha agreement negotiations, the Burundi Observer Mission (OMIB) in 1994–96 in connection with the Arusha mediation, and the Comores Observer Mission (OMIC) in 1997–99.[30] There have been no peacekeeping exercises by the subregional organizations. ECO-MOG tried on occasion to act as a peacekeeping force but it never received full agreement from all the parties, and it began and kept slipping into the role as peace enforcement. The largest peacekeeping efforts in Africa have been the Chapter VII UN Organization Mission in the Democratic Republic of the Congo (MONUC) and the UN Observer Mission in Sierra Leone (UNOMSIL), which stumbled into fruition in 2000; in both cases, there was a preliminary cease-fire immediately broken by the signatories. An additional peacekeeping (and implementing) force after the Ethiopian-Eritrean cease-fire was added in 2001 (UN Mission in Ethiopia and Eritrea [UNMEE]).

With no major examples, there is nothing to evaluate, except for the absence of examples itself. Since Africa's conflicts are mainly internal, the challenge to peacekeeping is substantial. In internal conflicts there are less likely to be sharp cease-fire lines to monitor and even the parties are not likely to be clear-cut under conditions of state collapse. The challenges of Congo and Sierra Leone were bigger than Africa's continental or regional organizations could handle; the Sierra Leone cease-fire was a false commitment by an undisciplined congeries of militias, and the Congo cease-fire was a pause of fatigue during which both sides rearmed, regrouped, and resumed attacks, until they got tired again two years later and the assassination of one of the principals, Laurent Kabila, opened new possibilities of a way out. Furthermore, the only relevant regional organization in the Congo case was SADC, engaged in both partisan peace enforcement and neutral peacemaking, a cause of considerable tensions. As the UN experience shows in these cases, peacekeeping was extremely difficult to organize, beyond the effective grasp of the UN and way beyond the capabilities of Africa's organizations.

Peacemaking

Peacemaking is necessarily an attempt at evenhandedness, concerned with mediation to end conflict—both through the establishment of a cease-fire and then through the resolution of the conflict. African continental and regional organizations have been frequently involved in the CCM effort. The record is spotty, but instructive.[31]

The OAU's charter obligation to pursue conflict resolution through peacemaking was to be accomplished by one of its major institutions, the Commission for Mediation, Arbitration, and Conciliation (CMCA). It was never fully constituted, never met, and never operated. Its story has been adequately analyzed[32] but it comes down to the fact that no judicial technician could have the standing to challenge the heads of the new states when they pursued their conflicts. It has only been when these heads of state themselves retired (in itself a rarity) and became available to join a council of elders that mediators of sufficient stature have become available to restrain younger successors. Suggested on numerous occasions, both within the OAU and without, such a council has not yet been constituted, but individual former heads of state have served in a mediating function on behalf of the OAU with helpful if mixed results.

In the absence of its Charter organ, the OAU turned to ad hoc committees to carry out its peacemaking obligation. Some thirty ad hoc committees were appointed during the first two decades of the OAU,[33] with a success ratio of about 1 in 3.[34] They then gradually fell into disuse and were replaced as the dominant means of handling conflict by the Mechanism, which was introduced in 1993 (discussed below), although ad hoc committees continue to be used on occasion, such as the Committee of Ten seeking to reverse the October 2000 elections in Ivory Coast. Batting .333 can be considered high or low depending on one's expectations, but the rise of internal conflicts in the OAU's third decade made its members consider the score low and look for alternatives; internal conflict, as a category, threatened them all and they hoped for better ways of handling it. Only five of the thirty conflicts handled by ad hoc committees were internal; several of them involved rival national liberation movements, one involved Biafra, and one (plus several non-OAU committees) concerned the internecine conflict in Chad in 1979–83.

Ad hoc committees have been constituted on the basis of a complicated and implicit formula. Membership has included "representatives" of regions, ideological groups, the camps around the conflicting states and neutrals, and the Anglo-French divide. Much of the work was be done by foreign ministers, with participation of the heads of state at crucial junctures. Persuasion and peer pressure have been the only means of leverage that the members could use; more tangible inducements have not been available. In two-thirds of the cases, this has not been enough: The disapprobation of fellow heads of state has not outweighed the stakes and prestige attached to the continuation of conflict. This is all the more remarkable given the fact that, in general, Africa's interstate conflicts have not produced any changes and have ended with the situation returning to the status quo. Only internal conflicts over domestic power have changed the status quo.

The committees—plus many other factors—might be considered enormously successful in that the frequency of the classical neighbor-against-neighbor interstate conflict has greatly diminished. But its replacement by regional conflict constellations and internal conflicts is no improvement and has made the work of ad hoc committees more difficult, since the heads of member states do not have the same hold over rebel leaders as they do over conflicting fellow heads of state.

This situation led to a number of attempts to reorganize the OAU's machinery for handling conflict at the end of the 1980s. Two stand out: the Kampala Movement, operating outside the OAU, discussed below,[35] and the Mechanism for the Prevention, Management, and Resolution of Conflict (hereafter "the Mechanism"), adopted at the 1993 OAU Summit in Cairo. The two are related; although the secretary-general does not like to admit it, the Mechanism seems to have been inspired by the competing pressure and ideas of the Kampala

Movement. The Mechanism has three components: the Central Organ or "Security Council" of nine OAU members who meet regularly at various levels and can act independently of the annual summit; the special representatives of the secretary-general (SRSGs); and the Division for Conflict Prevention, Management, and Resolution of the Secretariat.

The Central Organ has effectively replaced ad hoc committees and incorporated the annual summit as a means of handling conflicts. It meets annually at the head of state or government level at the summit, biennially at the foreign ministers' level at the Council of Ministers; and monthly at the ambassadorial level in Addis; thus, it appropriates existing times and levels of OAU meetings rather than instituting something new. What is new is its authorization to take action between summits.

The Mechanism has been supported by the Secretariat Division, which became the Conflict Management Center (CMC), part of the Political Department, in 1995; it is not clear to what extent its small staff of about twenty-five provides any effective intelligence or creative thinking.

The OAU's major peacemaking initiative in the 1990s was the cease-fire and conflict management agreement extracted from the warring parties in the Ethiopian-Eritrean war in 2000. The OAU president, Algerian President Abdulaziz Bouteflika, operated in combined cooperation and competition with other mediators, notably Libyan Moammar Qaddafi and the United States, primarily through Anthony Lake. The OAU mediation played two roles. Early on, it established the terms of a settlement, if there were to be one, even if those terms were rejected by each of the parties in turn for a year and a half.[36] At the end, abetted by a mutually hurting stalemate that the parties inflicted on each other, if unequally, it brought the parties to agree to those terms. The UN was tasked with providing a peacekeeping contingent (UNMEE).

The OAU has also dispatched eminent persons and special representatives of the secretary-general (SRSGs) to conflicted areas.[37] The most successful was the first mission, by SRSG Mohamed Sahnoun, to Congo-Brazzaville in 1993–94, where violence following the transition to a multiparty system was brought under control.[38] A similar exercise in the same country in 1997 ended in failure. Other SRSG missions to the Great Lakes region have not produced results. An exceptional case independent of any established organization, however, has been the ad hoc mediation effort in Burundi initiated by former U.S. President Jimmy Carter and taken over by former Presidents Julius Nyerere and then Nelson Mandela. African and great power support and dogged persuasion has brought about gradual movement to reconciliation and triggered a parallel peace process within the state,[39] again taking advantage of a growing sense of stalemate by at least parts of both sides of the conflict.

In the absence of effective mediation under the auspices of the OAU, the regional organizations proved a more active venue. ECOWAS provided the organizational framework for the Abuja Agreements of 15 August 1995 and 16 August 1996 ending the Liberian civil war, for the Abuja agreement of 2 November 1998 temporarily ending the Guinea-Bissau civil war, and for the Abidjan and Lome Agreements of 1997 and 18 May 1999, which did not end the Sierra Leonean civil war. In Liberia, a mutually hurting stalemate was in effect at the time of Abuja, the agreements were detailed enough to provide a plan for implementation, all the relevant parties were included, and Taylor saw the conditions for victory in the stipulated election. In Guinea-Bissau, the conflict was of a lower intensity and had reached an unproductive stalemate. In the case of Sierra Leone, the government was facing defeat at the time of Lome and the RUF obtained a power-sharing agreement. ECOMOG provided peacekeeping forces in Liberia between the agreements and the election the following year, and then military training for the next two years, and peacekeeping/enforcing forces in Sierra Leone until RUF broke the agreement and British and the UN forces of UNOMSIL arrived.

IGAD (in its earlier configuration as the Agency on Drought and Development) mediated an exemplary conflict management arrangement between Ethiopia and Sudan at its first meeting in Djibouti through the efforts of its secretary-general, consummated by an agreement on 3 April 1988.[40] It then turned to the Sudanese conflict in 1993 and mediated a Declaration of Principles (DOP) in 1994 that, like the OAU effort in the Ethiopian-Eritrean war, defined terms on which the conflict could be settled. However, the Sudanese government backed out of the principles. The IGAD effort then continued desultorily under uninterested Kenyan leadership, and was eventually consumed by wily Sudanese diplomacy during the Ethiopian-Eritrean war. The major missing element in the mediation effort was the hurting stalemate, which never affected both sides at the same time and so was never mutual.

SADC's major peacemaking triumph by Zambian President Frederick Chiluba was the Lusaka Agreement of 21 July 1999, signed over the next three months by the various parties after further mediation. The negotiations were enormously complicated for four reasons: the classical problem of status between the state and the rebel movements, exacerbated by the involvement of neighboring states whose presence buttressed the state status of the Congolese government to the exclusion of the rebel movements; the ambiguous role of SADC, three of whose members (Zimbabwe, Namibia, Angola) had intervened in the conflict in support of the Congolese government; the pluralist nature of each side, with each state's different issues and reasons for involvement, exacerbated by growing splits within the rebel movement; and the absence of a mutually hurting stalemate. The agreement came about when a temporary "soft stalemate" of fatigue set in and the parties' diverse interests were addressed, rendering the agreement so complex, long-term, and difficult to implement that it is in danger of becoming a dead letter. MONUC, the UN peacekeeping force needed to give it authority, to permit a withdrawal of neighboring troops, and to support an internal dialogue, was inadequate for the task in numbers and mandate and hesitant in forthcoming.

THE CHALLENGES FOR COLLECTIVE CONFLICT MANAGEMENT

Conflicts made of state collapse and regional confrontation contain characteristics that challenge the standard components of conflict management.[41] The contextual elements are resiliently unpropitious for resolution, by any agency. The conflict is not contained in one space or on one level, posing questions of precedence and priority. Despite the need to resolve on all levels, debate continues as to whether conflicts such as Congo, Sudan, or Sierra Leone should be managed first on the level of domestic dialogue between government and oppositions or on the level of foreign troop withdrawal (troops who would have no cause or opportunity to intervene if the political vacuum within the state were filled).[42] All parties need to feel the hurting stalemate at the same time for it to be mutual and effective, or else one party's stalemate becomes another's opportunity and the conflict ratchets on.[43] The result is more frequently a soft and stable stalemate, punctuated by violent outbreaks, where each party expects to prevail in the next round and where hanging on is possible and preferable to negotiating—a classic "prisoner's dilemma game."[44] The seesaw nature of the Sudanese, Angolan, Eritrean, Liberian, and Sierra Leonean conflicts is the most likely future for the Congolese conflict as well. In all these conflicts, the rebels' greatest ally is the government's general incapacity and selective discrimination, a characteristic of the process of state collapse and not of states capable of making and holding a peace agreement.

The appropriate formula for a conflict management agreement then also becomes difficult to identify because of the complexity of parties and contours to the conflict. While the multiple parties and issues facilitate trade-offs, they also make a broadly attractive package harder to assemble, and when assembled harder to implement. In addition, the conjunction of structural causes such as poverty and ethnicity with immediate grievances and power struggles means that mutually attractive opportunities to drive conflict management processes are caught in vicious circles. The 1999 Lusaka agreement on the Congo conflict touches every issue in the regional collision but without realistic procedures or timetables for their solution. The 1996 Abuja, 1999 Lusaka, and 1999 Lome Agreements provided settlements for the multiple parties in the Liberian, Congolese, and Sierra Leonean conflicts, respectively, as did the 1991 Bicesse and 1994 Lusaka agreements in Angola before them, but the underlying causes of squandered resources and undelivered services in these collapsed states were not and could not be addressed in a simple peace agreement.

Even when appropriate formulas are evident, parties and solutions are worn out by reneged commitments and betrayed opportunities. Federalism, a prominent solution to the Sudanese conflict, is no longer available because it was enacted by the Addis Ababa agreement of 1972 and then betrayed by the Sudanese government. Cooperation between the two halves of the country as a solution to the state's collapse was tried in Congo and betrayed under the first Kabila government of 1997–98, as it was in Angola in the 1991 Bicesse agreement and then all over again in the 1994 Lusaka agreement. Election of a president was tried but failed as a means to restore confidence in the state in Angola in 1992, in Congo-Brazzaville in 1993, and in Sierra Leone in 1996. For these various reasons, finding the right contents for a formula to pull the parties out of conflict and onto a path of reconstruction is unusually difficult.

In facing these problems for collective conflict management (CCM), Africa has been left to its own devices. Global coalitions and organizations, like regional ones, are not corporate actors but instruments of their members, and ultimately among them, of their strongest members or hegemons. The UN—which means the great powers who dominate the Security Council—has been wary of involvement, for lack of strategic interest in the continent, anxiety before the unmanageable elements in conflicts composed of collapse and contagion, and dread of body bags. With some partial exceptions, the post–Cold War and postcolonial leaders of the world have lost interest in Africa and have devoted little effort to conflict management either directly or through the UN Security Council.[45] The exceptions are perfunctory—support for the beleaguered government in Rwanda by the French through Operation Turquoise in 1994 or in Sierra Leone by the British in 1999, mediation effort in support of the OAU in the Eritrean-Ethiopian War by the United States in 1999–2000. The United States watched attentively and approved regional mediation efforts in Sierra Leone, Burundi, and Congo at the end of the decade but took no active role and worked to send late and inappropriately limited UN forces to Sierra Leone as UNOMSIL and Congo as MONUC in 2000. It did, however, call for a UN Secretariat study of causes and remedies for African conflicts, at the same moment as it apologized for inaction in Rwanda and vetoed low-cost authorization for a peacekeeping/enforcing force in Congo-Brazzaville;[46] in the event, the UN report was comprehensive and inconclusive.[47]

So Africa has to rely on its own CCM mechanisms. But its continental organization, the new African Union, has taken an irresponsible flight into supranationality, and the regional organizations are still too new, weak, and inexperienced to be able to contain deviant behavior and the processes of collapse in their conflicted members. Regional hegemons are weak and unable to supply leadership and have generally—and wisely—used at least the collective cloak to cover their actions.[48] Nigeria, at times near collapse itself, mobilized ECOWAS for its purposes, as South Africa and Zimbabwe competed to mobilize SADC. In the Horn, the potential hegemon, Ethiopia, has only recently emerged from its own collapse, and in central Africa the collapse of the potential hegemon, Congo, and the absence of a comprehensive regional organization constitute the problems and bar the solutions. The available CCM mechanisms have been institutionally incapable of meeting four important requirements to move the participants from conflict to its management: compulsion, enforcement, norm-building, and reconstruction.

1. As competing profiteers, the parties are not only fully occupied by their conflict but richly benefiting from it, uninterested in devoting attention and

imagination to the search for a solution. The OAU Mechanism and SRSGs, regional organization representatives and committees, and individuals mediators are able to provide creative and authoritative formulas that constitute standards for an acceptable agreement—such as the 1999 OAU resolution in the Eritrean-Ethiopian war, the 1981 Implementation Committee's proposals in the Western Sahara, the 1994 IGAD Declaration of Principles (DOP) in Sudan, the 1994 and 1999 Lusaka Agreements on Angola and on Congo, among others—but they cannot make the horse drink: They cannot compel the parties to accept these terms as a basis for ending their conflict. Primarily, they are unable to provide worse alternatives for the parties if they turn down the terms, or to block the abilities of the parties to profit from continued conflict. African conflict management characteristically relies on persuasion as its means, as noted, with no compelling alternatives at hand to their mediating démarches.

2. As partisan combatants, the parties are unable to provide an authoritative and impartial umpire to coordinate commitments, call fouls and delay-of-game, and monitor and enforce results. Even when the parties are sincere in reaching an agreement, it is in their interest to cheat slightly even when the agreement is in their interest and greatly when it is not. Normally, an intergovernmental organization (IGO) should provide such authority, but the absence of effective government is the source of the conflict. Since the continental and regional organizations are groups of member states, they too suffer the same debilitation. The OAU/AU's size, diversity of interests and outlooks, and broad range of activities render it inept at such functions. As membership organizations, SADC, IGAD, and ECOWAS have found it difficult to perform these functions in regard to the Lusaka Agreements on Angola and on Congo, the DOP in Sudan, and the half-dozen agreements on Liberia, respectively; the OAU never ventured into any of these conflicts.

3. As both potential subjects of collapse and potential exploiters of the negative externalities that derive from others' collapse, African states have been unable to create a system of norms to govern their internal and international relations and serve as guidelines for their collective conflict management. African norms embodied in the OAU Charter, now bypassed by the African Union, relate to a past anticolonial era. Within the AU, African states have neither the means of ideology and imposition used by the former Communist world nor the methods of concertation and consensus employed in the West to develop a normative system. Nor has public opinion or civil society been developed enough to oblige governments to devise such a sense of common standards.

4. As weakened conflictors, the parties are unable to provide the resources for reconstitution of the state and of peacebuilding necessary to the conclusion and implementation of their conflict management agreement and the prevention of recurrent conflict. Rebuilding a state and filling a vacuum are extremely daunting processes, far beyond the experience and capability of any organization.

Peacebuilding is the open-ended process of reconstructing a conflicted society—whether domestic or international—so as to prevent further conflict. The subject is enormous for analysis and for practice, and is generally beyond the scope of this study, in part because it is beyond the CCM capabilities of Africa. Yet it must be mentioned, not only because it is part of the standard array of conflict-related measures, but because it addresses the basic issues of state collapse and clustered conflicts that underlie and characterize Africa's problem. Within this broad topic, there is one aspect that is, paradoxically, both within the grasp of African states and outside the usual treatments of peacebuilding—the construction of norms and standards to constitute a regime of conflict prevention.

All of Africa's organizations constitute very splotchy regimes, in that their purposes and standards are directed toward the establishment of norms and procedures for managing conflict but are far from comprehensive, all for sound historical reasons. In the case of the OAU, its establishment in 1963 came soon after its members' independence and was focused above all on the protection of that independence, with the management of conflict among its members coming as a distant second. The successor AU is unclear in focus and seeks to become an African version of the European Union without any of the history of half a decade of common efforts, economic exchanges, or internal institutional development behind it. All regional organizations began as instruments of economic cooperation and only turned to conflict management when security imposed itself by its absence as a precondition to development.

However, at the beginning of the 1990s, the absence of security, stability, development, and cooperation and of standards of conduct for the attainment of these goals became the subject of attention across the continent, under the leadership of retired Nigerian president and general Olusegun Obasanjo. He mobilized a series of meetings of government and civil society representatives across the continent, culminating in a conference and document at Kampala that set out a regime for the achievement of security, stability, development, and cooperation in Africa (Conference on Security, Stability, Development, and Cooperation in Africa [CSSDCA]) inspired by the Conference (after 1994, Organization) on Security and Cooperation in Europe established in Helsinki in 1972.[49] Presented to the OAU summits in 1991 and 1992, the document was shelved, after the Mechanism for Conflict Prevention, Management, and Resolution was lifted from it and added to the OAU structure. The proposed regime posed a threat to the organization and many of its members.

Obasanjo's incarceration by the Nigerian government in 1995 brought a temporary halt to the Kampala movement, although planning continued on the level of civil society. His liberation and reelection to the Nigerian presidency in 1999 brought CSSDCA back to the OAU agenda as the primary plank of Nigerian foreign policy. It was again swallowed up by the OAU in 1999 and 2000, which endorsed its principles as an expression of the organization's already established purposes and handed it to a committee to organize the indicated conference. Instead, at its summit in 2000 the OAU reconstituted itself as an African Union, bypassing the Kampala regime and its principles. Organizers of the

Kampala movement, however, seek to continue their efforts within African civil society bodies and to press for the adoption of the principles by the regional organizations.

Principles are words but they are also formalized commitments. International relations theory and practice show that regimes have an important effect on state behavior (despite the skepticism of critics).[50] Regional organizations are both the subject and the embodiment of regimes, and their work in conflict management is greatly facilitated by the legitimizing, standardizing, and coordinating effects of agreed sets of principles. Adoption of standards of behavior to foster individual and state security, stability in governance, socioeconomic development, and continental and regional cooperation in Africa would be a major step in strengthening commitments and procedures for the management and prevention of conflict in Africa.

CONCLUSION

Jarred by Somalia in 1993, shocked by Rwanda in 1994, and rejected by Congo and Sudan after 1997, external powers have vowed to stay out of African conflicts, where they see entrapment rather than interests, leaving conflict management to Africans. Yet to expect much collective conflict management (as opposed to support for beleaguered governments) from African states working through the OAU/AU is unrealistic. The organization provides a regular meeting place for African states, a crucial center for the African concert system, an occasion for handling problems among heads of state, a forum to define standards for solutions, and an institution to protect the fragile sovereignty of member states. As such it is most useful, and is fully occupied pursuing these tasks. But as an organization dedicated above all to the protection of its members states' ever-fragile sovereignty, it has little role in conflict management. From time to time, incidentally, the OAU will be given a problem that it can handle, as it did in the Congo-Brazzaville case in 1993, or with some help from the United States in the Ethiopian-Eritrean case in 2000. But these accomplishments are almost accidental and attempts to build on or repeat the incidental success may prove the case to be exceptional, as the Congo-Brazzaville civil war of 1997–99 and the Guinea-Liberia war of 2000 show.

Instead, regional hegemons, the likely leaders in any conflict management efforts though themselves weakened, are more apt to work through a regional organization, but as dictated by their own interests.

There they have to take into account other members' interests but in a less absolute way and can mobilize their colleagues to support and legitimize their actions. Since the hegemons are working in a region of direct concern to them, they find it in their interest to deploy the leadership, pressure, and resources necessary to manage regional conflicts and respond to state collapse as needed. Such intentions and capabilities are necessarily limited and do not guarantee success: The region conflict clusters within ECOWAS, IGAD, and SADC had not yet been successfully managed at the end of 2001. The problems of state collapse and clustered conflict pose an enormous challenge to any would-be manager, individual or collective. All that is indicated is that, when efforts are deployed, they are led by the hegemon and conducted within the regional organization.

This situation is bound to continue, in all its aspects. Too consistent failures may change the pattern and discourage regional hegemons and organizations from any action, as it did with global hegemons' efforts in the mid 1990s, although it is harder for neighbors to turn their backs to the cancer of local conflict that invades their own bodies politic. Repeated failures or, less likely, occasional successes can turn regional leaders to join the Kampala Movement or its local variety and adopt codes of conduct for handling conflict. Such a change would be wonderful, but unfortunately less likely than a continuation of current trends.

NOTES

1. In the following discussion, when the analysis focuses on past characteristics, the term OAU will be used. When the entire African experience, past and future is discussed, reference will be to OAU/AU. When future possibilities are addressed, the continental organization will be referred to as AU.

2. Andrew Hurrell, "Explaining the Resurgence of Regionalism in World Politics," *Review of International Studies* XXI, no. 3 (October 1995): 354.

3. I. William Zartman, ed., *Collapsed States: The Disintegration and Restoration of Legitimate Authority* (Boulder, Colo.: Lynne Rienner, 1995), 1.

4. Samuel Huntington, *Political Order in Changing Societies* (New Haven, Conn.: Yale University Press, 1968), 266; Crane Brinton, *The Anatomy of Revolution* (New York: Vintage, 1958).

5. Brinton, *The Anatomy of Revolution*.

6. William Reno, *Warlord Politics and African States* (Boulder, Colo.: Lynne Rienner, 1998).

7. Paul Collier and Anke Hoeffler, "Justice-Seeking and Loot-Seeking in Civil War" (Washington, D.C.: World Bank, 1999); Paul Collier, "Economic Consequences of Civil War," *Oxford Economic Papers* LI, no. 1 (1999): 168–83; Paul Collier, "Doing Well Out of War," in *Greed and Grievance: Economic Agendas in Civil Wars,* ed. Mats Berdal and David Malone (Boulder, Colo.: Westview, 2000).

8. Morocco-Algeria 1963, Dahomey-Benin 1963, Ethiopia-Somalia 1964, Mali–Upper Volta 1965.

9. Mali–Upper Volta 1976, Somalia-Ethiopia 1978, Uganda-Tanzania 1979.

10. Chad-Libya 1980, Nigeria-Cameroon 1981, Senegal-Mauritania 1989.

11. Nigeria-Cameroon 1993, Eritrea-Ethiopia 1998–2000.

12. Francis Deng et al., *Sovereignty as Responsibility* (Washington, D.C.: Brookings, 1996), 145–58.

13. Waldemar Nielsen, *Africa's Battleline* (New York: Harper & Row, 1965).

14. I. William Zartman, "Mediating Conflicts of Need, Greed and Creed," *Orbis* (2000): 255–66; I. William Zartman, "Need, Creed and Greed," in *The Economics and Politics of Conflict,* ed. Cynthia Arnson (Washington, D.C.: Woodrow Wilson Center Press, pending).

15. Gilbert Khadiagala, *Allies in Adversity: The Front Line States in Southern African Security* (Athens: Ohio University Press, 1994); Douglas Anglin, "Conflict in Sub-Saharan Africa," *Southern African Perspectives* 81 (University of the Western Cape, 1999).

16. I. William Zartman, "Foreign Relations of North Africa," *Annals of the American Academy of Political and Social Sciences* 489 (1987): 13–27; I. William Zartman, "The Ups and Down of Maghrib Unity," in *Middle East Dilemma: The Politics and Economics of Arab Integration,* ed. Michael Hudson (New York: Columbia University Press, 1999).

17. After they intervened in Congo on government request, Zimbabwe, Angola, and Namibia signed an alliance on 15 April 1999, pledging to do what they had already done.

18. Tanzania's sin, in 1979, was as much that it acted unilaterally (in support of Ugandan exiles) as that it interfered in Ugandan internal affairs. Of course, Tanzanian President Julius Nyerere understood full well that had he turned to the OAU for legitimization, he would have been rebuffed for interfering in Ugandan internal affairs, and so he acted unilaterally, thus relieving Africa of an egregious ruler, which the criticizing OAU members acknowledged with gratitude—but only privately.

19. See Inis L. Claude, Jr., "Collective Legitimization as a Political Function of the United Nations," in *International Organization: A Reader,* ed. Friedrich Kratochwil and Edward D. Mansfield (New York: HarperCollins, 1994).

20. Inis L. Claude, Jr., *Power and International Relations* (New York: Random House, 1962); Arnold Wolfers, "Collective Defense vs. Collective Security," in *Alliance Policy in the Cold War,* ed. Arnold Wolfers (Baltimore: Johns Hopkins University Press, 1959); Marina Finkelstein and Lawrence Finkelstein, eds., *Collective Security* (San Francisco: Chandler, 1966).

21. William Foltz, "The OAU and the Resolution of Africa's Conflicts," in *Conflict Resolution in Africa,* ed. Francis Deng and I. William Zartman (Washington, D.C.: Brookings 1991); William Foltz and Jennifer Widner, "The OAU and Africa's Liberation Struggle," in *The OAU after Twenty Years,* ed. Yassin El-Ayouty and I. William Zartman (Westport, Conn.: Praeger, 1984).

22. I. William Zartman, "African Regional Security and Changing Patterns of Relations," in *Africa in the New International Order,* ed. Edmond Keller and Donald Rothchild (Boulder, Colo.: Lynne Rienner, 1996).

23. John Stremlau, *The International Politics of the Nigerian Civil War* (Princeton, N.J.: Princeton University Press, 1977).

24. Boutros Boutros-Ghali, *Agenda for Peace,* revised edition (New York: United Nations, 1992).

25. Thomas Mockaitis, *Peace Operations and Interstate Conflict* (Westport, Conn.: Praeger, 1999).

26. Dean Pittman, "The OAU in Chad," in *The OAU after Twenty Years,* ed. Yassin El-Ayouty and I. William Zartman (Westport, Conn.: Praeger, 1984).

27. Herman Cohen, *Intervening in Africa* (New York: St Martin's, 2000), chapter 5.

28. Saadia Touval, "Coercive Mediation on the Road to Dayton," *International Negotiation* I, no. 3 (1996): 547–70 (Special Issue on Negotiations in the Former Soviet Union and the Former Yugoslavia).

29. Paul Richards, "Rebellion in Liberia and Sierra Leone," in *Conflict in Africa,* ed. Oliver Furley (New York: St. Martin's, 1995).

30. Adekeye Adebajo and Chris Landsberg, "The Heirs of Nkrumah: Africa's New Interventionists," *Pugwash Occasional Papers* II, no. 1 (1995): 72–86.

31. I. William Zartman, "African Diplomacy," in *Africa in World Politics,* 3rd ed., ed. John Harbeson and Donald Rothchild (Boulder, Colo.: Westview, 2000).

32. C. O. C. Amate, *Inside the OAU* (New York: St Martin's, 1986).

33. Yassin El-Ayouty and I. William Zartman, eds., *The OAU after Twenty Years* (Westport, Conn.: Praeger, 1984), 379–83.

34. I. William Zartman, "African Diplomacy."

35. Francis Deng and I. William Zartman, *Africa in Search of a Vision* (Washington, D.C.: Brookings, 2001).

36. Gilbert Khadiagala, "Reflections of the Ethiopia-Eritrea Border Conflict," *The Fletcher Forum of World Affairs* XXIII, no. 2 (1999): 51–69.

37. Gilbert Khadiagala, "Prospects for a Division of Labour: African Regional Organisations in Conflict Prevention," in *Early Warning and Conflict Prevention,* ed. Klaas van Walraven (Dudrecht: Kluwer, 1998), 134.

38. I. William Zartman, "Prevention Gained and Prevention Lost: Collapse, Competition and Coup in Congo," in *Opportunities Missed, Opportunities Seized,* ed. Bruce Jentleson (Lanham, Md.: Rowman & Littlefield, 2000).

39. Mohammed Maundi et al., *Entry into Mediation* (Washington, D.C.: U.S. Institute of Peace, 2002).

40. I. William Zartman, *Ripe for Resolution: Conflict and Intervention in Africa* (New York: Oxford University Press, 1989), 122–24.

41. I. William Zartman, "Barriers to African Conflict Resolution," in *Conflict Resolution in Africa,* ed. Steven Metz (Carlisle, Pa.: U.S. Army War College, 2000).

42. Chester A. Crocker, *High Noon in Southern Africa* (New York: Norton, 1992).

43. I. William Zartman, *Ripe for Resolution*; I. William Zartman, "Ripeness: The Hurting Stalemate and Beyond," in *International Conflict Resolution after the Cold War,* ed. Paul Stern and Daniel Druckman (Washington, D.C.: National Academy Press, 2000).

44. I. William Zartman, ed., *Elusive Peace: Negotiating an End to Civil Wars* (Washington, D.C.: Brookings, 1996), 10.

45. For the last era of U.S. attention, see Herman Cohen, *Intervening in Africa* (2000).

46. I. William Zartman, "An Apology Needs a Pledge," *New York Times,* 2 April 1998.

47. Kofi Annan, *Report of the Secretary-General on the Causes of Conflict in Africa* (New York: United Nations, 1998).

48. David Meyers, *Regional Hegemons* (Boulder, Colo.: Westview, 1991); I. William Zartman, "African Regional Security."

49. Olusegun Obasanjo, *The Kampala Document* (New York: African Leadership Forum, 1991); Deng and Zartman, *Africa in Search of a Vision.*

50. Audie Klotz, *Norms in International Relations* (Ithaca., N.Y.: Cornell University Press, 1996); Andreas Hasenclever, Peter Mayer, and Volker Rittberger, *Theories of International Regimes* (Cambridge: Cambridge University Press, 1997).

4

The Dilemma of Regional Security in East Asia

Multilateralism versus Bilateralism

Victor D. Cha

In most American postwar international relations scholarship, the concept of regional security has been at best redundant and at worst irrelevant. In the former case, redundancy derived from the fact that many of these local security problems were inextricably linked to a more fundamental superpower conflict at the core. In the occasional instance when such linkages to the core did not exist, then regional security was, for the most part, ignored. With the end of the Cold War, however, regional security has emerged as a popular object of study. As Lepgold argues, there are three basic axes around which studies of how to manage regional security should sit: the nature and severity of the security problem, the availability of institutions and actors to act "regionally," and the presence of extraregional actors that affect choices.[1] This chapter, while touching on all three axes, focuses primarily on the second as it relates to regional security in Asia. I seek to explain the absence of regional institutions and multilateral security mechanisms, and I offer conceptual arguments for how such institutions can be created. One of the key tasks in this regard is understanding how regional security can be better integrated into the existing and predominant security institution in the region today, the U.S.-based set of bilateral alliances. I begin with a brief overview of the record of regional security institutions in Asia. I then present the research "puzzle" that regional security poses, followed by the argument for the enhancement of such institutions in the region.

THE RECORD OF REGIONAL SECURITY IN ASIA

Unlike Europe, the history of regional security in Asia has been unimpressive. There are no comparable institutions like NATO and the Warsaw Pact. States instead chose paths of security self-reliance, neutralism, or bilateralism (largely with the United States, but also with China or the Soviet Union). Attempts at constructing institutions did exist but these were largely subregional rather than regionwide (e.g., Southeast Asian Treaty Organization [SEATO, 1954], Australia–New Zealand–U.S. Pact [ANZUS, 1951], and Five Power Defense Arrangement [FPDA, 1971]) and met with limited success.[2] Largely profit-based "natural economic territories" (and their attendant positive security and political effects) were envisioned in Asiatic Russia, North China, Japan, Mongolia, and the Korean peninsula but these largely failed.[3] Efforts at a regionwide "PATO" equivalent of NATO failed miserably despite a compelling Cold War security environment and established venues for dialogue.[4] While more recent institutions at official and Track II levels have been more successful (e.g., ASEAN Regional Forum [ARF], Asian-Pacific Economic Cooperation [APEC], Council for Security Cooperation in the Asia-Pacific [CSCAP], Northeast Asia Cooperation Dialogue [NEACD], Asia-Europe Meeting [ASEM]), they differ fundamentally from these predecessors, exhibiting a "softer" quality not extending beyond dialogue and transparency building.[5] The most advanced of these at the regionwide level is the Association of Southeast Asian Nations (ASEAN) Regional Forum (ARF), formed in July 1994 and meeting annually with regard to cooperative security dialogue and preventive diplomacy.[6]

The absence of a NATO-type organization in Asia stems from a variety of factors. Unlike Europe, Asia was both a maritime and land theater without the same clearly identifiable geographical boundaries that separated contiguous Europe. Moreover, the two poles that defined NATO and Warsaw Pact membership were never as clear in Asia. On the one hand, Asia's balance of power was always complicated by a third pole in China whose geostrategic leanings varied throughout the Cold War. On the other hand, residual mistrust and animosity among Asian nations toward Imperial Japan ensured that any postwar leadership role for this key power in a NATO-type organization would be politically unsustainable. These disparate perceptions of external threat did not constitute ideal conditions for collective or multilateral security. Furthermore, any enthusiasm in the region for such institutions were dampened by domestic factors. Postcolonial nation building made anathema the notion of submitting new-found sovereignty to a larger external entity. Moreover, in many of these cases, the primary threat to security was internal rather than external. Initial choices by the United States were also important. The priority in American postwar planning was Europe. The United States put the best minds, political focus, and economic resources into creating a new set of institutions in Europe to ensure peace and economic recovery.[7] In Asia, however, the policy was more ad hoc and reactive (with the exception of Japan's occupation) with the priority on managing a process of decolonization in the context of the Cold War.[8] Another factor often unobserved for the absence of multilateral security in Asia is the region's peace. This is not to deny that wars in Asia occurred in the post-1945 era and during the Cold War, but they were never on a scale that commanded a bold push for multilateralism or regional security models.[9]

The Puzzle

While the structural and domestic factors described above provide an initial explanation for the absence of regional security institutions in Asia, they at best provide only the broad, permissive conditions. Indeed, upon closer analysis, there is a basic puzzle with regard to regional security and the American network of bilateral alliances in Asia. Despite regionalism's underwhelming record, the United States and its allies[10] generally agree on the tenets of regionalism in Asia. They agree that regional or multilateral security should be inclusive rather than exclusive. They agree that such institutions and practices should be seen as a complement to, and not replacement of, the bilateral alliance (or for that matter global multilateral institutions).[11] They value the basic norms of multilateralism (e.g., preservation of national sovereignty).[12] They also recognize, for the most part, legitimate security problems and negative security externalities in the region that require management at some level.[13] This general convergence of views should provide the conditions for regional security's thriving in the region. However, the empirical record as described above shows otherwise, raising a host of unanswered questions. Why has multilateral and regional security been relatively ineffective in East Asia? Why in spite of general agreement on multilateral principles and norms does participation in such institutions remain problematic for the bilateral alliances? Why do some see multilateral institutions as a threat to the alliances? Why do others see multilateralism as impeded by the alliances? And why do yet others see it as irrelevant to the alliances?

This chapter tries to address this puzzle. It makes three arguments. First, regional security's ineffectiveness in Asia is not easily explainable by focusing on external threats. Indeed, a threat-based explanation of regional security is *over determined*. One could plausibly argue that either high or low values of the threat variable could explain the absence of regional security initiatives. In the former case, this is because of the intervening variable of U.S. bilateral alliances. This leads to the second point: Enthusiasm among the United States and their primary allies for regional security is undercut by the perception of zero-sum trade-offs between bilateral and multilateral security arrangements. For this reason, regional security advocates face "twin dilemmas of appeal" vis-à-vis the American bilateral alliances: an asymmetry of need, and functional redundancy. In short, multilateral security dialogues (MSD)—as they are currently constituted—are ineffective and do not resonate loudly within the bilateral context because: (1) MSDs need the alliances more than the alliances need the MSDs, and (2) the MSDs duplicate rather than complement security functions already provided by the alliances.

Third, I argue that there are several ways that MSD advocates can mute these twin dilemmas of appeal and create greater complementarity between the needs of the alliances and the needs of MSDs. These have to do with broadening the underlying security conceptions operative among MSDs, creating "binding and reinforcing" rationales for MSD participation by the United States and its allies, and utilizing MSD participation as a means to facilitate "minilateral" security dialogues.

Why Regional Security?

Understanding how to create better convergence between bilateralism and multilateralism in Asia is important because it avoids pitting an old system of managing security against the new. In other words, it is incumbent on the traditional Cold War American network of bilateral alliances to cope with, rather than reject or ignore, the newer attempts at indigenous and multilateral regional security initiatives and institutions. As some experts have argued, previous multilateral efforts may have been disappointing, but there is no denying that such regional initiatives have gained traction in the post–Cold War era, and that the United States and its allies must anticipate change rather than adhere to a familiar but potentially anachronistic status quo.[14] These two variables, more than any other (barring major war), will determine the future security landscape of the region. Therefore, I seek to show how these two pieces fit together and what are their potential points of conflict. More important, I try to show how the two can be mutually reinforcing and what are the potential divisions of labor between multilateral security dialogues and U.S.–Asia bilateral alliance commitments.

THREATS AND PROBLEMS ON THE REGIONAL AGENDA

What is particularly interesting about the regional security puzzle in Asia is that external threat is not a good predictor of regionalism's success or ineffectiveness. The notion of a single, clearly defined threat to the region is highly contested. The natural inclination based on relative power capabilities might incline one to define this threat as China. China possesses the most advanced nuclear weapons and ballistic missile programs in Asia. Its ballistic missile infrastructure offers a wide variety of land- and sea-based systems. It is in the midst of a wide-ranging modernization program that aims to improve range, payload, and accuracy (through development of solid propellants, improved rocket motors, targeting technologies) to replace older systems deployed in the 1970s and 1980s.[15] China's nuclear arsenal consists of approximately 400 to 450 devices. Beijing relies largely on the land-based leg of the nuclear triad, reserving nearly 250 of these "strategic" warheads for medium- and long-range strike missions mated with the ballistic missile program.[16] Chinese efforts to modernize this arsenal were manifest in a series of tests completed in 1996, the information of which enabled finalizing weapons designs. China has conducted forty-five tests over thirty-three years, versus 1,030 tests conducted by the United States.[17]

In spite of these capabilities, there is no clear consensus in the region that China poses the most proximate threat. For some in the region, the more proximate threat is internal (e.g., Indonesia); for others, it is North Korea (e.g., Japan); and yet still for others, based on historical memory, the true threat is not a more powerful China but a militarily resurgent Japan (e.g., South Korea). The point to be made here is that material capabilities and threat perceptions in the region do not necessarily match. Moreover, with regard to the empirical puzzle for regional security, this disparity of threat perceptions renders the threat variable less useful in explaining regional security dynamics. The problem becomes one of overdetermination. On the one hand, one could explain regional security's ineffectiveness because threats perceptions are disparate (although underlying power capabilities may not be as diffuse). On the other hand, for those countries that do see China as the primary threat, one could explain the absence of regional security responses as a function of a power intervening variable—the U.S.-based bilateral alliance system in the region. Thus, both high and low values on the threat variable can be used to explain the regional security puzzle, which is not very helpful. In addition, the variable most likely to offer the most explanatory value—the bilateral alliances—is overlooked in a threat-based framework. I focus below on this intervening variable and the perceived zero-sum trade-offs between the bilateral alliances and multilateral security initiatives as a key explanatory variable in the puzzle. I begin with a discussion of the perceived trade-offs from American and Asian perspectives.

THE ZERO-SUM TRADE-OFF

The weakness of multilateral security in the region has not been helped by American and allied Asian attitudes. Traditionally, all have been conspicuously ambivalent and even outright opposed to such initiatives. U.S. disinterest particularly at the end of the Cold War stemmed from a combination of an "ain't broke, don't fix it" mentality and initial concerns that such regional initiatives were meant to undermine U.S. leadership. Whether these initiatives took the form of Mahathir's East Asian Economic Caucus (EAEC) or less radical alternatives (i.e., APEC proposals by Australia), the United States was decidedly ambivalent. In November 1990 Secretary of State James Baker criticized the notion of regional security dialogues replacing the American "hub and spokes" network of bilateral alliances in Asia that had been at the center of Asian security and prosperity for four decades.[18] Statements by then–assistant secretary for East Asia Richard Solomon in October 1990 typified the attitude: "[T]he nature of the security challenges we anticipate in the years ahead—do not easily lend themselves to region-wide solutions. When we look at the key determinants of stability in Asia . . . it is difficult to see how a Helsinki-type institution would be an appropriate forum for enhancing security or promoting conflict resolution."[19] This gave way (post-1991) to grudging acceptance that multilateral security dialogues could complement (but not replace) the U.S.-based bilateral architecture.[20] However, at the same time that American acceptance of a role for regional security grew, the rhetoric remained somewhat ambivalent for an alternative reason: If the United States were now *too* enthusiastic about multilateral security, this might be interpreted in the region as the pretext for American withdrawal.

The Key Ally: Japan

Among U.S. allies, Japan's attitudes toward regional security most critically affected security outcomes in the region. There were, of course, other allies that had voice opportunities on these issues, but Japan's stance, because of their material capabilities and their hosting of the mainstay of the American security presence in the region, mattered most. For example, as discussed below, allies like South Korea were strong advocates of multilateral security at certain points during the Cold War (spinning these off regional consultative bodies on the Vietnam conflict), but such initiatives fell flat because of the absence of support from Japan.

In this regard, Japan's interest in regional security was traditionally even less enthusiastic than that of the United States. In theory such an attitude derived directly from the Yoshida doctrine, which emphasized security bilateralism with the United States. In practice as well, the alliance provided all that Japan and other U.S. allies needed in security and economic goods thereby obviating any pressing need for alternative multilateral or bilateral partners. South Korea, although relatively more supportive in political rhetoric on regional security, only saw such institutions as secondary to the prized bilateral alliance with Washington. The cost of this dependence was persistent Japanese and Korean fears of becoming entrapped in military contingencies or political situations in which the allies did not share or shared only partially American interests, but this was acceptable.[21]

Japanese disinterest in multilateral security also stemmed from an acute sensitivity to the region's lingering historical suspicions. Any multilateral security architecture would by definition require a larger Japanese leadership role that would be deemed unacceptable by many in the region. For example, discussions of a Northeast Asian NATO equivalent ("PATO") in the 1960s could not advance past popular opposition and suspicion that this might spark a renewal of Japanese dominance in the region. Japanese attempts at a larger political and economic role in Southeast Asia in the 1970s also met with fiercely negative reactions and riots against Japanese Prime Minister Tanaka in 1974. Part of the problem in this regard stemmed from perceived zero-sum trade-offs of U.S. and Japanese leadership roles in the region. In other words, from the perspective of potential participants in MSDs, any enhancement of the Japanese role by definition meant a reduction in the American role and therefore looked like the United States was "handing off" the region to Japan.[22]

Current Enthusiasm for MSDs in Japan and Korea

This is not to deny that Japanese and Korean participation and enthusiasm for multilateralism exists today. The Koreans have been extremely proactive, proposing a variety of MSDs at the Track II level, as well as utilizing existing venues to create opportunities for security dialogue. While many of these endeavors are motivated by peninsular security issues (i.e., drawing North Korea into regional security groupings to increase transparency), they also have been undertaken for less self-serving purposes like creating dialogue among antagonists in the region.[23]

Japanese participation, at least initially, largely reflected reactive rather than proactive thinking. Participation in multilateral exercises like Rim of the Pacific (RIMPAC), or the extension of sea-lane defense to one thousand nautical miles (1981) only came with intense U.S. pressure. More recent enthusiasm is a function of generational changes in political leadership in Japan. China's rise in the region also made Tokyo's participation in multilateral institutions more attractive as a means of checking and restraining Beijing's influence as Tokyo had less leverage bilaterally to effect changes on issues of concern to it (e.g., nonproliferation).[24] Most important, international criticism of Japanese passiveness during the Gulf War provided the impetus for a more proactive Japanese interest in multilateral security. A bold manifestation of this was the 1991 Nakayama proposal for more open discussions of Japan's role in regional security (i.e., historical impediments to such a role) and for discussions on regional security structures.[25]

TWIN DILEMMAS OF APPEAL

From the region's perspective, regional security faces twin dilemmas of appeal with regard to the bilateral alliances. Receptiveness to multilateral security has grown in recent years relative to the initial skepticism that pervaded the Cold War and early post–Cold War years.[26] In spite of this recent turn in attitudes, a symmetry of needs between the alliances and multilateralism does not obtain. In the simplest of terms, the region still needs the alliances more than the alliances have traditionally needed the region. This observation is most apparent in the inability of MSDs to thrive (at least in Northeast Asia) without avid support from Washington and Tokyo. The bilateral alliances, by contrast, arguably do not require MSDs to remain resilient.

Advocates of regionalism might point to the region's record of MSDs, finding examples of functionally based groupings facilitated by middle and smaller powers in the region. However, without the support of the two most important economic and security powers in the region, these have been ineffective at best and irrelevant at worst. Many have argued that APEC—hardly an irrelevant institution—was founded and developed by powers in Asia like Australia and ASEAN despite American passiveness and Japanese reluctance,[27] but in actuality, Washington and Tokyo's tacit support (and lack of resistance) were indispensable, some have argued, to APEC's success.[28]

The region faces an additional dilemma deriving from the first one. The multilateral security groupings often seek to appeal to the alliances on as many levels as possible to elicit American, Japanese, and South Korean participation.[29] These levels have ranged traditionally (i.e., during the Cold War) from "hard" security issues (e.g., PATO proposals) to transparency building, confidence-building measures (CBMs), and preventive diplomacy. However, many of these appeals for participation are redundant—that is, their purpose duplicates what the United States and Japan and the United States and South Korea already can deal with, either in a bilateral context or in a global multilateral one. Or, participation in such institutions provides little value-added in terms of resolving salient security problems while at the same time imposing more constraints on freedom of action. For example, the three traits often trumpeted as virtues of multilateral security dialogues[30] do not necessarily offer the alliances better options or alternatives when it comes to dealing with traditional security issues like North Korean ballistic missiles and nuclear weapons, Taiwan straits, or chemical biological weapon (CBW) proliferation. The Democratic People's Republic of Korea (DPRK) attended the ARF meetings in Bangkok for the first time in July 2000 and held discussions on bilateral loans from members as well as support for the North's membership in the Asian Development Bank. While this was a positive development, its overall utility is questionable. The United States and Japan still deal with DPRK security problems in the bilateral context or trilaterally with the Republic of Korea (ROK). At the same time, the growing number of countries that deal with the North creates "a risk that preserving good ties with Pyongyang will be seen as an end in itself, or as a better means to an end than issuing threats or demonstrating a robust deterrence through military exercises."[31] The net assessment is therefore unfavorable to MSD participation on "hard" security issues: MSDs offer the alliances little marginal security and more marginal entanglement.

CREATING COMPLEMENTARITY

The challenge then is to conceive of ways to resolve the twin dilemmas of MSD appeal to the alliances and create greater complementarity between the needs of the bilateral alliances and multilateral security.

Defining Security Broadly

One way of doing this is to narrow the "overlap" between multilateralism and bilateralism in the region. This entails a circumscribing of the "traditional military" security roles played by multilateral institutions and broadening the focus on nontraditional or "new" security issues.[32] Setting collective security or collective defense as the conceptual endpoint of regional security dialogues in the region is a self-defeating exercise. Conceptually and historically, the conditions necessary for success are highly restrictive (i.e., well-defined threat or purpose, no free-riding, security as indivisible, aversion to war, etc.).[33] In addition, the region faces additional obstacles of historical distrust (vis-à-vis Japan), ambiguities with regard to membership (e.g., is China in or out?), and outstanding territorial disputes.[34] And perhaps most important, neither the United States, Japan, nor South Korea see such organizations as providing military security and protection of sovereignty more effectively than their current bilateral arrangements.

Having the MSDs appeal to the alliance on broader, nonmilitary security issues offers better promise. First, as in the case of the Commission on Security and Cooperation in Europe (CSCE), issues in "baskets" 2 and 3 (i.e., cooperation in the field of economics, science, technology, environment, and humanitarian issues) are easier and prior to those in basket 1 (cooperation on military and security issues). Second, in Asia there are a host of problems including piracy, environmental degradation, refugees, maritime safety, narcotics trafficking, disease, and terrorism that are considered salient nonmilitary security issues.[35] Third, the transnational nature of these problems makes them less easy to resolve through the mere application of resources within the bilateral alliance. Rather, the problems are more effectively addressed through the United States, Japan, and South Korea acting in larger coordinated regional efforts. Fourth, because such MSDs focus on nontraditional security issues outside the alliances' purview, they are not only helpful, but also nonthreatening to the alliances.

In July 1999 at the ASEAN postministerial conference (PMC), Secretary Albright explained how the United States saw one of the most important functions for multilateralism in Asia to be the prevention of transnational crime, maritime piracy, and the illegal trafficking of women and children. Devised at the Clinton-Miyazawa summit in 1993, the U.S.–Japan Common Agenda is a distinct document in the alliance (despite its relative obscurity today) because of its vision that allied cooperation should not be limited to just bilateral security but should extend over a wide range of global issues including climate change, disease prevention, science and technology research, and natural disaster relief. Despite disagreements on other issues, the Bush-Kim summit in 2001 made similar reference to the importance of regional security initiatives on transnational issues to the bilateral alliance.[36] These sorts of statements are indicative of the two necessary preconditions for greater complementarity between multilateralism and bilateralism. The United States, Japan, and South Korea must perceive MSDs as the appropriate venue for dealing with larger nontraditional and transnational problems. At the same time, the allies must agree that the definition of their bilateral security extends beyond the mutual defense treaties to encompass these larger issues. In short, Washington, Tokyo, and Seoul must see MSDs as the best instrument of dealing with nonmilitary security problems, yet also see the alliances' scope as not exclusive of such problems. If both conditions exist, then the alliances will value their participation in MSDs.

BINDING RATIONALES

Equally important to resolution of the twin dilemmas is tying participation in multilateral security dialogues in positive ways with the continued resiliency of the U.S.–Japan and the U.S.–ROK alliances. While the two alliances provide the mainstay of the U.S. security presence in Asia, concerns about their resiliency have always been salient. In the Korean case, the durability of the alliance was less contingent on military readiness and interoperability because of a very proximate security threat and a fully integrated joint and combined command structure. Instead, resiliency rested on the political conditions surrounding the alliance. These included maintaining decent civil-military relations with the host country by U.S. Forces–Korea (USFK) as well as "leveling-out" the relative positions of the allies in the partnership. In the former case, this meant issues like Status of Forces Agreement (SOFA) and host nation support. In the latter case, this meant decreasing Korea's asymmetric dependence (e.g., giving the ROK command of Combined Forces Command [CFC] in peacetime), as well as increasing Seoul's presence in the region generally.

The U.S.–Japan alliance, like the U.S.–ROK alliance, faced similar problems with regard to civil-military relations (arguably more than the ROK in Okinawa). But for Japan, resiliency issues went much deeper. Bilateral efforts at strengthening the alliance—starting from the 1978 Defense Guidelines through the Reagan years to the recent revision of the Guidelines—have focused primarily on ensuring that the necessary understandings, division of responsibilities, and legislation were in place that would enable the alliance to function in a military contingency (a problem less apparent in the ROK case because of the nature of the two commands [integrated versus independent]). Since then, alliance-watchers have talked about an "upgrading" of the alliance pursuant to the Guidelines Revision and missile defense cooperation. As the Armitage report put it, the future of the U.S.–Japan alliance should take the Guidelines as the "floor, not ceiling" of defense cooperation.[37] There are, however, two prerequisites to such an upgrading of the alliance.[38]

From Washington's perspective, a key component of the alliance's future robustness is Japanese enhancement of its military capabilities (within the alliance). Yet this is not possible as long as Japan suffers a "legitimacy deficit" in the region. One source of the legitimacy deficit is external. Memories of World War II still inform the region's reluctance to accept a larger Japanese military presence and political leadership role. The other constraint is internal. Overdependence on the United States created a postwar generation of relatively passive and reactive Japanese leadership, unwilling to take on a larger role.

Thus for the United States, key to facilitating an upgrade of the alliance is to mute regional security dilemmas emerging from a more active Japanese military and political role. A useful way of accomplishing this is to integrate Japan in multilateral regional institutions such that it can strengthen political ties, reduce suspicions, and legitimize its role as a leader. Others who were formerly fearful of Japan would grow accustomed to it through participation in these institutions. "Enmeshing Japan" thereby creates regional legitimization of Japan's enhanced presence. This, in turn, is good for alliance robustness.

Japanese MSD participation also addresses the internal constraints on Japanese leadership. Practitioners of the alliance say that one of the primary differences from the Cold War days and a new variable driving the future of the alliance is growing domestic sentiment for a "normal" Japanese diplomatic role in world affairs.[39] As one scholar put it, the younger generation chafes at Japan's "high aspirations but low status" predicament, and the desire to be a major player while remaining a middle, dependent power.[40] They abhor being considered a "nonfactor" with regard to issues on the Korean peninsula (i.e., four-party talks), South Asia, and the Gulf that matter dearly to Japanese national interests. One of the likely reactions to a prolonged period of frustration and stasis is to advocate cutting all Japan's dependencies and striking out on its own.[41]

Multilateralism can preempt such reactions. Encouraging Japanese participation in regional groupings becomes the cathartic means by which Japan expresses its new role and identity among a younger generation of leadership. On the one hand, it gives Japan the practice and confidence to surmount the insecurities of the postwar generation. On the other hand, it offers a release valve by which to deflate any pent-up frustrations and inclinations toward more radical reactions. To restate, the argument is not merely for greater Japanese participation in MSDs; instead it is that the United States should encourage Japanese *multilateralism* for the *bilateral* alliance's resiliency. In addition, by undertaking such support for regional security, the United States is de facto utilizing such institutions to promote its own interests in the region. As two experts have noted, "Washington's careful and selective use of multilateral diplomacy can be a 'force multiplier' to promote American interests in Asia."[42] In this sense, as Ikenberry has argued, multilateral institutions serve multiple functions:[43] (1) they legitimize the region's view of a larger Japanese leadership role, (2) they bolster Tokyo's confidence to assume this new identity, and (3) they implicitly bind and preempt frustrated negative reactions that might send Japan astray. Moreover, all of these functions are necessary prerequisites to any "bilateral upgrading" of the alliance.

From Japan and Korea's Perspective: Binding American Unilateralism

From Japan and South Korea's perspective, there are equally strong rationales for linking American MSD participation to the bilateral alliances' resiliency. For Tokyo and Seoul, the key concern with regard to the alliance's future is not just Japan-passing and Korea-passing, but more generally, American unilateralism. As the INSS/Armitage report notes, concerns abound in Asia that the United States is becoming increasingly arrogant and unable to recognize (or even worse, chooses not to recognize) that its prescriptions are not universally applicable.[44] Ambassador Hisashi Owada argues that while the United States practiced unilateral globalism after World War II in terms of providing security, aid for development, and so on, it is now pursuing "global unilateralism" where it acts without concern for others.[45] The Bush administration's cold treatment of ROK President Kim Dae Jung, his clear skepticism regarding the "sunshine" policy of engagement with the North, and determined plans to push forward with missile defense have raised similar concerns even among staunch alliance supporters in Korea about America's tendency to conflate allied "consultation" with merely informing the allies of its policy preferences. In a different but related way, some see America's overwhelming power at the end of the Cold War as creating dual incentives for the rest of the world akin to Microsoft's relationship with the market: everyone uses and benefits from its operating system but also feels the need to see this overwhelming dominance somehow checked and restrained.[46]

Thus for the allies, one of the keys to future bilateral alliance resiliency is to avoid and discourage American unilateralism. Encouragement of American participation in multilateral security dialogues is a means by which Korea and Japan can mute these unilateral tendencies. "Enmeshing America" in MSDs not only prevents rash behavior, but also reassures Seoul and Tokyo and the region that the United States is acting in good faith and is cognizant of others.

This dynamic was somewhat evident, for example, in Tokyo's views on APEC. Although Australia and ASEAN took the public lead, Japan behind the scenes strongly encouraged American involvement primarily for binding rationales. American involvement in APEC would undercut any tendencies toward unilateralism at the end of the Cold War and help ameliorate trade frictions in the bilateral alliance.[47] Similar thinking underlay Japanese and South Korean enthusiasm for U.S. participation in the ARF. As one foreign ministry official wrote, "[A] major goal for Japan [in the ARF] was to ensure constructive engagement of the major powers around the Asia-Pacific region. In order to keep the United States engaged in the region, development of concrete discussions regarding cooperation and burden-sharing through debate at ARF would be extremely important."[48] More recently, one of the successes of U.S. policy on North Korea has been the establishment of TCOG (trilateral coordination and oversight group) among Seoul, Tokyo, and Washington. The value of this institution for Japan and Korea stems in good part from the fact that U.S. participation in this group assures Tokyo and Seoul that the United States will not move unilaterally on policy toward the DPRK.[49] Indeed, with the change of administrations in Washington and uncertainty regarding future changes in U.S. policy, Seoul and Tokyo's heightened focus on convening TCOG as soon as possible (26 March 2001 meeting) reflected the value of the institution's binding and transparency-building functions.

From the region's perspective therefore, the need is to create "Gulliver" mentalities in the United States, Japan, and South Korea. Each sees their respective interests vis-à-vis the bilateral alliance served by encouraging the *other* to participate in multilateral institutions. As Ikenberry has argued, multilateral security dialogues become somewhat like mutually binding institutions. They keep the United States engaged, "honest," and nonunilateral; and they legitimize a larger Japanese (and Korean) leadership role beneficial to the alliance (and to those in Japan who seek a more proactive foreign policy).

TRADITIONAL SECURITY-ENHANCING MECHANISMS

As noted earlier, the appeal of multilateral security dialogues to the U.S.–Japan and U.S.–Korea alliances is most promising on broader, nonmilitary security issues rather than traditional "hard" security problems. Implicit in this view is that the alliances may value mutual participation in MSDs not just for tangible reasons (i.e., whatever particular issue the MSD is organized around), but also for less tangible ones having to do with mutually binding and evolving the bilateral alliances.

In addition to these important binding functions, this argument is not meant to imply that MSDs serve no useful purpose on traditional security issues. The effects of MSD participation are less direct but not less useful in at least two dimensions of traditional security issues. First, participation in multilateral security dialogues along with other regional allies and competitors can provide an arena in which interaction can help mute security dilemmas over things that make the U.S.–Japan bilateral alliance threatening to others. For example, one issue area where such dialogues might prove useful is missile defense.[50] Deployment of a U.S.–Japan based theater missile defense system (Navy theater) raises Chinese concerns about a potential Japanese role in Taiwan's defense (i.e., if the United States were to respond to Chinese missile coercion against Taipei).[51] Trilateral dialogue among Washington, Beijing, and Tokyo would be ideal, but in the absence of this, participation by the three in MSDs provide a useful venue in which the sides can gain greater transparency on each other's intentions. Participation in such MSDs also enable security experts from Beijing and Tokyo to continue small-scale and nonofficial initiatives on missile defense. On the Chinese side, for instance, these talks give voice to expert groups that understand Japan's need for some form of missile defense to defend against North Korean missiles. These experts could engage those on the Japanese side who understand Beijing's trepidations regarding Japan's potential engagement in a Taiwan straits crisis (and for this reason have called, for example, for explicit Japanese statements that Japanese cooperation in U.S.-based missile defense should not be construed as part and parcel of the revised U.S.–Japan Defense Guidelines).[52]

Second, multilateral security participation could be sold to the United States as a way to facilitate "minilaterals." This term refers to a form of security cooperation in the region that has emerged largely in the post–Cold War era. Minilaterals have three general traits: (1) they are small in number of participants relative to multilateral security (usually three or four parties), (2) they are ad hoc in formation, usually formed for a temporary period of time and disbanded without an institutional legacy, and (3) they usually deal with real or traditional security issues. As the 1998 East Asian Strategy Review described, these dialogues are functional, temporary, and U.S.-based: "[They] are intended to be overlapping and interlocking, complementing each other to develop an informal security framework for promoting understanding and mutual confidence, and facilitating bilateral ties between participants."[53]

The most well-known example of a minilateral at the official level is U.S.–Japan–South Korean trilateral coordination on North Korea nuclear proliferation (the institutional product of which has been the Korea Energy Development Organization [KEDO]). Other minilaterals include unofficial dialogue among the United States, Japan, and Russia, prior to the historic November 1997 Japan-Russia summit; the Four Party Talks among the United States, China, and the two Koreas; and proposed discussions between the United States, Japan, and China on the revision of the U.S.–Japan Defense Guidelines.

Despite U.S. acceptance of multilateral initiatives in the region, many critics would argue that the U.S. genuine interest in multilaterals to deal with the harder security issues does not extend beyond these minilateral groupings. These groupings have the advantage of being small in number, more focused, and more U.S.-centric than the larger multilateral groupings. Yet even in this regard, multilateral dialogues can provide a ready venue in which the United States could seek to "peel off" key participants and facilitate or enable the creation of smaller minilateral groupings.

CONCLUSION AND IMPLICATIONS: A SPECTRUM OF SECURITY

Four general conclusions emerge from this analysis of regional security in Asia. First, one can envision a spectrum of security in Asia, defined by three axes of multilateralism, minilateralism, and bilateralism:

Multilateral security dialogues	Minilateral security	Bilateral alliances
5+ participants	3–4 participants	2 participants
"New" security issues (environment, transnational crime, maritime piracy)	Traditional security issues harder to address through unilateral or bilateral channels	Traditional security

Second, while the value-added of participation in MSDs is that they enable participants to deal with new security issues that are difficult to address outside a regionwide context, I have argued that U.S. and allied participation in MSDs indeed have *second-order traditional* security effects. In particular, such participation in MSDs offer a means by which Washington, Tokyo, and Seoul can enhance the resiliency of their bilateral alliance. Through encouraging its ally's participation in these institutions, the three are each able to alleviate its own concerns about its counterpart. In Japan and Korea's case, American participation helps to prevent and remind the United States about the ill-effects of unilateralism. In America's case, allied participation helps promote a larger leadership role for the allies (Japan in particular) in the region, which is a necessary precondition for any "upgrading" of the bilateral alliance's political and security functions.

Third, at a functional level, if policy makers agree that there are synergies in multilateralism and bilateralism that are beneficial to the alliance (rather than seeing the former as undercutting or distracting to the latter), then a premium must be placed on coordination between these two tracks. For example, prior to major multilateral meetings, the United States and Japan through bilateral institutions (greatly enabled by those set up at the Bush-Koizumi June 2001 summit) could coordinate agendas and present united views in these larger fora. Efforts at U.S.–Japan coordination (bilateral arms control commission) prior to the Geneva Disarmament convention offer working precedents in this vein.

Fourth, at a conceptual level, this chapter has shown how multilateral institutions can have effects that go beyond merely the functional and transparency-enhancing characteristics normally associated with them in the international relations literature. In supporting the resiliency of the U.S.–Japan and U.S.–Korea alliances, multilateral institutions perform a variety of different functions. They legitimate power by facilitating new leadership roles in the region. They also mute "negative" (Japanese) power by directing pent-up frustrations for a more proactive Japan among younger generations in the direction of the MSDs and the bilateral alliance rather than in the direction of hyper-self-help reactions. These institutions also bind U.S. power by creating not only greater accountability to the region of any tendencies for American unilateralism, but also by tying these to the resiliency of the bilateral alliance.

NOTES

1. See Joseph Lepgold, "Regionalism in the Post–Cold War Era," chapter 1 in this collection.

2. SEATO was established at the Manila Conference of 1954 largely on the model of NATO, but failed because members found internal subversion rather than compelling external threats as their primary security concerns. ANZUS formed in 1951 as an extension of the U.S.–Australia treaty (the U.S.–New Zealand axis dissolved in 1986). FPDA was established in 1971 among Britain, Australia, New Zealand, Malaysia, and Singapore. Its function was consultative, based on historical legacies of the Commonwealth rather than any overt security purpose. See Leszek Buszynski, *SEATO: The Failure of an Alliance Strategy* (Singapore: Singapore University Press, 1983); Chin Kin Wah, "The

Five Power Defence Arrangement: Twenty Years After," *Pacific Review* 4, no. 3 (1991); Michael Yahuda, *International Politics in the Asia-Pacific* (London: Routledge, 1996); Gilbert Rozman, "Restarting Regionalism in Northeast Asia," *North Pacific Policy Papers*, No.1 (Program on Canada-Asia Policy Studies: University of British Columbia, 2000).

3. Although these visions existed earlier, they were popular in the late 1980s and early 1990s (e.g., in the form of the Tumen river project, gas pipelines, etc.). See Gilbert Rozman, "Flawed Regionalism: Reconceptualizing Northeast Asia in the 1990s," *Pacific Review* 11, no. 1 (1998), 1–27; and Robert Scalapino, "The Politics of Development and Regional Cooperation in Northeast Asia," in *Regional Economic Cooperation in Northeast Asia,* ed. Won Bae Kim, et al. (Vladivostok: Northeast Asian Economic Forum, 1992).

4. For example, the Vietnam War Allies Conference met regularly in Saigon in the late 1960s and early 1970s, providing a ready venue for multilateral security discussions on larger Cold War issues and strategy beyond Indochina, but nothing came of this. The Asia and Pacific Council (ASPAC) was established in 1966 as a forum for cooperation among Asian states on cultural and economic issues. Members included Australia, Taiwan, South Korea, Malaysia, New Zealand, Philippines, Thailand, South Vietnam, and Japan. Proposals in the early 1970s were floated by various countries (e.g., South Korea in 1970) to devise a new ASPAC charter based on collective self-defense with regionwide membership (including Laos, Indonesia, and Singapore), but these failed in part because of lack of support for an active Japanese leadership role in the group.

5. Higher degrees of institutionalization exist among the original ASEAN nations including proposals for national defense manufacturer associations, C-130 flight training centers, and F-16 joint training bases.

6. The ARF was formed pursuant to meetings of the ASEAN postministerial conference (PMC) in 1993.

7. G. John Ikenberry, *After Victory* (Princeton, N.J.: Princeton University Press, 2000), chapter 6.

8. See Philip Zelikow, "American Engagement in Asia," in *America's Asian Alliances,* ed. Robert Blackwill and Paul Dibb (Cambridge, Mass.: MIT Press, 2000), 19–30.

9. The region's relative peace in spite of the levels of historical enmity and armaments is often a factor overlooked in many international relations analyses foreboding of Asia's impending conflicts. In the former vein, see for example Kurt Campbell, "The Challenges Ahead for US Policy in Asia," presentation at the FPRI Asia Study Group, Philadelphia, Pa., 30 March 2001. In the latter vein, see Aaron Friedberg, "Ripe for Rivalry," *International Security* (Winter 1993/94): 5–33; Richard Betts, "Wealth, Power and Instability," *International Security* (Winter 1993/94): 34–77; Kent Calder, *Pacific Defense* (New York: Murrow, 1996); Paul Bracken, *Fire in the East* (New York: HarperCollins, 1999); and Michael Klare, "The Next Great Arms Race," *Foreign Affairs* 72, no. 3 (Summer 1993): 136–52.

10. Here I include Japan, South Korea, Australia, and Philippines, but the primary references in this chapter are to Japan (and to a lesser extent, Korea).

11. For the now-classic statement, see Joseph Nye, "The Case for Deep Engagement," *Foreign Affairs* 74, no. 4 (1995): 90–102; also see *United States Security Strategy for the East Asia–Pacific Region 1998* (Washington, D.C.: Government Printing Office, November 1998).

12. These are: the preservation of national sovereignty, the principle of noninterference in domestic affairs, pursuit of prosperity through markets, economic interdependence to enhance security, peaceful resolution of disputes, and adherence to global multilateralism.

See Stuart Harris, "Asian Multilateral Institutions and their Response to the Asian Economic Crisis," *Pacific Review* 13, no. 3 (2000): 502.

13. Lepgold, "Regionalism in the Post–Cold War Era," 17–19.

14. Kurt Campbell and Mitchell Reiss, "Korean Changes, Asian Challenges and the US Role," *Survival* 43, no. 1 (Spring 2001): 64–65.

15. Improvements are also being sought regarding the survivability of its forces; command, control, and communication capabilities; stealth technologies; as well as countermeasures to ballistic missile defense (decoy warheads, multiple reentry vehicles, electronic and infrared jammers).

16. The bomber leg of the triad are approximately 120 Hong-6 bombers (range of 3,100 km, each capable of delivering one to three bombs of 10kT–3MT) and thirty Qian-5A attack aircraft (range of 400 km, capable of delivering one nuclear bomb 10kT–3MT) deployed in 1965 and 1970 respectively. The sea-based leg consists of about twelve JL-1 SLBMs deployed in 1986 on one Xia-class submarine. Experts consider both the air- and sea-based legs of the triad less threatening. The bomber force is old, highly vulnerable to air defense, and incapable of reaching the United States. The SLBM program has proved less successful despite the four decades of development invested in it. In addition, China is believed to possess about 150 tactical weapons made up of low-yield bombs, artillery shells, atomic demolition munitions, and short-range missiles (although it does not officially acknowledge possession of tactical weapons). For a concise overview, see Robert Manning, Donald Montaperto, and Brad Roberts, *China: Nuclear Weapons and Arms Control* (New York: Council on Foreign Relations, 2000), 15–37.

17. China conducted its first nuclear test in 1964. It exploded a hydrogen weapon in 1966 and began production of nuclear weapons in 1968 and thermonuclear weapons in 1974.

18. See *Australian Financial Review*, 2 May 1991 ("Security, in Letter and Spirit").

19. Cited in Paul Midford, "Japan's Leadership Role in East Asian Security Multilateralism," *Pacific Review* 13, no. 3 (2000): 372.

20. See James Baker, "America in Asia: Emerging Architecture for a Pacific Community," *Foreign Affairs* 70, no. 5 (1991/92): 1–18; and quoting Baker, Philip Sheron, "Baker Asks Asians to Move Warily on New Pacts," *New York Times*, 25 July 1991, A14.

21. See John Welfield, *An Empire in Eclipse* (London: Athlone, 1988); and Victor Cha, *Alignment Despite Antagonism: The US-Korea-Japan Security Triangle* (Stanford, Calif.: Stanford University Press, 1999).

22. Japanese disinterest also traditionally stemmed from the implications multilateral participation would have on outstanding territorial issues. With its fair share of territorial disputes in the region, Japan was concerned that certain proposals for multilateralism entailed a de facto ratification of the territorial status quo, which worked against Japanese interests. For this reason, Tokyo opposed Soviet proposals in 1986 for a regionwide CSCE-type grouping in Asia as this would reinforce the status quo and Moscow's possession of the northern territories.

23. Reference NEACD, ASEM, and APEC meetings in Seoul where Ambassador Lee played a role in bringing Taiwan and China to the same venue. Also see *Peace Regime-Building on the Korean Peninsula and the Roles of the Regional Powers* (Seoul: Ministry of Foreign Affairs: Institute for Foreign Affairs and National Security, 1996).

24. For this point as tied to larger shifts in Japan toward a more strategically oriented rather than economic-based foreign policy, see Michael Green and Benjamin Self, "Japan's Changing China Policy: From Commercial Liberalism to Reluctant Realism," *Survival* 38, no. 2 (Summer 1996): 34–46.

25. Foreign Minister Taro Nakayama's proposal called for (1) a multilateral security dialogue component within the ASEAN postministerial conference (PMC), (2) a senior officials meeting (SOM), and (3) discussions of the region's concerns about Japanese remilitarization. This was Japan's first regional security initiative, largely emerging out of the fiasco of Japanese participation in the Gulf War. The proposal itself did not meet with popular acceptance (including opposition from the United States) but was an important impetus to the eventual thriving of the ARF (see Midford, "Japan's Leadership Role," 387–88).

26. Where this was manifest in the context of the bilateral alliance was in the April 1996 U.S.–Japan Defense Guidelines revision, which emphasized a larger Japanese regional security role. See Rajan Menon, "The Once and Future Superpower," *Bulletin of Atomic Scientists* (January/February 1997): 29–34.

27. For example, see Miles Kahler, "Institution Building in the Pacific," in *Pacific Cooperation*, ed. Andrew Mack and John Ravenhill (Boulder, Colo.: Westview, 1995).

28. For the argument, see Yoichi Funabashi, *Asia-Pacific Fusion: Japan's Role in APEC* (Washington, D.C.: Institute for International Economics, 1995), especially 192–95; and Ellis Krauss, "Japan, the US, and the Emergence of Multilateralism in Asia," *Pacific Review* 13, no. 3 (2000): 473–94. Both argue that Australian Premier Bob Hawke's ideas on an East Asian financial grouping was based on thinking and ideas that came out of Ministry of International Trade and Industry (MITI) and the Reagan-Takeshita summit in 1988.

29. Admittedly, it has been less difficult to elicit Korean support for such initiatives; however, the key participants are Japan and the United States.

30. These are (1) not a substitute for global multilateral institutions, (2) weighted toward semiofficial and Track II dialogues rather than formal ones, and (3) open regionalism and inclusive memberships, including China and North Korea (see Harris, "Asian Multilateral Institutions," 501).

31. Campbell and Reiss, "Korean Changes, Asian Challenges," 56.

32. This is a process that is already under way in Asia. One analytical distinction deserves mention here. The discussion of MSDs and transnational, lower-tier security issues has largely been in the context of making multilateral security more viable—that is, such issues are considered easier ones around which to organize regional security than a NATO-type agenda. I focus more on how an MSD-focus on these lower-tier security issues makes MSDs more appealing to the U.S.–Japan alliance because it fulfills functional needs that the alliance cannot. Thus I do not disagree with the first argument but seek to complement it.

33. See Robert Jervis, "From Balance to Concert," *World Politics* 38, no. 1 (October 1985): 58–79; Charles Kupchan and Clifford Kupchan, "Concerts, Collective Security, and the Future of Europe," *International Security* 16, no. 1 (Summer 1991): 114–61; and Mira Sucharov and Victor Cha, "Collective Security Systems," in *Encyclopedia of Violence, Peace and Conflict* (San Diego, Calif.: Academic Press, 1999), 343–53.

34. The last factor in particular is problematic for a collective security institution as the implicit assumption for participation is that all members are satisfied with the territorial status quo.

35. See William Carpenter and David Wiencek, eds., *Asian Security Handbook* (New York: M. E. Sharpe, 2000), esp. contributions in part II; Tetsuya Nishimoto, "Problems in Managing the Japan-US Security Treaty After the Guidelines," unpublished paper presented at the Atlantic Council meeting on the U.S.–Japan alliance, Tokyo, Japan, April

122 Victor D. Cha

2000; and Bonnie Jenkins, "Prospects for a Conventional Arms Reduction Treaty and Confidence-Building Measures in Northeast Asia," *INSS Occasional Paper* 34 (Colorado Springs, Colo.: USAF Institute for National Security Studies, August 2000).

36. Joint Statement by U.S. President George W. Bush and ROK President Kim Dae-jung, 7 March 2001.

37. "The United States and Japan: Advancing Toward a Mature Partnership," *INSS Special Report* (11 October 2000); Michael Green, "The Forgotten Player," *The National Interest* (Summer 2000): 42–49; Yoichi Funabashi, "Tokyo's Temperance," *Washington Quarterly* (Summer 2000): 135–44; and James Auer, "US-Japan Defense Ties: Excellence over Arrogance," *Japan Digest*, 13 October 2000.

38. Forward-looking visions of the U.S.–ROK alliance are not available (aside from blanket statements about regional security), which seems ironic given recent changes on the peninsula. At any rate, the discussion here focuses mostly on the U.S.–Japan alliance.

39. Kurt Campbell, "Energizing the US-Japan Security Partnership," *Washington Quarterly* (Autumn 2000), 128; Green, "The Forgotten Player," 43–46.

40. Matake Kamiya, "How to Gain Status on World Stage," *Nikkei Weekly*, 3 April 2000.

41. For example, one of the reasons Shintaro Ishihara won election as governor was not necessarily because the public agreed with his views, but because he was seen as someone who could shake things up. The point is that the potential for adverse directions are real in Japan and (as discussed below) multilateralism provides a means of closing off such negative paths.

42. Campbell and Reiss, "Korean Changes, Asian Challenges," 65.

43. G. John Ikenberry, "Institutions, Strategic Restraint, and the Persistence of American Postwar Order," *International Security* 23, no. 3 (Winter 1998/99): 1–35.

44. "The United States and Japan: Advancing Toward a Mature Partnership," *INSS Special Report* (Ft. McNair, Va.: Institute for National Strategic Studies, National Defense University, 11 October 2000), 2.

45. See Samuel Huntington, "The Lonely Superpower," *Foreign Affairs* 78, no. 2 (March/April 1999): 42; also see Funabashi, "Tokyo's Temperance," 135–44.

46. See Campbell, "The Challenges Ahead for US Policy in Asia."

47. See Krauss, "Japan, the US and the Emergence of Multilateralism in Asia," 483; and Funabashi, *Asia-Pacific Fusion*. Similarly, the United States wanted Japanese involvement in APEC to give Tokyo a larger leadership role in the region.

48. Masaharo Kohno, "In Search of Proactive Diplomacy," CNAPS Working Paper (Washington, D.C.: Brookings Institution, Fall 1999), 29.

49. For similar observations, see G. John Ikenberry, "Getting Hegemony Right," *The National Interest* 63 (Spring 2001): 124.

50. Campbell, "Energizing the US-Japan Security Partnership," 130.

51. A full discussion of missile defense is beyond the scope of this chapter. For an excellent overview, see Michael Green and Toby Dalton, "Asian Reactions to US Missile Defense," *NBR Analysis* 11, no. 3 (November 2000). For additional observations on the political "cascade effects" of missile defense, see Victor Cha, "Proliferation: Pessimism versus Optimism in South Asia and East Asia," *Journal of Strategic Studies* 29, no. 4 (2001): 78–122.

52. See Kori Urayama, "Chinese Perspectives on Theater Missile Defense," *Asian Survey* 40, no. 4: 599–621.

53. *United States Security Strategy for the East Asia–Pacific Region 1998*, 43.

5

Conflict Management in Latin America

Carolyn M. Shaw

The end of the Cold War has presented unique opportunities and challenges for conflict management around the world over the past decade. In Latin America,[1] the OAS, its member states, nongovernmental organizations (NGOs), and individuals have welcomed the changes in the international environment and attempted to address a number of regional concerns that have not previously been on the agenda. The collapse of the Soviet Union in 1991 resulted in many states struggling throughout the 1990s for a new framework on which to base their foreign policies. Security concerns were no longer shaped by Soviet threats and fears of communist subversion. Many policy makers and politicians were optimistic that the new world order would lead to greater cooperation among states to address broader global issues collectively.[2] Issues such as sustainable economic development, environmental protection, and migration became the focus of a number of regional forums. The aspiration to take greater collective action on transnational issues has been achieved to some degree. States throughout the hemisphere have recently ratified conventions on a wide range of issues in an effort to establish regional policies and guidelines and to articulate regional norms.[3]

The new effort at multilateralism on transnational issues has also affected the area of security in the hemisphere. The traditional concept of regional security based on geopolitical and strategic threats has gradually been expanded to include a number of concerns that had not previously been considered "security issues." The United States and Latin American states have developed a common agenda of security concerns that includes consideration of human rights, democracy, the environment, government reform, social equality, and a free market environment.[4] These issues have been of nominal concern to Latin American states for many years, but until the collapse of the Soviet Union they were not considered genuine security issues. After a decade of discussion and redefinition, in the new millennium, regional order and security have increasingly come to be defined in terms of collective defense of democracy and the promotion of liberal economic reform and regional integration. As the number of democratic countries in the hemisphere has increased, a growing consensus supporting democratic government has emerged.

The inclusion of economic reforms in security dialogues was linked to the growing importance of democracy for regional stability. Some policy makers believed that open markets would lead to more open political regimes as well, although this was not the case in some East Asian countries. Discussions of regional security concerns, thus, also included discussion of economic development of the region. In the 1980s, the international financial community recognized the limitations to import-substitution industrialization (ISI) that had been adopted in Latin America in the 1960s. A new consensus emerged among officials in the International Monetary Fund (IMF), the World Bank, and the U.S. Treasury that Latin American countries needed to significantly restructure their economies. This "Washington Consensus" had three prescriptions: (1) Reduce and revise the economic role of the state. Resources should be focused on economically productive areas, such as health, education, and infrastructure expansion. (2) Increase support for the private sector. States need to remove restrictions on foreign capital. (3) Revise trade policies. Latin American states should look outward for markets.[5] The proposed Free Trade Area of the Americas (FTAA) became an extension of the consensus as Latin American states sought to expand and open up their markets.

The justification for the expanded concept of regional security is based on several assumptions. The first assumption is that the promotion of political democracy is not merely a valued end in itself but also contributes to regional stability and security.[6] This assumption is based on the democratic peace theory that democracies rarely go to war with each other. Thus, the more democratic regimes there are, the fewer international conflicts that will arise.[7] Not only is there a pragmatic justification for upholding democratic governments based on the theory of the democratic peace, there is also strong normative support for democracy in the region. The principle of representative democracy has been a part of inter-American norms for over fifty years and was formally incorporated into the Charter of the OAS in 1948 (Articles 2 and 3). It was only recently, however, with the Santiago Commitment and Resolution 1080 (1991) that it became a top regional priority.

The second justification for a broader concept of regional security is based on the assumption that economic liberalization and regional integration can create a stable and secure regional order. Prosperity and progress will alleviate many of the social tensions that threaten domestic stability, thus promoting greater domestic and regional stability. The third assumption is that issues such as drug trafficking, environmental degradation, migration and refugees, and domestic insurgencies pose threats to the regional order, are transnational in nature, and thus ought to be addressed as security issues.[8] Andrew Hurrell notes that advocates of multilateralism argue that these issues are much greater than a single state can handle and that the most effective response is a coordinated multilateral one.[9] A final consideration that motivates states to embrace the broader concept of regional security is that they seek to avoid the negative externalities that arise from regional instability. Regional conflict can lead to human rights abuses, refugee flows, reduced trade, as well as other undesirable consequences that affect states beyond those directly involved in the dispute. By employing a broader definition of security and restructuring multilateral organizations to address these concerns, Latin American states hope to avoid such negative externalities stemming from regional conflict.

In addition to a broader concept of regional security, the end of the Cold War has led to a new prioritizing of regional norms. The Western Hemisphere has a long history of support for regional norms such as state sovereignty, nonintervention, pacific settlement of disputes, consultation between states during crises, and representative democracy. Although all of these principles are in the 1948 OAS Charter, the priorities placed on these principles have shifted over time. State sovereignty and nonintervention largely predominated security discussions from the 1940s to the 1990s. Recently, however, states have placed less emphasis on the principle of state sovereignty in conflicts in which democracy is threatened, or where human rights abuses have occurred, thus allowing for greater multilateral intervention to address these concerns. This new attitude toward intervention in support of democracy, combined with the broader definition of security concerns, has altered the security arena in the new century. It allows for a more active response from member states when regional security is threatened.

The redefinition of regional security has taken place at many levels and in many forums, but has been largely institutionalized within the OAS. The OAS has been an ideal forum for the discussions that have resulted in the broader definition of regional security issues because it is the only regional organization in which all states of the hemisphere are members (with the exception of Cuba). The first steps taken regionally to promote democracy in the hemisphere were taken in 1990 when the OAS General Assembly established the Unit for the Promotion of Democracy. It was created to provide advisory services and technical assistance to member states on issues of democratic government. A second step was taken in June 1991 in Santiago, Chile, when the General Assembly passed Resolution 1080, creating automatic procedures for convening the OAS Permanent Council in the event of a coup or other disruption of constitutional order. The Summits of the Americas, at which heads of state met in 1994, 1998, and 2001, placed new items such as drug trafficking, terrorism, corruption, and economic integration on the security agenda. They also "reaffirmed hemispheric commitment to preserve and strengthen [the] democratic systems for the benefit of all people of the hemisphere . . . to strengthen democratic institutions and promote and defend constitutional democratic rule in accordance with the OAS Charter."[10]

The restructuring of the security regime that has resulted from institutional and ideational/normative reforms has left the region better prepared to manage some of the conflicts that might be anticipated in the near future. There remain, however, several threats to hemispheric security that the region is not adequately prepared to address. I begin with an examination of the current and potential future threats posed to the hemisphere. I then explore the international and regional organizations, mechanisms, and actors available to address these security concerns. Finally, I analyze the threats to the region and evaluate the applicability and likelihood of success of four different conflict management strategies.

FUTURE THREATS TO REGIONAL SECURITY

Given the expanded concept of regional security espoused by states in the Western Hemisphere, potential and existing threats to regional security and stability fall into three general categories: (1) traditional strategic concerns, which include boundary disputes, arms races, and extrahemispheric threats; (2) situations that pose threats to the democratic order that member states have pledged to uphold (i.e., antidemocratic coups, tensions between the civilian government and the military over governing, and domestic insurgencies); and (3) transnational issues, especially narco-trafficking. Some of these threats pose a greater hazard to the region than others. Arguably, regional security leaders are most concerned with the violent, ongoing domestic insurgency in Colombia, which has strong connections to the drug trade in the hemisphere. Drug trafficking affects many states in the region through corruption of government officials, money laundering, scandals, and cartel-related violence. State leaders also remain alert to the instigation of antidemocratic crises, based on the occurrence of six coup attempts in the past decade. There is less concern about a potential arms race or an extrahemispheric threat to the region. The few remaining unresolved boundary disputes are not considered a major security threat. Whereas security issues were once focused on interstate conflicts such as border disputes, the two top security concerns in the region are now intrastate disputes and their transnational effects. Latin America is unique in comparison to other regions in that it does not face extensive ethnic conflicts or failed states. The absence of these types of situations makes the Western Hemisphere more secure than some regions and makes conflict management more manageable in many respects. I will now examine recent conflicts in each of the three noted threat categories, and assess the potential for similar future security threats to the region.

Traditional Strategic Threats

Although there has most recently been considerable focus on threats to democracy in the region, several traditional security threats remain. One of these concerns is the risk of an arms race between states in the hemisphere. Most notably, Brazil and Argentina have long been concerned about each other's level of militarization and have competed with each other in arms acquisitions. These two countries, however, have recently set aside such concerns to work more cooperatively together. In the early 1990s, before Argentina signed the Treaty of Tlatelolco and the nuclear Non-Proliferation Treaty (NPT), it reached an accord with Brazil to work in complete openness on their nuclear programs and to provide accessibility to each other's facilities. This reciprocal agreement was preferable to the inequality of states established by the NPT.[11] Additional regional mechanisms have continued to foster this less competitive relationship as well as reduce the risk of an arms race between other Latin American states. In 1999 the OAS General Assembly drafted the Inter-American Convention on Transparency in Conventional Arms Acquisitions, which aimed to build confidence among states by sharing information about purchases of conventional weapons.[12] Treaties also exist to reduce the risk of nuclear competition. The Tlatelolco Treaty (1967) establishes the region as a nuclear-free zone and has been signed and ratified by twenty-six states. Many Latin American states have also signed the NPT. In addition to these conventions and treaties, several military forces in the region have adopted global military operations (i.e., peacekeeping) that provide new missions for the military and that establish a global focus for the military rather than a narrow, local defensive purpose. All of these measures reduce the risk of a future arms race between Latin American states.

A second traditional strategic threat in the region is boundary disputes between states.[13] Although these disputes are usually bilateral and involve limited military engagements, there are negative externalities that affect other states as well as civilian populations. If a dispute results in a border being closed, then interstate trade and transportation is disrupted. During the "Soccer War" between El Salvador and Honduras (which remained unresolved for thirteen years), Honduras would close the Pan American Highway to El Salvador for long periods, making its reopening contingent on El Salvador's willingness to resolve the boundary dispute. In the current era of increased economic integration and trade, such tactics could be particularly disruptive. Refugee flows related to military engagements are also a concern for neighboring states. Final settlement of boundary disputes is likely to promote regional development, not only by keeping borders open, but by easing distrust or hostility between neighboring states over territorial issues. An easing of tensions can promote cooperation in a number of issue areas beyond boundary concerns.

Eight settlements regarding boundary disputes have been reached in Latin America in the past decade, resulting in more secure and stable borders.[14] Peru and Ecuador signed a final peace accord in 1999 resolving their long-standing border dispute.[15] The OAS secretary-general has been involved in facilitating negotiations between Belize and Guatemala, and Costa Rica and Nicaragua. In March 2000, Honduras and Nicaragua signed an agreement resolving a maritime boundary dispute in the Caribbean. Despite these steps, there are still ten outstanding active disputes.[16] One example is the dispute between El Salvador, Honduras, and Nicaragua over fishing rights in the Gulf of Fonseca. Until these disputes are resolved, there remains a slight risk of further militarized engagements that could threaten regional stability by disrupting trade and dislocating civilians. The risk is low, however, since states have resorted to the use of military force in only half of these disputes.

A third potential strategic threat to the region is posed by extrahemispheric actors. For the most part, Latin American states are not greatly concerned about extrahemispheric threats such as a missile launch by a rogue state. In fact, there is no real collective dialogue about such threats. The likelihood of any state other than the United States being the target of such a threat is minimal, thus the burden is on the United States alone to protect itself against such an occurrence. The United States acknowledges that deterrence and nonproliferation agreements are not enough to protect it from unconventional weapons of mass destruction, such as biological and chemical weapons. Accordingly, the United States has revised its policy to adopt "antiproliferation" efforts to try to reduce capabilities to produce such weapons.[17] In addition, the regional mechanisms established during the Cold War to address Soviet threats (the Rio Treaty and OAS Charter) are still in place and could presumably be invoked should an extrahemispheric threat arise that needed to be addressed collectively. States in the region are, however, much more concerned about threats to democracy, which are discussed below.

Threats to Democracy

Given the evolving nature of democracies in Latin America, many states face a fragile balance between competing forces in politics and society. Many democratic regimes are attempting to include opposition parties in governing coalitions, to address the social and economic needs of their citizens, and to find a viable role for the military outside of politics. Unsatisfactory performance of any of these tasks could result in a coup attempt against a democratic government in the region. There are two different scenarios that pose a threat to democracies in the region: antidemocratic coups and domestic insurgencies.

One threat to democratic governments is the risk of coups and coup attempts resulting from dissatisfaction with election results, economic inequalities, or government corruption. In the countries of Central America, where democratic institutions have recently been installed after prolonged civil wars, there remains a risk of backsliding into violent conflict when electoral outcomes are less than satisfactory to one side. An electoral loss could lead to a political faction taking up arms against the government. Economic inequalities and lack of progress toward improved social services can also lead to protests and uprisings that can destabilize a government. For example, Mexico has faced an uprising in the Chiapas region since 1994 with the Zapatista rebels demanding greater rights for the indigenous people in the region. The movement has disrupted governmental functioning in the region and has discredited the national government (although it has not posed a serious threat to the national government). Although historical trends indicate that coups are less likely today with democratic regimes in place, many countries in the region still face the threat of a coup as they strive to consolidate their democratic institutions.

One situation that is particularly worrisome for newly established democracies is their relationship with the military. Military challenges to civilian authority not only question the legitimacy of the government but also may lead to coup attempts. After playing an active role in politics historically, many Latin American militaries are still struggling to find a more limited professional role. They are seeking to define new "enemies" following the end of the Cold War and are gradually assuming new roles, but this has been a challenge. The professionalization of the military forces is important for providing them with a legitimate function outside of elective politics. Troops from Argentina, Brazil, Uruguay, and Venezuela have participated in international peacekeeping operations in such places as the Persian Gulf, El Salvador, Mozambique, Croatia, and Cyprus.[18] In addition to preventing the military from becoming overly active in politics, many regimes also face the challenge that military leaders are not subservient to elected government officials. This lack of respect for civilian authority can lead to political challenges to government leaders by the military. Military challenges to civilian authority remain a security concern in the region.

The greatest threat to Latin American security today is the domestic insurgency (i.e., guerrilla forces) in Colombia (the *Fuerzas Armada Revolucionarias de Colombia* [FARC], or the Revolutionary Armed Forces of Colombia).[19] Insurgents actually pose a threat to democracy at several levels. Not only is there the risk of a democratic government being overthrown by a guerrilla force, there is also the risk that democratic processes as well as human rights will be curtailed in order for the government to address the guerrilla threat. The threat of the Shining Path guerrillas in Peru in the early 1990s provides a good example of the risk such insurgencies pose to the democratic process. Prior to the capture of Abimael Guzman, the leader of the Shining Path, in September 1992, a number of observers believed that the guerrillas were on the verge of taking power in Peru.[20] In an effort to strengthen his hand against the guerrillas, and other domestic opposition, President Fujimori nullified congress, displaced the judiciary, and announced the suspension of key civil rights in April 1992. The international community responded by suspending nonhumanitarian economic aid to Peru. Fujimori offered some compromises, but essentially maintained control over the writing of a new constitution. The United States and other states were reluctant to pressure an ally in the drug war too strongly, and he had domestic support for his actions. Thus, democracy suffered a blow in order for the threat of the insurgency to be handled.

Colombia serves as an example of how human rights have been abused in relation to the government's response to the domestic insurgency. In order to control villages in the territories they hold, the FARC engages in brutal abuses of any villagers accused of supporting the government or its right-wing paramilitary fighters. These paramilitary groups are also guilty of human rights abuses of those suspected of supporting the FARC. Because the Columbian military is closely aligned with the paramilitary units, the paramilitaries have not faced any consequences for their brutal actions.

Not only do guerrilla forces threaten the democratic government of Colombia, they also pose threats to neighboring countries and contribute to regional instability. The violence being perpetrated on the civilian population has resulted in over a million refugees. The United Nations High Commissioner for Refugees (UNHCR) estimates that twenty-five to thirty thousand refugees crossed into Ecuador due to increased violence and crop fumigation efforts in the summer of 2000. Anticipating violence along the border, Ecuador moved additional police and military troops into the region.[21] The guerrillas have also kidnapped foreigners for ransom on a number of occasions in order to raise funds for arms.

An assessment of the situation in Colombia indicates that the conflict and violence are likely to continue in the near future. The Colombian government has not been successful in fighting the guerrilla forces. The FARC forces are approximately the same size as the Colombian military (not including the forces guarding key facilities).[22] They are well armed and well financed through the ransoming of kidnapped victims and taxes on the drug trade (more on this below). In the past few years they have come to control large sections of the country, especially in the southeastern jungles, forcing the Colombian military to withdraw from almost a third of the country.

Although the international community had been disturbed by the human rights abuses in Colombia previously, an increasing number of successful attacks by the FARC on government military installations in 1998 resulted in growing concern about the very survival of the Colombian government. Andres Pastrana, elected president in May 1999, had campaigned on the pledge to seek a peace accord with FARC. FARC, however, demanded some disconcerting concessions before consenting to talks. FARC then gained control of a four-county area east of the capital. The government was forced to negotiate from a weak position. Eventually the settlement talks stalled. When the United States agreed to supply $1.3 billion in aid to the government to fight the guerrillas in August 2000,[23] there was little indication that the confrontation between forces would end soon.[24] Countries in the region anticipate continued conflict and violence in the future and continue to work toward multilateral solutions.

Transnational Threats: The Drug War

The domestic insurgency in Colombia continues to disturb other states in the hemisphere because of its intractability, the violation of human rights, and the threat it poses to the democratically elected government of Colombia. Furthermore, the threat it poses to the hemisphere is compounded by the links the guerrilla groups have to the drug trade. Intelligence officials estimate that 60 percent of the financing for the FARC comes from taxing the drug trade. Farmers and transport planes are taxed. The guerrillas often guard coca fields and processing labs for a share of the profits. They use these profits to arm themselves.

The greatest security threat is to democracy in Colombia, but narco-trafficking has additional negative externalities affecting many other countries in the hemisphere. The United States faces domestic crime problems associated with the drug trade and drug use. The Caribbean nations are affected by the drug trade as narcotic shipments pass through their countries. Issues of government corruption and money laundering touch many of the governments in the region. A number of Latin American states are concerned with the human rights abuses perpetrated by the cartels and the insurgents linked to the drug lords. The threat posed by narco-trafficking remains a regional problem, with no indication of a quick remedy or easy solution in sight. The problem has a broad impact on the region, suggesting the need for a multilateral approach to a solution.

REGIONAL ACTORS, ORGANIZATIONS, AND MECHANISMS

Latin America does not have as many organizations as Europe does that address security concerns. Although there are small subregional organizations such as the Organization of East Caribbean States (OECS) that occasionally take up security issues (i.e., the coup in Grenada in 1983), the OAS is the primary organization in which hemispheric security concerns, as well as regional economic, development, and cultural issues, are addressed. The OAS is the only regional organization that includes all states in the hemisphere (with the exception of Cuba). There are formal mechanisms as well as regional norms that determine and shape the way the OAS responds to regional threats. Both the OAS Charter and the Inter-American Treaty of Reciprocal Assistance (The Rio Treaty) embody mechanisms to respond collectively to regional or extrahemispheric threats and conflicts.

Latin American states have traditionally preferred to respond to threats diplomatically. This preference is embodied in the OAS Charter and Rio Treaty, which both advocate pacific settlement of disputes. Signatories of the Rio Treaty are part of a collective security arrangement. The Rio Treaty recognizes that an attack on one member is equivalent to an attack on all members who are expected to come to the defense of the victim state. Acts of aggression are subject to sanctions that may include the recall of diplomatic missions, the breaking of diplomatic relations, the partial or complete interruption of economic relations, and the use of armed force (Article 6). A member state may invoke the Rio Treaty, calling for a meeting of the Organ of Consultation (Council of foreign ministers), if the sovereignty or political independence of any American state is affected by armed or unarmed attack, or if any other situation endangers the peace of the Americas. The treaty has been invoked eighteen times since the OAS was founded in 1948. Given the variety of mechanisms available to members to respond to a crisis, some cases lead to economic sanctions while others lead to more militarized responses. For example, in the Dominican Republic–Venezuelan case (1959), economic sanctions were levied against the Dominican dictator Rafael Trujillo following an assassination attempt on Venezuelan President Romulo Betancourt. The sanctions were finally lifted following the assassination of Trujillo two years later. In another case involving the Dominican Republic (1965), multilateral military measures were taken following a coup attempt in the country. The OAS put together an inter-American peace force to help restore law and order on the island.

In addition to the economic and military options available for resolving conflicts, the OAS has a number of diplomatic options and resources at its disposal. Chapter Five of the Charter lays out provisions for the pacific settlement of disputes, including direct negotiation, good offices, mediation, investigation and conciliation, judicial settlement, and arbitration. Member states place a high value on diplomatic efforts at conflict resolution. Such efforts are often carried out by the secretary-general, or by an investigating committee selected by the Permanent Council. In addition to OAS personnel and representatives, there are a number of individual diplomats and mediators who can play a role in managing regional conflicts. Diplomats from the Vatican (or the papal nuncio within a state), senior statesmen of member states, and members of the academic community have contributed historically to many settlements reached in the region. Occasionally statesmen will work together outside the OAS framework if the OAS is not making progress in resolving a dispute. For example, in the 1980s the OAS went through a period of decline and was unable to effectively address the ongoing conflicts in Central America. The Contadora Group, consisting of Mexico, Venezuela, Colombia, and Panama, put forward a plan for a negotiated settlement. The Contadora process eventually stalled and was replaced by the Esquipulas II Accords proposed by Oscar Arias. The group's early efforts, however, contributed to the final agreement and helped bring regional states together to find a peaceful settlement.

The principle of consultation also shapes the security environment in Latin America. By supporting pacific settlement and promoting consultative procedures when threats to the peace occur, states are able to gain a more comprehensive understanding of the dispute and to address the issue collectively. The consultation process tends to promote consensus among member states and thus legitimates and strengthens the actions of the OAS. The region has a strong history of inter-American multilateral consultations and actions. In 1994, 1998, and 2001, thirty-four heads of state met at the Summit of the Americas to discuss extensively regional security concerns and economic development issues. Although further progress on establishing the Free Trade Area of the Americas (FTAA) has slowed in recent years due to lack of U.S. leadership, the consultative spirit remains as states in the hemisphere struggle to address new transnational issues in a multilateral framework.[25] Differences remain on issues such as the drug war, but because this issue affects regional stability and security, dialogue continues as members seek to reduce the threat to the region posed by narco-trafficking.[26]

States in the Western Hemisphere have several incentives to use the wide variety of conflict management mechanisms available to them to address regional security threats. The most influential motivation is the desire to reduce tensions and prevent the spread of the conflict in the region. Boundary disputes, potential arms races, interruptions to democracy, and narco-trafficking all have negative externalities that affect neighboring states, not just those directly involved. Refugee flows, increased violence and human rights abuses, and disrupted diplomatic and economic relations affect all states in the region when tensions increase or conflict erupts. It is in the interest of OAS members to bring these issues before the organization and seek solutions before they adversely affect other states in the region. Increased democratization and economic integration have linked states more closely together such that instability in one state places others at risk. Thus, members have put a strong emphasis on defending democracy in addition to addressing traditional security concerns.

Since the OAS has established mechanisms for addressing many of these threats (traditional security concerns and newly defined threats to democracy), it is an ideal forum through which to attempt conflict management. This is particularly true since a number of the newer "security" issues that concern members require multilateral action to be addressed most effectively (such as anti-narcotics policies). In addition to being motivated to manage conflict in a timely and effective manner to avoid spillover effects, Latin American members also support OAS actions for a second reason. They prefer to work cooperatively through the OAS to avoid U.S. dominance or unilateral action in the region. In many instances, however, the OAS is dependent on resources supplied by the United States to carry out conflict resolution efforts, especially those with a militarized component.

Although the OAS is the most active regional organization in managing regional conflict, the newly expanded definition of security to include issues of economic integration has opened the door for a number of financial organizations and trade regimes to play a role as well. There are several regional trading organizations such as Mercosur and the Andean Pact that have an active interest in seeing disputes among or within member states resolved. In addition, Mercosur has clear political goals to consolidate democracy and maintain peace throughout the southern cone.[27] The international finance community is represented by the IMF and World Bank as well as the Inter-American Development Bank (IADB). These organizations are particularly relevant when considering economic sanctions as a conflict management strategy. These groups tend to follow the lead of the OAS in condemning unacceptable regional aggression and taking appropriate punitive actions. For example, Mercosur denounced General Oviedo's behavior in Paraguay in 1996 when he threatened to invade the presidential palace. If the FTAA were to be established and institutionalized in the future, it would provide a second, strong regionwide forum for managing conflicts.

INTERNATIONAL ACTORS

In addition to the OAS playing an active role in the Western Hemisphere, there are two additional actors to consider when examining conflict management potential in the region: the United Nations and the United States. Both the UN and the United States have the ability to strongly influence disputes in the region if they should choose to get involved. The UN has many financial, military, and diplomatic resources at its disposal to use in mediating and resolving conflicts around the world. It also has the moral authority to intervene, particularly when human rights are being violated.[28] Article 52 of the UN Charter provides for action by regional organizations, but also retains for the UN the authority to engage in conflict resolution efforts. Despite its capabilities and authority, however, the UN has not historically played an active role in Latin America. On the few occasions when it was asked to intervene, it ultimately took little action. For example, in the case of Guatemala (1954), the Guatemalan president requested the UN Security Council to consider the open aggression of Honduras and Nicaragua against Guatemala when rebels crossed the border intending to oust President Arbenz. The USSR supported Guatemala's request for an observer mission, but the United States argued that the case fell under the jurisdiction of the OAS and did not require UN action. The Security Council ended up issuing an ineffective resolution calling on the parties to end any actions likely to cause bloodshed. The United States was able to block any further UN action and President Arbenz was overthrown before the OAS could take action.

More recently, the UN has been slightly more active in the region. It intervened in Central America in cooperation with the OAS after the Esquipulas II Accords were signed in 1987 and in Haiti following the coup in 1991. The United Nations Observer Group (ONUCA) conducted a peacekeeping operation in Central America from 1989 to 1993. A similar force, the United Nations Observer Mission in El Salvador (ONUSAL) was present from 1991 to 1995. In 1997, the General Assembly authorized the United Nations Verification Mission in Guatemala (MINUGUA), which continues its work verifying the demobilization of combatants and compliance with the Agreement on Human Rights. Whereas the UN took an active role in Central America only after peace accords were signed, it was directly involved with forcing Raul Cedras from power in Haiti in 1994. Following the Haitian military's last-minute rejection of the Governors Island Agreement in October 1993, the UN authorized the use of a multinational force to intervene in Haiti using "all necessary means" to restore Aristide to power. Last-minute shuttle diplomacy by former President Jimmy Carter gained cooperation from Cedras and prevented direct engagement of the UN forces with the Haitian military. In 1997, following the restoration of the democratically elected government, the military mission was superseded by the Civilian Police Mission (MIPONUH).

Despite this recent activity, the UN has few incentives to act to address potential disputes in Latin America. One reason is that it is needed more urgently elsewhere in the world. The demands on the UN throughout the 1990s were quite high as a number of brutal civil wars broke out around the globe. The peacekeeping priorities of the UN have thus been focused on these new violent crises. Barring a significant outbreak of violence or human rights violations, it is unlikely the UN would give much attention to Latin American disputes in the near future. Even if such an event were to occur, it is likely that the UN would first turn to the United States to address the problem before taking action. U.S. hegemony in the region essentially ensures that it will take care of its "own backyard." The UN does not have this luxury in some other regions of the world where there may not be a hegemon capable of (or willing to) engage in conflict management and help restore law and order. In addition to the strong presence of the United States, the UN also relies on the OAS to resolve disputes among its member states. The OAS has played an active role in managing conflict for over fifty years. It has only been circumvented in favor of the UN in a few cases where the disputants didn't trust the OAS because of U.S. dominance (e.g., Guatemala, 1954). Overall, UN involvement in Latin America has not been high. It has been most active in cases where the United States has demanded action, such as in Haiti (1993). For the most part, however, it has been willing to let the United States and the OAS take care of disputes in the region.

In contrast to the UN, the United States has been more active in the hemisphere historically. However, these periods of activity have alternated with periods of benign neglect when U.S. attention has been focused elsewhere (Soviet Union, Middle East, East Asia). In the early 1990s, U.S. foreign policy focused once again on Latin America for trade issues (NAFTA, FTAA) as well as security issues (i.e., Haitian refugees, narco-trafficking). The United States demonstrated a willingness to work multilaterally on a number of transnational concerns in the region. The Clinton administration was able to push through the North American Free Trade Agreement (NAFTA) and continued to pursue FTAA at the Summit of the Americas (1994, 1998). Domestic electoral politics in 1996, however, shifted the president's attention away from Latin American concerns, and tensions over some policies limited the spirit of cooperation seen earlier in the decade. The United States and Latin American states do not have convergent interests on the problem of drug trafficking, nor on environmental and immigration issues. In addition, the policy making process in Washington has become quite balkanized, leading to contradictory policies that further increase tensions with neighboring states.[29]

Despite these tensions and disagreements on some regional issues (as well as a shift in foreign policy priorities away from Latin America), the United States remains committed to maintaining security and, by extension, democracy in the

Western Hemisphere. The strongest incentive for the United States to remain committed is that events in Latin America directly affect U.S. interests. Transnational issues such as immigration, environmental protection, and narco-trafficking cannot be ignored by the United States. Instability in the region can exacerbate these problems and raise additional security concerns, including dealing with refugee flows. Based on the proximity of the United States to Latin America, the United States has clear reasons for helping manage conflict in the region. The means used for doing so, however, are not defined as clearly. The United States has the ability to act not only multilaterally, through the OAS, but also unilaterally if it should choose to. Historically, U.S. intervention in the region has often been unilateral. For example, in 1989, the United States acted unilaterally to remove Panamanian President Manuel Noriega from power based on his alleged participation in narco-trafficking.

As the regional hegemon, the United States has the resources to carry out enforcement measures or sanctions on its own, although these may not be as effective as they would be if they were carried out multilaterally. The United States, however, has also endorsed many multilateral efforts made by the OAS over the years. Most recently, the United States has supported OAS actions to help restore democracy when it was threatened in Haiti (1991), Peru (1992), Guatemala (1993), and Paraguay (1996 and 2000). It seems likely that the United States will continue (perhaps reluctantly) supporting multilateral efforts to strengthen democracy in the future, particularly since such efforts can be more effective through cooperative multilateral actions.[30]

Although the United States has demonstrated strong support for maintaining democracy in the region through the efforts of the OAS, it has not been as willing to act multilaterally in the case of the drug war in Colombia. The United States has chosen to act bilaterally in cooperation with Colombia to address the threat of narco-trafficking. Although the OAS has taken some limited steps to address this threat, they have not been particularly effective.[31] It is likely that the United States will continue to pursue stronger actions bilaterally with Colombia to address the threat of narco-trafficking to the region.

The actions of these international actors, the UN and United States, have in most instances been complementary to the efforts of the OAS to manage regional conflict. The UN has worked closely with the OAS in Central America in the 1990s to help build democracy in the region. The United States has also supported OAS efforts to strengthen democracy in the region. On the issue of drug trafficking, however, different perspectives concerning cutting supply levels versus reducing demand have led to bilateral U.S. actions and minimal OAS policies.

REGIONAL CONFLICT ISSUES AND
CONFLICT MANAGEMENT OPTIONS

Throughout the 1990s, a number of strategies have been employed to address conflicts in different regions stemming from the end of the Cold War. These strategies include collective enforcement, peacekeeping and related operations, economic sanctions, and peacemaking/diplomacy. Some conflict management strategies, such as economic sanctions and peacekeeping operations, are best suited to handle low- to mid-level threats, whereas situations in which the threat to the region is high might require collective enforcement measures. Diplomatic measures are usually used in combination with the other strategies. For example, peacekeeping forces may not begin their operation until diplomatic arrangements have been made to insure their safety and the legitimacy of their mission by receiving permission from the host country for their presence. In many cases the mission of the peacekeeping force is to facilitate and help implement agreements reached by the diplomats (i.e., monitoring demobilization, disarmament, and elections). Economic sanctions can also be used effectively in combination with the other strategies. For example, economic sanctions and diplomatic negotiations were used to put pressure on Peruvian President Alberto Fujimori to restore democratic institutions following the coup in 1992. Different combinations of strategies can be used to address the variety of threats facing Latin American states.

Given the potential and existing security threats to the Western Hemisphere, boundary disputes and arms races pose the lowest level of threat to the region and will likely be managed through diplomatic efforts and economic sanctions, with the possible use of a limited peacekeeping force. Antidemocratic coups pose a greater threat to the region and require a higher level of response, such as the intervention of a peacekeeping force. When there are tensions between the civilian government and the military, prior to an actual coup, the dispute may best be addressed regionally through diplomatic measures. It is difficult for third parties to intervene in these disputes. There is a fine line between support for the regional norm of democracy and upholding the principle of nonintervention. Regional leaders can be most effective when the challenged civilian leader seeks international support for his position. Domestic insurgencies and drug trafficking are the two greatest threats to regional stability and security. Such threats may best be handled by a collective enforcement effort, but even this strategy may not be an adequate response to remove the threat that the guerrillas in Colombia currently pose to the region.

Latin American states have used three of the four noted conflict management strategies in the last decade. The strategy used most frequently is peacemaking, reflecting the region's commitment to pacific settlement of disputes and nonintervention. Although the United States has historically used military force when security issues are at stake, Latin American states prefer nonmilitarized responses to conflicts because of the tendency for the United States to dominate any collective military operations. Economic sanctions are used less frequently than peacemaking. Sanctions can be effective in cases where a coup has occurred, but are not as effective in many of the other situations that potentially threaten the hemisphere today. Peacekeeping has been used on occasion, most notably in cooperation with the United Nations in Haiti and in Central America in the 1990s. The region has never engaged in any collective enforcement efforts.

Boundary Disputes

Despite several long-term territorial disputes, such as the one between Ecuador and Peru dating back to 1955, disputes over borders have not been a major source of tension among Latin American states in the past decade. Bilateral boundary disputes have not posed significant threats to other states in the region. The periodic clashes between the military forces along some borders have generally been very limited. The greatest regional impact has usually been economic, when trade and transportation have been disrupted along a border. In some cases, the risk of military engagement has been actively reduced by both sides seeking a negotiated agreement prior to such an outbreak when tensions increased. For example, in order to ease tensions in late 1999 over a territorial dispute in the Caribbean, Honduras and Nicaragua agreed to meet with a special representative appointed by the OAS secretary-general to facilitate dialogue between the two countries.[32] In February 2000, Honduras and Nicaragua reached an agreement to reduce troops in the region to the precrisis level, to engage in joint patrol maneuvers, and to coordinate rescue operations and drug interdiction efforts in the disputed region of the Caribbean.[33] The agreement was intended to help maintain peaceful relations while the parties waited for the International Court of Justice (ICJ) to rule on the dispute. The secretary-general has also been active in facilitating talks between Costa Rica and Nicaragua on navigation rights on the San Juan river, and between Belize and Guatemala on their long-standing border dispute. Progress is being made in many of the remaining boundary dispute cases.[34]

The most notable recent diplomatic success in resolving boundary disputes came in October 1998, when Peru and Ecuador signed a peace treaty settling a border dispute that had lasted almost half a century. President Fujimori noted that the settlement not only resolved traditional issues involving border demarcations, trade, and shipping, but also laid the foundation for true and effective economic integration between Peru and Ecuador.[35] The agreement emphasized not only the value placed on pacific settlement of disputes by states in the region, but also the new importance of economic integration issues, which are also affected by boundary disputes. The diligent effort of diplomats to negotiate settlements for the few remaining boundary disputes is further reducing the threats, both economic and military, posed by these disputes to the region.

The diplomatic efforts of the OAS secretary-general have been successful based on the context of the disputes and the attitudes of regional and local actors. The secretary-general has been able to call on a number of skilled diplomats to serve as impartial facilitators in recent negotiations. In addition, negotiations have benefited from the neutrality of other states in the region that have not had a direct stake in the outcome of these bilateral disputes. Other regional actors such as the United States and the UN have, in fact, been quite supportive of OAS efforts to facilitate settlements. An end to boundary disputes not only promotes regional stability, but also aids efforts at economic integration, which are disrupted by such disputes.

Diplomats face two challenges when attempting to resolve territorial disputes. Not only must they address the division of territory, they must also consider the symbolic and historic value of the land to the people of both countries.[36] The context of current Latin American disputes makes the first element a little less difficult than it might be in Africa for example. The boundary disputes are focused on challenges to the placement of borders between two states, but do not question the sovereign right of other states to exist or to control territory. On the face of it, these disputes are fairly straightforward; agreements must be reached on new borders. The symbolic or historic value of the land to the people, however, must also be addressed in negotiations. In some cases there are trade-offs that can be made to reduce tensions and promote a settlement on boundaries. Trade-offs can include division of natural resources within the disputed territory. They can also include resettlement of citizens based on altered borders. Trade-offs may include combined or cooperative efforts to achieve common goals in the region. For example, in the case of a recent Nicaraguan/Honduran dispute in the Caribbean, they established a joint "patrol mechanism" in cooperation with third parties to prevent clashes between naval forces and to verify compliance with the recent agreement.[37] It is easier for diplomats to find trade-offs on division of resource issues than on less tangible issues concerning the significance of the land (i.e., its symbolic value).

In order to resolve conflicts such as boundary disputes and other potential security threats, the element of timing is critical. If the parties have not reached a "hurting stalemate," then the conflict may not be "ripe for resolution."[38] Ultimately the disputants themselves must be prepared to reach a settlement rather than perpetuate the conflict. Because boundary disputes usually involve only limited military engagements, with relatively low costs (in lives and resources), it is sometimes difficult to determine when both sides have had enough and are ready to come to the negotiating table. Paul Huth examines why leaders become involved in territorial disputes with their neighbors, and by extension, why those disputes continue.[39] He explains that military security interests frequently play a role as leaders promote and defend national security. Such logic makes leaders cautious about raising disputes with their allies within the OAS as a security organization. They are also reluctant to reject prior international agreements on borders because a rejection might jeopardize stable borders with other neighbors. In addition, some of the domestic political motivations that drive these disputes make negotiations difficult. Leaders are often motivated to try to gain control over valuable economic or natural resources in order to use them for development. They may also make territorial challenges to protest the prior loss of national territory and to generate popular support by seeking to recover the lost land. Finally, leaders may resist negotiations in order to avoid the political controversy of *not* maintaining the long-standing dispute (i.e., to avoid losing face).[40] All of these motivations make negotiations difficult, because the disputants many not be particularly motivated to reach a settlement. Ironically, these motivations for why Latin American border disputes continue also provide some explanation for why many disputes do not escalate. Leaders recognize that such engagements can be costly in terms of lives and resources, and furthermore, the conflict is frequently more symbolic than security related, thus not worth an escalation.

Because most Latin American boundary disputes are not heavily militarized, peacemaking is the most useful conflict management strategy. In those few cases, such as Ecuador/Peru, however, there may be a limited role for peacekeepers. For example, when tensions were high along the Ecuadoran/Peruvian border in 1995, the Rio Protocol guarantors[41] were asked to provide a military observer mission to oversee implementation of a cease fire, separation and withdrawal of troops, and creation of a demilitarized zone. This operation had a clear mandate and the support of the host states who wanted to avoid further military engagements. The peacekeepers were well suited to perform these tasks and carried out a successful operation.

Arms Races

Diplomacy has been employed recently to reduce the risk of an arms race in the region, putting into place regional measures to promote transparency and reduce the risk of arms races in the future. In early 1999, the OAS General Assembly, in a move designed to increase trust and security among nations, adopted a treaty requiring governments to report acquisitions of conventional weapons. The Inter-American Convention on Transparency in Conventional Weapons Acquisitions was cosponsored by Brazil and the United States and signed by nineteen states right away. U.S. Under Secretary of State Thomas Pickering remarked at the signing, "With the convention now in place, countries in the region will be better able to evaluate their security situation in an environment that allows democratic governments to maintain and modernize defense forces without triggering suspicions that could lead to an arms race."[42]

If an arms race were to develop despite the new convention on transparency, it is likely that it could be headed off in the early stages through diplomatic measures. Without any active military engagements, a peacekeeping force or collective enforcement measures would not be options. Economic sanctions, such as an arms embargo, would be ineffective without compliance by all arms-supplying states internationally. It is unlikely that all states would comply with the call for an embargo unless there were an active military dispute (and some might not even comply under those circumstances). Fortunately, the conditions are ideal for successful diplomatic handling of any potential arms races.

Although Latin America has a number of subregional groupings and affiliations, all the states (except Cuba) are members of the OAS, which serves to promote collective security in the region. United by this common security regime, it is likely that member states would choose to remain impartial to reduce tensions, rather than siding with one of two competing states. As in the case of OAS management of boundary disputes, there are also a number of impartial diplomats available to facilitate talks between countries competing in an arms race. Diplomatic efforts would likely receive clear support from regional actors for preventing arms races and stabilizing the region. It is less certain that the competing countries would support diplomat efforts to end an arms race, but given the urgent social needs in many Latin American countries, if security could be guaranteed, then competitors should be willing to end a costly arms race. The provisions are already established for such security guarantees both with a hegemonic member state, and with the collective security arrangements of the Rio Treaty. The presence of such guarantees help explain why arms races have not historically been much of a threat in the region. In addition, with the collapse of the Soviet Union, there is less of a need today for strong deterrent forces, thus further reducing the motivation for states to maintain large (and potentially threatening) military forces.

ANTIDEMOCRATIC COUPS

When considering the threat posed to the region by antidemocratic coups, it is useful to consider the threat in two stages: (1) tensions between the democratic government and the military, and (2) actual attempts at or successful coups. Prior to coup attempts, there are often incidents of tension between the civilian government and the military. These tensions may be reduced successfully through domestic and international efforts, or they may lead to a coup. The threat to regional security posed by such antidemocratic coups is higher than that of limited boundary disputes and potential arms races. Several recent incidents between civilian governments and military have threatened the fragile democratic regimes that are undergoing consolidation in the region. In Paraguay in 1996, just three years after the first civilian president was elected in a free and fair election, President Wasmosy was in a standoff with army commander General Lino Cesar Oviedo. Wasmosy had called for Oviedo's resignation. The general responded by threatening to invade the presidential palace. Faced with an immediate popular and regional outcry giving support to the president, Oviedo backed down.

Recent events in Peru also sparked concerns about a possible military intervention in the civilian government by Vladimiro Montesienos when President Fujimori first announced his decision to dismantle the intelligence service and to call for new elections in July 2001. After several days of silence, the Armed Forces Joint Command and the National Police released a reassuring statement saying they respected Fujimori's authority and his decisions. Neither the crisis in Peru, nor the one in Paraguay resulted in a coup, but the increased tensions between the civilian government and the military created that risk. With the new emphasis on democracy, such an interruption to democratic government has been defined by states in the region as a security threat to be addressed rapidly by the OAS and its member states.

Diplomacy appears to be the strongest strategy for handling such threats to the region posed by tensions between civilian governments and the military. Economic sanctions are not useful in the early stages of a democratic crisis because they cannot be targeted to reduce the threat to the democratic government posed by the military.[43] If economic sanctions are imposed on a country facing challenges from the military, such sanctions are likely to weaken the democratic government rather than strengthen it. Sanctions are often felt most keenly by the poorer segments of the population, which can lead to diminished popular support for the government. Similarly, peacekeeping and collective enforcement are not strategies to be adopted in such situations.

The conditions that exist in such standoffs between the military and civilian government favor diplomatic intervention. In order for diplomacy to be effective, impartial facilitators must be available. As noted above in the discussion of arms races and boundary disputes, there are skilled, impartial regional diplomats available to aid in negotiations between civilian government officials and the military.[44] Whereas states were neutral concerning boundary disputes and arms races, they are unlikely to remain impartial when democracy is threatened. Because states in the region have placed such importance on maintaining democratic processes, any military actions that threaten that process are likely to put states in direct opposition to the military leaders' position. Regional leaders will support the democratically elected government if its authority is challenged by the military. Such one-sided support, rather than complicating negotiations, however, may actually aid in settling the dispute by isolating the military leaders. It was clear in the case of Paraguay, when the international community stood strongly behind President Wasmosy, that General Oviedo would face considerable difficulties if he persisted in challenging the president. Thus, diplomatic efforts are aided by the availability of impartial facilitators as well as the *lack* of neutrality on the part of member states.

If military challenges to civilian authority are to be addressed before events result in a coup, then the timing of the international response is also critical. The OAS recognizes the need for a rapid response to these crises. In 1991 the General Assembly adopted Resolution 1080 of the Santiago Commitment to Democracy. Resolution 1080 instructed the secretary-general of the OAS to immediately convoke an emergency meeting of the OAS Permanent Council "in the case of any event giving rise to the sudden or irregular interruption of the democratic political institutional process . . . in any of the Organization's member states." The Council would then convene a meeting of the foreign ministers within ten days to look into the events collectively and adopt appropriate decisions in accordance with the Charter and international law. The resolutions adopted in Haiti (1991), Peru (1992), Guatemala (1993), and Paraguay (1996) included a wide range of measures but did not include direct military action to restore constitutional rule. In the case of Haiti, the OAS decided to recognize Aristide as the only legitimate government of Haiti and to diplomatically and economically isolate the country. Following the coup in Peru, the OAS appointed a special mission to travel to Peru and mediate between Fujimori and the opposition forces.[45]

These response mechanisms have worked well, allowing the OAS to meet quickly and to unanimously condemn threats to democracy. In May 2000, when a group of retired and active military officers in Paraguay surrounded the National Congress building with tanks, the Permanent Council met in special session within hours and vehemently condemned the assault on democratic and constitutional order in Paraguay. Shortly thereafter the government succeeded in arresting the insurgents and restoring order. In addition to regional leaders responding rapidly to the situation and supporting diplomatic initiatives to resolve it, there is also motivation on the part of the disputants to resolve the crisis. A standoff between the government and the military itself is unproductive. Eagerness on the part of military challengers and the civilian government to resolve the dispute provides ideal conditions for diplomatic settlement.

Another factor that promotes a diplomatic solution is the availability of options. Prior to an actual coup, there are several options available to settle such disputes between military and civilian leaders. Military challenges are linked to the issue of power sharing. Several options for satisfying the military's demands for greater authority include giving military leaders greater control over promotions, training, and the purchase of equipment. Such decision making can occur without impinging on civilian authority or threatening the democratic government. The one issue that may produce the most difficulty in negotiations is the future status of those military leaders who challenged the civilian government. In order for civilian officials to agree to give the military greater authority over security issues, it is likely that they will demand that the perpetrators face the consequences of their actions and be removed from office. This was the case in Paraguay in 1996 when General Oviedo resigned after the standoff with President Wasmosy.

The availability of impartial diplomats, the procedures for a rapid response, the willingness of all actors involved to reach a settlement, and the variety of options available to settle power sharing disputes all contribute to diplomacy being a strong mechanism to resolve disputes between civilian government and military leaders.

If tensions between the government and military are not resolved and result in an eventual coup, they are even more of a threat to regional stability and may require additional strategies to address them. From 1990 to 2000, there have been six coups and attempted coups in the region. Such crises for democratically elected governments pose varying degrees of threat to the security of the region. In some cases, such as Paraguay in May 2000, the coup attempt was quickly put down by the government. The OAS condemned the attempt and the issue was quickly resolved. In other cases, such as Haiti (1991–94), democratic government has not been so easily restored. Only the combined efforts of UN and OAS peacekeeping forces were able to restore the legitimate government of Haiti. Thus, in some cases, when the legitimate government is able to retain or regain control quickly, there is little need for more than a general statement of support for the regime from states in the region. When the coup is successful, however, a stronger response is needed. In such cases, peacekeeping forces, in cooperation with diplomats and the use of economic sanctions, can play a productive role in restoring democracy. Because peacekeeping forces rarely enter a country without permission from the host state, however, peacekeepers are most active once a settlement has been reached.

In cases where society has become divided following a coup, peacekeepers have a vital role to play following a negotiated settlement. In such cases, diplomats cannot fully restore law and order to the country because of distrust, tensions over power sharing among factions, and concerns about retaliation and physical safety. Thus, peacekeepers are needed to maintain law and order in the transition period so the coup leaders can leave power safely and the restored government can gain its footing before facing further challenges. Prior to the restoration of law and order by peacekeeping forces, however, diplomats must find a negotiated solution to the crisis so the peacekeepers can safely enter the country. The conditions diplomats face, however, are not ideal for settlement. Many of the conditions that promoted diplomatic settlement in boundary disputes, potential arms races, and tensions between civilian governments and the military are not present when a democratic government has been overthrown.

One challenge that negotiators face is the element of timing. When a coup occurs, a quick, strong, unambivalent response is necessary. If the international community unanimously condemns the coup and threatens further actions before the coup leaders can solidly take control of the government and country, then there is a possibility that democracy may be restored in a timely manner. For example, on 21 January 2000 a coup of indigenous peoples with support of some military elements ousted Ecuadoran President Jamil Mahuad. Democracy was restored when Vice President Gustavo Noboa took power and was confirmed by the Congress and acknowledged by Mahuad as the new president. The Ecuadoran ambassador stated that the OAS's condemnation of the coup and threats of international isolation brought the swift restoration of constitutional democracy with the installation of the vice president.[46]

If international actions and condemnation do not deter the coup leaders from consolidating their power, however, negotiations become more difficult. Because it is not an ongoing, two-sided conflict (the civilian government either loses power or arrests the coup leaders), there is no opportunity for a stalemate to develop. Thus, coup leaders have no incentive to negotiate because they have successfully attained power. An additional challenge to diplomats is that there are not as many options available regarding the main issue at stake (i.e., control of the government). If a democratic government is to be restored, the coup leaders must unconditionally surrender and hope to gain asylum elsewhere. This is a losing scenario for them. Thus, diplomats are not likely to have the support of the coup leaders when attempting to negotiate the restoration of democracy. Each of these factors makes the job of the diplomats difficult.

There are, however, two conditions that aid a diplomatic settlement: the availability of impartial negotiators, and the support of regional powers for an agreement. The support of regional powers is particularly important. If regional leaders are unified in their intentions to oust the coup leaders and restore democracy, they can bring considerable diplomatic and economic pressure to bear on the coup leaders.

The use of economic sanctions is more successful in some cases than others in getting coup leaders to reach a settlement based on the vulnerability of the regime. For example, in the case of the coup in Peru in 1992, while there was not a forceful call for a general trade embargo, many countries cut aid to Peru. The United States suspended all nonhumanitarian aid and suspended $2.5 billion in pending loans to Peru.[47] Fujimori's popularity was built on his ability to generate economic growth and control inflation, thus making him vulnerable to such economic sanctions. Given this vulnerability, the international community was able to put considerable pressure on Fujimori to make some concessions in restoring democratic rule in Peru.[48] Economic sanctions are not always so effective, however. General Raoul Cedras in Haiti was less vulnerable to the international pressure of economic sanctions. The coup leaders had considerable economic resources at their disposal and held no pretensions of governing by popular acclaim. Thus, the fact that the sanctions hurt the Haitian people did not greatly move the coup leaders toward a negotiated settlement.

If regional powers are able to pressure the coup leaders to reach a settlement, then there is a strong possibility that the conditions will exist for peacekeepers to successfully carry out their mission. With the goal of restoring a democratically elected government, peacekeepers should be able to operate under a clear mandate that will likely include provisions for restoring law and order, training a new police force, disarming former militants, protecting political candidates, monitoring elections, and helping in institution-building efforts to strengthen democracy in the long run. OAS peacekeeping forces should be well suited to these tasks. The OAS has had experience in performing these tasks in several countries in the past decade. For example, the OAS, through the Unit for the Promotion of Democracy, worked closely with the government of Guatemala from 1996 to 1999 to support democratization. In addition to helping demobilize combatants and reintegrate them into society, the OAS program provided technical electoral assistance, strengthened political parties, and removed land mines in the country.[49] In any conflict where peacekeepers might play a role, their work would be facilitated by the existence of a negotiated agreement, preventing them from becoming targets in an active conflict.[50]

The peacekeeping forces would also have the advantage of being supported by regional powers and neighboring states. The states in Latin America have declared their support for democracy and have proven their commitment in condemning past coups and coup attempts. Such support and unified action provides additional legitimacy to the actions of the peacekeeping force. Although diplomats are likely to face considerable lack of cooperation from the coup leaders in negotiations, peacekeepers should not face the same resistance if they enter the country only after an agreement has been reached.

One challenge facing peacekeepers involves the separation of forces following the negotiated settlement. In the case of a coup, it may be easy to identify the coup leaders, but identifying all of the subordinates who were involved is more difficult. In addition, in a coup, there may not be two identifiable military forces to keep separate. Peacekeepers may be most concerned about protecting civilians and the military forces from each other as law and order are restored. This task requires spreading peacekeepers throughout the cities and countryside because there are no obvious physical lines of demarcation to separate the forces.

Domestic Insurgencies and Drug Trafficking

Among the most significant security threats to Latin America today are the domestic insurgencies linked to international drug trafficking in Peru and Colombia. The OAS member states have taken several measures to address this threat, including establishing a new multilateral evaluation mechanism to be used by the Inter-American Drug Abuse Control Commission (CICAD) to analyze antidrug efforts in all thirty-four member states. Efforts are also being made to reduce corruption linked to the drug trade. Twelve countries are participating in a new program to implement the Inter-American Convention Against Corruption designed to help strengthen anticorruption laws in the region. In addition to these multilateral efforts, the United States has taken an active role in addressing the threat by providing antinarcotic assistance to the Colombian government. In August 2000, President Clinton signed a waiver freeing up $1.3 billion in antidrug assistance to train and equip the Colombian army and police forces, and to promote economic development, judicial reform, and human rights improvements. The president stated that a "drug emergency" exists and such aid was important for U.S. national security interests.[51]

Although diplomatic efforts have been successful in addressing some of the other security threats to the region, the conditions surrounding the drug war, and domestic insurgencies in Colombia in particular, are less than optimal. The important factors of impartiality and the cooperation of the combatants are lacking. Although it is still possible to find individuals who can negotiate in good faith with the parties, all countries in the region have taken a stand against the guerrilla forces. This clear regional support for the Colombian government places the guerrillas in a difficult position at the bargaining table and can influence the degree of cooperation they exhibit. There is also little evidence that the timing is right for diplomatic intervention. Even though the war has dragged on for decades in Colombia, apparently neither side has accepted that a hurting stalemate has been reached. Most recently, the government of Colombia has appeared to be more willing than the guerrillas to make concessions and reach a final settlement. The guerrillas, on the other hand, have been increasing their demands and offering few concessions. Similar circumstances have existed in the past as both sides have lost and gained ground, altering their bargaining positions but not resulting in a final settlement. Overall losses on both sides are high, but neither side seems prepared to acknowledge a stalemate. Despite strong support for an end to the conflict on the part of regional actors, the lack of cooperation from the combatants and lack of regional impartiality that contribute to successful diplomatic negotiations are not present at this time. Given these difficulties faced by the diplomats, other strategies might serve better in reducing the threat to the region posed by the guerrilla forces.

In coup situations in which a negotiated settlement has been reached, one would expect peacekeeping troops to perform well. One of the key factors to such an assessment is that the peacekeepers would not enter the country until an agreement had been reached. Such a situation would provide the peacekeepers with a clear postconflict mandate to restore law and order, provide for elections, and help strengthen the democratic institutions of the government. The peacekeepers would also have the consent of the disputants to carry out these activities. In the case of Colombia, none of these advantages are available to a potential peacekeeping force. Diplomats have not been able to negotiate a settlement thus far between the guerrillas and the government. It is unlikely that the guerrillas would be willing to cooperate with any peacekeeping force prior to reaching a settlement. This would put the peacekeepers in a dangerous situation. Furthermore, it would be difficult to establish a clear mandate for the troops to protect themselves and attempt to reduce the violence in the country. The presence of government troops, paramilitaries, guerrillas, and drug traffickers would make the operational environment quite complex, particularly if the peacekeepers were sent to prevent human rights abuses, because all sides in the conflict have been accused of such acts. Because Latin American peacekeepers have more experience with postconflict activities such as election monitoring and nation building, they may not be suitable for more militarized operations, especially when there is no real peace to keep. The ruggedness of the terrain would also make the separation of forces and any monitoring of troop movements quite challenging. Unless a negotiated settlement can be reached, it is unlikely that a peacekeeping force could be effective in reducing the threat to region posed by guerrilla forces in Colombia.[52]

Given the unsuitable conditions for a successful diplomatic mission or peacekeeping force, collective enforcement may be the only option left for the region to address the threat posed by guerrilla forces in Colombia. The presence of the United States in the hemisphere provides several advantages to regional forces when considering the option of collective enforcement. A force supported by the United States would have the military strength to engage in enforcement activities and the ability to act against all aggressors in the conflict. The coordination of such a force would likely be quite strong, particularly with the United States taking a leading role. Many of the military forces in Latin America have trained with the U.S. military. Historically, Latin American leaders have turned to the United States when there were serious extrahemispheric threats to the region, particularly during the Cold War. The physical capacity for strong collective enforcement is present.

Coordinating military actions with political goals, however, might be more difficult. Although there is the capacity to mount a collective enforcement effort, many Latin American states would likely resist such an obvious U.S. "invasion" of another sovereign state. Latin American states have traditionally resisted U.S.-dominated intervention in the region in domestic affairs, and would not likely support such a mission even in order to wipe the guerrillas. Furthermore, there are no precedents for collective enforcement in the hemisphere, so all of the actions to be considered would have significant political implications. In fact, political considerations would likely prevent such a force from ever acting because of the interventionary precedents it would set. There is not enough political will in the region currently to put together a collective enforcement operation. There is no agreement on what strategy to adopt to reduce the threat posed by narco-trafficking. The United States favors efforts to reduce the supply of drugs flowing north. Many Latin American countries prefer strategies to reduce consumption within the United States and thus weaken the market and power of the producers. Because few multilateral strategies have been adopted for dealing with the guerrillas and narco-traffickers, the United States has continued to provide strong unilateral support to the Colombian government in the hopes that the military can eventually overcome the guerrillas.

CONCLUSION

Given the existing and potential security threats in Latin America today, the use of peacemaking appears to be the strongest strategy available to states in the region to manage conflicts. When boundary disputes arise, the conditions are good for diplomatic efforts to succeed. There are impartial negotiators available through the OAS or other neutral states. Although the disputants and other regional actors are likely to prefer a diplomatic settlement over a militarized conflict, diplomats may face a challenge in overcoming domestic incentives to perpetuate the dispute. Conditions are also good for the successful diplomatic resolution of an arms race should one develop in the future. Additional steps have already been taken to prevent such an occurrence through greater transparency and collective security arrangements.

Tensions between civilian governments and the military pose a greater threat to the region than boundary conflicts and potential arms races, but again, the best strategy to address these challenges to the democratic order is peacemaking. Economic sanctions cannot be adequately targeted to reduce the threat to democracy posed by the military. Peacekeeping and collective enforcement measures are too forceful and intrusive into domestic affairs in such a crisis. If an antidemocratic coup does occur, however, diplomatic efforts, economic sanctions, and peacekeeping forces can work in combination to help restore law and order and a democratically elected government. Peacekeeping troops are more likely to successfully carry out their mandates if diplomats are able to arrange a negotiated settlement prior to their entry into the country. Economic sanctions and political pressure can be used effectively to secure such a settlement.

Latin American states have strong mechanisms to address most threats to the region and have used peacemaking well to secure negotiated settlements in nearly all cases of regional conflict. In some cases the use of economic sanctions and peacekeeping forces have helped to promote and implement agreements. The conditions surrounding the guerrilla insurgencies and drug war in Colombia and Peru, however, are far from ideal for achieving a diplomatic settlement. Without a negotiated settlement, the tasks of a peacekeeping force would be difficult to carry out. Collective enforcement may be the only method for addressing the threat, but conditions are also not ideal for such a force to be effective. Although there is sufficient military strength and potential for coordination through U.S. leadership, the political will for such forceful multilateral action is lacking. If there is no consensus on what multilateral actions might be taken to address this threat, it appears likely that the United States will act bilaterally with Colombia to reduce the threat that drug traffickers pose to the region. Regional organizational mechanisms would only play a secondary role, by monitoring antidrug efforts on the part of member states and coordinating less interventionist efforts.

Despite their inability to fully address the threat posed by drug traffickers, Latin American states have been largely successful in resolving regional threats through diplomatic efforts. The United Nations has, for the most part, not been needed in the region to address security concerns. Because the UN's attention and resources have been focused elsewhere, the OAS has continued to rely on its own members and mechanisms to manage conflicts in the region. Increased U.S. attention to the region and emphasis on multilateralism in the early 1990s has promoted consensus among members and provided an impetus toward greater cooperation and integration. It remains to be seen whether this multilateral spirit will continue if U.S. attention to the region diminishes in the future.

The norms of pacific settlement of disputes, consultation, and nonintervention that are embodied in the OAS Charter and Rio Treaty have led member states to seek diplomatic solutions to conflicts in the region. Diplomatic efforts are preferred over militarized solutions, and most of the threats posed to the region exhibit conditions that are ideal for diplomatic settlement. With a number of impartial negotiators available, alternatives and trade-offs possible, and strong regional support for negotiated settlements, peacemaking (supported at times by use of economic sanctions and peacekeeping troops) is an ideal tool to manage regional conflict. Member states are unified through the Organization of American States, and share many common security concerns and development goals that promote cooperation. Past experiences in managing regional conflict have prepared the region well for addressing most threats in the future.

NOTES

1. I use the term Latin America in a broad sense to include all of the Western Hemisphere: Central America, the Andean states, the Southern cone, North America, and the Caribbean.

2. Cleveland Fraser, "International Relations," in _Understanding Contemporary Latin America_, ed. Richard Hillman (Boulder, Colo.: Lynne Rienner, 1997), 169.

3. Some of these conventions include: the Inter-American Convention against Corruption; the Inter-American Convention against the Illicit Manufacturing of and Trafficking in Firearms, Ammunitions, Explosives, and Related Materials; the Inter-American Convention to Prevent and Punish Torture; and the Managua Protocol establishing the Inter-American Council of Integral Development. _OAS News_ (Washington, D.C.: Department of Public Information, Organization of American States, March–April 1999; May–June 1999; July–Aug 1999; Sept–Oct 1999; Nov–Dec 1999; Jan–Feb 2000; March–April 2000; May–June 2000; July–Aug 2000).

4. Howard J. Wiarda, "After Miami: The Summit, the Peso Crisis, and the Future of U.S.-Latin American Relations," _Journal of Interamerican Studies and World Affairs_ 37 (Spring 1995); Tom J. Farer, "Collectively Defending Democracy in a World of Sovereign States: The Western Hemisphere's Prospects," _Human Rights Quarterly_ 15 (November 1993).

5. Peter H. Smith, _Talons of the Eagle_ (Oxford: Oxford University Press, 2000), 255.

6. Andrew Hurrell, "Security in Latin America," _International Affairs_ 74 (Fall 1998).

7. Bruce Russett, _Grasping the Democratic Peace: Principles for a Post–Cold War World_ (Princeton, N.J.: Princeton University Press, 1993).

8. Hurrell, "Security in Latin America."

9. Andrew Hurrell, "Latin America in the New World Order: A Regional Bloc of the Americas?" _International Affairs_ 68 (Spring 1992).

10. First Summit of the Americas, _Declaration of Principles_ (1994). www.summit-americas.org/miamidec.htm (26 August 2002).

11. Raul Alfonsin, "Banning the Bomb: A Good Idea for Latin America?" _New Perspectives Quarterly_ 15 (Summer 1999).

12. _OAS News,_ May–June 1999.

13. Boundary disputes include both land and maritime territorial disputes. Some involve challenges to sovereignty (i.e., the right to exist as a nation), while others simply contest where the border is actually drawn between the two countries. No Latin American states face the first type of challenge.

14. David R. Mares, "Boundary Disputes in the Western Hemisphere: An Overview of Where We Stand," paper presented for the conference of Boundary Disputes in Latin America at the Inter-American Dialogue, Washington, D.C., February 2001.

15. It is interesting to note that this accord also included elements of economic integration, emphasizing again the new importance of integration for Latin American states.

16. In his research, David Mares ("Boundary Disputes in the Western Hemisphere") lists an additional eight "nonactive" disputes. These nonactive cases involve disagreements among states on boundaries that have been raised in the past but are not currently being discussed by the states publicly or through diplomatic channels.

17. Wyn Q. Bowen and David H. Dunn, _American Security Policy in the 1990s— Beyond Containment_ (Brookfield, Vt.: Dartmouth Publishing Company, 1996).

18. Deborah L. Norden, "Redefining Political-Military Relations in Latin America: Issues of the New Democratic Era," _Armed Forces & Society_ 22 (Spring 1996); Paul

Zagorski, "The Military," in *Understanding Contemporary Latin America,* ed. Richard Hillman (Boulder, Colo.: Lynne Rienner Publishers, 1997), 114.

19. *Sendero Luminoso* (the Shining Path) in Peru posed a considerable threat to Peru in the late 1980s and early 1990s, but President Alberto Fujimori was largely successful in weakening the guerrillas and regaining control of the country. The Shining Path was weakened after its founder (Abimael Guzman) was captured in 1992, but it has not been defeated. The guerrillas have continued to stage attacks on government facilities and to embarrass the Fujimori government. It will be up to President Alejandro Toledo, elected in June 2001, to continue the government's efforts to defeat *Sendero.*

20. Jo-Marie Burt, "Shining Path after Guzman," *NACLA Report on the Americas* 28 (Nov–Dec 1994).

21. U.S. Committee for Refugees, "The Crisis in Colombia," 18 July 2000.

22. Linda Robinson, "Is Colombia Lost to Rebels?" *U.S. News and World Report,* 11 May 1998.

23. President Clinton defended his decision to waive restrictions requiring the Colombian government to curb paramilitary human rights abuses that Congress had placed on the aid package, declaring that a "drug emergency" exists in Colombia and that President Pastrana is making progress on human rights (Marc Lacey, "Clinton Defends the Outlay of $1.3 Billion to Colombia," *The New York Times,* 24 August 2000).

24. Since 1998, the aid has increased to nearly the level given to El Salvador in the 1980s (Ryan Beiler, "Deja Vu in Colombia," *Sojourners* 29 [March 2000]).

25. Richard E. Feinberg, *Summitry in the Americas: A Progress Report* (Washington, D.C.: Institute for International Economics, 1997).

26. There are also considerable differences between Latin American states and the United States on the issues of immigration and the environment. Debate on these issues clearly affects U.S.–Latin American relations, but does not directly influence the security of the region.

27. Smith, *Talons of the Eagle,* 332.

28. Following the end of the Cold War, the UN has taken unprecedented interventionary steps despite the principle of state sovereignty. Such intervention has been justified based on support of human rights.

29. Peter Smith cites the example of U.S. relations with Mexico. Relations are more open in terms of trade following the NAFTA agreement, yet the border patrol continues to build more walls and fences, which Mexican officials find offensive. Different bureaucracies in Washington, D.C., clearly have different agendas in terms of U.S.–Mexican relations (Peter H. Smith, "Trouble Ahead? Prospects for U.S. Relations with Latin America," in *The United States and the Americas: A Twenty-First Century View,* ed. Albert Fishlow and James Jones [New York: W. W. Norton and Company, 1999]).

30. Abraham F. Lowenthal, "United States—Latin American Relations at the Century's Turn: Managing the 'Intermestic' Agenda," in *The United States and the Americas: A Twenty-First Century View,* ed. Albert Fishlow and James Jones (New York: W. W. Norton and Company, 1999).

31. Members have been working through the Inter-American Drug Abuse Control Commission (CICAD) to design and implement a new Multilateral Evaluation Mechanism to measure national progress against narco-trafficking.

32. *OAS News,* Jan–Feb 2000.

33. *OAS News,* March–April 2000.

34. *OAS News,* May–June 2000.

35. *OAS News,* March–April 1999.

36. Paul R. Hensel, "Contentious Issues and World Politics: The Management of Territorial Claims in the Americas, 1816–1992," *International Studies Quarterly* 45 (March 2001).

37. *OAS News,* Jan–Feb 2000.

38. I. William Zartman, *Ripe for Resolution* (New York: Oxford University Press, 1985).

39. Paul K. Huth, *Standing Your Ground* (Ann Arbor: University of Michigan Press, 1996).

40. Huth, *Standing Your Ground,* 101.

41. Argentina, Brazil, Chile, and the United States.

42. *OAS News,* July–Aug 1999.

43. Sanctions can be useful, however, as a threat to the military to restore democratic government if they succeed in taking power.

44. These diplomats are skilled professionals who have often served for years in the OAS. One such diplomat who has been active in negotiating boundary disputes in the region is Luigi Enauldi. He has served as the U.S. Ambassador to the OAS, worked in the U.S. Department of State, and is currently a visiting scholar at the Inter-American Dialogue.

45. Dexter S. Boniface, "Defending Democracy in the Western Hemisphere: A Behavioral Analysis of the Organization of American States," paper presented at the International Studies Association Convention, Washington, D.C., February 1999.

46. *OAS News,* March–April 2000.

47. Boniface, "Defending Democracy in the Western Hemisphere."

48. Ultimately, however, because the coup was quite popular among Peruvians, Fujimori did not fully meet international demands.

49. *OAS News,* May–June 1999.

50. Peacekeepers may still face some hostility while carrying out their mandates, but once a settlement has been reached, it is unlikely that they would be caught in the middle of active fighting between the factions.

51. U.S. efforts have focused on Colombia most recently. President Fujimori has been successful in reducing the power of the Shining Path guerrillas in Peru over the past few years, but Colombian President Pastrana has not been as effective; Lacey, "Clinton Defends the Outlay of $1.3 Billion to Colombia."

52. Given Peru's relative success in dealing with its guerrillas, it is highly unlikely that the government would even accept the presence of an intervention force in the country. Thus, peacekeeping would not be a viable option in the case of Peru either.

6

Conflict Management
in the Middle East

Between the "Old" and the "New"

BENJAMIN MILLER

As the recent crisis in the Middle East (ME) shows, despite the post–Cold War expectations for a "New Middle East," which will engage the region in peaceful cooperation, the ME is still unstable and prone to violence. My argument is that the underlying source of these dangers is the high extent of the state-to-nation imbalance in the region as compared to most other regions. Such an imbalance shapes, to a large extent, the security agenda in the region and creates numerous security problems and intense security dilemma.[1] The severity of these security issues and the dangers inherent in them provide strong incentives for regional conflict management. These incentives are closely related to the logic of a rational status-quo state seeking security and economic prosperity based on cost-benefit calculations. At the same time, the high extent of the state-to-nation imbalance in the region, which produces ideological motives, emotionally laden issues, and domestic constraints, makes it difficult for the regional actors and institutions to manage regional conflicts by themselves. As a result, international actors from outside of the region become a key for managing regional conflicts. Yet, the ability of international forces to shape regional conflict management is limited and thus the security situation in a region that depends on conflict management from the outside is problematic.

I start with a short conceptual discussion of the implications of the state-to-nation imbalance for regional security problems. Then I apply this analysis to the Middle East to show that it accounts for the severity of the different levels of security problems in the region. Such severity provides for powerful security and economic incentives to manage the regional conflicts. Indeed, this was the logic behind the conception of a "New Middle East." But the extent of the imbalance also makes such management extremely difficult. This has constrained the applicability of the "New ME" and maintained strong elements of the "Old Middle East" (revisionist ethnic nationalism).

Thus the role of international/global forces ("the new world order") has become crucial for conflict management in the Middle East. But in light of the constrained ability of the global elements to manage conflicts in the region, it continues to be unstable and prone to violence. Because of the regional incentives and the role of global forces, conflict management can be successful, but so long as the state-to-nation imbalance persists, it will be more in the form of the lower levels of conflict management: crisis management, avoidance of escalation and spread of violence, and cessation of hostilities and at best conflict reduction rather than the higher levels of conflict resolution, let alone conflict transcendence.

IMPLICATIONS OF THE STATE-TO-NATION IMBALANCE

I argue that the extent of the state-to-nation imbalance in a certain region determines the severity of the security problems in that region by producing major issues for conflict and by increasing the security dilemma and transborder violence. The severity of the security problems produces, for its part, major incentives for regional conflict management but the state-to-nation imbalance makes it difficult. Global factors can be helpful but only in the sense of mitigating rather than resolving the problems.

Following are the key propositions of the study:

1. The greater the state-to-nation imbalance in a certain region, the more severe the regional security problems are.
2. Severe regional security problems produce powerful political, economic, and security incentives to manage conflicts.
3. A sharp state-to-nation imbalance handicaps the ability of the regional actors to manage conflicts.
4. Under these circumstances, global management becomes a necessity. However: (a) Its effectiveness depends on the type of global engagement in the region, and (b) even the more effective forms of global engagement lead, at best, to limited and somewhat shaky conflict management in the region, namely crisis management and conflict reduction rather than conflict resolution, let alone conflict transcendence.

I discuss the second and third propositions in the context of the empirical section. Following the introduction of the outcomes, I present briefly the logic behind propositions 1 and 4.

THE OUTCOMES: PATTERNS OF
REGIONAL CONFLICT AND ITS MANAGEMENT

How does a region deal with its conflicts and security problems? There are three major potential ways: violence, conflict management, and conflict resolution (or reconciliation).

One potential avenue is by resort to violence, that is, the eruption of hot wars. Another avenue is through conflict management, namely, attempts to prevent or at least to minimize the duration, scope, and frequency of the resort to violence in addressing conflicts in the region. There are two major forms of such attempts:

1. Cessation of hostilities, termination of war, or crisis management: Within a protracted conflict, the most that can be done might be only to manage crises or to stop the hostilities after they have already erupted and establish a cease-fire without addressing the underlying sources of the conflict. The situation in the region will be then a "cold war"—although hot war may erupt at any time, it might last a relatively short period, so that there are long periods without violence.
2. Conflict reduction and crisis prevention: reaching agreements on certain aspects of the conflict. This is sufficient to prevent the onset of regional crises but insufficient to fully resolve the conflict. Thus, the danger of war declines considerably but does not disappear completely. This situation might be called "cold peace." Under a regionwide cold peace, there might be localized low-intensity violence (lower-level hostilities such as communal violence), but it is unlikely to escalate to a regionwide war.

The third road of addressing conflicts is by reconciliation and conflict resolution. This can be accomplished by either one of the following ways:

1. Settlement: direct resolution of all outstanding issues in conflict among the states in the region, thus reducing drastically the threat of war.
2. Conflict transcendence: the conflict is transcended by regional cooperative engagements like joint economic endeavors, trade relations, regional institutions, or coping with common problems like the environment. Settlement or transcendence leads to a "warm peace" in which the likelihood of resort to violence declines dramatically.

THE EFFECTS OF REGIONAL AND GLOBAL
FACTORS ON THE MANAGEMENT OF REGIONAL CONFLICTS

I argue that the two ends of the continuum—the "hot or warm" outcomes of proneness to violence (1) and conflict resolution (4)—are determined by regional domestic factors, most notably by the extent of the state-to-nation compatibility in the region. However, the in-between "cold" outcomes of conflict management (2 and 3) are affected by systemic factors, notably the type of great-power involvement in a region (see figure 6.1).

This is the result of the differential effects of two different sets of balances (balance of motivations and interest, and balance of capabilities), two different sets of actors (regional states and external powers), on two different types of outcomes (hot or warm outcomes [violent conflicts and reconciliation or

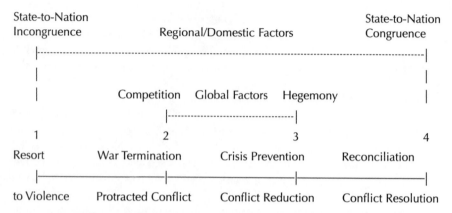

Figure 6.1.   Patterns of Regional Conflicts and the Factors Explaining Them

conflict resolution] and cold ones [two types of conflict management]). The more intense or hot the outcome (that is, violence or reconciliation), the larger the influence regional states will exert because of their superior motivation. In contrast, the great powers' superiority in capabilities over regional states is reflected in the great powers' influence on the less intense outcomes of conflict management. The specific influence of the great powers on regional conflict management is conditioned by the type of great-power involvement in regional affairs. I distinguish between two ideal types of great-power regional involvement: hegemony and competition. Great-power competition may prolong and aggravate the regional conflict, making it more susceptible to punctuation by regionally inspired hot wars. Yet, competition may bring about the lower level of conflict management—war-termination resulting (in the absence of conflict resolution) in cold war. Hegemony can facilitate higher levels of conflict management: escalation control, crisis prevention, and conflict reduction, resulting in cold peace and diminishing the prospects for regionwide hot wars.

The sources of regional violence are independent of great-power effects. Hot wars derive from regional, rather than global-systemic, factors relating to underlying problems in the state-to-nation congruence. The greater the imbalance, that is, the greater the number of powerful revisionist-irredentist states and secessionist national groups within states, the stronger the regional war propensity. I discuss these issues in greater detail elsewhere.[2]

Great-power effects, however, are prominent in conflict-prone regions with high war-propensity, either in aggravating the level of conflict—which is the case when the great powers compete in the region—or in reducing the intensity of the conflict—which happens under conditions of great-power hegemony. Thus, the shift of the Middle East from being a tense war zone to one of emerging cold peace was the result of the systemic change vis-à-vis the region: from U.S.–Soviet competition during the Cold War to U.S. hegemony in the post–Cold War period (see table 6.1). The superpower rivalry—which had ex-

Table 6.1.   The Effects of the Type of Great Power Involvement on Regional Conflicts in the War-Prone Region of the Middle East

Type of Great Power Involvement	Regional Outcomes	Empirical Cases
Competition	Cold War (Protracted Conflict/War Termination)	The Middle East During the Cold War
Hegemony	Cold Peace (Conflict Reduction/Crisis Prevention)	Post–Cold War Middle East

acerbated the Arab-Israeli conflict during the Cold War—ended, reducing the level of the regional conflict. The second factor was the rise of U.S. hegemony, which further facilitated a transition to cold peace (see table 6.1).

Yet, the sharp state-to-nation imbalance in the Middle East poses a tough challenge for regional conflict management either by the regional actors or by the global ones, including the U.S. hegemon.

THE STATE-TO-NATION INCONGRUENCE AS THE UNDERLYING CAUSE OF REGIONAL WAR-PROPENSITY

In order to go to war, regional states need both motivation and capabilities to do so. The state-to-nation imbalance provides an underlying motivation for war and therefore makes certain regions more war-prone than others. The state-to-nation congruence refers to the degree of compatibility between the existing division to territorial states and the national aspirations and political identifications of the people in the region. The balance moves on a continuum between symmetry and asymmetry. Symmetry means that there is a compatibility or congruence between the regional states (as entities or institutions administrating a certain territory) and the national sentiments of the peoples in the region (as political aspirations to live as national communities in their own states).[3] In other words, there is a strong identification of the people in the region with the existing states and their territorial identities. The result is that the demand for states and their supply are more or less balanced.

State-to-nation asymmetry prevails when there are nationalist challenges to the existing state-system in a certain region either from below the level of the state (i.e., subnational ethnic groups aspiring for secession from the state) or from above (i.e., pan-national movements of unification or irredentist-revisionist claims to territories held by other states on the grounds of national affiliation of the population or national-historic rights on the territory). The secessionists claim that there are too few states while the pan-nationalists argue that there are too many states in the region on national grounds. The result is that the supply-demand ratio of states is imbalanced: either the demand considerably exceeds the supply, leading to wars of secession, or the supply far outnumbers the demand, resulting in wars of national unification.[4] Thus, the state-to-nation ratio is measured by the power of secessionists, irredentists, nationalist-revisionists and pan-national unifiers in a certain region. Two particular groups who support the revisionist/ nationalist agenda are settlers who reside beyond the state boundaries and advocate, with the support of irredentist groups in the homeland, their annexation to the homeland; and refugees who claim the right of return to their homes in their previous places of residence. The more powerful these nationalist forces are in relation to the status-quo states, the greater the state-to-nation incongruence and vice versa. The greater the state-to-nation incongruence, the more prevalent is the presence in the region of two types of states: incoherent and revisionist. Revisionist states are dissatisfied from the current regional order and are willing to use force to change the territorial status quo based on nationalist claims. Incoherent states are states in which there is a low level of identification of the citizens with the state and with its territorial identity, as reflecting their national identity and aspirations.[5]

Regions with high state-to-nation asymmetry are more prone to wars than others because of three reasons, which are not elaborated here.[6] First, this is due to the emergence of substantive issues of conflict on national grounds (territories and boundaries and also demographic issues such as refugees and settlers).[7] Second, such a high asymmetry provides fertile grounds to the enhancement of other causes of war such as the security dilemma and power rivalries in the region. Because of that, the likelihood of arms race and proliferation of weapons of mass destruction increase drastically. Third, such an asymmetry produces regional insecurity through the effects of spreading transborder instability like guerrilla, insurgency, and terrorism. Moreover, incoherent states produce regional instability because they provide targets for external intervention either out of temptation for profit and expansion or due to insecurity and fear of spreading instability out of the incoherent states. Pan-national forces especially tend to intervene in domestic affairs of other states, and such intervention will be most feasible in incoherent states. Ethnic alliances—cases in which a majority group in one state is a minority group in a neighboring state—increases the likelihood of international conflict[8] where the coethnics in one state (the majority group) are propelled by feelings of solidarity with their ethnic kin in a proximate state (the minority). Incoherent states produce secessionist movements, which also affect neighbors' security. Because of its weakness, an incoherent state may host, frequently involuntarily, guerrilla forces that attack neighboring states, or such state may cause problems of refugees in the region.[9]

Because the state-to-nation incongruence increases the likelihood of the spread and the escalation of war, it generates incentives for rational status-quo actors to manage regional conflicts. But this incongruence also produces domestic and ideological constraints on the regional ability to manage conflicts.

In the absence of effective regional mechanisms for conflict management, global actors, especially the great powers, become highly relevant for conflict management. But different types of regional engagement of the great powers might have different consequences for security management, depending on whether a number of great powers compete in the region or whether there is a single hegemon vis-à-vis the region.

APPLICATION TO THE MIDDLE EAST

The Security Problems in the Middle East: Types, Severity, and Sources

In contrast to expectations during the 1990s that a "new ME" is emerging, recent developments both in the Gulf and the Arab-Israeli conflict show that the Middle East is still unstable and prone to violence. In the Gulf there have been rising challenges posed by Saddam Hussein, while the Gulf coalition is in decline. The Arab-Israeli arena was dominated in the last year by the recent violence in the West Bank and Gaza and the fear of its escalation and spread to other fronts, especially South Lebanon, involving Syria. Yet because of global changes, namely the post–Cold War "new world order" reflecting U.S. hegemony, especially vis-à-vis the Middle East, there is a possibility for conflict management, even if only a partial and limited one.

Types of Security Problems

The state-to-nation imbalance in the Middle East makes the region highly prone to violent conflicts on a number of levels: territorial and border interstate disputes; the threats posed by revisionist states and their destabilizing transborder effects; the presence of incoherent or weak states, the eruption of civil wars and external intervention in these conflicts; the occurrence of low-intensity conflicts such as guerrilla warfare and terrorism; and proliferation of weapons of mass destruction

In the Third World in general there have been numerous challenges to the legitimacy of the postcolonial order because of the absence of legitimate boundaries,[10] artificial division into states, and arbitrary allocation of peoples and territory to states, leading to interstate conflicts out of irredentism.[11] This process of artificial state formation also took place in the Middle East in the post–World War I era.[12] Yet, while in most of the Third World there was, on the whole, an acceptance of the colonial borders despite their artificial nature, or at least a rejection of the use of force as a method for border change,[13] the problem of the regional order's legitimacy was aggravated in the Middle East because of the special strength of ideological revisionism in the region, challenging state sovereignty, in addition to the presence of incoherent states.[14] Thus, regional interstate wars also concentrated in the Arab-Israeli section of the Middle East because the state-to-nation problems, due to powerful revisionism, were especially prevalent there. The challenges to legitimacy were the underlying causes of the eruption of regional wars, which led to specific wars either through the externalization of domestic conflicts or through the aggravation of the proximate causes of war, notably the security dilemma and power rivalries.

These proximate causes can explain the timing and context of the eruption of specific wars. At the same time, changes in the underlying factors can account for the variations in war-proneness between different periods in the same region. Thus, decline in revisionism and strengthening of the states should lead to reduction in the frequency of wars. Indeed, this has happened in the Middle East in the post-1973 period. Yet, state-to-nation problems have remained powerful enough to prevent comprehensive conflict resolution or the emergence of normal, let alone warm, peace. The best outcome that could be achieved is a limited "cold peace"—and this only under U.S. hegemony.

While the Arab-Israeli conflict is by no means the sole conflict with a potential for a major violent escalation, it reflects an enduring major state-to-nation incongruence and thus includes a number of levels of conflict: interstate, low-intensity, and the transborder threat of weapons of mass destruction. The Arab-Israeli conflict is also interrelated with other regional conflicts, notably in the Gulf and the Northern Tier, and is closely related to major state-to-nation processes in the region such as Pan-Arabism and state strength and regime stability and the questions of refugees and settlers. However, there are also other dangerous security problems in the Middle East, notably in the Gulf, which have manifestations in different levels of violence: interstate, domestic, and nonconventional.

THE MIDDLE EAST DURING THE COLD WAR

The post–World War II Middle East was characterized by shifting between situations of hot and cold wars and high proneness to conflict and violence. The combination of revisionist-nationalist ideologies (Pan-Arabism, Nasrism, the Ba'th, and Zionism in different stages), radical regimes (especially the revolutionary regimes in Egypt, Iraq, and Syria and since the late 1970s the Islamic Republic of Iran), and incoherent weak states (notably Jordan and Lebanon) led to a multiplicity of conflicts in an unstable region. The conflicts have been both interstate and domestic civil wars.[15] There have been four main types of conflicts in the region:

1. The enduring Arab-Israeli conflict has led to a series of short interstate wars between 1948 and 1982.
2. There were a number of other conflicts between Arab and non-Arab states in the Middle East, the most notable of them generated the protracted Iran-Iraq war in the 1980s. One enduring point of quarrel here is the control over the strategic Shat al Arab waterway. There were also enduring rivalries between Turkey and Syria and Turkey and Iraq, revolving around questions of boundaries, water, and transborder ethnic minorities (particularly the Kurds).
3. Inter-Arab rivalries over hegemony, notably between Egypt and Iraq and the "Arab cold war" between the radicals states and the conservative

monarchies,[16] have been intense and led to interference in the domestic affairs of other states, but did not generate hot interstate wars until the Iraqi invasion of Kuwait in 1990.

4. The domestic weakness of states brought about civil wars in which neighboring revisionist states intervened. Even if specific cases of intervention by Arab states in other Arab states were motivated first of all by particularistic state interests rather than by a concern for the general Arab cause,[17] Pan-Arabism has provided a certain degree of legitimacy in the eyes of Arab opinion for interventions in the domestic affairs of other Arab states such as the Egyptian intervention in the civil war in Yemen in the 1960s,[18] the Syrian intervention in Jordan in 1970 and in Lebanon in 1976, the Iraqi threat vis-à-vis Kuwait in 1961, and many other cases of nonmilitary transborder intervention in domestic affairs.[19]

The Effects of the Global Cold War

The global Cold War and the superpower competition in the Middle East in the 1948–73 period prolonged the Arab-Israeli conflict and made it difficult to move beyond a regional cold war to cold peace, that is, to reduce the level of the regional conflict. Thus, the superpowers supported opposite sides in the Arab-Israeli conflict and helped to sustain it by arms supply and diplomatic and economic support of their respective clients. What's more, a strategic backing of their clients by the superpowers, namely the commitment to come to their aid in times of crisis by arms resupply and issuing threats of intervention when the clients were attacked and the survival of their regimes was threatened, reduced the costs and risks of continuing the conflict for the client states, including by resort to force.

Although the United States helped to establish peace between Israel and Egypt in 1978–79, so long as the Cold War persisted, the radical forces in the Arab world were able to form a counterbalancing coalition against the U.S.-led peace process. This coalition, supported by the Soviets, was led by Iraq, Syria, and the Palestinians. Jordan, Saudi Arabia, the small Gulf states, and North African states either tilted toward this coalition or at least were constrained, by nationalist domestic and regional pressures, from joining openly the peace process with Israel. Thus, following the 1979 peace treaty with Israel, Egypt was expelled from the Arab League and returned only with the end of the Cold War in the end of the 1980s.

The "Arab cold war" between the conservative and radical forces was also reinforced by the respective superpower patrons—the United States supported the conservative Saudis and Jordan while the Soviets were allied, in different degrees of intensity in different periods, with Egypt (until 1972–73), Syria, and Iraq. But the Arab cold war was transcended already before the end of the Cold War by the post-1967 rise of the Arab-Israeli conflict over the occupied territories and in the 1980s by the Iran-Iraq war.

POST-COLD WAR CHANGES

The end of the Cold War, Soviet disintegration, and the Gulf War brought about major changes in the security landscape of the region. One set of changes had a stabilizing effect, reducing the likelihood of major regional wars. The other set of changes had destabilizing effects. There were two major pacifying developments:

1. The emergence of a vigorous bilateral and multilateral Arab-Israeli peace process; and
2. The formation of a broad antirevisionist coalition led by the United States, which was interested in containing the radical forces in Iran and Iraq. Specifically, the United States established a multidimension containment strategy vis-à-vis Iraq[20] and Iran.

Whereas these developments reduced the threat of interstate conventional war, there have also been three destabilizing patterns:

1. The danger of conventional war was not completely eliminated due to remaining interstate disputes,[21] especially among neighbors, over territories, boundaries, water, and ethnic nationalism. These conflicts took place in three theaters: the Arab-Israeli, the Gulf, and the Northern Tier. All these theaters were inflicted by sharp state-to-nation incompatibilities. Being part of the same regional security system, there were interrelations among the conflicts in these theaters. Such interrelationships might have even increased in the post–Cold War era. Two destabilizing developments have increased the likelihood of nonconventional violence:
2. Fear of spread of WMD (weapons of mass destruction: nuclear, biological, chemical).
3. The problem of low-intensity conflict such as guerrilla warfare and the growing threat of terrorism, especially by militant Islamic groups.

Post-Cold War Changes in the Arab-Israeli Conflict

The end of the Cold War and especially the Iraqi defeat by the U.S.-led coalition in the Gulf War led to a vigorous Arab-Israeli peace process that seemed to transform the region from a conflictual to a cooperative one, and at the very least to reduce the likelihood of war quite substantially. The U.S. hegemony became more complete with the end of the Cold War and Soviet disintegration, when other Arab parties to the conflict, notably the Palestinians and Syria, lost the possibility of recourse to a rival superpower patron who could shield them from the adverse effects and costs of opposition to U.S.-led peacemaking efforts. The weakening of Iraq reduced the possibility of forming a radical countervailing coalition against the U.S.-led peace coalition, which included the status-quo states in the region. Thus, the combined effect of the Soviet disintegration and

U.S. victory in the Gulf was to bring about a "bandwagoning" of rational actors toward the United States based on realpolitik and economic considerations. One of the key manifestations of this bandwagoning was joining the U.S.-led peace process, not so much out of a sudden desire to make peace with Israel and to recognize its legitimacy, but out of an expectation of getting tangible security and economic benefits from the hegemon. The United States has always been interested in making peace between Israel and the Arabs because this is the most effective way of maximizing U.S. influence in the region and because advancing the peace process reconciles the U.S. dilemma between ensuring the flow of oil (which necessitates maintaining good relations with the Arabs) and its special commitment to Israel.

Thus, it is no coincidence that about eight months after the end of the Gulf War, Israel, Palestinian representatives, and most of the Arab states met for the first time around the negotiations table. In October 1991, the Madrid conference, cochaired formally by the United States and the USSR but led by the United States, initiated the peace process in the Middle East. Following the conference, multilateral working groups composed of Israelis, Arabs, and various states outside of the region started to discuss a variety of functional issues like security and arms control, economics, water, refugees, and the environment.

The major breakthroughs took place in 1993–95 with the interim Oslo accords between Israel and the Palestinians and the 1994 peace treaty between Israel and Jordan. There were also active bilateral negotiations with the Syrians on Israeli withdrawal from the Golan Heights in exchange for normalization of relations and security arrangements.

Especially important were the Oslo accords, which established a Palestinian National Authority (PNA) in those parts of the West Bank and the Gaza Strip that were evacuated by Israel. Following the Hebron Agreement of 1997 and the 1998 Wye accord, most of the Palestinian population lived in the territory of the Palestinian Authority, although it lacked territorial contiguity and controlled only about 40 percent of the territory of the West Bank and about two-thirds of the Gaza Strip. The Oslo accords conveyed a mutual recognition between Israel and the Palestinians and a commitment to resolve conflicts peacefully. The essential bargain was based on Israeli territorial concessions in the occupied territories, leading eventually to a Palestinian state there, in exchange for security cooperation, which would minimize terrorist threats and violent actions against Israel. This process was severely tested by the terrorist actions committed by the radical Islamic organizations against Israel, culminating in a bus bombing campaign in spring 1996, which led to the emergence of a right-wing government in Israel that slowed down the peace process. The Palestinians, for their part, were dissatisfied from the continued expansion of the Jewish settlements in the territories and the presence of the Israeli army in checkpoints and roadblocks there.

When Ehud Barak was elected prime minister of Israel in summer 1999, negotiations were accelerated, initially with the Syrians on a bilateral peace accord, and later with the Palestinians on a final-status agreement. The negotiations seemed promising and the parties appeared to be willing to make considerable concessions.

Since 2000, however, major negative developments have taken place in the various fronts of the Arab-Israeli conflict, both diplomatically and with regard to the resort to violence. On the whole, they highlight the difficulties in reaching a comprehensive Arab-Israeli peace and the possibilities at best for interim agreements. These developments also point out the danger of a continuous low-intensity conflict with some danger of escalation depending on the developments in South Lebanon and in the longer-term in Iraq. The major destabilizing developments are:

1. Violence. Since fall 2000 there has been protracted low-intensity violence between the Israeli army and Palestinian militias and demonstrators in the occupied territories. The Palestinian militias also conduct an attrition war against Jewish settlers in the territories and some militant groups resort to terrorist attacks inside Israel's major cities. Following the May 2000 Israeli withdrawal from its self-declared security zone in South Lebanon there has been a reduction in the level of the transborder violence but it was not terminated. There is still a potentially serious danger of escalation involving also Syria.
2. Diplomacy. The failure of the unprecedented negotiations on a final-status accord that took place between Israel and the Palestinians under active U.S. mediation from summer 2000 and until the end of the Clinton presidency and the Israeli elections in February 2001. The Syrian-Israeli negotiations also collapsed in early 2000.
3. The likelihood of escalation. As recent events have shown, the lack of resolution of the outstanding state-to-nation issues is likely to lead to violence, at the very least in the form of protracted low-intensity conflict and guerrilla and terror warfare. Although less likely for the foreseeable future, continuation of the Israeli-Palestinian conflict could potentially also lead to an escalation to a broader regional war, which might include additional state and nonstate actors.

The Israeli-Palestinian Conflict

During the Camp David summit and in the subsequent months far-reaching diplomatic negotiations took place aiming at reaching a final-status agreement between Israel and the Palestinians. For the first time, all the fundamental issues of the conflict related to the state-to-nation problem were addressed:

1. the future boundaries of the Palestinian state and its territorial scope and contiguity;
2. the future status of Jerusalem, including Arab East Jerusalem and the Old City and especially the holy places for both Jews and Muslims in Temple Mount and Haram El Sherif;

3. the right of return of the Palestinian refugees to pre-1967 Israel;
4. the future of the Jewish settlements in the Palestinian territories;
5. the type of security arrangements between the Palestinian state and Israel including the extent of the demilitarization of the Palestinian state and how and by whom it is going to be enforced. Related issues are the extent and location of the Israeli military presence in the new state, especially in the strategic Jordan valley that separates Palestine and Jordan, and beyond that, Iraq; and
6. the degree of economic cooperation and integration or separation between Israel and Palestine.

The parties were reported to make some important concessions in relation to their previously held positions. Arafat was willing to consider that some blocs of Jewish settlements would be annexed to Israel in exchange for major Israeli concessions including the establishment of a Palestinian state, whose capital would be in Arab East Jerusalem, in the Gaza Strip, and on about 95 percent or so of the West Bank. Barak was also willing to compensate the Palestinians for the annexation to Israel of the 5 percent or so from the West Bank territory by giving them some territories in the Negev part of pre-1967 Israel. The most far-reaching change in the Israeli position concerned the willingness to divide Jerusalem whereas the unity of the holy city under Israeli sovereignty was before a sacred cow in Israeli domestic politics and foreign policy.

But at end of the day the gaps were too wide to be bridgeable for the time being. The key points in dispute were the future sovereignty of the holy sites in Jerusalem and the right of return of the Palestinians refugees to Israel proper. This claim of the Palestinians was rejected by Israel. The Palestinians were reluctant to accept Israeli demands to station their troops in the Jordan Valley for some years and it is unclear how many of the settlements could stay in their place as a part of peace deal.

The disputes were not confined, however, to the negotiating table. The frustration with the continued Israeli control over substantial parts of the territories together with the persistent expansion of the settlements led to the eruption of violence following Ariel Sharon's visit to Temple Mount in late September 2000. While the Palestinians claim that the violence was provoked by the visit and the killing of Palestinian demonstrators in its aftermath, Israel argues that the violence was premeditated. In the Israeli view, Arafat wanted to bring about an internationalization of the conflict following the Kosovo precedent: the greater firepower of Israel would bring about disproportionately higher level of Palestinian casualties (especially children). This would exert pressures on the international community, through the "CNN effect" to apply pressures on Israel and even to consider military intervention that would isolate Israel and force it to make much more concessions than what it offered in the negotiations. Some observers argued that Arafat endorsed this line following the Camp David summit in which Israel, through the major Barak's concessions, seemed to be capturing the high moral grounds as indicated by Clinton's statement that Israel showed a greater degree of flexibility than the Palestinians.

Another Palestinian motivation to resort to violence might be to affect the Israeli public: to bring about concessions through inflicting casualties. Here the Palestinians might have been influenced by the South Lebanon analogy: Hizballah showed that violence can presumably pay off because of the great Israeli sensitivity to casualties. Thus, because of the supposed greater Palestinian willingness to sacrifice, their advantage in the balance of motivation will compensate for disadvantages in the balance of power.

Moreover, even if these outstanding issues are resolved in a formal peace accord, which seems unlikely in the near future, two major questions in this state-to-nation conflict are, on the one hand, whether the Palestinian state will be an irredentist state with continuing territorial and demographic (the "right of return") claims vis-à-vis Israel and, on the other hand, to what extent the Palestinians will feel that the settlement fulfills their right of self-determination in a viable, contiguous, and independent state of their own or whether Israel continues to be a "neocolonial" power that controls their life militarily, politically, and economically. Major Israeli concessions, especially in East Jerusalem and on the settlements, might lead, in turn, to Jewish irredentist-nationalist movements, which would resort to force against the Palestinians and the Israeli government. The relative strength and the democratic nature of the Israeli state as compared to the Palestinian state leads us to expect that the problem might be more serious on the Palestinian side, which at least until now has been the major revisionist/dissatisfied party.

At any rate, the Israeli public endorsed a hard-line approach to the Palestinians as a result of the combined effect of the rejection of the Clinton's plan and Barak's concessions by the Palestinians and the resort by them to violence. In the eyes of most Israelis, Barak's concessions were very generous so their rejection and the escalating violence indicated a lack of Palestinian interest in peace. Thus, the situation now is of continued violence with great difficulties in resuming the failed security cooperation between the two parties and in returning to the peace negotiations. External assistance, especially by the United States, is crucial for the two areas as well as for establishing a permanent cessation of hostilities.[22]

Syria-Lebanon-Israel

The negotiations conducted under U.S. mediation during the 1990s failed to reach a peace agreement[23] because of the disagreement on the scope of the Israeli withdrawal from the Golan Heights and the security arrangements following the withdrawal and also the type and degree of normalization of relations between the two countries. Thus, the Golan Heights remains a potential flash point. The Syrian regime under Basher Assad continues to insist on a complete Israeli withdrawal to the pre-1967 borders while Israel would like at the minimum to maintain full control of the Lake of Galilee, which supplies a major portion of its water resources. The danger in Syrian-Israeli relations is further reinforced by the situation in South Lebanon.

South Lebanon

The Israeli pullout from South Lebanon in May 2000 led to a major reduction in the level of violence on the border between the two states, although a number of violent incidents have taken place in recent months. Yet, this border remains a potential flash point because the Lebanese state did not extend its authority to the evacuated area while radical militias, related to Iran and Syria, are active there against Israel. President Emile Lahoud has refused to send his army down to guard the border, apart from a symbolic joint force of twelve hundred army and internal security personnel that was deployed under pressure from the UN and the West, but they have proved impotent in the face of the two Shiite militias—Amal and the Iranian-backed Hizballah. Thus the two militant groups filled the vacuum created by the Israeli evacuation. More recently, Palestinian militant groups also began to stage attacks on the Israeli army from South Lebanon. Palestinian refugee leaders stated that they cannot look upon "their lands just a few meters away from the border fence and do nothing about it."[24] Underlying all of this is Syria's desire to keep up the pressure on Israel in the absence of a deal that would return the Golan Heights to Syrian control. Syria is the true ruler of Lebanon and that at least partly explains the inaction of the Lebanese government in taking control over the south. Faced with the Lebanese government's lack of cooperation in containing the situation in the south, Israel had sent warnings to Syria, both public and via proxy diplomatic channels, that it would not tolerate any further attacks, and that it would hold Syria responsible and retaliate accordingly, "both in Lebanon and in Syria itself if necessary."[25] Indeed, the Israeli air force attacked Syrian installations in Lebanon in mid-2001 in response to Hizballah's shootings at Israeli forces in a disputed border area. The situation may get out of control, especially in light of the role played by the irregular forces supported by Iran. Yet, thus far Syria did not respond and an escalation is not very likely so long as Syria is weak in the absence of an external patron like the role played by the USSR during the Cold War.

GULF SECURITY

This oil-rich region has become volatile in the recent three decades following the 1973 oil embargo and the related rise in oil prices, the 1979 Islamic revolution, the 1980–88 Iran-Iraq war, and the 1991 Gulf War. In the post-1979 era Iran's Islamic revolution was seen as posing the greatest threat to the status-quo states in the region. Thus, the oil-rich Gulf states supported Iraq in the Iran-Iraq war. Since the Iraqi invasion of Kuwait, Iraq is seen as a key threat, although the perception of the Iranian threat also did not disappear. Iraqi power has been weakened and contained since the Gulf War. Both the Islamic Revolution and the Iran-Iraq war weakened the conventional power of Iran, although it gained in transnational ideological appeal. Recently both Iran and Iraq seem to be building their conventional and nonconventional capabilities, posing potential threats to the Gulf and to the region as a whole.

The main problem in the Gulf is the asymmetry between a group of weak and vulnerable status-quo oil-rich states (Kuwait, Qatar, Oman, Bahrain, the United Arab Emirates [UAE] and the largest and strongest in this group—Saudi Arabia) and two relatively strong and revisionist neighbors—Islamist with a Shiite flavor in Iran and Pan-Arabist with Ba'thist undertone in Iraq.[26] The small oil-rich states are extremely worried about their survival and territorial integrity in a neighborhood that includes revisionist powers and also domestic and transnational (Pan-Arabist and recently especially Islamist) threats to their regimes as well as some territorial conflicts among themselves. The Pan-Arabist challenge declined in recent decades, although Iraq tried to manipulate it and to mobilize support in the Arab world in favor of its 1990 occupation of Kuwait. Since the 1979 revolution Iran had a transnational appeal to Shiite and Islamist forces in the Arab world.

Both of the revisionist states have aspired, to various degrees in different times, for hegemony in the Gulf and beyond in the Middle East as a whole. They are hostile to Israel and to the peace process, have a multiplicity of border conflicts with their neighbors and restive/dissatisfied ethnic groups at home, try to reach WMD capabilities, and support terrorist organizations. At various times they tried to destabilize regimes of other regional states and to challenge their legitimacy and even, especially Iraq, the legitimacy of the states themselves, most dramatically in the case of Kuwait, manifested in the Iraqi occupation in 1990 (and earlier in the 1961 challenge). Iran and Iraq have used a wide range of destabilizing tools (propaganda, support of local opposition groups, terrorism, territorial claims, threats) in order to affect their neighbors' policies.[27] Iran and Iraq do not fully accept that the smaller states are sovereign members of their region, and, in many cases, refuse to address issues important to their smaller neighbors. Thus, Iran refused to accept that there is a legitimate UAE view on the two strategically located islands it occupied: Abu Musa and the Greater and the Lesser Tumbs.[28] Iran has also claims vis-à-vis Bahrain. Similarly, Iraq has been traditionally insensitive to Kuwaiti concerns despite Kuwait's financial and logistical support during Iraq's war with Iran. The strongest of the conservative group, Saudi Arabia, also demonstrated insensitivity to Doha's complaints and there has recently been a rift between Saudi Arabia and Qatar.

The mismatch between oil-rich states with small population and a combination of poor neighbors with relatively large population (Yemen, Egypt) and oil-rich with relatively large population (Iraq and Iran) becomes explosive because of the mismatch between states and nations and the lack of legitimacy to recently established boundaries because people on different sides of the border share the same national identity (Arab) and language or the same religion (Islam or a certain sect like Shiites). This increases the legitimacy of the claim to share in the benefits of the oil richness.[29] The problem becomes an acute military threat because the two neighbors with relatively large populations and revisionist agendas are able to build substantial military machines, including WMD, due to their own oil resources.[30]

Although most of the serious conflicts with a potential for a violent escalation are between Arab and non-Arab countries, notably between Iran and Iraq[31] and Iran and UAE, there are a number of boundary disputes between Arab states. Yet, most of these disputes are likely to be resolved by peaceful means.[32] These are the disputes between Saudi Arabia and Qatar and Saudi Arabia and Yemen, and also the tensions between Qatar and Bahrain, Oman and Saudi Arabia, and Kuwait and Saudi Arabia.[33]

But the most serious conflict is between Iraq and Kuwait.[34] The UN Security Council has insisted that Iraq should accept the Iraqi-Kuwaiti border, which the UN demarcated after the Gulf War. The redefinition of the boundary from its original de facto to de jure status, which has also involved some realignment, has been rejected not only by the Iraqi government but also by the vast majority of the Iraqi opposition movement. Iraq agreed to respect the newly aligned boundary without recognizing it. This suggests that unless Iraq and Kuwait find a mutually acceptable formula, the boundary between them remains a powerful potential source of conflict in the future. A key problem that Iraq faces, quite apart from irredentist-nationalist claims over the frontier region, is that without some adjustment of the maritime boundaries, it is effectively a landlocked state. Such a state tends to be extremely sensitive over boundary issues, especially if it is located in an unstable neighborhood. Being landlocked would also require Iraq to abandon its objective to function as a state with strategic interests in the Gulf—a position it has held since at least 1971. This appears most unlikely to take place either under the present or any conceivable successor regime. The challenge is how to balance Iraq's aspiration for access to the Gulf with the legitimate concerns of Kuwait and Iran.

The Northern Tier

In the post–Cold War era, with the disappearance of the Soviet threat and the difficulties of integration into Europe, Turkey has increased its involvement in the Middle East, including, on the one hand, the intensification of conflicts between Turkey and its Arab neighbors and, on the other hand, a potential emergence of a U.S.-supported Israeli-Turkish axis.

The Gulf War signaled a new Turkish orientation toward a greater involvement in the Middle East by joining the anti-Iraqi coalition and allowing the coalition forces to use air bases on its territory also in the aftermath of the war. The

Gulf War also increased the Turkish fears about the establishment of Kurdish state in Northern Iraq, which might encourage separatism in its own Kurdish minority. Indeed, the rising conflict with the Kurds raised tensions with the neighboring states, which also have Kurdish population: Iran, and especially Syria and Iraq. The growing usage of the Euphrates and Tigris rivers by Turkey further increased the water conflicts with the latter two downstream states.[35] At the same time, Turkish security cooperation with Israel increased in the 1990s including intelligence sharing, some limited joint exercises, and allowing the training of Israeli jets in the Turkish airspace.[36]

Proliferation of Weapons of Mass Destruction and Ballistic Missiles

The high degree of insecurity in a state-to-nation imbalance provides fertile grounds for proliferation of WMD because of mutual fears of revisionism. The ME is considered to be one of the most dangerous regions in terms of WMD proliferation.[37] No less than seven countries have WMD programs, in various stages of development, production, and deployment. Because of the increasing capabilities to launch WMD the threat transcends regional security considerations and poses a potential threat to European countries and even, according to recent prognosis, to the U.S. territory.

The illegitimacy of Israel has led to its acquisition of nuclear weapons in light of the asymmetry in conventional resources and its fear of being attacked by a grand coalition of Arab states, which will include all its neighbors and Iraq. In more recent years the Israeli nuclear deterrence is designed to deter also the growing threat of nonconventional missile attack by the Arabs and Iranians.

Thus, Israel views its nuclear option as purely defensive for deterrence of Arab aggression and as a crucial component of its security.[38] The Arabs, however, fearing Israel's quest for domination and expansion, see Israel's nuclear monopoly as posing a major threat to their security. They are concerned that Israel might use it for blackmailing them, especially in times of crisis. As a result, they demand denuclearization of Israel, most notably Egypt's pressures on Israel to join the Non-Proliferation Treaty (NPT).[39]

Israel, for its part, opposes these demands as long as there is no comprehensive peace in the region that includes also the revisionists—Iraq and Iran. Israel is worried about the latter's plans for acquisition of WMD, notably nuclear weapons. The Gulf War showed Israel's vulnerability to missile attacks, even if they were only with conventional warheads. But Israel might believe that its nuclear deterrence discouraged Iraq's use of its chemical and maybe biological weapons. Due to the big concentration of its small population along the coast, Israel is extremely vulnerable to nonconventional attack, particularly by nuclear weapons. Such a scenario has seemingly become more feasible after the end of the Cold War because the breakup of the Soviet Union made nuclear smuggling (both material and knowledge) to radical forces in the ME more likely as a result of the spreading fear of "loose nukes."

Despite signing the NPT, Iraq was probably very close to reaching nuclear capability before the Gulf War. The Arabs attempt to counterbalance, or at least to deter Israel's abuse of its superiority, by arming themselves with WMD, mostly the relatively cheap chemical weapons and ballistic missiles and in the case of the two major revisionist states—Iraq and Iran—also attempt to acquire nuclear weapons. Being oil-rich makes it possible for them to do that. Their motivation is related not only to their anti-Israeli ideology and fears of Israel's nuclear capabilities, but also their other regional concerns, including of each other.

Two major events have influenced dramatically the course of proliferation in the ME. The first was the Iran-Iraq war during the 1980s and the second was the Gulf War of 1991.[40] In both cases ballistic missiles were used against civilian centers—during the "war of cities" in 1988 and the Iraqi offensive against Saudi Arabia and Israel in 1991. The lesson seems to be that missiles cannot guarantee victory but can save from utter defeat.[41] Another important milestone of proliferation was Saddam's use of chemical weapon against the Kurds in Iraq. These experiences have proven the utility of WMD and ballistic missiles, in terms of deterrence, coercive diplomacy, and prestige, especially when resources for military expenditure are limited.

The end of the Cold War has facilitated and accelerated the process of proliferation, mainly by Russian scientists (with or without formal consent of the government), China, and North Korea.[42] According to the American intelligence community, "during the next fifteen years the United States most likely will face ICBM threats from Russia, China, and North Korea, probably from Iran, and possibly from Iraq."[43] This assumption reversed previous intelligence assessments arguing there was no direct threat to the United States.[44]

Low-Intensity Conflicts

In the post–World War II era the thirty-one politically active minorities of North Africa and the Middle East initiated greater magnitudes of communal protest and rebellion than groups in any other world regions.[45] In the post–Cold War era there has been destabilizing developments in the case of the Kurds in Turkey and especially Iraq. In the Arab-Israeli front the conflict between the Hizballah and Israel intensified in South Lebanon until May 2000 with further potential escalation in the future. After some moderation of the Palestinian struggle with the end of the Cold War, there has been aggravation more recently of the low-intensity conflict between Israel and the Palestinians in the occupied territories.

A major case of an enduring guerrilla insurgency is the struggle of the Kurds for independence or at least autonomy in Turkey and Iraq.[46] The rebellion against Iraq peaked between 1961 and 1975 so long as the Kurds received assistance from Iran and Israel, both of which had an interest in weakening Iraq. When Iraq reached a border agreement with Iran, the latter stopped its assistance for the Kurds and the rebellion was suppressed. The rebellion was renewed during the Iran-Iraq war and especially following the Iraqi defeat in the Gulf War. The no-fly zone in Northern Iraq, imposed by the United States and Britain, has become an autonomous Kurdish region, but infighting and the opposition of the neighboring states and the West to Kurdish independence weakens considerably their struggle.[47] From the mid-1980s until the late 1990s Turkey tried to suppress the Kurdish insurgency in its southeastern region led by the Kurdish Workers' Party (known by its Turkish initials as PKK). The capture in 1999 of its leader, Abdhallha Ocelan, seemed to calm the situation.

Islamic Fundamentalism and Terrorism

Following the 1979 Islamic revolution in Iran,[48] Islamic movements challenged secular regimes in a great number of Middle Eastern states such as Egypt,[49] Jordan, Turkey, Syria, North Africa, and the Gulf and the Arabia Peninsula. Islamic forces captured the government in only one state, Sudan, although they are still a powerful social and political force in many Arab and Islamic countries. One of the enduring consequences has been the emergence of terrorist organizations that are anti-U.S. and anti-Israeli.

"Arab Afghan" is a label widely used by ME governments to refer to Arabs recruited to fight in Afghanistan in the 1980s. Thousands of such recruits were later transferred to Yemen and established Islamic terror groups linked to attacks on U.S. targets already before the attack on the USS *Cole* on 12 October 2000.[50] Thus Afghanistan has become a central training camp for Islamic terrorist organizations around the world, and the Afghanistan alumni have become a significant factor in the development of terrorism in the ME and beyond. Their return to the ranks of their organizations has led to an escalation of terrorist activity in various countries, threatening the stability of their regimes. Afghanistan alumni have also played major roles in some of the principal terrorist attacks on the international scene during the 1990s.[51]

The best-known anti-American terrorist, located in Afghanistan, is Osama Bin-Laden. In the fight against Israel, Islamic organizations replaced nationalist-secular forces in the forefront of the battle: Hizballah in South Lebanon, the Hamas and the Islamic jihad in the occupied territories.[52]

THE SOURCES OF THE SECURITY PROBLEMS: MANIFESTATIONS OF STATE-TO-NATION IMBALANCE IN THE MIDDLE EAST

Explaining the High War-Proneness of the Middle East: A State-to-Nation Incongruence Produces Revisionist Ideologies and Incoherent States

The high level of illegitimacy in the ME was derived from the strength of the revisionist ideologies and the presence of weak states. Two main manifestations of revisionist ideologies are two rivals: Zionism and Arab anti-Zionism. A third revisionist ideology is the broader framework to which the second is related: Pan-Arabism. The fourth ideology—Pan-Islam—has been on the rise in the last two decades.

The state-to-nation compatibility in the ME is problematic in two major senses. On the one hand, there are "too many states" in the region according to supra/pan-national revisionist ideologies, mainly Pan-Arabism and, to a lesser extent, Pan-Islam. "Too many states" refers both to the artificial, illegitimate division of the Arab world into separate states and to the illegitimate existence of Israel. In both cases, Arab nationalists claimed that Western colonialism was the perpetrator, or guilty party. On the other hand, for a number of key dissatisfied national groups, which lacked states of their own, there are too few states. Examples are the stateless Palestinians, the Kurds, and other ethnonational groups, especially in the Fertile Crescent.

Many states in the region have been incoherent due to a combination of supranational and subnational challenges and ineffective domestic institutions and unstable regimes. There are strong interrelationships between revisionism and incoherent states. Some of the main manifestations of these relations include the Palestinian refugees; Pan-Arabism as a major source of revisionism, which as a supranational ideology has also weakened the Arab states; and the weakness and illegitimacy of the Arab states has also increased the power and appeal of Pan-Arabism.[53] Some of the sources of the state-to-nation problem in the Middle East are:

1. "illegitimate states" or "artificial nations that do not deserve a state";
2. nations without states: Palestinians and Kurds;
3. states without nations;
4. ethnic fragmentation and the endorsement of radical Pan-Arab positions[54];
5. incoherent, weak states[55];
6. "too many states": pan-nationalism transcending boundaries, most notably, the Pan-Arabist revisionist challenge to the Arab State-system;
7. pan-religion; and
8. stateless refugees and the right of return: the Palestinian refugees.

"Illegitimate States" or "Artificial Nations that Do Not Deserve a State"

These are due to irredentist-nationalist claims by at least some of their neighbors, such as the Arab claims vis-à-vis Israel, Iraqi claims toward Kuwait, Syria toward Lebanon, and the claims at different times of Syria, Iraq, Israel, and the Palestinians vis-à-vis Jordan. The illegitimacy of Israel in the eyes of all its Arab neighbors (at least until the 1978 Camp David accords) was an underlying source of the Arab-Israeli conflict that brought about most of the hot wars in the region. The other key dimension is the Palestinian issue discussed below. There are three key questions in this conflict:[56]

1. Should Israel exist? A major component of Pan-Arabism was to view Israel as an illegitimate state in the midst of the Arab world.
2. To the extent that the right of Israel to exist is accepted by the Arabs, then the major question is where should its boundaries be?

3. Who will control the territories on the other side of the frontier with Israel: a Palestinian state, Jordan, or another Arab state like "Greater Syria" or Egypt (which until 1967 controlled the Gaza Strip)?

In the 1948–73 era the Arab-Israeli conflict vacillated between hot and cold war. The source of the conflict was related to state-to-nation problems affecting regional legitimacy. On the one hand, these concerned the illegitimacy of Israel in the eyes of its Arab neighbors. The Arabs did not recognize the legitimacy of the Zionist claim that the Jews should have the right to immigrate from all over the world and settle and establish a Jewish state in what the Arabs saw as Arab Palestine. The basic Arab concern since the early Zionist settlement in Palestine in the late nineteenth century has been that the Zionists are bent on continuous territorial expansion at the expense of the Arabs and on achieving dominance in the region. After 1967 the problem was magnified by the Israeli occupation of the West Bank and the Gaza Strip, thus supposedly confirming the Arab fears about Zionist expansion. The stateless status of the Palestinians compounded Israel's illegitimacy in the eyes of the Arabs.

On the other hand, the fundamental Israeli nightmare since the establishment of the state in 1948 is that due to continuing illegitimacy of its existence in the Middle East, a grand coalition of Arab states might initiate a surprise two-front attack taking advantage of its asymmetrical manpower resources vis-à-vis the Israeli vulnerabilities of a lack of strategic depth and the limitations to its military manpower, composed largely of reserve soldiers. Such mutual fears on both sides produce an intense security dilemma.

Nations Without States: Palestinians and Kurds

The presence of two stateless nations has major effects on the security situation in two major parts of the Middle East: the Palestinians on the Arab-Israeli sector, and the Kurds on the Iraq-Iran-Turkey triangle.

The Kurds are a non-Arab national people, mostly Sunni Muslims who number about twenty million and live in Turkey, Iran, and Iraq—also Syria and the former USSR.[57] Most Kurds are reluctant to be assimilated into dominant groups; instead they promote their own culture, preserve their own identity and language, and are determined to win regional autonomy, if not independence.

At different times the Kurds have conducted various levels of insurgencies, particularly against Iraq and Turkey. But this has major implications also for Iranian and Syrian security. In southeastern Turkey, the PKK has used guerrilla and terrorist tactics to pursue independence and during the recent decade was the target of bombings and reprisals both in Turkey and in villages and camps in northern Iraq.

Due to the spread of the Palestinian refugees in many Arab states, especially those bordering Israel, and Pan-Arab commitments to the Palestinian and the anti-Israeli cause, the Palestinian issue had major implications for Arab-Israeli wars and terrorist and guerrilla operations against Israel. In the aftermath of the establishment of Israel during the 1948 war, the Palestinians remained without a state and thus became a revisionist-irredentist force that did not have a stake in the stability of the regional order.[58]

The 1967 war increased the number of Palestinian refugees and led to a growing Palestinian demand for an independent state of their own in the occupied territories of the West Bank and the Gaza Strip. The Palestinians tried to achieve their objectives through the guerrilla and terrorist actions of the Palestine Liberation Organization (PLO) and other Palestinian organizations, culminating in the Intifada in the occupied territories in the late 1980s and early 1990s, and the eruption of a second round of Intifada in September 2000.

At least until the Oslo Accords of 1993 there was an intensive debate in Israel whether the Palestinians and their Arab supporters aim only at the occupied territories or also at pre-1967 Israel proper. Even following Oslo, the right wing in Israel has continued to be skeptical about the Palestinian ultimate intention. This view was reinforced in the Israeli public by the recent Intifada and the advocacy of the right of return of the Palestinian refugees to their former homes inside Israel proper (see below).

States Without Nations

The nation-building enterprise has not been successful in most Fertile Crescent states like Lebanon, Jordan, Iraq, and Syria. This is partly due to ethnic fragmentation. Moreover, the dominant ethnic groups in each state tend to exclude the other groups and to discriminate against them while controlling the state resources and privileges. The Pan-Arabist loyalties of large shares of the population also pose difficulties for constructing coherent nations in each state. In addition, the presence of a large population of stateless Palestinian refugees, especially in Jordan and Lebanon, made the nation building a difficult task and led to the eruption of civil wars in Jordan (1970) and Lebanon (1975–90).

Ethnic Fragmentation and the Endorsement of Radical Pan-Arab Positions

Members of minority groups, when in power, have sought to demonstrate their nationalist credentials by endorsing militant Pan-Arab stances regarding Arab unity and the Palestinian question. One example refers to leading members of the Syrian Ba'th party from the minority Alawi sect, who were opposed by the majority Sunni public. Especially unpopular was the radical faction of the Ba'th party, which took power in February 1966. In addition to its ethnic composition, there were also socioeconomic sources of tension between the secular, socialist group and large segments of the more conservative public. The ruling group itself was intensely factionalized. To strengthen domestic control, these tensions were externalized in a militant policy against the pro-Western Jordan and Saudi Arabia, but the main target was Israel through both rhetoric and military actions,[59] leading to the escalation culminating in the Six-Day War. The Alawites still control Syria, and their minority status continues to encourage them to adopt radical nationalist positions.

Externalization of domestic conflict also played a role in Iraqi hegemonic quest. Iraq is highly fragmented with ethnicity in the north running parallel to sectarianism elsewhere. Whereas the Kurds are separatist, the Shiites seek a change in the regime but not in the territorial identity of the state. Still, there is a permanent threat of partition of a state that was created seventy years ago from the unification of three distinct Ottoman districts and in which there has been constant interference of neighbors, especially Iran and Turkey.[60]

The prospect of Arab leadership was expected to induce the Shi'a majority to support the Sunni Arab rulers.[61] Although Iraq had no common border with Palestine before 1948 and with Israel after that, Iraq has been consistently engaged in the Arab-Israeli dispute. This can also be explained by the relationships between state incoherence and revisionist and hegemonic aspirations, related to Pan-Arabism. The Sunni elite tries to legitimize its dominant position by highlighting the Arab identity of Iraqis (rather than sect or religion) as the basis for national identity. Thus, every Pan-Arab issue, notably the Palestine question, has become a major domestic issue for Iraq. The first mass anti-Zionist demonstration anywhere in the Arab world took place in the Iraqi capital in 1928. Since the 1930s, Iraqi elites saw the Palestinian issue both as an important element in the vision of an Iraqi-led Fertile Crescent and an ideological common denominator for the Sunni and Shi'a inside Iraq. Thus, Iraqi regional behavior has been closely intertwined with the building of an Iraqi nation-state and the persistent domination of the Sunni Arab elite.

Incoherent, Weak States

This factor is not unique to the Middle East, as numerous regimes and states in the Third World have faced domestic challenges to their legitimacy.[62] The European colonial powers exported the institutional structure of the territorial state and the idea of nationalism to the Third World, including the Middle East. Both the European state and nationalism were alien in these regions. In the Middle East, these structures and ideas were strange to those accustomed to the Islamic universalism of the Ottoman Empire.[63] While Israel and Iran, and to some extent Egypt,[64] enjoy a historical sense of identity that facilitates civic loyalty to the state, none of the other Middle Eastern states can make that claim.[65] Most states in the region, especially in the Fertile Crescent, are superficial colonial constructs and many of their inhabitants have not identified with them and with their colonially drawn artificial boundaries.[66]

What is unique about state legitimacy in the Middle East are the powerful pressures exerted on it from both above the state—due to the power of Pan-Arabism—and from below—by subnational, ethnic, and communal forces. As Hudson argues, "legitimate authority is hard to develop within state structures whose boundaries are inherently incompatible from those of the nation."[67] Almost all Arab regimes and states have faced the problem of low domestic legitimacy.[68]

The legitimacy problems have often been translated into threats to the security of state structures or regimes, both from Pan-Arab nationalist forces within and outside the boundaries of particular states (see below)[69] and from local ethnic forces (such as the Kurds or the Shiites in Iraq) who have opposed the imposition of artificial political boundaries and, having in many cases a strong territorial basis, demanded secession.[70] Arab political culture is permeated with primordial sentiments and includes stigmatized groups—racial, tribal, religious, ethnolinguistic, and class. Minorities in the Arab world lack either the Arab or the Islamic character, or both, that define the majority community. At least half of the Arab states are heavily fragmented with conflict-ridden divisions: Iraq, Syria, Lebanon, Jordan, Yemen, Morocco, Oman, Bahrain, and Sudan. There are a number of examples of extremely violent conflicts between Arab-Sunni majorities and minority groups, which appear to be primordial in nature, even though political and economic interests were involved in the conflict. Examples include the civil war in Yemen during the mid-1960s (between the ruling Zaydi imamate and the orthodox Shafi'is who supported the Republicans), the Lebanese civil war of 1975–91 (between the ruling Maronites and a coalition of mostly Muslim groups), Kurdish struggle for self-determination in Sunni-dominated Iraq in the 1960s and 1970s, revived following the Gulf War of 1991 (joined at that time by a Shiite rebellion in the south), and a secessionist struggle in South Sudan up to these days.[71] Although supposedly internal conflicts, in all these cases there was an intense involvement by neighboring states: Saudi Arabia and Egypt in the Yemeni civil war, Syria and Israel in Lebanon, Israel and Iran in the Kurdish rebellion (which, in turn, is also related to Turkey because of the Kurdish insurgency on its territory), and Israel and neighboring African states in the Sudanese case.[72] Thus, these conflicts show the close relations between domestic illegitimacy and regional conflicts so that domestic weakness leads to external intervention[73] and as a result to confrontations between regional neighbors such as Syria and Israel in Lebanon.[74]

As a result of the low levels of legitimacy and the weak and fractured national identities, a major mission of the armed forces has been the defense of the regime or a particular ruling elite against domestic threats to its control that emerge from its narrow base of support, or from a fragmented political system.[75]

The Palestinian Authority is the most recent example of the ultimate weak state, which lacks monopoly over the means of violence in its territory. There is a multiplicity of competing armed militias in the Palestinian Authority while it is unclear whether Arafat's Authority is able to control Palestinian violence against Israelis even if he wants to. However, it is also uncertain whether Arafat is interested in stopping the violence or uses it to get more concessions from Israel.

"Too Many States": Pan-Nationalism Transcending Boundaries

There have been powerful relations between Pan-Arabism and state weakness in the Arab world. On the one hand, Pan-Arabism has challenged the autonomy of the individual Arab states and undermined their legitimacy and the state formation process. On the other hand, the weakness, permeability, and illegitimacy of the Arab states increased the appeal of Pan-Arabism at the expense of territorial state identity and made it easier for a transnational ideology, and the powerful Arab states championing it, to penetrate the domestic systems of other Arab states. This appeal was both to elites, who were unable to consolidate their hold on power and were pushed in a Pan-Arab direction in search of legitimacy and support,[76] as well as to minorities who saw in Pan-Arabism an instrument for their integration in the larger Arab nation and hoped that their support of Pan-Arabism would demonstrate their nationalist credentials and thus facilitate their social mobility.

The challenge to the legitimacy of the regional order has been sharper in the Middle East than in other regions because the challenge has not been only from the substate, subnational level, as is common in the Third World, notably Africa. In the Middle East, the challenge has also been on the supranational level due to the strength of the revisionist ideology of Pan-Arabism, at least until the 1970s. Even if this challenge has become weaker today than it was until then, it is still stronger than in other regions. Pan-Arabism saw the Arab world as one nation sharing a common identity and a feeling of belonging, a single language, a shared glorious heritage, and one culture, while the various sovereign Arab states and their boundaries were perceived as artificial colonialist constructs that only divided the culturally homogeneous Arabs.[77] Accordingly, Pan Arabism posed a tough challenge to the separate existence and legitimacy of individual Arab states by underlying the unity of one Arab nation that supersedes the different Arab states.[78] Thus, the Arab agenda was full of calls for redrawing the regional political map, guided by the belief that there were too many colonially constructed states in the region. As a result, proposals for and attempts at unification of various Arab states,[79] besides the advocacy of the elimination of Israel, dominated regional politics.

On the whole, the effects of Pan-Arabism were both to increase the power of revisionism and to weaken the Arab states and thus to contribute to the problem of regional and domestic legitimacy in the region.[80]

Pan-Arabism has made the Palestinian issue both a constraint and an opportunity for Arab states, leading to hard-line policies. Pan-Arabism constrained the ability of Arab states to reach a comprehensive Arab-Israeli peace.[81] At the same time, radical policies vis-à-vis the Palestine issue provided a shield against threats to the legitimacy of the regime. Even if leaders striving for hegemony in the Arab world, like Nasser, Assad, and Saddam Hussein, manipulated the Pan-Arabist cause for their own particularistic power purposes,[82] it shows that Pan-Arabism has been a potent transborder political resource that has provided incentives for radical policies. Thus, Pan-Arabism exerted pressure on the individual Arab states to be loyal to the Palestine cause,[83] that is, to be hard-liners in the Arab-Israeli dispute and to adopt more intransigent positions than they would otherwise endorse,[84] including willingness to resort to military force, for example, regarding the Jordan River issue in the 1960s.[85] This led to radicalizing Arab positions in the Arab-Israeli conflict, encouraging the resort to force against Israel and thus also increasing Israel's sense of insecurity and use of force.

Despite the decline of Pan-Arabism as a force for Arab unification in recent decades and despite the expectation of rising state strength, as the recent Intifada shows, the support of the Palestinians constrains Arab leaders and moderate states from making peace with Israel, or at least from warming the relations with it. Thus, even Jordan and Egypt, which signed peace treaties with Israel, had to return their ambassadors from Israel, and other states had to sever their relations with the Jewish state.

A recent development is the emergence of the all-Arab El-Gazira cable television, widely watched in the whole Arab world. Such a creation of a Pan-Arab audience strengthens the nation at the expense of the particular state, which used to have a monopoly and full control over the sources of information.

Pan-Religion

A more recent source of domestic illegitimacy in the Middle East is Islamic fundamentalist movements opposing secular Arab regimes, notably in Egypt, Algeria, and Jordan. These movements are inspired and supported, most notably, by the Islamic republic of Iran since the Islamic revolution of 1979 (and later also by the Islamic regime in Sudan). Iran has challenged the legitimacy of the regimes in Saudi Arabia, Bahrain, Kuwait, Egypt, Iraq, and Jordan. Its questioning of the norm of sovereignty was not to redraw state boundaries in the region, as was Nasser's quest, so much as to change the character and sources of legitimacy of domestic regimes in existing states.[86] The Islamic revolution, and Islamic movements throughout the Arab world, also challenge the legitimacy of Israel, support violence against it, and oppose the peace process with it. The most active of these movements in the resort to violence are located in the occupied territories and in the weak states neighboring Israel: Jordan and Lebanon.

Stateless Refugees and the Right of Return: The Palestinian Refugees

The stateless Palestinian refugees raised both the levels of revisionism and of incoherence, especially among Israel's Arab neighbors. By proclaiming their right to return to their homes in what they defined as occupied Palestine, the refugees constituted an irredentist-revisionist force that undermined the legitimacy of the regional order and of the post-1949 boundaries. Since, on the whole, they maintained their separate Palestinian identity and were not allowed to integrate into the local societies in the Arab states in which they resided,[87] the refugees also jeopardized the coherence of these states, which included all of Israel's neighbors. Moreover, as the Palestinians organized themselves in political-military movements to fight Israel, they also presented a challenge to the sovereignty of the host Arab states.[88] These states were, in turn, constrained in their ability to control the Palestinian guerrillas because too tight a control would contradict the Pan-Arab commitment to the Palestinians to regain their occupied homeland.

Thus, they were a major burden for attempts at state-building in these states, most notably the most incoherent and weakest of Israel's neighbors—Jordan and Lebanon—where the refugees constituted a large portion of the population. They were also a revisionist-irredentist force in Syria and Egypt (especially before the 1967 war when Egypt still controlled the Gaza Strip, which was densely populated by refugees) and in a different way, they were also a restive element in the Israeli occupied territories after the 1967 war. The Palestinian paramilitary insurgent challenge to state authorities led to a civil war in Jordan (Black September in 1970) and made a major contribution to the eruption and longevity of the protracted civil war in Lebanon (1975–1991). These civil wars, in turn, brought about regional escalation since both Israel and Syria became involved in one way or another in these wars. The stateless Palestinians also revolted in the Intifada against the Israeli occupation between 1987 and the early 1990s. Palestinian revisionism contributed to the eruption of wars between Israel and Egypt (1956) and Syria and Egypt (1967) and the Israeli invasion of Lebanon (1982). The escalatory dynamics involved cross-border infiltrations and raids by Palestinian guerrillas against settlements inside Israel and Israeli retaliatory actions against targets in the Arab host countries. Such action-reaction dynamics raised the level of the security dilemma between Israel and its neighbors, which in turn contributed to large-scale violence in 1956, 1967, and 1982.[89]

Other related phenomenon that increase the state-to-nation imbalance in the ME include:

1. A conflict between "my state and my nation" as in the case of the Arab citizens of Israel.
2. The strength of revisionist ethnic nationalism-irredentism manifested by the "Greater state": "Greater Iraq"; "Greater Syria"; "Greater Israel."
3. From a seeming emergence of a post-Zionist Israel back again to Zionist Israel: the differences in this respect between the outcome of the May 1999 victory of the moderate Barak versus the victory of the nationalist Sharon are striking.
4. Israel also does not seem to be willing or able to make concession regarding the settlers and their right to stay in the occupied territories. This aggravates the conflict between Israelis and Palestinians.

INCENTIVES FOR REGIONAL CONFLICT
MANAGEMENT: THE RATIONAL-LIBERAL INDUCEMENTS

Because of the great dangers of a resort to violence and its transborder spread in a region with a high degree of state-to-nation incompatibility, there are powerful incentives for the regional states to cooperate in conflict management and to attempt to resolve their conflicts or to transcend them.[90] The incentives follow a liberal logic of a rational-egoist state that is interested in protecting its security and territorial integrity, but also in maximizing its "absolute gains" derived from economic development and social welfare.[91]

The idea of a "New Middle East" suggests that the post–Gulf War Middle East of the 1990s is in a similar situation to post–World War II Europe of the 1950s: fatigue from the costs involved in nationalist rivalry and supposedly a mutual desire to move away from the road of wars toward negotiated solutions. Thus it was reasonable to expect that the Middle East will also make a transformation from a focus on military power to economic considerations and from territorial nationalism to a quest for prosperity and from conflict-dominant region to cooperative arrangements with mutual benefits to all the parties involved.

Negative Security Externalities: Fears of Transborder Spread of Violence

State-to-nation incompatibility produces a great fear of negative security externalities,[92] namely, of a transborder spillover of conflicts that may spread from one state to another or escalate from communal violence to the regional level because of the transborder national linkages between the population in the different states. This produces incentives for cooperation among the regional states in escalation control and conflict reduction.

Such a fear of negative security externalities is especially powerful in the Middle East due to the national and religious transborder linkages among the Arabs who are split among a great number of states and also between the Palestinians in Arab states and under the Israeli occupation. Thus there are great fears of the spread of violence from the Israeli-Palestinian conflict to other arenas in the region. The Syrian presence in Lebanon leads to a concern about the escalation of violence in Lebanon to a Syrian-Israeli confrontation. Such concerns produce strong incentives to manage these conflicts.

There are also transborder linkages among the Kurds who live in Iraq, Iran, and Turkey. Thus, any one of these states is worried that any change in the status of the Kurds in one of these states will influence the Kurds in its own backyard. For example, a greater Kurdish autonomy in one state may lead to comparable demands in the others or that Kurdish refugees will destabilize their neighbors. This creates an incentive for cooperation among these states despite the numerous differences and conflicts among them.

The Lessons of the Cold War Period in
the Middle East: Limitations to Military Power

Although war is likely under state-to-nation incongruence, it did not solve the many dimensions of this incongruence in the Middle East. Thus, the Middle East parties have learned the futility of resorting to military power as a mechanism to resolve political conflicts.[93] Especially sobering in the Israeli case were the post-1967 conflicts, starting with the surprise and enormous casualties suffered by Israel in the 1973 war; the domestically disputed expansion of war aims in the 1982 Lebanon war; the surprise of the popular Palestinian rebellion in the Intifada in 1987–93; and the vulnerability demonstrated by the missile attacks on Israel's cities in the Gulf War.

The Arabs have learned that they are unable to defeat the militarily superior Israel,[94] which also enjoys U.S. support. Moreover, Israel's nuclear deterrence further raised the costs of attacking Israel.[95]

Fear of War and Its Consequences, Especially WMD

The costs involved with modern warfare have increased the fear of war. Such fears increased dramatically following the use of missile attacks against civilians in the Iran-Iraq war and the Gulf War.[96] There has been a growing sense of war weariness due to a "hurting stalemate."[97] Arabs and Israelis and others became tired of protracted conflicts and their heavy toll in blood and treasure, including the high economic costs of the arms race. The fear of spread of WMD following the Iran-Iraq war, the Cold War, and the Gulf War has especially increased the interest in regional conflict management.

From Military Nationalism to Economic Development

The image of a "New ME" seemed to be appealing and to provide incentives related to the "peace dividend" expectations for economic prosperity and social welfare—the economic benefits of peace and declining military costs.[98] This seemed to be linked to value change: from a world view of romantic heroism focusing on territorial nationalism to desires for economic prosperity and consumer goods and also quality of life and democratization.

Strengthening of the Arab State vs. the Arab Nation

Many observers agree that two related processes took place in recent decades:[99] Pan-Arabism declined while the individual territorial Arab state and its institutions strengthened at its expense. This has led to a much greater inclination to promote particular state interests rather than pan-national commitments. Such pragmatic orientations focused on economic considerations and as a result also on greater ties to the West. Pragmatism also means greater acceptance of Israel; hostility toward it was the major banner of the Arab nationalism.

Even on the Palestinian side there seemed to be a growing pragmatism and the victory of state over nation following the Oslo process: learning to coexist with Israel, learning from past mistakes about the failure of extremism, and the rise of a more pragmatic approach that focuses on state building and the control of the radicals rather than on an all-out jihad (holy war) with the Jewish state.

The Emergence of a "Post-Zionist Israel"?

In the 1990s Israel seemed to be going through an ideological-cultural shift that meant greater preference for the good life of economic prosperity at the expense of a nationalist-territorial agenda. Even if national-religious symbols still had powerful appeal to some sectors, secular-Western oriented values seemed to be on the ascendance. Indeed, the conflict between the secular and the religious camps in Israel appeared to be transcending the conflict with the Arabs. The works of the "New Historians" undermined nationalist myths and led to some changes in school textbooks. The concept of security appeared to be changing—less importance to control over territory and more to peacemaking and economic interdependence with the western economy and potentially also with the Middle East. In this context the rise of high-tech economy played a key role in raising the standard of living of many Israelis, increasing focus on material goods and greater integration with the West. The result of these cultural changes was the massive victory of Barak, as the leader of the peace camp in May 1999. This victory seemed to convey a departure from the ideals of "Greater Israel" and much greater willingness to compromise with the Arabs and the Palestinians.

Changing Balance of Threat

The peace process was to a large extent equated with the Gulf coalition and more generally as a coalition of status-quo actors against the common radical threat (Iraq, Iran, Islamic extremism). One of the foundations for the peace process was the belief that progress on the peace front would weaken considerably the power and appeal of extremists and radical forces and vice versa, namely, irresolution of the Israeli-Palestinian conflict will strengthen the standing of the radicals in the region.

THE RESPONSE: COLLECTIVE CONFLICT MANAGEMENT IN THE POST–COLD WAR ERA

These incentives created greater opportunities for regional conflict management in the post–Cold War era than was the case during the Cold War when regional institutions and cooperation were weak.

Weakness of Regional Organizations Under State-to-Nation Incongruence

For one thing, strong and coherent states are a prerequisite for effective organizations. Under state-to-nation incongruence, there is a prevalence of weak states, which lack of institutional capacities.

For regional institutions to be effective, states must be willing to transfer some authorities to the regional organizations. But certain conditions make them too insecure to be willing to do that. As noted, the state-to-nation incongruence increases the security dilemma in the region. Authoritarian states, which face domestic challenges to their regimes, will be especially reluctant to transfer authorities because they are concerned about external intervention in their domestic affairs. This is also true for incoherent states confronting secessionist/irredentist threats to their sovereignty. This will be especially the case if there are powerful revisionist/irredentist forces in the region that are inclined to intervene in the internal affairs of other states and pan-national (or pan-religious) forces that pose threats to the state's sovereignty.

In contrast to economic liberal expectations, under state-to-nation incongruence, states are less likely to behave according to economic rationality. The issues, which dominate the regional and domestic environments, are ideological and emotionally laden. This poses considerable domestic constraints on the freedom of action of leaders to make the compromises necessary for conflict resolution. It is much more difficult to make compromises once nationalist commitments and symbols are involved because these tend to be zero-sum indivisible goods. Such concerns might even provide incentives for some politicians to initiate diversionary strategies by externalizing domestic conflicts so as to shift the attention of public opinion from socioeconomic difficulties in the domestic arena to foreign threats and thus to mobilize domestic support for their hold over power.[100]

Many analysts argue that the Arab League (AL) was not only irrelevant to Arab-non-Arab conflicts but also faced great weaknesses regarding inter-Arab conflicts.[101] The Gulf Cooperation Council (GCC) was established in 1981 in order to promote cooperation and security and economic coordination among the six Gulf states. Yet, even jointly they were too weak to face either Iraq or Iran—the two key states in the Gulf. Instead, they had to rely on external assistance—from Egypt and Syria (the Damascus declaration of 1991) but mainly from the United States.[102]

On the one hand, these organizations are more alliances against common enemies than regional collective security organization. The exclusion of key states prevents effectiveness. The AL excludes key non-Arab regional states such as Iran, Turkey, and Israel,[103] while the GCC does not include the key Gulf states of Iran and Iraq.

On the other hand, the member states were unwilling to concede much authority to these organizations because they were insecure:

1. The domestic regime: authoritarian states, like all the Arab states, are insecure about the support of their public.

2. Weak states seek to build their own authority rather than to concede to supranational organizations.
3. Ideological rivalries in the Arab world between the revolutionary-radical and the conservatives.
4. Pan-national threats to sovereignty are especially powerful in the region and thus make the states even less inclined to concede authorities to the regional organizations.

The Arab League did not receive any supranational tools for imposing its decisions, and no Arab state was willing to concede its sovereignty for the Arab League. The structure of the AL reflected the Arab balance of power and the inter-Arab disputes. The League either did not intervene or was only effective in a limited way, for example in the Iraqi attempts to annex Kuwait in 1961 and 1990—there needed to be also international interventions in the two crises (by Britain in 1961 and the United States in 1990) in order to prevent such annexations. In the Jordanian civil war of 1970—the United States and Israel exercised deterrence versus Syria. In the Lebanese civil war Syria played the key role as the local hegemon and policeman.

A "NEW MIDDLE EAST": THE 1990S TRANSFORMATION—A MORE STABLE ORDER IN THE POST-COLD WAR AND POST-GULF WAR ERA

Two avenues of conflict management have become more available with the end of the Cold War: a liberal road of cooperative security and regional peacemaking and a realistic way of alliances facing common threats, based partly on the idea that the "neighbor of my neighbor is my friend." These alliances transcended previous patterns of ideological/nationalist rivalries.

Conflict Management through Cooperation and Peacemaking

Following the Gulf War the regional peace process was institutionalized starting from the 1991 Madrid Conference in which for the first time, most Arabs and Israelis met around the negotiating table. This led to the emergence of a status quo peace coalition, which used the following means to advance regional peace:

1. bilateral talks
2. Egypt as the regional broker
3. multilateral talks
4. economic cooperation.

The Bilateral Talks

The main avenue of discussion has been the bilateral negotiations on resolving the territorial and other conflicts between Israel and each of its neighbors.

The key accomplishments were the peace treaty with Jordan (1994) and the moderation of the key issue—the Palestinian track—through the Oslo process that transferred all the big cities of the West Bank and the Gaza Strip to the Palestinian National Authority (PNA) rule, creating a state-in-the-making that controls 98 percent of the Palestinian inhabitants of the occupied territories. The Oslo process persisted even under the nationalist Nethanyou government with the Hebron accord (1997) and the Wye Agreements (1998), but still did not go beyond the stage of interim agreements. Expectations became high following the electoral victory of Barak in 1999, who sought to transform the interim accords into a final-status agreement. The outline of such an agreement seemed to revolve around the so-called Beilin-Abu Mazen compromise, which included Palestinian control over the Gaza Strip and 92 to 94 percent of the West Bank, the annexation to Israel of a few blocs of big Jewish settlements, and a Palestinian capital on the outskirts of Jerusalem. The main accomplishment seemed to be an agreement by all status-quo parties, including Israel and the Palestinians, to resolve all outstanding issues by peaceful means.

Egypt as the Regional Broker

On the regional level there has been a special role for Egypt as a broker. This is due to the combined effect of a number of its attributes: the most powerful and populous Arab state; the first Arab state to make peace with Israel; a key pro-Western status-quo state while maintaining leadership aspirations in Arab world; and a stable state with a high extent of state-to-nation congruence. This places Egypt in a unique position to play the role of the regional broker. Indeed, Egypt is active in various mediation efforts between Israel and the Palestinians, most recently the Egyptian-Jordanian initiative to revive the negotiations between Israel and the Palestinians. Yet, as an Arab state, Egypt has a bias in favor of the Arab cause—or at least there are strong domestic constraints on its ability to play the honest unbiased broker. Egypt is also concerned about a potential Israeli hegemony, based on its superior military and economic resources, in case of a comprehensive regional peace that will pose a threat to its leadership role in the region. On the whole, as a key U.S. ally in the region, Egypt plays a moderating role in preventing an escalation to a regionwide war; but as leading Arab state, it also works against a full-blown normalization of relations between the Arab world and Israel.

The Multilateral Talks

Multilateral functional talks[104] were conducted between 1992 and 1996 in the framework of the Madrid Conference on arms control, economic cooperation, water, refugees, and the environment. This was an American idea for creating an environment conducive to regional peacemaking and especially for having spillover effects on the key bilateral negotiations through confidence building and Israeli integration into the region.[105] Thus, apart from addressing some important functional issues, the multilaterals were designed to facilitate the resolution of the difficult bilateral issues. The key regional participants were Israel, Egypt, Jordan, and the Palestinians. Most of the Gulf and North African states also took part. Syria and Lebanon were willing to take part only in the bilateral talks, while the rejectionist camp, including Iran, Iraq, Libya, and Sudan, opposed any talks with Israel. Such a boycott limited the ability to reach regionwide agreements. But the talks enjoyed wide international support including the sponsors—the United States and Russia and also the leading industrialized states—Japan, Canada, and the EU.

The talks peaked following Oslo in 1993–95 but collapsed in the aftermath of the rise to power of the Nethanyou government and the resultant slowdown in the peace process. Although the negotiations did not accomplish the expected deepening of the regional peace, they helped to broaden it. More states engaged in peaceful negotiations with Israel and some in the Gulf and North Africa established diplomatic relations with it.

Economic Cooperation

A key idea informing the peace process and its multilateral-functional aspect was Shimon Peres's "New Middle East" (1993). It was influenced by the process of European integration and the logic behind it: economic interdependence as providing powerful incentives for consolidating regional peace and creating constraints against defection and unilateral actions. From 1994 to 1997 a number of international economic meetings were held in the region and many suggestions were made for joint projects and regional cooperation in tourism and infrastructure and other economic fields. While Israel seemed to be eager for such cooperation, many Arabs, especially Egypt, became worried about Israeli economic domination and were reluctant to go ahead with cooperative plans, at least so long as the bilateral conflicts with Israel are not resolved.

Security Cooperation

Terrorism

A key component of the Oslo accords was to promote cooperative security between the Israelis and Palestinians so that the security coordination between the parties will be institutionalized through liaison offices and joint patrols, and especially so they will fight jointly against terrorism. Although this cooperation was important because of the great Israeli sensitivity to terrorist actions by the radical Islamic organizations, both sides became highly dissatisfied from it. The Palestinians felt misled by the Israeli policies to expand settlements and maintain its occupation. Israel was dissatisfied by the too-limited crackdown by the PNA against the radical organizations, especially when there is tension between the Palestinian Authority and Israel as is the case since the outbreak of the recent Intifada. Thus, measures that are taken by Israel for enhancing its security such as establishing checkpoints or blockades are seen by the Palestinians as oppressive occupation. Steps that are taken by the Palestinians to build a national consensus, such as not arresting or releasing militants from jail, are seen by Israel as posing a threat to its security. As a result, precisely when the security cooperation becomes especially important, it is not carried out effectively.

Arms Control in the Middle East

Although the issue of proliferation in the ME[106] has troubled the international community, relatively little was done to counter this trend and even the activities that did take place have had only limited effect. So far regional actors have never initiated any common policy to address the problem of proliferation, while all efforts to manage nonproliferation activities started by nonregional actors. Major regional actors did not sign the relevant nonproliferation treaties and if they did, they did not ratify them. Moreover, even countries that did sign and ratify these treaties ignore them while pursuing WMD, most notably Iran and Iraq.

Multilateral Working Group on Arms Control and Regional Security

The main achievement of the multilateral group on arms control and regional security was that both Israel and Arab states had discussions on such sensitive issues and tried to design regional security guidelines.[107] But the discussions reached a deadlock in 1995. Although there was an ambitious initiative to formulate a joint paper called "the vision paper" setting the guidelines for security regime in the Middle East, the draft was never concluded.[108] Egypt insisted on addressing the issue of Israel nuclear capabilities and its refusal to join the Non-Proliferation Treaty (NPT) before formulating any regional security mechanism.[109] Egypt also refused to join the Chemical Weapon Convention as long as Israel maintains the Arrow program, and avoids the NPT and the Missile Technology Control Regime (MTCR).[110] Israel has agreed to join the NPT two years after forging a comprehensive peace in the Middle East conditioned by strict and direct verification mechanism.[111] While Israel is most interested in opening the Arab's and Iranian's WMD programs and wishes to set them under international inspection, it wants to keep its own programs and facilities under secrecy. Recently a new idea was brought up, the "code of conduct" that calls for the limitation of ballistic missiles proliferation and transparency of missile programs.[112]

Proliferation of ballistic missiles and WMD in the Middle East has become one of the distinctive characteristics of the region. The phenomena has grown in scope and sophistication, and regional actors invest more and more in this field at the expense of conventional arms. This trend was intensified by the growing availability of materials and technology following the end of the Cold War. Despite increased nonproliferation efforts during the 1990s, these initiatives can be seen at most as partially successful. Although without these mechanisms countries like Iran and Iraq would have possessed nuclear capabilities by now, they still manage to promote their programs. The willingness of the supplier countries to enforce the regime seems limited, while in the case of China and North Korea such willingness does not exist. Thus the implications for the region are grim as the growing nonconventional capabilities, in the absence of any regional mechanism to regulate the situation, would destabilize the region even further.

Conflict Management through Alliances: The Changing Balance of Threat, and Linkages Among the Different Parts of the Middle East Security System

One manifestation of the idea of a regional security system is that based on geographical proximity as enhancing conflict among neighbors,[113] enduring rivalries among neighbors lead to alliances among the neighbors' neighbors irrespective of ideology and based on the logic that "the neighbor of my neighbor is my friend." In other words, two states that border a third state share a common threat in the third state; thus they tend to form an alliance against that state. Examples of alliances from the Middle East based on this realpolitik logic are:

1. The Iran-Iraq and Iraq-Syria rivalries led to the Iran-Syria alliance that has been in place since the 1980s (which has also a partial convergence of interests in Lebanon against Israel) despite the conflicting ideologies of the secular Ba'th in Syria versus the Iranian Islamic Fundamentalism.
2. The conflicts between Syria-Turkey and Syria-Israel led to the Turkey-Israel strategic partnership, which is implicitly anti-Syrian. This alliance also serves as an alternative security strategy for Israel instead of the Arab-Israeli peace process, especially substituting Israel-Syrian reconciliation. Two countervailing coalitions seemed to emerge: the pro-U.S. Israel-Turkey axis (which to a much more limited extent includes also Jordan) versus the alliance among the radicals—Iran-Syria, which recently made a rapprochement with Iraq.[114]

   The alliance between Turkey and Israel demonstrates the utility of the realist/alliance avenue for conflict management but also its limitations. On the one hand, it further reduces the likelihood of the Arabs to defeat Israel and thus reduces the likelihood of war and raises the chances of peace.[115] On the other hand, the alliance with Turkey can be viewed as dangerous and destabilizing because it increases the Arabs' security dilemma due to their fear of the Israeli-Turkish axis, which might be directed against them in the future. Thus, the Arabs might respond by countervailing moves such as armament and the formation of a balancing coalition. The result

of such moves could be the escalation of Middle East tensions and a growing danger of a regional war.

3. The Iraqi threat to Kuwait and Saudi Arabia has led to an alliance between
    the latter and Egypt and Syria (the Damascus Declaration of March
    1991),[116] although it has especially generated security dependence on the
    United States.

4. Interrelationships between the Arab-Israeli conflict and the Gulf: Security
    in the Arab-Israeli sector is connected with other parts of the Middle East,
    notably the Gulf.[117] What makes this connection especially strong are two
    related manifestations of the state-to-nation incongruence in the region,
    namely the transborder Pan-Arabism with its shared national, cultural, and
    linguistic links; and the centrality of the Palestinian problem in the Arab
    world and its effects on regime legitimacy. Pan-Islamic forces further in-
    crease the scope of the regional system to include Iran, which is con-
    nected, for example, to radical Islamic forces in Lebanon such as Hizbal-
    lah, who fights against Israel in south Lebanon and might entangle also the
    Syrians in potential escalations. Thus, the growing power of the revision-
    ist forces in the Gulf increases the dangers in the Arab-Israeli arena and
    vice versa—the weakening of the radical forces in the Gulf reinforces the
    chances for progress in the Arab-Israeli peace process. At the same time,
    progress in the Arab-Israeli peace process weakens the regional appeal of
    the Gulf revisionists, while slow-down of the process strengthens their re-
    gional influence. The linkage between the different parts of the ME was
    reinforced due to technological advances in the power-projection capa-
    bilities of airplanes and longer-range missiles. Thus, the Iraqi defeat in the
    1991 Gulf War made possible the initiation of the Arab-Israeli peace
    process, starting with the October 1991 Madrid Peace Conference. The de-
    feat of Iraq weakened the radical camp in the Arab world and so enabled
    the progress in the peace process under a U.S.-led coalition that was
    formed at the start of the Gulf crisis and after the Iraqi defeat was joined
    by Jordan and the Palestinians who allied with Iraq during the crisis. In the
    absence of the U.S. victory in the Gulf War, there would have been no
    progress in the Arab-Israeli peace process. Continued Iraqi control of
    Kuwait could have brought about major deterioration in regional stability.
    Progress in the peace process in the mid-1990s further weakened Saddam
    Hussein's standing in the Arab world and made it easier to apply and
    maintain the sanction and inspection regime vis-à-vis Iraq and also to con-
    tain Iranian and Islamic influence in the region.

**The Recent Crisis: Limitations to Regional Conflict Management Due
to the Continuing State-to-Nation Incongruence of the "Old Middle East"**

The major changes, which took place in the post–Cold War Middle East, were
in the regional balance of capabilities due to the defeat of the radical forces in

the Gulf War and the loss of Soviet support. The result was an inability to form a regional countervailing coalition against the peace process. Thus third parties like Jordan and the Palestinians "bandwagoned" with the U.S.-led peace process. But there has been insufficient change of intentions regarding revisionist aspirations and ideologies or the strengthening of incoherent, weak states.

The forces of ethnic nationalism, religion, and the derived territorial aspirations are still powerful, while there is a relative weakness of the state and its economic and pragmatic considerations. Thus, despite the decline of Pan-Arabism, transborder support for the Palestinians and anti-Zionist resentment still constrain moderate leaders in the Arab world and poses difficulties for the peace process. There is a persistent and some might even argue an increasing power of religion as manifested by the conflicts over the holy sites in Temple Mount and Haram El-Sharif.

In contrast to the expectations about the emergence of a post-Zionist Israel, the issues of the unity of Jerusalem under Israeli control and the Jewish settlements in the territories still constrain the diplomatic flexibility of Israeli leaders. On the Palestinian side, anti-Zionism is still strong as well as nationalist-religious passions and commitments to Jerusalem and other symbols. Thus, the anti-Israeli propaganda in textbooks and the intransigent positions regarding the final-status agreement. The gulf between the parties is so big that the highest extent of violence erupted after the greatest Israeli concessions. This shows that the internal debate inside Israel between doves and hawks might have been at least partly irrelevant for the Palestinian positions. This applies especially to a major state-to-nation incongruence: the Palestinian demand for the right of return of the Palestinian refugees to Israel—which the Palestinians see as their homeland. There is almost a consensus in Israel rejecting such a demand because it will transform the nature of the state from a Jewish state to a binational state.

At the same time, the problem of state weakness is also still relevant. The presence of Palestinian refugees weakens the Jordanian and Lebanese states. The weakness of the Lebanese state is reflected in its lack of control over the militias in the border area with Israel; this can lead to an escalation that might involve Israel and Syria. Iraq is fragmented and in Syria the rule of the Alawite minority makes it more difficult to make concessions on nationalist issues. Despite its relatively high level of modernization even Israel is not a coherent state in two respects—the difficulties to rein in the settlers beyond the green line, and the Arab minority, which is torn between its identity as citizens of the state of Israel and its nationalist identification with the Palestinians and the resentment at its discrimination in Israel.

The ultimate weak state is the Palestinian authority with its absence of a monopoly of the use of means of violence and the multiplicity of armed militias, both Islamic radicals (Hamas and jihad) and from Arafat's own organization (the Tanzim—the Fatah Hawks) and also a great number of competing security organizations. The big question is whether Arafat is unwilling or unable to rein in violence.

Under this kind of conflict the security dilemma is especially intense: what Israel perceives to be self-defense, the Palestinians see as oppressive, hegemonic, and aggressive behavior. What the Palestinians view as a struggle for national liberation, the Israelis see as a threat to their security and even existence. At any rate, in contrast to "the decline of territory" thesis, both sides seem still to be excited by religious and nationalist symbols and as a result to attribute crucial importance even to small inches of territory. At the very least there are severe domestic constraints on their ability to make concessions on these issues.

In contrast to the mutually moderating effects between the outcome of the Gulf War and the Arab-Israeli peace process in the first half of the 1990s, more recently there seem to be mutually reinforcing destabilizing effects between the endurance of the revisionists in the Gulf and the problems in the peace process. Cracks in the inspection regime in Iraq, growing opposition in the Arab world to the suffering of the Iraqi people as a result of the sanctions, and the endurance of Saddam in power undermined the U.S.-led Gulf coalition in the late 1990s and thus also reduced the support in the peace process and renewed hopes among Palestinian radicals that a countervailing anti-U.S. and anti-Israeli coalition might be formed in the region against the peace process, with some support of external powers like Russia, France, and China, which oppose U.S. global hegemony and its application to the Middle East.

On the other hand, the eruption of the Al-Aqsa Intifada in fall 2000 emboldened Saddam Hussein to further challenge the sanctions and the no-fly zones, and more generally U.S. hegemony in the region. Saddam encouraged radicalization of the Intifada and the resort to violence against Israel. This violence severely jeopardized the peace process and, in turn, made it more difficult to apply the sanctions against Iraq because of rising opposition in the Arab world to the supposed "double standard" applied by the West vis-à-vis Israel in contrast to the harsh treatment of the Iraqi people. Following the eruption of the Intifada, there has been some rapprochement between key Arab states (notably Egypt and Syria) and Iran with Iraq in November 2000.

The deterioration of the sanction regime and the total collapse of the Gulf Coalition might enable Saddam Hussein to play a more central role in ME politics. He might then take advantage of the violence in the Israeli-Palestinian and Israeli-Lebanese fronts for his own power aspirations. The great danger for the future is that this scenario might destabilize the region and lead to a regionwide escalation that might involve Israel and a number of Arab states and would also challenge the stability of pro-U.S. regimes in the Arab world, like Egypt and Jordan and the oil-rich countries—Saudi Arabia and the small Gulf states.

THE GLOBAL CONFLICT MANAGEMENT: THE "NEW WORLD ORDER" AND ITS RESTRAINING EFFECTS

Under the shadow of the weakness of regional conflict management, global management becomes crucial. There are two variants of global influences in the post–Cold War era. The first variant is transborder economic globalization and the derived loss of importance of nationalism and territory in contrast to the rising importance of economic prosperity, trade, markets, and high-tech. Although these forces are influential also in the ME, especially in Israel, on the whole they are insufficient to overwhelm the state-to-nation forces.

Much more relevant is the second global variant—the diplomatic-strategic: the emergence of U.S. hegemony and its moderating effects. In the post-1973 period the United States gradually managed to exclude the Soviet Union from involvement in the Arab-Israeli conflict and to establish a partial hegemony over the region, becoming the common great-power patron of Israel, Egypt, Jordan, and the Gulf states. The U.S. hegemony became more complete with the end of the Cold War and Soviet disintegration[118] when other Arab parties to the conflict, notably the Palestinians and Syria, lost the possibility of recourse to a rival superpower patron, who could shield them from the adverse effects and costs of opposition to U.S.-led peacemaking efforts.

The United States has played a leading role in cooling the Arab-Israeli conflict since the 1973 war. U.S. leadership helped to moderate the conflict, to initiate an Arab-Israeli peace process, and specifically to establish a cold peace between Israel and Egypt in 1978–79.[119] Following the Gulf War, a more comprehensive cold peace was established, manifested in the Madrid process involving Israel, the Palestinians, Jordan, and most Arab states.[120] It is extremely hard to imagine the progress in the Arab-Israeli peace process since 1973 without the active mediation and the financial assistance of the United States to Israel and to the two parties that signed peace treaties with it—Egypt and Jordan. The end of the Cold War, the collapse of Soviet power, and the blow inflicted by the United States to Iraqi military power, and thus to Arab radicalism, in the Gulf War, are essential for understanding the accomplishments in Arab-Israeli diplomacy in the 1990s. The Gulf War dramatically demonstrated the security dependence of both Israelis and most Arab states on U.S. military power. U.S. economic power also provides it with important leverage both through direct financial assistance to key regional players and through the provision of credit and technology transfers. Thus, U.S. hegemony has created a powerful realpolitik logic in favor of peace, even if only a cold one: those who join the peace camp benefit in the security, economic, and diplomatic fields, while those who oppose the peace pay a heavy price in these domains without being compensated by a countervailing force. This explains why pragmatic, rather than idealist, leaders "bandwagoned" with Pax Americana in the 1990s, while ideologues on both sides (Arab radicals and Islamic elements and right-wing nationalists in Israel) rejected the peace process and indeed faced heavy diplomatic, economic, and military sanctions imposed by the hegemon. Thus, the Arabs interested in joining the new world order had to join the U.S.-led peace process: "If the price of joining the new world order was a begrudging accommodation with Israel, it seemed just about worth paying—particularly as the old currency of belligerent rhetoric was now evidently worthless."[121]

The Gulf War demonstrated that regional threats are as serious, if not more so than external ones. As a result, the Gulf states realized that a U.S. presence is an essential element in any security scheme. For these states, regional security is tightly connected to the American power-projection capability. But Iran and Iraq view this presence as a major threat to their independence and interests.

The United States has employed the various strategies available to a hegemonic power for promoting a transition from a regional cold war (crisis management) to cold peace (conflict reduction):

1. Restraining its client Israel (notably in times of local wars, when it posed a threat to Arab capitals, such as at the end of the 1967 and 1973 wars, or when its use of force could potentially cause an escalation of the conflict, such as during the 1956 war and the Gulf War) and applying diplomatic and economic pressure to induce its moderation in the regional peace process, for example, during the reassessment crisis of spring 1975.[122]
2. In recent years, and especially after the outbreak of the Intifada in recent months, the United States restrains Israeli reactions to the provocative acts committed against it from Lebanon and the Palestinian territories so as to prevent escalation in these two fronts.[123]
3. Reassuring its allies through arms supply and security cooperation and military assistance (to Israel, Jordan, the Gulf states and post–Camp David Egypt), crucial financial assistance (to Israel, Egypt, and Jordan) and security guarantees (to the Gulf states). The reassurance to Israel is designed to make it easier for Israel to make territorial concessions to its Arab neighbors.
4. Coercing revisionist regional powers by sanctions and use of force: In contrast to its attitude toward its friends in the region, the United States has imposed economic sanctions and arms embargoes on states perceived to be hostile toward it, its regional interests, and the advancement of the peace process, specifically Iraq, Libya, Iran, and Sudan.[124] A notable example of a containment strategy toward revisionist powers by the imposition of diplomatic and economic sanctions and an arms embargo is the Clinton administration's dual containment vis-à-vis both Iran and Iraq.[125] When diplomatic and economic means were insufficient for defending its key interests, the United States was willing to resort to military means to maintain the regional order. Washington exercised deterrence,[126] later compellence, and when both of these strategies failed to prevent aggression, ultimately was willing to fight and defeat a regional aggressor (Iraq in the Gulf War).[127]
5. Establishing a regional security regime in the Gulf following the 1991 war. The failure of the regional balance of power to deter Iraq, the inability to establish regional collective security due to revisionist status quo split and the conditions in the aftermath of the war led to the internationalization of security arrangements. Some of the U.S. objectives in the Gulf included

preserving regional stability, preventing a WMD buildup by either Iran or Iraq, containing Iraqi aggression and Iran's support of radical Islamic forces in the region, and toppling Saddam Hussein. The United States employs a number of instruments to meet its objectives: economic sanctions, weapon inspection, pressures on external suppliers (notably China and Russia), a powerful military presence, no-fly zones in northern and southern Iraq, limited military strikes against Iraq, and support for the Iraqi opposition.[128]

6. Playing an active mediating role in moderating the level of the Arab-Israeli conflict. Since 1967 successive U.S. administrations have undertaken a long series of unilateral diplomatic efforts intended to promote the reduction of this conflict under exclusive U.S. auspices.[129] Moreover, the United States serves, in fact, as the guarantor of the accords reached between Israelis and Arabs since 1973 and as a final arbiter/referee in case of disagreements among the parties about the interpretation of a settlement. For example, an important component of the Israeli-Egyptian disengagement agreements in the Sinai in the aftermath of the Yom-Kippur war has been the U.S. role in monitoring and verifying the implementation of the agreements, including an American commitment to administer early-warning stations at the buffer zone and to conduct regular reconnaissance flights over the demilitarized area established by the accord. In the Camp David accords the United States was active in the establishment and manning of the international force that was deployed in the Sinai.[130]

7. Providing financial compensations to those who join the peace process and are willing to make concessions. Thus, Israel and Egypt have become the beneficiaries of generous assistance following the Camp David accords.[131] To a lesser degree, this is also true for Jordan and the Palestinians after signing accords with Israel in the 1990s.

As for the U.S. willingness to play the role of the hegemon in the Middle East, it stems from the intrinsic importance of the region to U.S. interests due to the location of vast oil resources there. This produces an American interest in maintaining good relations with the Arab states. Such an interest conflicts with the U.S. political, ideological, moral commitment to Israel's security. The United States tries to reconcile this conflict of interests by advancing the Arab-Israeli peace process.

U.S. attempts during the Cold War to construct an Arab-Israeli grand alliance against the supposedly shared Soviet threat failed because local parties diverge from great powers by tending to focus on regional threats rather than on global ones. In contrast to the highly dubious and disputed Soviet threat to the regional states, following its 1990 invasion of Kuwait, Iraqi revisionism has posed a true shared threat to the United States (because of the threat to the regional oil resources), Israel, and status-quo Arab states. Thus, the United States was able to lead a multinational coalition, which included most Arab states, and in the aftermath of its victory over Iraq, to promote the Arab-Israeli peace process.

While U.S. involvement has been conducive to the establishment of cold peace in some parts of the Middle East, peacemaking has not progressed much beyond this level. Thus, the threat of war has not disappeared completely from Israeli-Egyptian relations (despite their having been at peace since 1979), let alone from the Israeli-Syrian arena, where there are still many unresolved substantive issues related to the recognition of Israel, normalization of Syrian-Israeli relations, security arrangements, and the legitimacy of boundaries. Even in the two Arab states that have signed peace agreements with Israel (Egypt and Jordan), there are still significant elites who continue to regard Israel as illegitimate and oppose the development of transnational relations with it, at least partly because of the lack, thus far, of a permanent settlement of the Palestinian problem. Moreover, the progress made in the Middle Eastern peace process is still reversible and vulnerable to domestic changes and to changing strategies by the leadership of the respective parties. Thus the peace process at its current stage is still heavily dependent on U.S. mediation in both the Syrian and the Palestinian tracks. Continued Egyptian and Jordanian commitment to the peace process and to broker between Israel and its adversaries is conditioned by the expectation of persistent U.S. assistance to them. U.S. coordination is also essential for the security cooperation between Israel and the Palestinians against the militant/terrorist elements; and U.S. monitoring seems to be essential for ensuring the compliance of the Palestinians and Israelis with the U.S.-brokered cease-fire agreement of mid-June 2001.

The Limitations to the U.S. Hegemonic Management

1. There are inherently greater difficulties for an external power to pacify communal, nationalist, religious violence under state-to-nation incongruence like the Israeli-Palestinian clashes, in contrast to the somewhat more manageable interstate conflicts.
2. Countervailing forces that oppose U.S. hegemony are emerging, even though they are still weak: Russia, Iraq, Iran, Islamic forces, radical movements, and terrorist forces like Bin-Laden. In a different way the Europeans, notably the French, also oppose U.S. hegemony and seek a greater role in Middle East diplomacy. At any rate, there is an increasing economic and diplomatic engagement of the EU in the Middle East.
3. Rising resentment against the United States in the ME leads to the weakening of the anti-Iraqi Gulf coalition.[132] This is derived from a combination of a growing opposition in the Arab world to the sanctions regime against Iraq and to its isolation and sympathy to the suffering of its people and the perception that there is a "double standard" in the attitude to Israel, especially following the eruption of the Intifada because of the supposedly

pro-Israeli bias of the United States under the influence of its domestic politics.

Potential Sources of Future Instability

The following are some of the potential sources of instability:

1. U.S. disengagement from the region will deprive the region of the most effective broker, banker, policeman, referee, and monitor. Following the overcommitment of the Clinton administration, the Bush administration showed some signs of disengagement, which had destabilizing effects, although most recently it seems that the administration is returning to the regional arena as the "peacemaker."[133]
2. Collapse of the sanction regime vis-à-vis Iraq and renewal of its build-up of WMD and its aggression vis-à-vis its neighbors.
3. Rise of an antihegemonic, countervailing coalition that might include Russia, China, Iran, Iraq, and other radical forces.
4. Growing split between the Europeans and the United States on the management of the ME, which might be affected also by a potential deterioration in other issues of their relations.
5. Spread of WMD, most likely from Russia, China, and North Korea to Iran and Iraq.
6. Water scarcity will aggravate existing conflicts, notably between Turkey, Iraq and Syria, and Israel and its neighbors.
7. No progress in the peace process and further deterioration in the Israeli-Palestinian violence might lead to regional escalation if the following events take place:

   • Major terrorist actions against Israel
   • Collapse of the Palestinian authority
   • Success of an Islamic revolution in the Palestinian territories or in a key Arab state, notably Egypt
   • Escalation at the Lebanese border that would involve also Syria
   • These scenarios are especially likely to lead to escalation if U.S. hegemony collapses. If that does not happen, the likelihood of a regionwide confrontation (rather than protracted low-intensity warfare between Israelis and Palestinians) is unlikely in the foreseeable future

CONCLUSION

This chapter has shown that there is a multiplicity of security problems in the Middle East. The state-to-nation incongruence leads to problems on a number of levels: interstate, transborder/transnational, and subnational/domestic. The threats include conventional wars, spread of WMD, civil wars, intervention in domestic affairs of other states, and forms of low-intensity conflict such as guerrilla warfare and terrorism. The dangers apply to the three main theaters of the region: the Arab-Israeli, the Northern Tier, and the Persian Gulf. Being part of a single regional security system means that there are interrelationships among the three arenas, especially in affecting the balance of threat and alliance formation.

The intensity of the security problems produces powerful incentives for rational status-quo states to cooperate in collective conflict management and to resolve regional conflicts. Indeed, in the recent decade there were numerous attempts to resolve conflicts in the region or even to transcend them through multilateral-functional cooperation. Yet, the state-to-nation incongruence generates powerful domestic and ideological constraints on the possibilities for effective conflict management and resolution. Thus, the attempts at regional conflict resolution and conflict transcendence in the Middle East face major difficulties.

As a result, global forces and actors become important for regional management. Under great-power hegemony, the global management becomes more effective than in other types of great-power regional engagement. Thus, U.S. hegemony in the aftermath of the Cold War and the Gulf War has made some headway in regional conflict management. But even a hegemon is quite limited in its managerial abilities and it is, at best, able to bring about crisis prevention and conflict reduction (cold peace) rather than conflict resolution (warm peace). When the state-to-nation incongruence is especially extreme and conflict management is very problematic, as in the Israeli-Palestinian case, the hegemon might have to focus on the lower forms of conflict management: crisis management and cessation of hostilities besides the efforts to resolve the conflict or, at least to reduce it. When the hegemon faces revisionist powers like Iran and Iraq, who pose threats to regional conflict management, it might resort also to coercion and military means and use containment, deterrence, and compellence strategies.

A potential decline of U.S. hegemony in the ME will bring greater levels of instability and spread of violence. At the same time, the current hegemony, despite all the major problems and limitations that it faces, offers some prospects for effective regional conflict management and conflict reduction to the extent that the hegemon persists in an active engagement in the region. Yet, in order to reach successful conflict resolution, the regional parties will have to overcome the various elements of the state-to-nation incongruence through strengthening the status-quo states and their full control over their territory, including a Palestinian state and Lebanon, and weakening the nationalist/revisionist elements by reining in militants, and by resettling, on the one hand, Jewish settlers from the occupied territories inside the boundaries of the state of Israel, and, on the other hand, Palestinian refugees in the Palestinian state rather than inside Israel.

NOTES

1. Saad Eddin Ibrahim, "Ethnic Conflict and State Building in the Arab World," in *Powderkeg in the Middle East*, ed. Geoffrey Kemp and Janice Stein (Washington, D.C.: American Association for the Advancement of Science, 1995), 45. With only 8 percent of the world's population, the Arab world and ME had some 25 percent of all the world's armed conflicts since 1945. Most of these conflicts have been ethnically based. Moreover, in contrast to Ibrahim, many conflicts of what he considers as "interstate" and not ethnic conflicts, like the Arab-Israeli conflict, are also ethnic or, more precisely, what I call here state-to-nation conflicts.

2. Benjamin Miller, "Explaining Regional War-Propensity: The Middle East in a Comparative Perspective," paper presented at the annual meeting of the International Studies Association, Washington, D.C., 16–20 February 1999; idem, "The Sources of Regional War and Peace: Integrating the Effects of Nationalism, Liberalism, and the International System," paper presented at the annual meeting of the American Political Science Association, Atlanta, 2–5 September, 1999; idem, "When Regions Become Peaceful: Explaining Transitions from War to Peace," *REGIS Working Papers* (McGill University, 2001); idem, "The Global Sources of Regional Transitions from War to Peace," *Journal of Peace Research* 38, no. 2 (March 2001); idem, "Between War and Peace: Systemic Effects on the Transition of the Middle East and the Balkans from the Cold War to the Post–Cold War Era," *Security Studies* 11, no. 1 (Autumn 2001): 1–52. See also James Mayall, *Nationalism and International Society* (Cambridge: Cambridge University Press, 1990); Stephan Van Evra, "Hypotheses on Nationalism and War," in *Global Dangers—An International Security Reader*, ed. Sean M. Lynn-Jones and Steven E. Miller (Cambridge: MIT Press, 1995), 251–85.

3. On the definition of state and nation, see Walker Connor, *Ethnonationalism: The Quest for Understanding* (Princeton, N.J.: Princeton University Press, 1994), 90–117; and Lowell W. Barrington, "'Nation' and 'Nationalism': The Misuse of Key Concepts in Political Science," *PS: Political Science and Politics* (December 1997): 712–16. Especially useful is Barrington's distinction between state and nation.

4. For an elaborate discussion, see the sources cited in footnote 2.

5. See Barry Buzan, *People, States and Fear: An Agenda for International Security Studies in The Post Cold War Era* (Chapel Hill: University of North Carolina Press, 1991), chapter 2; Stephan R. David, "Explaining Third World Alignment," *World Politics* 43 (1991): 233–56; Stephan R. David, *Choosing Sides: Alignment and Realignment in the Third World* (Baltimore: Johns Hopkins University Press, 1991); Brian Job, *The Insecurity Dilemma: The National Security of Third World States* (Boulder, Colo.: Lynne Rienner, 1992); Mohammed Ayoob, *The Third World Security Predicament* (Boulder, Colo.: Lynne Rienner, 1995); K. J. Holsti, *The State, War and the State of War* (Cambridge: Cambridge University Press, 1996).

6. For an elaborate discussion, see Miller, "Explaining Regional War-Propensity."

7. For studies that show that ethnic/national claims are major sources of territorial conflicts, see Robert Mandel, "Roots of Modern Interstate Border Dispute," *Journal of Conflict Resolution* 24 (1980); and David Carment, "The International Dimensions of Ethnic Conflict: Concepts, Indicators and Theory," *Journal of Peace Research* 30 (1993): 137–50; Paul Huth, "Enduring Rivalries and Territorial Disputes, 1950–1990," in *A Road Map to War*, ed. Paul F. Diehl (Nashville, Tenn.: Vanderbilt Univ. Press, 1999), 53–57.

8. Will H. Moore and David R. Davis, "Transnational Ethnic Ties and Foreign Policy," in *The International Spread of Ethnic Conflict: Fear, Diffusion, and Escalation*, ed. David Lake and Donald Rothchild (Princeton, N.J.: Princeton University Press, 1998).

9. See the useful studies in David Lake and Donald Rothchild, *The International Spread of Ethnic Conflict*; and David Carment and Patrick James, eds., *Wars In The Midst of Peace* (Pittsburgh, Pa.: University of Pittsburgh Press, 1997).

10. Notably in Asia such as Kashmir, China-India, Iran-Iraq, Iraq-Kuwait, and Syria-Turkey.

11. Especially in Africa: including conflicts between Ethiopia and Somalia, Libya and Chad, and over the Western Sahara. See Mohammed Ayoob, "Unrevealing the Concept: National Security in the Third World," in *The Many Faces of National Security in the Arab World*, ed. Bahgat Korany, Paul Noble, and Rex Byrnen (London: Macmillan, 1993): 42–43.

12. On the artificial creation of states and borders in the Middle East by colonialist powers, see David Fromkin, *A Peace To End All Peace: Creating the Modern Middle East 1914–1922* (New York: Holt and Company, 1989) and others cited in Ayoob, *The Third World Security Predicament*, 44, footnote 35; Avi Shlaim, *War and Peace in the Middle East: A Concise History* (New York: Penguin, 1995); and Avraham Sela, *The Decline of the Arab-Israeli Conflict: Middle East Politics and the Quest for Regional Order* (Albany: State University of New York Press, 1998).

13. See Mark Zacher, "The Territorial Integrity Norm: International Boundaries and the Use of Force," *International Organization* 55, no. 2 (Spring 2001): 215–50; Robert Jackson, *Quasi-States: Sovereignty, International Relations and the Third World* (Cambridge: Cambridge University Press, 1990).

14. As Gause suggests: "unlike other post-colonial areas , however, in the Middle East the challenges to the state have been as likely to advocate amalgamation of the existing states into a larger entity as their fragmentation into smaller units" (Gregory F. Gause, "Sovereignty, Statecraft, and Stability in the Middle East," *Journal of International Affairs* 45 [1992]: 444).

15. In a recent comprehensive work on war-proneness, Singer and Geller cite a number of quantitative studies that underline the especially high war-proneness of the Middle East as compared to other regions in the post–World War II era (Daniel S. Geller and J. David Singer, *Nations at War* [Cambridge: Cambridge University Press, 1998], 98–100). See the table in Holsti, *The State, War and the State of War*, 22; and K. J. Holsti, *Peace and War: Armed Conflicts and International Order 1648–1989* (Cambridge: Cambridge University Press, 1991); see also Martin Sherman and Gideon Doron, "War and Peace as Rational Choice in the Middle East," in *Regional Security in The Middle East: Past, Present and Future*, ed. Zeev Maoz (London: Frank Cass, 1997), 72; and the sources cited in Maoz, *Regional Security*, 35. Contrasted with other regions, the risk of international war in the Middle East does not seem to have diminished. Three of the five international wars that took place since 1980 were in the ME (Iran-Iraq, Lebanon, and the Gulf War), and a fourth (the Afghanistan War) was on the fringes of the region. The 1980s and 1990s have also witnessed the spread of civil wars throughout the region, which have caused substantially more human suffering than the civil wars in other regions. See Maoz, *Regional Security*, 14. For the costs of ME wars see Kemp and Stein, *Powderkeg in the Middle East*, 46.

16. On the struggles for hegemony, see Elie Podeh, *The Quest For Hegemony in the Arab World: The Struggle Over the Baghdad Pact* (Leiden: Brill, 1995); and Sela, *The De-*

cline of the Arab-Israeli Conflict. On the Arab cold war, see Malcolm Kerr, *The Arab Cold War 1958–1967: A Study of Ideology in Politics,* 2d ed. (London: Oxford University Press, 1967).

17. Sela argues that the most important Pan-Arabist leader, Nasser, was more interested in Egyptian hegemony in the Arab world than in a radical change of the regional state system (*The Decline of the Arab-Israeli Conflict,* 19–20). For a critical overview of the debate on the national interests versus ideological reasons for Nasser's advocacy of Pan-Arabism, which reaches a similar conclusion to Sela's, see Shibley Telhami, *Power and Leadership in International Bargaining: The Path to the Camp David Accords* (New York: Columbia University Press, 1990), 92–93.

18. Sela, *The Decline of the Arab-Israeli Conflict,* 47–48.

19. Gause, "Sovereignty, Statecraft, and Stability in the Middle East," 448–51; Sela, *The Decline of the Arab-Israeli Conflict,* 44–47.

20. Daniel Byman, "After the Storm: U.S. Policy Toward Iraq Since 1991," *Political Science Quarterly* 115, no. 4 (Winter 2000–2001): 493–516.

21. On the multiplicity of territorial and boundary conflicts among states, see Geoffrey Kemp and Jeremy Pressman, *Point of No Return: The Deadly Struggle for Middle East Peace* (Washington, D.C.: Brookings Institute Press, 1997), 37, 163–74. On the Gulf, see Richard Schofield, "Border Disputes in the Gulf: Past, Present, and Future," in *The Persian Gulf at the Millennium,* ed. Gary Sick and Lawrence Potter (New York: St. Martin's Press, 1997), 127–65; and George E. Joffe, "Disputes Over State Boundaries in the Middle East and North Africa," in *The Middle East in Global Change,* ed. Laura Guazzone (New York: St. Martin's Press, 1997), 58–94. On the danger of interstate conventional wars and preparation for it by an arms race, see Kemp and Pressman, *Point of No Return,* 200–202.

22. Indeed, some recent limited progress due to the U.S. role is reported in the *New York Times* (25 April 2001). Following the killing of twenty Israeli youngsters at a Tel Aviv discotheque in early June, the Israeli threat of retaliation and massive international pressure led Arafat to accept an unconditional cease-fire. The CIA director came to the region to arrange a stable cease-fire agreement that is intended to lead to confidence-building measures and eventually to peace negotiations if the cease-fire holds.

23. Helena Cobban, *The Israeli-Syrian Peace Talks: 1991–1996 and Beyond* (Washington, D.C.: U.S. Institute of Peace Press, 1999).

24. Joseph Matar, "The Lebanon Trap," *The Jerusalem Report* (26 February 2001), 26–27.

25. Joseph Matar, "The Lebanon Trap," 26–27.

26. Anwar Gargash, "Prospects for Conflict and Cooperation in the Gulf Toward the Year 2000," in *The Persian Gulf at the Millennium,* ed. Gary Sick and Lawrence Potter (New York: St. Martin's Press, 1997), 321–23.

27. Kemp and Stein, *Powderkeg in the Middle East,* 69.

28. On the Iran-UAE conflict see Kemp and Stein, *Powderkeg in the Middle East,* 21.

29. Kemp and Stein, *Powderkeg in the Middle East,* 71.

30. On Iran, see Sick and Potter, *The Persian Gulf at the Millennium,* 22–23. On the Gulf, see Gargash, "Prospects for Conflict and Cooperation in the Gulf Toward the Year 2000," in Sick and Potter, 319–40.

31. On the current disputes between Iran-Iraq, see Kemp and Pressman, *Point of No Return,* 163–65; and Kemp and Stein, *Powderkeg in the Middle East,* 19–20.

32. Joffe, "Disputes Over State Boundaries in the Middle East and North Africa," 68–69.

33. Kemp and Stein, *Powderkeg in the Middle East,* 21, 73.

34. Kemp and Pressman, *Point of No Return,* 165–66; Kemp and Stein, *Powderkeg in the Middle East,* 20; Joffe, "Disputes Over State Boundaries in the Middle East and North Africa," 69–70.

35. On conflicts over water, see Kemp and Stein, *Powderkeg in the Middle East,* 16–19. On Syria-Turkey disputes over boundaries, water, and the Kurdish problem, see Kemp and Pressman, *Point of No Return,* 119.

36. See Efraim Inbar, "Regional Implications of the Israeli-Turkey Strategic Partnership," *The Middle East Review of International Affairs (MERIA)* 5, no. 2 (June 2001).

37. See Kemp and Stein, *Powderkeg in the Middle East,* 30–35; Kemp and Pressman, *Point of No Return,* 197–200; Feldman, *Nuclear Weapons and Arms Control in the Middle East*; Gerald Steinberg, *Arms Control and Non-Proliferation: Developments in the Middle East,* Security and Policy Series Paper #44 (Israel: Bar Ilan University, BESA Center for Strategic Studies, 2000).

38. Simor Hersh, *Samson Option* (New York: Vintage Books, 1993); Shai Feldman, *Israeli Nuclear Deterrence: A Strategy for the 1980's* (New York: Columbia University Press, 1982); Yair Evron, *Israel's Nuclear Dilemma* (London: Routledge, 1994).

39. See Famaz A. Gerges, "Egyptian-Israeli Relations Turn Sour," *Foreign Affairs* 74, no. 3 (May/June 1995): 69–78; Bruce Jentelson and Dalya Dassa Kaye, "Security Status: Explaining Regional Security Cooperation and Its Limits in the Middle East," *Security Studies* 8, no. 1 (Autumn 1998): 204–38.

40. This section draws on the research report written for this project by Ram Erez, "Proliferation of Weapons of Mass Destruction in the Middle East" (Jerusalem: Hebrew University of Jerusalem, 2001).

41. Aaron Karp, "Ballistic Missiles in the Middle East: Realities, Omens and Arms Control," *Contemporary Security Policy* 16, no. 1 (April 1995): 155. On ballistic missiles use during wars in the Middle East, see Martin Navias, *Going Ballistic: The Build Up of Missiles in the Middle East* (London: Brasseys, 1993), 128–44.

42. Western countries were also involved in sales of relevant components to developing WMD capabilities (Germany, France, Israel).

43. National Intelligence Council (NIC), *Foreign Missile Developments and the Ballistic Missile Threat to the United States through 2015,* September 1999, available online: www.cia.gov/cia/publications/nie/nie99msl.html [accessed 29 August 2002].

44. In 1995 the CIA concluded, "No Country, other than the major declared powers, will develop or otherwise acquire a ballistic missile in the next fifteen years that could threaten the contiguous states or Canada," NIC, *Emerging Missile Threats to North America During the Next Fifteen Years* (NIE–95–19), November 1995. "Panel Rebuts Charges That Nuclear Threat to U.S Was Played Down," *New York Times,* 5 December 1996.

45. Barbara Harff, "Minorities, Rebellion and Repression in North Africa and the Middle East," in *Minorities At Risk,* ed. Ted R. Gurr (Washington, D.C.: U.S. Institute of Peace Press, 1993), 217.

46. Kemp and Stein, *Powderkeg in the Middle East,* 27–28, and chapters 9–10, 211–48.

47. James Ciment, *The Kurds: State and Minority in Turkey, Iraq and Iran* (New York: Facts on File INC, 1996).

48. On Islamic fundamentalism, see Bassam Tibi, *The Challenge of Fundamentalism: Political Islam and the New World Disorder* (Berkeley: University of California Press, 1998). On terrorism, see Yoram Schweitzer, "Middle East Terrorism: The Afghanistan

Alumni," in *The Middle East Military Balance,* ed. Shlomo Brom and Yiftah Shafir (Tel Aviv, Israel: Jaffee Center for Strategic Studies, 2000), 121–33; Kemp and Stein, *Powderkeg in the Middle East,* 34–35.

49. On Egypt's Islamic fundamentalists, see Kemp and Pressman, *Point of No Return,* 92–94.

50. *New York Times,* 23 November 2000, A18.

51. Schweitzer, *The Middle East Military Balance,* 121.

52. On the Hamas, see Shaul Mishal and Avraham Sela, *The Palestinian Hamas: Vision, Violence and Coexistence* (New York: Columbia University Press, 2000). On Palestinian terrorism, see Kemp and Pressman, *Point of No Return,* 78–80.

53. Malik Mufti, *Sovereign Creations: Pan Arabism and Political Order in Syria and Iraq* (Ithaca, N.Y.: Cornell University Press, 1996).

54. For details on the ethnic fragmentation in the ME, see Ibrahim, "Ethnic Conflict and State Building in the Arab World," in Kemp and Stein, *Powderkeg in the Middle East,* 48; Gabriel Ben Dor and Ofra Bango, eds., *Minorities and the State in the Arab World* (Boulder, Colo.: Lynne Rienner, 1999).

55. On weak states, see Tibi, *The Challenge of Fundamentalism*; and Kemp and Stein, *Powderkeg in the Middle East.* On instability related to ethnic and religious minorities, see Kemp and Stein, 27–30. On Syria, see Kemp and Pressman, *Point of No Return,* 116. On Iraq, see Daniel Byman, "Divided They Stand: Lessons about Partition from Iraq and Lebanon," *Security Studies* 7, no. 1 (Autumn 1997): 1–29. On civil wars, see the list in Ibrahim, "Ethnic Conflict and State Building in the Arab World," in Kemp and Stein, 46; and Maoz, *Regional Security,* 9.

56. Bernard Lewis, *The Middle East: 200 Years of History from the Rise of Christianity to the Present Day* (London: Meidenfield and Nicholson, 1995), 368.

57. See Kemp and Stein, *Powderkeg in the Middle East,* 27–30. For background on the Kurds, see Gurr, *Minorities At Risk,* 226–30.

58. Ayoob, "Unrevealing the Concept," 42.

59. Janice Stein, "The Security Dilemma in the Middle East: A Prognosis for the Decade Ahead," in *The Many Faces of National Security in the Arab World,* ed. Korany, Noble, and Byrnen (1993), 62–63.

60. Kemp and Stein, *Powderkeg in the Middle East,* 70.

61. Amazia Baram and Barry Rubin, eds., *Iraq's Road to War* (New York: St. Martin's Press, 1993), introduction.

62. Buzan, *People, States and Fear*; David, "Explaining Third World Alignment," and *Choosing Sides: Alignment and Realignment in the Third World*; Ayoob, *The Third World Security Predicament*; Holsti, *The State, War and the State of War.*

63. Gabriel Ben Dor, *State and Conflict in the Middle East: The Emergence of a Post Colonial State* (New York: Praeger, 1983), 231. Elie Kedourie, "The Nation-State in The Middle East," *Jerusalem Journal of International Relations* 9 (1987), cited in Mufti, *Sovereign Creations,* 9, note 16.

64. Yet, the boundaries of even the strongest Arab state, Egypt, were affected by the colonial powers. See Warburg cited in Ben Dor, *State and Conflict in the Middle East,* 259, footnote 16.

65. Gause, "Sovereignty, Statecraft, and Stability in the Middle East," 461.

66. Sela, *The Decline of the Arab-Israeli Conflict,* 4, 11, 14; Abbas Kelidar, "States without Foundations: The Political Evolution of State and Society in the Arab East," *Journal of Contemporary History* 28, no. 2 (April 1993): 315–22.

67. Michael Hudson, *Arab Politics: The Search For Legitimacy* (New Haven, Conn.: Yale University Press, 1977), 6.

68. Hudson, *Arab Politics*; Ayoob, "Unrevealing the Concept," 34–35; Shlaim, *War and Peace in the Middle East.*

69. Holsti, *The State, War and the State of War,* 112, cites the results of a survey that show that 80 percent of the respondents believed there is a single Arab "nation" that is artificially divided and ought to be unified into a single state (Bahgat Korany, "Alien and Besieged, Yet Have to Stay: The Contradictions of the Arab Territorial State," in *The Foundations of the Arab State,* ed. Ghassan Salamé [London: Croon Helm, 1987], 54–55).

70. Ghassan Salamé, "Strong and Weak States," in *The Arab State,* ed. Giacomo Luciani (London: Routledge, 1990), 29–64; and Iliya Harik ("The Origins of the Arab State System," in *The Arab State,* ed. Luciani, 21) cited in Holsti, *The State, War and the State of War,* 112; Philip Khoury and Joseph Kostiner, eds., *Tribes and State Formation in the Middle East* (London: T. B. Tauris, 1990); and Milton Estman and Itamar Rabinovich, eds., *Ethnicity, Pluralism and the State in the Middle East* (Ithaca, N.Y.: Cornell University Press, 1988).

71. Civil wars in the 1990s include the civil war that erupted in spring 1994 in Yemen and the violence in Algeria since the elections of 1992.

72. Hudson, *Arab Politics,* 11, chapter 3.

73. Ibrahim, "Ethnic Conflict and State Building in the Arab World," in Kemp and Stein, *Powderkeg in the Middle East,* 59.

74. Kemp and Pressman, *Point of No Return,* 118–19.

75. Keith Krause, "Insecurity and State Formation in the Global Military Order: The Middle Eastern Case," *European Journal of International Affairs* 2, no. 3 (September 1996): 333–34.

76. Mufti, *Sovereign Creations.*

77. Bahgat Korany and Hillal E. Dessouki, eds., *The Foreign Policies of Arab States* (Boulder, Colo.: Westview Press, 1991), 33; Sela, *The Decline of the Arab-Israeli Conflict,* 10–11.

78. Sylvia G. Haim, *Arab Nationalism: An Anthology* (Berkeley: University of California Press, 1976), 147–53; Ben Dor, *State and Conflict in the Middle East,* chapter 4; Gause, "Sovereignty, Statecraft, and Stability in the Middle East"; Michael Barnett, "Sovereignty, Nationalism, and Regional Order in the Arab States System," *International Organization* 49, no. 3 (1995): 479–510; Stephan Walt, *The Origins of Alliances* (Ithaca, N.Y.: Cornell University Press, 1987); Sela, *The Decline of the Arab-Israeli Conflict,* 6–7; Hassan Nafaa, "Arab Nationalism: Response to Ajami's Thesis on the End of Pan-Arabism," in *Pan-Arabism and Arab Nationalism,* ed. Farah Taufic and Bill Jang (Boulder, Colo.: Westview Press, 1987), 149–50; Mufti, *Sovereign Creations,* 3.

79. Mufti, *Sovereign Creations,* 40; Sela, *The Decline of the Arab-Israeli Conflict*; Ben Dor, *State and Conflict in the Middle East,*; Gause, "Sovereignty, Statecraft, and Stability in the Middle East"; Yehoshua Porath, *In Search of Arab Unity 1930–1945* (London: Cass, 1986); Patrick Seale, *The Struggle for Syria* (London: Oxford University Press, 1965, second edition 1986).

80. Ben Dor, *State and Conflict in the Middle East,* 197–98; Miller, "Explaining Regional War-Propensity."

81. Ben Dor, *State and Conflict in the Middle East,* 212.

82. Ayoob, "Unrevealing the Concept."

83. Barnett, "Sovereignty, Nationalism, and Regional Order in the Arab States System," 499.

84. Nadav Safran, *From War to War: The Arab-Israeli Confrontation, 1948–1967* (New York: Pegasus, 1969), 40.

85. Sela, *The Decline of the Arab-Israeli Conflict,* 59.

86. On the Islamic challenge to Arab states, see references cited in Gause, "Sovereignty, Statecraft, and Stability in the Middle East," 446, 449–51; Barnett, "Sovereignty, Nationalism, and Regional Order in the Arab States System," 509, footnote 108; Lewis, *The Middle East,* 376–87.

87. The most receptive state was Jordan, which was the only one where they were granted citizenship and became involved in the kingdom, but even there they did not dissolve their refugee identity, which they needed for getting Western and UN aid, and in order to work for promoting their political objective of returning to Palestine. Moreover, the Palestinians were discriminated against in Jordan as well (Benny Morris, *Israel's Border Wars, 1949–1956* [Tel Aviv: Am Oved, 1996], 20).

88. Hudson, *Arab Politics,* 295–96.

89. For a detailed study on this pattern before the 1956 war, see Morris, *Israel's Border Wars.*

90. On such incentives in the Middle East, see Shimon Peres, *The New Middle East* (New York: Henry Holt, 1993); Sela, *The Decline of the Arab-Israeli Conflict;* Michael Barnett, *Dialogues in Arab Politics: Negotiations in Regional Order* (New York: Columbia University Press, 1998); Efraim Inbar and Shmuel Sandler, "The Arab-Israeli Relationship: From Deterrence to Security Regime," in *Regional Security Regimes,* ed. Efraim Inbar (Albany: State University of New York Press, 1995), 273–97; Kemp and Pressman, *Point of No Return,* 15–31, 121–22.

91. On absolute versus relative gains, see David Baldwin, ed., *Neorealism and Neoliberalism: The Continuing Debate* (New York: Columbia University Press, 1993).

92. On negative security externalities, see David Lake, "Regional Security Complexes: A Systems Approach," in *Regional Orders,* ed. David Lake and Patrick Morgan (University Park: Pennsylvania State University Press, 1997), 49–57; Lepgold, "Regionalism in the Post–Cold War Era," chapter 1 in this collection.

93. Janice Gross Stein, "The Widening of Negotiations," *Occasional Papers* 68 (Jerusalem: Hebrew University of Jerusalem, Leonard Davis Institute for International Relations, 1999).

94. Efraim Inbar, "Arab-Israeli Coexistence: The Causes, Achievements and Limitations," *Israel Affairs* 6, no. 3–4 (Spring–Summer 2000): 236–70.

95. On Arab perceptions of Israel's nuclear option, see Ariel E. Levite and Emily B. Landau, *Israel's Nuclear Image: Arab Perceptions of Israel Nuclear Posture* (Hebrew) (Tel Aviv: n.p., 1994).

96. See Kemp and Pressman, *Point of No Return,* 24.

97. See I. William Zartman, *Ripe for Resolution: Conflict and Intervention in Africa* (New Haven, Conn.: Yale University Press, 1982).

98. Michael Hudson, ed., *Middle East Dilemma* (New York: Columbia University Press, 1999), 307. On Syria, see Kemp and Pressman, *Point of No Return,* 121–22.

99. Among those who highlight the growing strength of the institutions of Arab states are Mufti, *Sovereign Creations;* Harik, "The Origins of the Arab State System," 26; Roger Owen, *State Power and Politics in the Making of the Modern Middle East* (London: Routledge, 1992); Ben Dor, *State and Conflict in the Middle East;* Barnett, "Sovereignty, Nationalism, and Regional Order in the Arab States System"; Sela, *The Decline of the Arab-Israeli Conflict;* Telhami, *Power and Leadership in International Bargaining,* 95. Brief

summary and citations in David Pervin, "Building Order in Arab-Israeli Relations: From Balance to Concert?" in *Regional Orders,* ed. Lake and Morgan, 278–79; Ghassan Salamé, "Inter-Arab Politics: The Return of Geography," in *The Middle East: Ten Years after Camp David* (Washington, D.C.: Brookings Institution, 1988), 344–53; Fouad Ajami, "The End of Pan-Arabism," *Foreign Affairs* 52, (1978–79): 353–73; Fouad Ajami, *The Arab Predicament* (Cambridge: Cambridge University Press, 1981); Gause, "Sovereignty, Statecraft, and Stability in the Middle East," 453–54, 456–62; Giacumo Luciani, ed., *The Arab State* (London:Routledge, 1990); Rex Brynen, *Echoes of the Intifada: Repercussions of the Palestinian-Israeli Conflict* (Boulder, Colo.: Westview Press, 1991). More skeptical are Kedourie ("The Nation-State in The Middle East"), who claims that the Arab state is still weak; Joel Migdal, *Strong Societies and Weak States: State-Society Relations and State Capabilities in the Third World* (Princeton, N.J.: Princeton University Press, 1988) argues that Egypt and Syria are weak by the late 1980s; for a similar view, see Ayoob, *The Third World Security Predicament* and "Unrevealing the Concept."

100. On diversionary wars, see Jack Levy, "The Causes of War: A Review of the Theories and Evidence," in *Behavior, Society, and Nuclear War,* ed. Philip Tetlock (New York: Oxford University Press, 1989), 271–85.

101. Maoz, *Regional Security,* 19–20. For an overview of regional organizations in the ME, see Charles Tripp, "Regional Organizations in the Arab Middle East," in *Regionalism in World Politics,* ed. Louise Fawcett and Andrew Hurrell (Oxford: Oxford University Press, 1995), 283–308.

102. On the adverse effects of the high dependence on the United States for the GCC, see Yezid Sayigh, "Globalization Manqué: Regional Fragmentation and Authoritarian-Liberalism in the Middle East," in *The Third World Beyond the Cold War,* ed. Louise Fawcett and Yezid Sayigh (Oxford: Oxford University Press, 1999), 204–5.

103. Tibi, *The Challenge of Fundamentalism,* 37.

104. For a comprehensive treatment, see Dalya Kaye, *Beyond the Handshake: Multilateral Cooperation in the Arab-Israeli Peace Process 1991–1996* (New York: Columbia University Press, 2001).

105. On the theoretical neofunctional ideas of spillover from "low politics" to "high politics," see Ernest Haas, *The Uniting of Europe: Political, Social and Economical Forces 1950–1957* (London: Stevens, 1958).

106. Ariel Levite in Maoz, *Regional Security,* 159–68; Jentelson and Kaye, "Security Status," and Kaye, *Beyond the Handshake,* on the Arms Control Regional Security (ACRS) talks. This section draws on Ram Erez, "Proliferation of Weapons of Mass Destruction in the Middle East."

107. Shai Feldman, "The Middle East Arms Control Agenda: 1994–95," *The International Spectator* 29, no. 3 (July–September 1994): 73–82.

108. Peter Jones, "Arms Control in the Middle East: Some Reflections on ACRS," *Security Dialogue* 28, no. 1 (March 1997): 61.

109. Sayigh, "Globalization Manqué," 204; Ahmed Abd Al-Halim, "Middle East Regional Arms Control and Security," in *Confidence Building and Verification: Prospects in The Middle East,* ed. Shai Feldman, JCSS Study No 25 (Jerusalem: The Jerusalem Post, 1994), 179.

110. Interview with Amr Moussa, Foreign Minister of Egypt, *Defence News* (1–7 February 1993).

111. Shimon Peres, then Foreign Minister, introduced this new Israeli position for the first time on 13 January 1993 in Paris during his speech before the Chemical Weapon

Convention: see Feldman, "The Middle East Arms Control Agenda," 70; and Jones, "Arms Control in the Middle East," 60.

112. Aluf Ben, "Israel Is Ready for Inspection, on Condition It Will Also Apply to Iran and Iraq," *Haaretz*, 23 November 2000.

113. Walt, *The Origins of Alliances*; Buzan, *People, States and Fear*; Miller, "Explaining Regional War-Propensity."

114. Daniel Pipes, "The Real 'New Middle East,'" *Insight Turkey* 1, no. 3 (July–September 1999): 44; Sayigh, "Globalization Manque," 204.

115. Inbar, "Arab-Israeli Coexistence," 257–58.

116. Bruce Maddy Weitzman and Joseph Kustiner, "The Damascus Declaration: An Arab Attempt at Regional Security," in *Regional Security Regimes*, ed. Efraim Inbar, 107–26.

117. Kemp and Stein, *Powderkeg in the Middle East*, 32.

118. Michael C. Hudson, "To Play the Hegemon: Fifty Years of U.S. Policy Toward the Middle East," *Middle East Journal* 50, no. 3 (1996): 329–43; Miller, "Between War and Peace."

119. Saadia Touval, *The Peace Brokers: Mediators in The Arab-Israeli Conflict 1948–1979* (Princeton, N.J.: Princeton University Press, 1982), chapters 9, 10; Telhami, *Power and Leadership in International Bargaining*; Avraham Ben Zvi, *The United States and Israel: The Limits of a Special Relationship* (New York: Columbia University Press, 1993).

120. Martin Indyk, "Watershed in the Middle East," *Foreign Affairs* 71, no. 1 (1991/1992): 70–93; William Quandt, *Peace Process, American Policy, and the Arab-Israeli Conflict* (Washington, D.C.: Brookings Institute, 1993); Robert Lieber, "The American Role in a Regional Security Regime," in *Regional Security Regimes*, ed. Inbar; Miller, "When Regions Become Peaceful," "The Global Sources of Regional Transitions from War to Peace," and "Between War and Peace."

121. "Things Fall Apart: Why Have Recent Events in the Middle East Inflamed the Whole Arab World?" *The Economist*, 21 October 2000, 27.

122. Steven Spiegel, *The Other Arab-Israeli Conflict: Making America's Middle East Policy from Truman to Reagan* (Chicago: University of Chicago Press, 1985), 291–305; Ben Zvi, *The United States and Israel*, chapter 4.

123. "Hopeless in Gaza," *The Economist*, 21 April 2001, 39–40: "Without ceremony, the United States stepped in on April 18 to ease the latest escalation between Israel and the Palestinians. The Americans virtually ordered Israel to withdraw its troops from positions they had taken in Palestinian held Gaza the night before." See also Jane Perlez, "Troops Pull Out After Harsh Criticism," *New York Times*, 18 April 2001, 1, 6.

124. Shai Feldman, *The Future of U.S.-Israel Strategic Cooperation* (Washington, D.C.: Washington Institute for Near East Policy, 1996), 35.

125. Hudson, *Middle East Dilemma*, 340; on U.S. policy toward Iraq, see especially Byman, "After the Storm."

126. Gordon Craig and Alexander George, *Force and Statecraft: Diplomatic Problems of Our Time*, 3d ed. (New York: Oxford University Press, 1995).

127. For an analysis, see Richard Herrman, "Coercive Diplomacy and the Crisis over Kuwait, 1990–91," in *The Limits of Coercive Diplomacy*, ed. Alexander George and William Simons (Boulder, Colo.: Westview Press, 1994), 229–66; Benjamin Miller, "The Logic of U.S. Military Intervention on the Post–Cold War Era," *Contemporary Security Policy* 19, no. 3 (1998): 72–109.

128. Byman, "After the Storm"; Kemp and Stein, *Powderkeg in the Middle East,* 323–24; Ibrahim, "Ethnic Conflict and State Building in the Arab World," in Kemp and Stein.

129. For details, see Miller, "The Global Sources of Regional Transitions from War to Peace," and "Between War and Peace."

130. Brian Mandell, "Anatomy of a Confidence Building Regime: Egyptian-Israeli Security Cooperation," *International Journal* 45, no. 2 (1990): 202–23; Brian Mandell and Brian Tomlin, "Mediation in the Development of Norms to Manage Conflict: Kissinger in the Middle East," *Journal of Peace Research* 28, no. 1 (1991): 43–55; Quandt, *Peace Process, American Policy, and the Arab-Israeli Conflict.*

131. William Quandt, *Peace Process: American Policy toward the Arab-Israeli Conflict since 1967,* revised edition (Washington, D.C.: Brookings Institution, 2001), 380.

132. For details, see "Things Fall Apart," *The Economist,* 27–30, especially 28–29; "Saddam Chips His Way to Freedom," *The Economist,* 25 November 2000. Old foes, such as Iraq and Syria, talk of resuming diplomatic ties. Six Arab states have already done so with Iraq. Syria reopened the Iraqi oil pipeline through its territory, renewed trade and flights, and held secret discussions with Saddam about Iraqi backing for Syria in the event of an Israeli attack (Thomas L. Friedman, "Clinton's Syria Memo," *New York Times,* 1 December 2000, A31).

133. Jane Perlez, "The Peacemaker Takes Up Another Line of Work," *New York Times,* 22 April 2001, Week in Review section, 1, 3. More recently, the director of the CIA played a key role in establishing a cease-fire between Israel and the Palestinians, and the United States is exerting pressure on the parties to obey it and then to return to peace negotiations. However, at this point, it is uncertain whether the cease-fire is going to hold, let alone a return to diplomacy.

7

Managing Conflict in South Asia

KANTI BAJPAI

After the Cold War, there was expectation mixed with hope that the world would be a safer and happier place. The record is, however, rather mixed. Some regions, it is true, have become more peaceful, but others have become more violent, and yet others have remained as violent as before. South Asia exhibits contrary trends. This region, composed of Bangladesh, Bhutan, India, Pakistan, the Maldives, Nepal, and Sri Lanka—the seven member countries of the South Asian Association for Regional Cooperation (SAARC)—has seen increasing violence as well as peacefulness. Between India and Pakistan there has been greater conflict and violence; between India and its smaller neighbors, there has been greater convergence and cooperation. How have South Asians tried to manage conflict? Why have India and Pakistan done less well and India and the smaller states done better in this regard?

This is largely unexplored intellectual territory, and few have focused on the history of cooperation and conflict management in the region, preferring to highlight conflict instead.[1] Most of the writings on cooperation and conflict management have been prescriptive rather than analytical. This chapter begins by summarizing the nature of regional conflict in South Asia. It then goes on to consider the structure of incentives and disincentives for conflict management in the post–Cold War period and how this has led to an uneven record of cooperation amongst South Asians. The third section deals with the interests of nonregional agencies and powers in furthering an agenda of conflict management in South Asia and the limits of their involvement. The chapter concludes with some thoughts on future prospects.

REGIONAL CONFLICT IN SOUTH ASIA

South Asia comprises two distinct "theaters" of conflict: between India and Pakistan, on the one hand, and between India and its smaller neighbors, on the other. The first is a theater of war where military hostilities are always a distinct possibility; the other is a theater of less militarized conflict in which hostilities are virtually ruled out. India is at the center of both sets of conflict as a result of the geographical structure of the region: India borders all the countries in the region; none of its neighbors shares a border with anyone else in South Asia.

There is no single fault line in South Asia. India and its various neighbors are in conflict over a number of issues. The most important sources of conflict are the power asymmetry between India and the rest, territorial disputes, cross-border intervention in each other's affairs, and identity clashes.

One of the most important sources of conflict in South Asia is the power asymmetry between India and its neighbors. India is roughly four times the size of the rest of the region put together, either in land area or population terms. Its economic superiority is also about the same. Militarily, it has more force at its disposal than the rest of the region combined. India's neighbors live in fear of Indian intimidation. India lives in fear of its neighbors reaching out to outsiders to balance against Indian power. New Delhi would love to integrate the region under its leadership and keep the great powers out. The other governments see the great powers as checks on Indian power and want them to be involved in regional affairs.[2] Thus, India signed a series of bilateral treaties with its neighbors that, in effect, made India the pivot of a regional security regime. Only Pakistan has remained outside that framework, but even here the Simla Accord of 1972 stands as a partial success for New Delhi in the sense that Islamabad agreed to a process of bilateral conflict resolution with India as against its earlier insistence on mediation by the UN or third parties.

Second, territorial disputes are a key element of conflict between India and its neighbors. The most important of these disputes is the India-Pakistan quarrel over Kashmir. The two countries are still at odds over other territorial issues: Siachen and Sir Creek.[3] Between 1989 and 1993, the two countries made progress on the smaller quarrels.[4] From 1996 onward, India and Pakistan once again began discussions on Kashmir and the lesser territorial issues, in the so-called six-plus-two dialogues. The talks foundered on substance and also on differing perceptions of a peace process. India's preference is for a peace process that deals with all bilateral issues simultaneously without giving priority to any one issue, especially Kashmir. Pakistan's preference, by contrast, is for a process in which Kashmir is recognized as the "core issue," and all other agenda items, particularly economic relations and people-to-people contacts, are secondary.[5] After the Kargil war in May–July 1999, India insisted that it would not resume negotiations until Pakistan stopped aiding the militants in Kashmir. Pakistan has equivocated, sometimes offering talks unconditionally and at other times hedging by insisting that it will negotiate only when India is serious about a Kashmir settlement.[6] In spite of their hard stands, in July 2001 the leaders of the two countries eventually met in India. The summit was inconclusive with both sides basically holding to the same positions.

India and the smaller states also are divided over a number of territorial disputes. India and Bangladesh have still not been able to resolve their differences over territorial enclaves left over from Partition as also ownership of South Moore/Talpatty sandbars in the Bay of Bengal. India and Nepal have recently found themselves quarreling over Kalapani, at the intersection of India, China, and Nepal. While these disputes have generally not been militarized, in 2001 Indian and Bangladeshi forces clashed over some of the enclaves. A contingent of Indian forces was brutally killed by Bangladeshi forces, leading to an outcry in India.[7] In the 1980s, Indian and Bangladeshi forces fought briefly over the sandbars.

Third, relations in South Asia are complicated by the involvement—or fear of involvement—of the smaller states in the domestic quarrels of India and vice versa. There is considerable evidence of Islamabad's complicity in the Punjab and Kashmir violence in India in the 1980s and 1990s. India is convinced that Pakistan also stirs up trouble in its turbulent northeast and is behind urban violence and terrorism in other parts of the country.[8] Islamabad's response has varied—from denials that it has provided real material assistance to suggestions that the violence, at least in the Kashmiri case, is legitimate because it is a "jihad" or a "national liberal struggle" and not terrorism. Pakistan also claims that Indian intelligence organizations have helped Sindhi and other disaffected Pakistani groups.[9] New Delhi accuses its other neighbors of tolerating subversive activities carried out from their soil against India. Thus, it has argued that Bangladesh is a haven for dissidents from the Indian northeast as well as for Pakistani agents; and Nepal has allowed Maoists and Pakistani subversives to operate in India across the open border. India's neighbors accuse New Delhi of exactly the same kind of behavior.

Fourth, identity clashes add another layer of conflict. Below the surface, there is a religious dimension to the differences between India and Pakistan. There is also a not so subtle competition between the two over secular and religious nationalism as the proper basis of nation building.[10] Indians have come to regard the Kashmir issue as a test case of its secular nationalism. For many Pakistanis, exactly the reverse argument applies. Pakistanis regard the accession of Kashmir to their country as being natural given that the subcontinent was divided on the basis of separate nationhood for the Muslim majority areas in western and eastern India.[11]

Identity differences also bedevil India's relations with its smaller neighbors. In general, India wants the smaller countries to affirm their basic South Asianness and not to look outward to affiliations in neighboring regions. Some Indians feel that the neighboring states are offshoots of the "mother" country—India—and that their rejection of this identity is the cause of conflict. The smaller states insist that they have legitimate ties to other regions and communities. So, Bangladesh has suggested that it is a bridge between the Islamic world, South Asia, and Southeast Asia. Nepal argues that, in addition to its South Asian identity, it has a Central Asian identity. And Sri Lankans cite Buddhism as their link to Southeast Asia.[12]

Power asymmetries, territorial quarrels, cross-border interference in domestic instabilities, and identity clashes are the basic sources of conflict in South Asia. In addition, India and its smaller neighbors are in conflict over economic and hydrological issues.[13] The India-Bangladesh trade balance favors India, and Bangladeshis complain that New Delhi is not doing enough to correct the situation. India wants transit rights across Bangladeshi territory to send goods across to its northeast. Dhaka fears that this could allow India to penetrate its internal politics. As a landlocked country, Nepal wants a better trade and transit agreement with India. India complains that Nepal takes advantage of its relationship with India, allowing goods to be imported into Nepal, which are then smuggled into India. India also has long had differences with the smaller states over water. The great Himalayan rivers are shared with Bangladesh and Nepal. India and Bangladesh periodically accuse each other of violating water-sharing norms and agreements and of not doing enough to combat the perennial problem of flooding. India and Nepal find it difficult to reach accords on the harnessing of hydrological power in the upper Himalayas.[14] For all three countries, the rivers are a vital resource, crucial for economic and ecological security reasons.

South Asia is rich in conflicts. How each of these conflicts is managed, within what limits, and exactly by what means is beyond the scope of this chapter. What follows rather is an analysis of the incentives and disincentives that have operated on, and in large measure continue to operate on, the regional states and on external agents who might intervene to manage conflict.

REGIONAL ACTORS AND CONFLICT MANAGEMENT

Conflict management in South Asia depends on a set of incentives and disincentives facing the regional actors. The disincentives have so far trumped the incentives in the India-Pakistan case, so that the moments of cooperativeness between the two countries have given way to contention, crisis, and war. On the other hand, with India and its smaller neighbors the incentives have trumped the disincentives and allowed them to cooperate in crucial disputes.

Regional Organization and Track II Diplomacy

In South Asia, conflict management is essentially a bilateral possibility. Thus far, regional organization has played an extremely small role in attenuating conflict. This is ironic because the South Asian Association for Regional Cooperation (SAARC), from its inception in 1985, was viewed not only as a mechanism for cooperation in various functional and economic areas but also as an instrument of conflict management. In the SAARC view, cooperation in these "noncontentious" areas would be the basis for conflict management, reduction, and resolution.[15]

SAARC has failed to fulfill this function, and while it has some accomplishments to its name, these are relatively minor. No major forms of cooperation in functional and economic areas have occurred, not even the preferential tariff arrangement that was signed more than five years ago. The only real security-related agreement, the convention on terrorism, remains a paper accord. The association has provided a venue for bilateral diplomacy at the highest political levels. Indian and Pakistani leaders have often convened talks during regional summits.[16] These have helped improve regional atmospherics, but not much else. One of the constraints on SAARC is that the Charter specifically bans discussion of bilateral and contentious issues.

After the Kargil war, India refused to allow any SAARC meetings to be convened. SAARC has therefore been almost completely moribund since the summer of 1999. In 2001, India finally relented, and official level contacts in SAARC resumed. It remains unclear whether political level contacts will be restored.

Conflict management in South Asia is also fundamentally an interstate possibility. The region has a growing Track II process. However, it is far behind some other regions in this regard.[17] Track II processes are constrained by governmental reluctance to permit freer travel in the region. The restrictions on travel are greatest between India and Pakistan, who fear that a more open travel regime will make subversion easier. Track II is also constrained by the reluctance of governments to take it seriously as a tool of diplomacy. At the same time, many Track II participants are suspicious of governmental interest in their activities. Some refuse to become involved in discussions on interstate disputes, choosing to focus instead on common social and development problems. In addition, Track II participants are often hostile to their own governments, seeing them as the primary cause of strife and deprivation.

India and Pakistan

What accounts for the undulating course of relations between India and Pakistan, with negotiations and discussions giving way to invective and tensions? In the India-Pakistan case, one answer is to say that there are both incentives and disincentives for conflict management, with the incentives ultimately more powerful than the disincentives. On the positive side are *geopolitical change*, *democratization*, and *economic pressures and reforms*. On the negative side are *problems of political control/legitimacy* and *growing internal extremism*.

Geopolitical Changes

The end of the Cold War led to changes that left India and Pakistan facing a very different geopolitical environment. Essentially, India lost its great-power partner in the Soviet Union/Russia, and Pakistan lost its great-power protector in the United States and to a lesser extent China. This encouraged a conflict management sensibility in the region.

For India, the collapse of the Soviet Union meant that New Delhi no longer had a "proxy" veto in the UN Security Council. For years, Moscow had used its veto in the Security Council to protect Indian interests. With the end of the Cold War, India could no longer count on Russian protection. The Kremlin had its own worries and was increasingly dependent on the cooperation and largesse of the Western states, particularly the United States. Most of India's concerns arose from its fear of a hegemonic America that was no longer fettered by its competition with the Soviet Union. Along with this diplomatic loss was the disruption of military spares, supplies, and major weapon systems from Moscow. Given that the Indian armed forces were 70 percent dependent on Soviet systems, this was a major problem for India's military preparedness. The chaos of the former Soviet Union (FSU) and Eastern Europe was also a serious blow to sectors of the Indian economy that were tied to the communist economies.[18]

Pakistan too faced a quite different geopolitical landscape. With the end of the Cold War, the United States was no longer interested in Islamabad as a frontline state against communism, and Washington's support could no longer be taken for granted. Indeed, as the Afghan war turned in favor of the Taliban, U.S. suspicion of Pakistan increased. The Taliban's Islamic crusade was worrisome and became linked in Washington's mind with fundamentalism and terrorism on a global scale. Pakistan's other strategic partner, China, also began to drift away. Islamabad had counted on Beijing for support against India. By the late 1970s, China was equivocating on the issue of Kashmir and urging Pakistan to come to a settlement with India.[19] Worse, China's relations with India continued to improve throughout the 1990s.

By the early 1990s, therefore, both India and Pakistan found themselves in a world without reliable great-power friends. India was in some ways affected more seriously than Pakistan. Strategically, New Delhi had tied itself so decisively to Moscow that it was without a prop of any kind. Islamabad had lost leverage over the United States, but Washington was the triumphant power at the end of the Cold War, and there was still reason to think that it would be supportive of Pakistan. In particular, the U.S. fear of Islamic extremism could be exploited to retain Washington's interest in Pakistan.[20] Pakistan could also count on a rising China in a way that India could not look upon the Soviet Union/Russia, which was in precipitous decline. Even Pakistan, though, could no longer count on its erstwhile protectors as before, primarily because with the removal of the Soviet Union, Western interest in Islamabad's cooperation had waned.[21]

Two effects flowed from this geopolitical change. First of all, both India and Pakistan had an incentive, as in other regions, to explore the possibility of stability and cooperation. This was partly a psychological effect: New Delhi in particular had for years argued that once the Cold War overlay of great-power rivalry disappeared, India and Pakistan would be able to engage in rational discussions. More important, though, without external providers and protectors, India and Pakistan faced an uncertain situation. For India, there was no effective counterweight to the United States and China. If either or both of these powers sought to interfere in the region, New Delhi could no longer count on Moscow to ride to the rescue. Better, then, to stabilize the region so as to reduce the opportunities for intervention. For Pakistan, without the automatic support of the United States and China, India's greater size and power was a danger. Some degree of accommodation and understanding with India was therefore necessary.[22]

The end of the Cold War and the collapse of the Soviet Union meant that the United States was the dominant power in the international system. Once it was clear that Moscow would no longer "return" phoenix-like to balance the United States, both New Delhi and Islamabad had to ensure that the Americans did not tilt decisively against them. The U.S. nonproliferation crusade after the Cold War made the triangular relationship a complex one. India felt that the United States had focused its attentions on the Indian nuclear program and was determined to cap, rollback, and eliminate its capabilities. New Delhi had to resist U.S. pressures, push ahead with its nuclear program, and at the same time not alienate Washington. Pakistan also had to ward off American nonproliferation pressures, continue to develop its nuclear and missile capabilities, and keep Washington reasonably happy. One way of reassuring Washington was to improve relations in South Asia. Thus, both countries projected an image of reasonableness so as to limit American interference in their nuclear plans.[23]

The second effect of the strategic loss for both countries was to increase their search for strategic autonomy. The nuclear tests of May 1998 must be seen in this context. Both countries had steadily built up their nuclear programs, and evidence suggests that they had at least crude deliverable nuclear devices in the late 1980s, probably in the period 1988–90. However, the tests were of cardinal importance. They laid to rest any remaining doubts about the capacity of the two countries to produce nuclear weapons and to defend their security against not just each other but also in relation to others. With nuclearization came the understanding that the two countries would have to exercise a degree of caution in military matters. Nuclear weapons were extraordinary weapons and could be "used" strategically, but within limits: for instance, they could be used, as they were by Pakistan in Kargil, to escalate subconventional conflict. These limits had to be defined, through mutual dialogue if possible, so that accidental war did not occur. Here was an incentive to evolve stabilization measures, at least in the military realm.[24]

The Rise of Democracy in Pakistan

While global change was an important factor in encouraging conflict management, the rise of democracy in Pakistan was another key incentive. After General Zia's unexpected death in 1988, Pakistani politics became more complex and contentious.[25] Nevertheless, those who came to power after Zia's death—Benazir Bhutto and the Pakistan People's Party (PPP) as well as Nawaz Sharif and the Pakistan Muslim League (PML)—did attempt a rapprochement with India, in part because they saw an improved relationship as a way of reducing the influence of the military in Pakistan.[26] In Nawaz's case, there were financial interests involved as well. Representing a new breed of Pakistani businesses, he saw advantage in a more normal economic relationship with India. Every time Nawaz has come to power since 1988, he has stressed that relations with India were a crucial item on his agenda and that he favored fuller commercial and trade interactions.[27]

On the Indian side, the rise of democracy in Pakistan was welcomed. A step-by-step approach and sensible diplomatic course with Pakistan was one way of strengthening civilian forces and of reducing the influence of "hard-line" military officers. India had gone down this road with Pakistan before, after the 1971 war, without great success; but here was an opening after eleven years of military rule, and it was worth making the effort to improve relations with India's old adversary. Increasingly, New Delhi has come to the view that democracy in Pakistan is the worst system except for the alternatives—military rule and fundamentalism.[28] As the role of Islamic extremists has grown, India has come to see Pakistan's uneven democracy as the lesser evil. This has continued to be a factor in India-Pakistan relations, with New Delhi hoping that democracy will at some point make a vital difference to Pakistani perceptions and choices in respect of its foreign policy.

Economic Pressures and Reforms

The 1990s were the decade of profound economic changes in India and Pakistan. In 1990–91, India faced a severe balance of payments and fiscal deficit simultaneously accompanied by negative growth and inflation. Under strictures from the IMF, the Indian government embarked on a process of reforms with deregulation and trade liberalization as the centerpiece. Pakistan initiated similar reforms. Throughout the 1990s, the two economies were under pressure to reduce unproductive expenditures and investment and to reduce the size and role of the state in order to attract foreign private investment. One area that both governments targeted for expenditure cuts was defense.[29] In order to reduce defense spending, it was necessary to lower tensions in the neighborhood. The success of the economic reforms also depended on foreign investors. Since foreigners were unlikely to invest in a region where there was conflict and violence, India and Pakistan had an incentive to improve relations in the region. For India, this meant better relations with China and Pakistan principally; for Pakistan, this meant stabilizing relations with India.

India has always argued that normalizing economic relations with Pakistan was a tool of conflict management, at least for the long term. The Indian argument is that economic profit will give the two societies a stake in each other's well-being and will contribute to peace and cooperation.[30] For the most part, Pakistani elites have opposed trade, precisely for the reason that India endorses it, namely, that groups within Pakistan may have a stake in better relations. However, even in Pakistan, attitudes have changed. Unofficial trade with India—smuggling, routing products through third countries particularly in the Gulf—is estimated at $1.5 billion; formal trade could become much larger.[31] This will profit not only the Pakistani business community but also the government, which will be able to levy duties and taxes on formal trade. Islamabad faces a variety of demands relating to social welfare but also to defense and therefore must generate more resources. Amongst the factors leading to the dismissal of the Benazir Bhutto government in November 1996 was the inability of her government to carry through a program of reforms that would fix the fiscal crisis. As noted earlier, Nawaz Sharif, who succeeded Bhutto twice in the 1990s, had a strong interest in more normal economic relations with India.

The Limits of India-Pakistan Cooperation

The changed geopolitical situation globally and the primacy of the United States, the return of democratic politics in Pakistan, and economic pressures and reforms should have combined to produce a period of sustained stabilization and cooperation between India and Pakistan in the 1990s. Unfortunately, this was at best an intermittent feature of the bilateral relationship. At least two factors, both related to the course of domestic politics, undercut the pressures exerted by these more positive inducements.

In both India and Pakistan, the political control and legitimacy of elected governments was precarious at best and this limited the room for decisive foreign policy initiatives. From 1989 to 1999, India had six prime ministers and five governments in New Delhi, only one of which lasted its five-year term. It had three different parties (coalitions) in power nationally: the Congress, the National Front, and the National Democratic Alliance. These formations were constantly under threat of collapse. Political instability was matched by violence. In 1990, there was widespread urban unrest over the new reservations policy for Other Backward Classes. The following summer, Tamil militants assassinated former prime minister Rajiv Gandhi. The mobilization of Hindus over the Babri Masjid climaxed in December 1992 with the tearing down of the mosque. There were riots all over India, and a series of bomb explosions rocked Indian cities. Finally, until the middle of the 1990s, Sikh separatist violence wracked India. In this troubled situation, it was difficult to maintain any coherence in foreign policy. Most important, it was impossible for any government in New Delhi to make any "concessions" to Pakistan, fearing that this would be exploited by political rivals.

In Pakistan, the competition between the two major political parties and their allies led to massive extraparliamentary actions in the form of street protests, disruptions of parliamentary proceedings, intimidation of political opponents, corruption, and coercion of the press and judiciary. Both parties at the same time feared the military and attempted to limit its influence. In doing so, they intervened in military affairs beyond what was acceptable to the Pakistani forces. The two parties lost public support as well as support from other sectors of civil society, including the press. Their relations with the presidency and the military deteriorated. When it departed the political stage in 1988, the army had made clear that it would not countenance any major changes in foreign policy, defense spending, and the nuclear program without the permission of the military. It might have been possible to gradually loosen the military's veto in these areas had the civilian governments been stronger and more confident of their survival and support base. In the end, the shadow of the military over external policy pushed Pakistan to fall back on its usual conservative and contrarian stand with India.

The second domestic factor that impinged on India and Pakistan's ability to manage conflict rationally was the rise of political extremism in both countries. In India, the rise of the Hindu right was part of a more general drift to political conservatism that swung electoral support to the Bharatiya Janata Party (BJP). While the BJP presents itself as a moderate political force, it is firmly part of the "Sangh Parivar," a coalition of Hindu groups led by the Rashtriya Swayamsevak Sangh (RSS). The Hindu right has generally been supportive of a hard stand on relations with Pakistan. No one in power in New Delhi during this period was able to ignore the influence of the Sangh Parivar and its mobilizational capacity, and this was felt in foreign policy as much as in domestic policy.[32]

Political extremism in Pakistan in the 1990s grew perceptibly. Iranian-influenced Shia groups, Wahabi groups inspired and funded by Saudi sources, and the Jamaat was one set of extremist formations, often mutually in conflict. In addition, in the backwash of the Afghan conflict and the rise of the Taliban, Pakistan became home to a more militant Islam. These *jehadis* have focused their energies on the "liberation" of Kashmir from India and on propagating a crusade on "Hindu" India. For them, there can be no compromise with India. The strength of political extremism in Pakistan cannot be judged quantitatively. Electorally, Islamic extremism has almost no power. However, in terms of "street power," it is a potentially formidable force. Whoever is in power in Pakistan—the mainstream political parties or the army—must reckon with it. Policy toward India is not completely captive to the preferences of Islamic extremists, but these groups are capable of disrupting any accords with New Delhi by raising the level of violence in Kashmir or by accusing Islamabad of "selling out."[33]

The incentives-disincentives structure has caused South Asia to oscillate between cooperation/stability and confrontation/instability. With Pakistan's return to democracy in 1988, relations temporarily improved. By the summer of 1990, however, the two were nearly at war over Kashmir. After the crisis, relations once again improved, and a flurry of confidence-building measures were agreed upon. In 1992, the two resumed discussions on bilateral negotiations and presented each other with a series of "nonpapers." The following year, India and Pakistan were reputed to be on the verge of signing a series of agreements on the Siachen, Sir Creek, and Wullar conflicts. However, in 1994–95, relations deteriorated. India was in the midst of a full-blown insurgency in

Kashmir and held Pakistan responsible. Pakistan charged India with maltreating Kashmiris and campaigned for international mediation in the dispute. Nonetheless, in 1996, the two countries began the so-called six-plus-two talks that covered Kashmir, security, trade, and other bilateral issues. By 1997, India's problems in Kashmir had perceptibly eased. India's security forces seemed to have gained the upper hand against the militants. Elections had returned a civilian government to Kashmir, and this further reduced tensions.

The nuclear tests of May 1998 caused India and Pakistan to once again trade charges. The two governments then surprised the world by agreeing to a historic summit in the Pakistani city of Lahore in February 1999. The summit produced a number of accords on nuclear weapons, confidence building, trade and economic relations, and, most importantly, resuming a dialogue on Kashmir.[34] Within months, however, the two countries were at war. Pakistani troops and Kashmiri militants crossed the line of control in Kashmir along the heights in Kargil and a short, sharp war ensued. In the aftermath of the war, both sides took strong stands. India insisted that Pakistan stop aiding the Kashmiri militants and Pakistan repudiated the Lahore agreements. The military coup in Pakistan in October 1999 and the hijacking of an Indian civilian aircraft from Kathmandu to Kandahar by Kashmiri militants led to further tensions.[35] In the summer of 2000, relations once again improved. A series of cease-fires in Kashmir (led off by a Kashmiri militant group in July and extended by the Indian government in November 2000), military retrenchment by Pakistan along the line of control, and Track II contacts between India and Pakistan led to a perceptible warming of relations. In July 2001, Indian and Pakistani leaders finally resumed negotiations. The summit in Agra did not, however, produce an accord, and once again relations deteriorated.

It seems safe to predict that the zigzag we have seen over the past decade will continue to set limits to negotiations, even in respect of a minimal agenda of arms control and confidence building. This latter point is worth investigating further here. Conflict management should at least mean agreements, tacit or explicit, on the nature and intensity of violence. The presence of nuclear weapons would seem to make this imperative. Yet, in the wake of the Kargil war, India and Pakistan show little signs of being galvanized even by this factor. Have political weakness (i.e., illegitimate governments) and political extremism gone so deep that they prevent further cooperation in managing conflict?

The answer on balance is yes. Internal political weakness simply does not allow a government to take forward a rational, systematic agenda of conflict management with the other side for fear that domestic rivals will exploit foreign policy moves for internal advantage. Political extremism compounds the problem. A hypermobilized minority, willing to take to the streets and to use extraparliamentary methods, can wield virtual veto power on domestic and foreign policy issues. This bears out Jack Snyder and Edward Mansfield's insight that democratizing powers are not particularly pacific and indeed may be more war- and crisis-prone than authoritarian powers.[36]

The other factor of importance is the view among strategic elites in both India and Pakistan that they have already done enough to manage conflict. This view rests on several beliefs and arguments. First, decision makers and analysts on both sides point to the restraint shown by India and Pakistan in earlier wars. The crucial factor here is that neither side has resorted to strategic bombing in war.[37] Second, both countries have erected strong defenses along the borders and in the plains where they expect the major military engagements to occur. These defenses, they expect, will have a sufficiently dissuasive effect on thoughts of military adventurism.[38] Third, with nuclear weapons on both sides, the threat of massive punitive retaliation will prevent both large-scale conventional war as well as nuclear war. Fourth, over the past decade, they have put in place a series of confidence-building measures to prevent accidental war and reduce the fear of surprise attack.[39] To summarize: history, defense, deterrence, and confidence building together should suffice to manage conflict.

In sum, India and Pakistan seem to have reached a plateau in terms of conflict management possibilities. If it is a plateau, it is a very small one, one that either side could fall off, as the Kargil war of 1999 demonstrated.

India and the Smaller States

While India and Pakistan seem to be locked into a familiar pattern of discord, India and the smaller states have embarked on a different path. The *retrenchment of the major powers from South Asia* since the early 1980s, a trend that was reinforced by the end of the Cold War, the *growing political convergence* between India and the small states, and *economic change* created the conditions for conflict management. In addition, a more accommodative pattern of *Indian diplomacy* and *nonofficial contacts* led to greater cooperation between New Delhi and its neighbors, especially on economic and hydrological issues.

Great Power Retrenchment

A key incentive to manage conflict between India and the smaller states from the late 1980s onward was the gradual retrenchment of nonregional powers from the region. China, the Soviet Union, and the United States had an interest in the India-Pakistan relationship given the East-West struggle. However, the smaller states of South Asia had never been of any great strategic importance. There was some sympathy for them, particularly in China, as small states next to gigantic India, but by the late 1980s even Beijing had signaled that it supported cooperation between the smaller countries and India.[40] When New Delhi took action against Nepal in 1988–89, Beijing refused to intervene.[41] The Soviets were solidly behind India in any case, and the smaller states could expect no support from Moscow in their disputes with India. The United States, from 1982 onward, drew closer to India and began to describe it as the major power in the region. Washington was therefore not overly critical when Indian forces went to Sri Lanka in 1987 and indeed was supportive when Indian forces averted a coup in the Maldives in 1988. During the action against Nepal in 1988–89, too, Washington was silent.[42] The effect of retrenchment from South Asia was that the smaller states could no longer count on the great powers against India; and India became less concerned about great-power interference in the region on behalf of the smaller states. In this situation, bilateral conflict management became a necessity for the smaller states, and it became more attractive to India.

Political Convergence

A second regional change that promoted thoughts of cooperation and conflict management between India and the smaller states was political convergence between India and the smaller states. First, the transitions to democracy in Bangladesh and Nepal in 1988–89 eased the ideological divide with India. While democratization produces instabilities that often adversely affect foreign policy, a perceptibly more accommodative language marked India-Bangladesh and India-Nepal interactions after elected governments took power. Second, the change of governments in Bangladesh, Nepal, and India brought into power parties and personalities that found it easier to work with each other. The victory of Sheikh Hasina in Bangladesh, of the Nepali Congress–Rashtriya Prajatantra Party–Sadbhavana Party combination in Nepal in the same year, and of the Deve Gowda government in India, all of whom came to power in 1996, helped shape the Ganges and Mahakali treaties between India and Bangladesh and India and Nepal, respectively. New governments without commitments to well-worn positions allowed for a fresh approach. Moreover, these governments consisted of parties with ideological or personal links. For instance, in all three countries, the governing parties were left-of-center ideological formations. In the case of the Mahakali treaty, the fact that the Nepali Congress and the Rao Congress in India were in power at the same time in the early 1990s, two parties with links going back to pre-Independence days, helped broker an agreement. So also the appointment of I. K. Gujral as Indian foreign minister brought to the helm a political figure someone who had traveled widely and was well liked in South Asia. Gujral's presence was critical in the case of the Ganges treaty with Bangladesh.

Economic Change

A third incentive for cooperation and conflict management was economic change. For one thing, the increasing regionalization of global trading arrangements and the exclusion of South Asians from these arrangements brought home to the region the importance of economic cooperation.[43] The direction of economic reforms in the major South Asian states also helped. Sri Lanka had begun to open its economy up in the late 1970s. In the 1990s, it was the turn of

Bangladesh, India, and Pakistan. The four major countries joined the World Trade Organization (WTO) and were therefore formally committed to liberalization. Finally, within SAARC, signing a regional trade regime made a difference. The South Asian Preferential Tariff Agreement (SAPTA), signed in 1995, is not yet operational, mostly due to Pakistani opposition. From the point of view of the small states, however, the fact that there was a regional accord on trade made it easier for their governments to sell the idea of deeper economic ties with India to their publics. The regional accord served as a kind of "cover" under which they could conduct trade legitimately with India.[44] Thus, in 1998, India and Sri Lanka signed a free trade agreement. India and Bangladesh may well sign a similar accord in the near future.

The Limits of Cooperation

India and the smaller states managed to contain their differences and indeed have gone on to negotiate cooperative agreements on economic and hydrological issues. India and Bangladesh are working on a free trade arrangement. They are also discussing a possible transit agreement that would allow India to transship goods across Bangladeshi territory to its northeastern states. Most importantly, they signed a thirty-year accord on the sharing of the Ganges river. India and Nepal have revised their trade and transit agreements and are in the midst of yet another review of these arrangements. The two countries also signed the Mahakali treaty, which involves joint development of hydropower. India's and Sri Lanka's signing of a free trade agreement led to the opening of India-Bangladesh talks on free trade.

Conflicts remain, however. India and Bangladesh remain divided over how to deal with territorial enclaves in each other's territories as well as the South Moore/Talpatty islands. Allowing India transit facilities is a controversial issue in Bangladesh, and no agreement has yet been reached. India and Nepal differ over the Kalapani trijunction (where India, China, and Nepal intersect) and smuggling from Nepal into India. In the years to come, the movement of people across national boundaries could become a serious bone of contention. There is concern already over the flow of Bangladeshis into India. India and Nepal are worried about the free flow of people between their two countries even though this is permitted by the 1950 treaty. While India says little publicly about the outflow of Tamils from Sri Lanka, it is worried about political and social pressures arising from the presence of Sri Lankan Tamils in southern India.

What are the factors that hold back cooperation in these areas? In the case of India and Pakistan, we suggested that the biggest hurdle to managing conflict was domestic instability in two forms—the lack of political control (that is, legitimacy of elected leaders) and the rise of political extremism. Both factors influence relations between India and the smaller states as well. We have already seen how in the 1990s, India and Pakistan had their share of domestic political turbulence and how this affected their ability to deal constructively with each other. The smaller countries too were wracked by disorder. In Bangladesh, the high-voltage competition between Khaleda Zia and Sheikh Hasina from the 1980s onward polarized the political order. Strikes, protests, street violence, and boycotts of the national assembly frequently paralyzed political and economic life. Fifteen years on, little has changed. Khaleda Zia's electoral victory in the 2001 general elections has been challenged by Sheikh Hasina, who refuses to take part in the national assembly's deliberations, and there is turmoil once again in the streets. Relations with India have been an issue in domestic politics, and both parties, in varying degrees, adopt hard approaches in dealing with New Delhi in order to enhance their legitimacy. In Nepal, one government after another has come to power since the return of democracy in the late 1980s: the Nepali Congress was replaced by the leftists; and the leftists were replaced by the Nepali Congress. In the tumult of domestic politics, relations with India, as in Bangladesh, is very much a live issue, and every agreement with New Delhi is portrayed as a sellout by the opposition parties. In the Sri Lankan case, internal political competition is also severe as between the two major political parties—the Sri Lanka Freedom Party (SLFP) and the United National Party (UNP). However, except in the 1980s, relations with India were not important in the cut and thrust of domestic politics.

Political extremism has compounded the crises of legitimacy. In Bangladesh, the rise of right-wing Islamic parties and groups has affected the conduct of both domestic and foreign policies. The return to power of Khaleda Zia with the cooperation of the Islamic parties promises to complicate India-Bangladesh relations. In Nepal, it is the Maoist left that has been the most strident critic of Nepalese foreign policy. The assassination of the royal family in the summer of 2001 and the subsequent turmoil has strengthened the hands of extreme leftists, and this may well worsen relations with India. Once again, Sri Lanka is atypical. While the right-wing Sinhala nationalist Janatha Vimukthi Peramuna (JVP) was a political force in the 1980s and is showing signs of resurgence, it has not posed a major challenge over the past fifteen years. In any case, anti-Indianism, except briefly, has not been a feature of Sri Lankan politics. It was most evident when New Delhi was behind the Tamil rebels. With the change in India's attitude in 1987, Sinhala anger toward India began to ameliorate. Since the withdrawal of Indian troops in 1991, anti-Indianism has almost completely disappeared.

In aggregate, we can see that India's relations with its smaller neighbors are conditioned by factors that are similar to the India-Pakistan case. What is striking is the relatively cordial and rational diplomacy between New Delhi and the smaller states. This is in part because the power asymmetry is so large that the small states must seek accommodation. The power asymmetry is also so large that New Delhi need not worry about the distribution of gains from cooperation. However unequal the gains from cooperation may be, the asymmetry between India and the others remains more or less unaltered. This gives India much greater latitude in dealing with the smaller states.

Two other, more idiosyncratic factors meliorated relations between India and the smaller states: an accommodative turn to Indian diplomacy, and growing

nonofficial contacts. First, the Indian government's noticeably more concessionary attitude in the 1990s was pivotal in managing conflict and boosting cooperation. The Deve Gowda government got an agreement with Dhaka by taking a much softer line. It went out of its way, for example, to separate two
issues—the sharing of the river waters and obtaining a corridor to the Northeastern states through Bangladesh. Previous Indian governments had implicitly
linked a river water agreement with the corridor, a demand that had made it virtually impossible for any government in Dhaka to come to an agreement with
India. The Gowda government built on the predecessor government's approach toward the Mahakali treaty. Earlier, the Narasimha Rao government had
made a number of concessions on the construction and financing of the Panch-
eswar and Karnali dams—the key projects in the Mahakali treaty—as also the
sharing of hydroelectricity from those projects.

Second, while nonofficial dialogues and diplomacy have generally not been
terribly successful in South Asia, they did help pave the way for the India-
Bangladesh and possibly for the India-Nepal hydrological agreements. The return of democracy in Bangladesh and Nepal opened up a political space within
which these alternate diplomatic modes of communication on water issues
could flourish. Especially on hydrological issues, Bangladeshi, Indian, and
Nepali nongovernmental experts played a significant role in brokering differences at key moments.[45]

Why were these two factors not in play in the India-Pakistan case? India did
attempt to extend its conciliatory diplomacy to Pakistan in some measure.
However, the problem is that the power asymmetry with Pakistan being much
smaller, the relative gains problem is more severe, and this makes it harder for
India to take a generous view. In addition, the very charged nature of India-
Pakistan conflict makes it difficult for any Indian government to persist with
a softer line of policy. In particular, the quarrel over Kashmir, which has be-
come so central to the overall relationship, limits the room for maneuver in
India. When Pakistan supports militants in Kashmir, it makes it virtually impossible for Indian leaders to justify concessions and cooperation. The more
Indians die in Kashmir, the more passionate are the calls not to yield, so that
those who were killed did not die in vain. As for nonofficial contacts between
India and Pakistan, these intensified in the 1990s but were largely ineffective.
Both governments were suspicious of Track II and were unhelpful in granting
visas for the meetings. Those involved in the meetings tended to be former
diplomats rather than problem-solving technocrats and academics: given that
the issues were more "political" in nature here (e.g., Kashmir rather than hy-
drology), this was not surprising. Why were the two governments so conservative? In the end, the kinds of issues that were at stake (territory) and the
high degree of suspicion and fear in both countries combined with domestic
weakness (political illegitimacy and extremism) made bolder action unthinkable. It should be noted here that, even with the small states, India has not
been terribly successful in resolving highly visible, highly symbolic territorial

issues such as South Moore/Talpatty and the enclaves with Bangladesh and Kalapani with Nepal.

NONREGIONAL ACTORS AND CONFLICT MANAGEMENT: THE UN AND THE GREAT POWERS

Nonregional actors have tried over the years to manage conflict in South Asia. In particular, the United States, Russia, and China have attempted to play a role in regulating the India-Pakistan relationship. This section deals with the interests of these three powers during and after the Cold War in managing conflict in South Asia and the successes and limits of involvement in the region. Before we deal with that, it is worth adverting briefly to the UN's largely unsuccessful role in the region.

The United Nations

In the early years of the Cold War, the UN was a major player in trying to manage and to resolve conflict between India and Pakistan. By the mid 1960s, its role was greatly diminished and restricted to posting a very small contingent of peacekeepers in Kashmir. While the UN's role in conflict management has increased in many regions in the post–Cold War period, in South Asia it has remained virtually unchanged.[46]

After the 1948 war between India and Pakistan over Kashmir, UN troops were deployed in the contested territory to separate Indian and Pakistani troops and to report on cease-fire violations. More importantly, for a decade, the UN attempted to broker a solution to the dispute. By the late 1950s, these attempts had all foundered on the objections of either India or Pakistan. Since then, the UN has only played an occasional and limited role. During the 1965 and 1971 wars, it called for a cease-fire. In both cases, the two countries did eventually stop hostilities. In doing so they cited UN resolutions, although the real reasons for their restraint went beyond respect for the international community's wishes. A crucial factor in their decisions to stop fighting was the limit on war-making capacity, particularly on the Pakistani side (e.g., shortages of ammunition and spare parts, which came from foreign suppliers and were often embargoed as soon as hostilities broke out). In addition, India had reason to fear that as the military tide turned in its favor (as it eventually must given its much greater size and power), the chances of Chinese or U.S. military intervention on Pakistan's side would increase. India has also feared that international diplomatic involvement in the region would increase should it prolong hostilities beyond a limit. After the Simla accord of 1972, the two governments agreed to settle bilateral differences amongst themselves. From 1972 to 1989, the Kashmir dispute receded from world view and India-Pakistan interactions. However, in 1989, a rebellion broke out in Kashmir and India and Pakistan once again found themselves arguing over the disputed territory. From that time, the UN has done little to resolve the resurgent conflict beyond exhorting the two countries to settle the matter peacefully and offering its good offices. Even Pakistan, which has criticized India's Kashmir policy in various forums, has not formally asked the UN to mediate.[47]

Why has the UN not played a greater role in the India-Pakistan conflict over Kashmir? First of all, the organization seems not to have forgotten the interminable negotiations of the 1950s and 1960s. This was the first dispute to be brought to the UN, and despite several exhaustive efforts neither party to the quarrel was moved to implement UN recommendations.[48] Second, South Asia was never very central to the Cold War, and so the great powers gradually lost interest in having the UN do much more than it had initially done. The region remained a strategic backwater for the major powers after 1989. Third, the stalemate in the UN between the United States and Soviets meant that the organization became increasingly powerless to proceed in South Asia during the Cold War. Moscow, given its quasi-alliance with India, was unwilling after the mid 1960s to support any UN moves to discuss the subject.[49] After the Cold War, both Washington and Moscow do not seem to want to antagonize India in this matter. Even China, since the late 1970s, has supported a bilateral solution to the problem.[50] Fourth, during the Cold War, India and Pakistan themselves gradually turned away from the UN. India saw the Anglo-American powers as tilting toward Pakistan as a consequence of Cold War partnerships with Islamabad and therefore did not trust the UN to be neutral over Kashmir.[51] India's suspicion of the UN remains strong. Pakistan saw little advantage in going to the UN after a point, given the Soviet veto, and reconciled itself to either snatching Kashmir away militarily (as in 1965) or ignoring the issue as far as it could (from 1972 to 1989). Since 1989, it is back to supporting a military option in respect of Kashmir. It also recognizes that none of the major powers, China included, is interested in making Kashmir an issue in the UN.[52]

The Great Powers

During the Cold War, the United States and Soviet Union tried to regulate the relationship between India and the smaller states, primarily Pakistan, for a number of reasons. First, they sought to prevent the South Asian countries from drifting into the strategic sphere of the other side. Second, in order to play a role in the U.S.-led or Soviet-led alliance system, India and Pakistan in particular had to be freed from South Asian preoccupations. Third, the United States and Soviets wanted to ensure that hostilities between India and Pakistan did not drag them into the fray on behalf of their partners. Fourth, conflict in South Asia, on the flanks of the Gulf and Southeast Asia, might affect U.S. and Soviet interests in these nearby and more important regions.

After the Cold War, the United States and Russia came to look at South Asia rather differently. A competition for partners in South Asia was no longer a factor in U.S. and Russia calculations. Nor did either India or Pakistan have a larger role in the strategic plans of the two powers. The United States had some interest in Pakistan as a moderate Islamic state helping to curb Muslim fundamentalism and shoring up Gulf security, but this was a far cry from its frontline role after 1979. India might become a counterweight to China eventually but was not particularly important since it was no longer a quasi-ally of the Soviet Union. The fear of being dragged into a South Asian conflict and the effects on nearby regions remained. However, conflict came to be seen not in terms of conventional war but instead as a nuclear confrontation between India and Pakistan.[53]

What incentives did the United States, the sole superpower, as well as the other major powers, especially China, have in managing conflict in South Asia given this changed situation? The *proliferation* of nuclear weapons, the desire for *stability* in the region, and the threat of *Islamic fundamentalism* encouraged these powers as well as other outsiders to encourage cooperation and conflict management.

Nuclear Weapons

With the end of the Cold War, the United States came to see South Asia primarily as a nuclear flashpoint. Washington was hopeful of stopping the nuclearization of India and Pakistan and to strengthen the nuclear nonproliferation regime by doing so. Beyond the fate of the nuclear order, Washington feared that, armed with nuclear devices, India and Pakistan might find themselves in a nuclear standoff. This might then drag outside powers in, led by China. To the extent that China became involved in a South Asian nuclear standoff, Russia might be drawn in. The United States would then face some very difficult choices. Worse still, if either India or Pakistan or both actually came to use nuclear weapons, then the nuclear taboo in operation since 1945 would be violated. This also was not in the U.S. interest. Conflict management therefore was a necessary adjunct to nonproliferation policy. The international community had to find a way to reduce differences between India and Pakistan and to ensure that they did not drift into crisis. This required more than nonproliferation controls.[54]

Regional Stability

For the United States, stability in South Asia after the Cold War is important for the simple reason that, with a population of a billion and a half souls, this could be a massive zone of turbulence. The effects of this turbulence would be felt far afield. Stability in South Asia is threatened by many factors—economic deprivation, social tensions, malgovernance, internal conflict, and interstate tensions. The combination of these could result in massive internal or external violence or both. With nuclear weapons, violence could escalate to catastrophic levels. Even if violence is contained, there could be a slow economic, social, and political collapse that could culminate in state failure. In such a situation the United States, and the international community at large, would be hard pressed to stay aloof. South Asia's deterioration into another Africa—only bigger and with nuclear weapons around—would be a strategic and humanitarian calamity, not just for the subcontinent but also for Asia as a whole.[55]

As China looks at South Asia, it too sees the specter of instability. Chinese calculations about the region are complex, but on balance Beijing would like India and Pakistan to avoid hostilities. From the late 1970s, therefore, Chinese policy toward South Asia emphasized regional cooperation and bilateral conflict management. At the same time, it has sold arms and transferred nuclear and missile technology to Islamabad. Chinese motivations appear to be to help construct a military balance between India and Pakistan while building bridges with New Delhi. Thus, since the late 1970s, Chinese policy has followed a dual track: strengthening Pakistan militarily and cultivating India diplomatically. The diplomatic track with India has involved five sets of policies: normalizing diplomatic ties; resuming negotiations over the border dispute; increasing the frequency of high-level political contacts—at the Foreign Ministers, Premier/Prime Minister, and Presidential levels; instituting confidence-building measures (CBMs) for military stability; and, most recently, starting a security dialogue on issues not covered by the border negotiations and CBMs.[56]

China's interest in a stable South Asia arises from not wanting to be dragged into a confrontation in a theater that is a low priority.[57] It especially does not want an India-Pakistan confrontation to become a larger conflict that would draw in the Russians and Americans. However, China also has its own very distinct concerns. For example, it does not want the United States in particular to become entrenched in the region. An American presence along its southern periphery is in China's view dangerous, particularly given the Tibet problem. Specifically, it does not want the United States and India to become partners in Asia. A policy of engagement with India is therefore vital.[58] However, for China to be taken seriously in New Delhi requires Beijing to move away from its reflexive support of Pakistan and its anti-Indian diplomacy. The most productive way of doing this, from China's standpoint, is to bring about some degree of reconciliation between the two South Asian neighbors.[59]

Islamic Fundamentalism

Both China and the United States have a common interest in stabilizing South Asia from the point of view of their fear of Islamic fundamentalism and militancy. One of China's internal vulnerabilities is Xinjiang where Muslim Uighurs militants are fighting for independence. Beijing's interest is to dampen Islamic extremism throughout this area—Central Asia, Afghanistan, and Pakistan. Pakistan has played a role in encouraging Islamic forces and could expand its support of various militant organizations in the future, particularly if it becomes more Islamic itself.[60] China is therefore increasingly worried about the future of its erstwhile ally. Greater stability and cooperation in South Asia would reduce the influence of Islamic forces in Pakistan and is therefore in China's interest. The United States fears that the epicenter of radical Islam is shifting from North Africa and the Gulf to Afghanistan, Central Asia, and Pakistan.[61] The terrorist attacks in the United States on 11 September 2001 have only underlined this shift. Pakistan's Islamic parties, *madrassahs*, Kashmiri *jehadi* groups, and links to the Taliban make it a particular concern. If Pakistan came to be ruled by radical Islamic forces, the spread of Muslim fundamentalism would be greatly increased. Pakistan's assets are its size, the much greater resources and organization of its Islamic groups, and its conventional and nuclear forces. A nuclear Pakistan could become an unparalleled protector and promoter of radical Islamic forces. Regional stability would help in this situation. Liberal forces in Pakistan would have greater room for political maneuver and might be strong enough to hold Islamic forces at bay.[62]

The Limits of Outside Involvement

The United States and China as well as others such as the European Union and Japan have attempted to bring about a measure of cooperativeness between India and Pakistan and India and the smaller states.

First of all, the outside powers have counseled India and Pakistan to institute confidence-building measures to avoid military instability and to control their nuclear programs in the interest of regional peace. After the nuclear tests of 1998, they urged the two countries to avoid deploying nuclear weapons, to stop testing, to sign and ratify the Comprehensive Test Ban Treaty (CTBT), to end fissile material production, and to strengthen their export controls on dual-use technologies.[63] Both countries have been repeatedly asked to make public their conception of a minimum deterrent and to reassure the world about command and control systems.

Second, Islamabad and New Delhi have been asked to find a long-lasting settlement of the Kashmir dispute since this is the origin of their conflict. Proliferation and war arise from the quarrel over Kashmir. In the end, therefore, there must be a just settlement. Given the long and seemingly unproductive history of Kashmir negotiations, particularly in the UN, outsiders are aware that the multilateral track to a solution is fraught with difficulties. India's well-known opposition to a multilateral process is the most serious hurdle and has thus far not been seriously challenged. Outsiders have been supportive of bilateral negotiations between India and Pakistan and have, at most, offered their good offices.[64]

Third, the outside powers have urged both India and the smaller states to settle their outstanding bilateral disputes. The Europeans in particular have encouraged India and Pakistan to get SAARC unstuck and to foster regional cooperation so that the smaller states are stabilized. Regional cooperation in South

Asia, in this view, could evolve structures of peace on the model of the EU and thereby foster the conditions for military stability between the two principal powers as well.[65]

The attempts of outsiders to manage conflict in South Asia over the past decade have, however, produced a very mixed record. The international community was unable to stop either India or Pakistan going nuclear. After the 1998 tests, the United States adopted the most punitive approach by enacting sanctions. Japan followed suit. However, far more important has been the attempt to begin a process of dialogue with Islamabad and New Delhi in the service of nuclear moderation.[66] In these dialogues, the outside powers have not only counseled military restraint on the part of both India and Pakistan, they have also urged direct talks between the two neighbors. The India-Pakistan summit of February 1999 seemed to vindicate this approach.

However, within months the two countries were at war, not at peace. The Lahore agreement stands repudiated by the military government of Pakistan. India-Pakistan relations have scarcely ever been worse in its wake. The coming to power of General Musharraf, the person thought to be responsible for the Kargil war at least in India, and the hijacking of an Indian civilian airline from Kathmandu to Kandahar by Kashmiri militants later in 1999 caused relations to plummet to an all-time low. Prior to the nuclear tests and under the terms of the Lahore agreement, the two sides were committed to a dialogue on eight issues, including Kashmir. By the end of 1999, the prospects of a Kashmir dialogue had dimmed. India made talks conditional on Pakistan stopping its interference in Kashmir. Pakistan in turn refused to talk to India until India was serious about a Kashmir dialogue. In 2001, they nevertheless resumed negotiations, though with no great success.

Having said that, outside pressures and engagement have not been completely ineffective. The fear of alienating outside powers completely has both constrained and channeled Indian and Pakistani choices and actions. New Delhi and Islamabad's covert and protracted nuclearization, stretched out over decades, is testimony in part to the power of external pressures. The India-Pakistan CBMs agenda of the 1990s grew out of U.S. suggestions made at the time of the 1990 Kashmir crisis that the two countries might avoid future crises and, in any case, manage future difficulties better if they set up a process by which communication and transparency was enhanced.[67] As noted above, the Lahore summit was partly a response to the criticism of the nuclear tests of May 1998 and the fear that nuclear weapons would cause greater tensions in South Asia. The Lahore agreement outlined a series of nuclear arms control and confidence-building measures for the future. During the Kargil war, the United States and other Western powers in particular but also China played a role in containing the degree of violence and in getting Pakistan eventually to withdraw its troops from the Indian side of the line of control (LOC). In particular, the Clinton-Sharif summit in June 1999 produced the so-called Washington agreement by which Islamabad undertook to pull its troops back and end the war.[68] The summit between Prime Minister Vajpayee and President Musharraf in Agra in July 2001 was also in part a response to pressures from the international community, particularly on Pakistan to restart the process of dialogue. The point is not that every cooperative initiative in South Asia can be traced back to outside pressures and suggestions. Outsiders have not always been the prime movers behind conflict management, but they have been a force of some significance.

In respect of India's relations with the smaller states, outside powers have urged India to be more accommodative and the smaller states to be more pragmatic as well. They have applauded New Delhi's more concessionary approach over the past decade and they have made it clear to the smaller states that they cannot support these countries against India. Virtually all the major outside powers, except China, have indicated that India is the major power of the region and is increasingly important in global calculations. The smaller states have therefore been put on notice that they should be more cooperative with New Delhi. Outside pressures have probably been more influential with the smaller states than India. Since the late 1980s, Indian policy was inclined to be more concessionary anyway, and outside advice to this effect was in many ways unnecessary. Outside pressures were more effective with the smaller states given their *dependence*—economic dependence in particular—on powerful nonregional states.

Why have the outside powers not been a greater force for stability and cooperation in South Asia, especially between India and Pakistan? Clearly, the nonregional powers such as the United States and China dispose of enormous capabilities. As the sole superpower, the United States alone dwarfs India and Pakistan. Its diplomatic, economic, and military capacities should be more effective, especially after the Cold War when there is no oppositional power. Similarly, China should have been in a position to exert greater influence over Pakistan to manage conflict in South Asia. A number of factors have limited outside influence.

First of all, South Asia is unique among regions in terms of the power aggregation that India and Pakistan represent. India and Pakistan are no ordinary regional states. They are also the second largest and the seventh largest in population terms. India's economy is the fourth largest in the world in terms of Purchasing Power Parity (PPP).[69] The Indian armed forces are the fourth biggest and the Pakistani forces are the eighth biggest. Both now have nuclear weapons. In sum, it is not easy to coerce or co-opt these two powers. Their capacity to resist and to chart their own course is much greater than most states in the international system.

Second, neither South Asian power is so strong that it could not, at the limit, be cajoled and coerced into managing conflict in ways that reflect the preferences of the great powers, but the will of the outside powers to deploy their resources to do so is questionable. No power has such great stakes in South Asia. South Asia is not the Middle East for instance. It has no natural resources that make it a global asset. Nor do powerful outsiders have deep historical or ethnic links to India or Pakistan or any of the smaller states. The U.S. interest in the Middle East is a function not only of the need for oil but also of the stakes in Israel's survival and well-being, which have their roots in recent Judeo-Christian history and the tragedy of the Holocaust. South Asia does not excite such involvement.

Third, forces in civil society in both India and Pakistan have great mobilizational capacity, both against the state and against foreign influence. These forces, especially religious and political extremists, are particularly effective on matters of India-Pakistan relations. Ironically, it is the greater democratization of these countries that makes it possible for such groups to be effective. Secret deals and diplomacy and dramatic changes in policy, which might occur in authoritarian societies, are virtually impossible in India and Pakistan.

Fourth, larger strategic differences between the outside powers, in particular the United States and China, get in the way of a coherent and concerted approach. While U.S. and Chinese interests in South Asia are roughly parallel, their own bilateral difficulties have intruded into the region's affairs. For instance, U.S. arms sales to Taiwan may over the years have caused China to transfer nuclear and missile technologies to Pakistan in reaction.[70] Most analysts have explained Chinese policy in this matter in terms of balancing Indian power. While this is not altogether incorrect, it is only a partial analysis at best. China's motives go much deeper including the desire to react to U.S. policies that offend it, particularly in East Asia. The U.S.–China rivalry has not therefore left South Asia untouched: the China-Pakistan nuclear and missile relationship was cited by India as a reason for its nuclear tests in May 1998. The Bush administration's recent promise to resume arms sales to Taiwan was greeted by a Chinese statement to the effect that it might be forced to go back on proliferation undertakings it had given Washington.[71] This could well have implications once again for South Asia and could raise tensions between India, Pakistan, and China.

CONCLUSION: FUTURE PROSPECTS

What is the future of conflict management in South Asia? The events of 11 September 2001 and the U.S. attacks in Afghanistan are new elements in regional politics. Judged by the conclusions we have drawn on the incentives and disincentives for conflict management and cooperation in South Asia, what are the prospects?

First of all, there is little hope that either regional organization or the UN will play any great role in South Asia in the future. Nothing has changed in terms of their ability and willingness to get involved.

Second, in terms of bilateral conflict management, the India-Pakistan situation is critical. The most important factor is the future of Pakistan. If as a result of Pakistan's alliance with the United States in the fight against terrorism, the legitimacy of the Musharraf government is undermined and extremist forces in that country gain significant ground, and certainly if they overthrow moderate groups altogether, then relations with India will worsen, perhaps dramatically so. On the Indian side, the calls for a more "proactive" policy against Pakistan over Kashmir will only compound the dangers of confrontation.

Between India and the smaller states, the situation may also deteriorate with various domestic political changes in motion domestically. In Bangladesh, the rise of Islamic forces and the coming to power of the more conservative Khaleda Zia government could make relations with India more difficult. In Nepal, the shaky status of the new king and the increasing power of the Maoists does not bode well for stability. In Sri Lanka, the Kumaratunga government faces a rebellion within its own ranks. Finally, India too must confront a number of challenges. The war in Afghanistan may well spark communal clashes between Hindus and Muslims. If there are terrorist strikes against India by Islamic groups related to Al Qaeda, the pressures on India to retaliate in some way and the provocation to Hindu groups would be intense. In March 2002, right-wing Hindu groups have promised to build a temple on the site of the Babri Masjid mosque. As that date approaches, clashes between the two communities could well increase independent of what happens in Afghanistan.

Third, the outside powers have an interest in South Asian stability as never before. The United States in particular as also China and Russia do not want to see India and Pakistan square off in a fight at a time when they are trying to combat and contain Islamic extremists in Afghanistan. Washington in particular is trying hard to convince both New Delhi and Islamabad to keep talking and avoid taking any actions against the other's interests. To this end, Secretary of State Colin Powell made a two-day trip to India and Pakistan in October 2001. Whether under U.S. pressure or not, Pakistan has invited the Indian foreign minister to visit Pakistan. The Indian foreign minister has accepted. No dates have been set, and there is little optimism that the two will actually meet. However, India has said it will not take advantage of Pakistan's difficulties: the Indian government has rejected calls in India for military strikes across the line of control in Kashmir against terrorist camps. Pakistan, under pressure from the United States, has said it will conduct an inquiry into terrorism against India. Whether the United States and the other powers can do more to manage India-Pakistan conflict remains to be seen. Given Pakistan's difficulties with its Islamic extremists, it is doubtful that Islamabad can seriously engage India. However, the United States will have succeeded if it merely avoids a serious deterioration in relations in South Asia.

Should Pakistan collapse into anarchy or fall into the hands of religious extremists, the whole regional picture could change. India might then become a frontline state against terrorism. Conflict management mechanisms will at that point have almost completely collapsed. With nuclear weapons in the hands of a radical government in Pakistan, this could be an extremely dangerous situation—

necessitating conflict management more than ever and yet never further from conflict management.

NOTES

1. There is a large literature on the South Asian Association for Regional Coopera-tion (SAARC). The journal *South Asian Survey* publishes this regionalist literature. On confidence building, see Michael Krepon and Amit Sewak, eds., *Crisis Prevention, Con-fidence Building, and Reconciliation in South Asia* (New York: St. Martin's Press, 1995), as well as Ted Greenwood and Sumit Ganguly, eds., *Mending Fences: Confidence- and Security-Building Measures in South Asia* (Boulder, Colo.: Westview, 1996). Also see Jasjit Singh, "Conflict Prevention and Management: The Indian Way," in *Asian Strategic Review, 1995–96* (New Delhi: Institute for Defense Studies and Analyses, 1996), 9–26; and P. Sahadevan, ed., *Conflict and Peacemaking in South Asia* (New Delhi: Lancer's Books, 2001) for a collection of essays.

2. Stephen P. Cohen, *India: Emerging Power* (Washington, D.C.: The Brookings In-stitution, 2001), 232–45.

3. See A. G. Noorani, *Confidence Building Measures in Siachen Glacier, Sir Creek, and Wular Barrage: Easing the Indo-Pakistani Dialogue on Kashmir*, Occasional Paper No. 16 (Washington, D.C.: Henry L. Stimson Center, 1994).

4. Ashutosh Mishra, "Beyond Kashmir: The Siachen, Sir Creek, and Tulbul/Wular Disputes," in *Kargil and After: Challenges for Indian Policy*, ed. Kanti Bajpai, Afsir Karim, and Amitabh Mattoo (New Delhi: Har Anand, 2001), 196–241, for a review of the negotiations on the two disputes.

5. This was evident during the India-Pakistan summit in Agra in July 2001 where Pakistan insisted that Kashmir was the "core" issue and at best Islamabad could accept that other issues would be discussed "in tandem." See Harinder Baweja and Shishir Gupta, "Kashmir on the Mind," *India Today* (New Delhi), 16 July 2001, 34.

6. For India's stand on resuming talks after Kargil, see "Vajpayee Reaffirms Refusal to Talks With Pakistan," *Taaza News,* at http://news.zeenext.com/links/articles.asp?aid= 1507&sid=VAV, 11 September 2000. On Pakistan's view of resuming the dialogue, see a series of reports summarized by the Institute for Peace and Conflict Studies, New Delhi, in November 1999, at its website, www.ipcs.org/archives/a-p-index/99-11-nov.html.

7. Nitin Gokhale, Saba Naqvi Bhaumik, and Murali Krishnan, "Home-made Fiasco," *Outlook* (New Delhi), 7 May 2001, 22–25.

8. See Vijendra Singh Jafa, "Administrative Policies and Ethnic Disintegration," in *Faultlines: Writings on Conflict and Resolution*, vol. 2, ed. K. P. S. Gill and Ajai Sahni (New Delhi: Bulwark Books and Institute for Conflict Management, 1999), 50; and Ved Marwah, "Threats to Internal Security," in *Securing India's Future in the New Millen-nium,* ed. Brahma Chellaney (New Delhi: Orient Longman 1999), 304–5.

9. Cohen, *India: Emerging Power,* 220, notes that India and Pakistan accuse each other of the use of covert violence.

10. See Ashutosh Varshney, "Three Compromised Nationalisms: Why Kashmir Has Been a Problem," in *Perspectives on Kashmir,* ed. Raju G. C. Thomas (Boulder, Colo.: Westview, 1992), 192–234.

11. Sumit Ganguly, *The Origins of War in South Asia: Indo-Pakistani Conflicts Since 1947* (Boulder, Colo.: Westview, 1994), chapter 1, makes this argument neatly.

12. Kanti Prasad Bajpai, "The Origins of Association in South Asia: SAARC, 1979–1989" (Ph.D. diss., University of Illinois, Urbana-Champaign, 1990), chapter II, 61–86.

13. India and Pakistan solved their most important hydrological issues when they signed the Indus Rivers Treaty in 1960. New Delhi and Islamabad remain in dispute over the Wular Barrage/Tulbul project.

14. See Cohen, *India: Emerging Power*, 232–45, for a survey of these and other problems.

15. Ross Masood Hussain, "SAARC 1985–1995," in *The Dynamics of South Asia: Regional Cooperation and SAARC*, ed. Eric Gonsalves and Nancy Jetly (New Delhi: Sage Publications, 1999), 27.

16. See Kanti Bajpai, "Security and SAARC," *South Asian Survey* (New Delhi) 3, nos. 1 and 2 (1996): 295–307, on SAARC's security role.

17. On South Asia's Track II, see Navnita Chadha, Paul Evans, and Gowher Rizvi, *Beyond Boundaries: A Report on the State of Non-Official Dialogues on Peace, Security and Cooperation in South Asia* (Toronto: University of Toronto Press, 1997). See also Aabha Dixit, "India-Pakistan Relations: A Survey," in *Securing India's Future*, ed. Chellaney, 460–63.

18. J. N. Dixit, "Changing Strategic Environment and India's Security," *Strategic Analysis* (New Delhi) 17, no. 8 (November 1994): 932, for an understanding of some of these factors by a retired Indian diplomat.

19. See Rosemary Foot, "The Sino-Soviet Complex and South Asia," in *The Great Powers and South Asian Insecurity*, ed. Barry Buzan, Gowher Rizvi, Rosemary Foot, and Nancy Jetley (London: Macmillan, 1986), 197. During the Kargil war of 1999, China took a very balanced view of India-Pakistan relations and indeed in crucial respects sided with India. See Bhartendu Kumar Singh and Satyajit Mohanty, "Contextualizing Kargil Within China's Security Paradigm," in *Kargil: The Tables Turned*, ed. Ashok Krishna and P. R. Chari (New Delhi: Manohar, 2001), 222.

20. This is noted in Thom A. Travis, "Advantages and Disadvantages for Pakistan in the Post Cold War World," in *Readings in Pakistan's Foreign Policy, 1971–1998*, ed. Mehrunnisa Ali (Karachi: Oxford University Press, 2001), 428.

21. Travis, "Advantages and Disadvantages for Pakistan," 430–31, on U.S. loss of interest in Pakistan.

22. Marvi Memon, "Reorientation of Pakistan's Foreign Policy After the Cold War," in *Readings in Pakistan's Foreign Policy*, ed. Mehrunnisa Ali, 409–11.

23. For New Delhi's calculations with regard to U.S. nonproliferation policies, see J. N. Dixit, *Across Borders: Fifty Years of India's Foreign Policy* (New Delhi: Picus, 1998), 291–94. For Pakistan's concerns, see Memon, "Reorientation of Pakistan's Foreign Policy After the Cold War," 412–14.

24. On the importance of military stability after nuclearization, see Amitabh Mattoo, "Military and Nuclear CBMs in South Asia," in *The Challenge of Confidence-Building in South Asia*, ed. Moonis Ahmar (New Delhi: Har Anand, 2001), 210–12; and Lt. Gen. Talat Masood, "Confidence Building Measures: Concepts and Applications," in *The Challenge of Confidence-Building*, ed. Ahmar, 28, 30, and 32–33.

25. On the relationship of democratization, internal instabilities, and war, see Edward D. Mansfield and Jack Snyder, "Democratization and the Danger of War," *International Security* 20, no. 1 (Summer 1995): 5–38.

26. S. Akbar Zaidi, "Economic CBMs in South Asia: Trade as a Precursor to Peace with India," in *The Challenge of Confidence-Building*, ed. Ahmar, 345–49, shows how the

Pakistani military has an interest in perpetuating tensions with India. Zaidi is a Pakistani economist.

27. Zaidi, "Economic CBMs in South Asia," 339, on why trade with India is economically beneficial for Pakistan.

28. Dixit, *Across Borders*, 197, on how India welcomed the return of democracy in Pakistan in 1988.

29. Jasjit Singh, "Trends in Defense Expenditure," in *Asian Strategic Review, 1995–96*, 49, 61.

30. Aabha Dixit, "India-Pakistan Relations," 458–59, is instructive on this point.

31. Pran Chopra, "Prospects for Peace with Pakistan," in *Securing India's Future*, ed. Chellaney, 484–85, on Pakistan's general reluctance to go along with economic and other forms of cooperation. The figure of $1.5 billion comes from the World Bank economist Mahbub ul Haq. See his "Indo-Pak Relations: Proposals for a New Beginning," *Journal of Peace Studies* (New Delhi) 3, no. 14 (January–February 1996): 69. For a Pakistani view of the benefits of trade, see Zaidi, "Economic CBMs in South Asia."

32. Aijaz Ahmed, "The Hindutva Weapon," in *Out of the Nuclear Shadow*, ed. Smitu Kothari and Zia Mian (New Delhi: Lokayan and Rainbow Publishers, 2001), 209, shows how quickly the anti-BJP opposition parties jumped on the BJP nuclear bandwagon.

33. On the disproportionate power of Pakistani extremists, see Irfan Hussain, "Waiting to Exhale: Pakistan Can Pull Back from the Abyss," *Times of India*, 28 September 2001. The author is a well known Pakistani columnist.

34. See "Lahore Declaration, February 21, 1999," Appendix 11, *Strategic Analysis* (New Delhi), Special Issue, "The Highway Beyond Agra," vol. XXV, no. 7 (October 2001): 877–80.

35. See Kanti Bajpai, "Making South Asia Into a Flashpoint: Bombs, Wars, Coups and Hijacks," in *Kargil and After*, ed. Bajpai, Karim, and Mattoo, 15–31, on how these events are linked.

36. Mansfield and Snyder, "Democratization and War."

37. Sumit Ganguly, "Discord and Cooperation in India-Pakistan Relations," in *Interpreting World Politics*, ed. Kanti P. Bajpai and Harish C. Shukul (New Delhi: Sage Publications, 1995), 408–9.

38. Ashley Tellis, *Stability in South Asia: Prospects of Indo-Pak Nuclear Conflict*, A RAND Report (Dehra Dun, India: Natraj Publishers, 2000), 21.

39. Krepon and Sewak, eds., *Crisis Prevention, Confidence Building, and Reconciliation in South Asia*, appendix I, 239–61, for the text of the various CBMs.

40. Bajpai, "The Origins of Association in South Asia," chapter V.

41. See John W. Garver, *Protracted Contest: Sino-Indian Rivalry in the Twentieth Century* (Seattle: University of Washington Press, 2001), 157–61, on Beijing's very modest support to Kathmandu.

42. Denis Kux, *Estranged Democracies: India and the United States, 1941–1991* (New Delhi: Sage Publications, 1993), 412–16.

43. Zaidi, "Economic CBMs in South Asia," 343, quotes the eminent Pakistani economist Shahid Javed Burki on how South Asia's exclusion from regional economic groupings is an incentive to cooperate amongst themselves.

44. Bajpai, "The Origins of Association in South Asia," 283–88, for how SAARC functions as a "cover."

45. See Ramaswamy R. Iyer, "Three River Water Treaties," in *Conflict and Peacemaking in South Asia*, ed. Sahadevan, 394, note 10.

46. For a useful overview of the UN's involvement in India-Pakistan relations, see C. S. R. Murthy, "The United Nations and the India-Pakistan Conflict," in *Conflict and Peacemaking in South Asia*, ed. Sahadevan, 458–82.

47. During the July 2001 summit, President Pervez Musharraf of Pakistan conspicuously avoided any mention of a possible UN role in the India-Pakistan dispute.

48. Murthy, "The United Nations and the India-Pakistan Conflict," 458–59. The UN held 148 meetings and passed nineteen resolutions on India-Pakistan relations over five decades.

49. Murthy, "The United Nations and the India-Pakistan Conflict," 462–63 and 474.

50. See Garver, *Protracted Contest*, 227–34, on the nuances of China's position but its basic support for bilateral conflict resolution between India and Pakistan.

51. Murthy, "The United Nations and India-Pakistan Conflict," 474; and Kux, *Estranged Democracies*, 116.

52. A Pakistani scholar, Moonis Ahmar, recognizes this clearly. See Ahmar, "Gains and Costs of Third Party Mediation," in *Conflict and Peacemaking in South Asia*, ed. Sahadevan, 498.

53. Three out of four major reports on South Asia by U.S. think tanks focused on nuclear weapons: *Nuclear Weapons and South Asian Security*, Report of the Carnegie Task Force on Non-Proliferation and South Asian Security, Carnegie Endowment for International Peace, Washington, D.C., 1988; *South Asia and the United States After the Cold War*, A Study Sponsored by the Asia Society, New York, 1994; *Preventing Nuclear Proliferation in South Asia*, A Study Sponsored by the Asia Society, New York, 1995; and *After the Tests: U.S. Policy Towards India and Pakistan*, Report of an Independent Task Force, Co-sponsored by The Brookings Institution and the Council on Foreign Relations, 1998.

54. See *After the Tests,* which suggests that nonproliferation controls can only be one part of the effort to control the spread of nuclear weapons.

55. See *South Asia and the United States*, vii and viii, on the U.S. interest in a stable South Asia.

56. Garver, *Protracted Contest*, 216–42, deals with China's dual track policy in the region.

57. Garver, *Protracted Contest,* 381.

58. Garver, *Protracted Contest,* 225–26, 378, and 389, on Chinese concerns about the United States. See also Maqsudul Hasan Nuri, "China and South Asia in the 21st Century," *Peace Initiatives* (New Delhi) V, nos. III-IV (May–December 1999): 206–7.

59. Garver, *Protracted Contest*, 220, 227–34, and 240.

60. Anil Joseph Chandy, "India, China and Pakistan," in *The Peacock and the Dragon: India-China Relations in the 21st Century,* ed. Kanti Bajpai and Amitabh Mattoo (New Delhi: Har Anand, 2000), 330; and Fazal-ur-Rahman, "Pakistan's Relations with China," *Peace Initiatives* (New Delhi) V, nos. III-IV (May–December 1999): 185–87, on China's concern over Xinjiang and Islamic fundamentalism.

61. See "Lashkar Ought to Be on U.S. Blacklist: India," *The Times of India,* 2 May 2001. The story notes that the U.S. State Department's report, "Patterns of Global Terrorism," identifies a shift in the epicenter of terrorism from the Middle East and Gulf to South Asia.

62. U.S. academics and policy makers argue that India should cooperate with Pakistan so that Pakistani liberals can be strengthened politically. This would redound to India's advantage in the long run.

63. *After the Tests,* 7–8.

64. The United States has stated that it does not seek a mediatory role but would consider such a role if asked by both countries.

65. See, for instance, K. B. Lall, H. S. Chopra, and Thomas Meyer, ed., *The European Community and SAARC* (New Delhi: Radiant Publishers, 1993).

66. India, for instance, has security/strategic dialogues with Australia, China, France, Germany, Japan, Russia, Saudi Arabia, the United Kingdom, and the United States.

67. George Perkovich, *India's Nuclear Bomb: The Impact on Global Proliferation* (New Delhi: Oxford University Press, 1999), 309–10.

68. Suba Chandran, "Role of the United States: Mediator or Mere Facilitator?" in *Kargil: The Tables Turned,* ed. Ashok Krishna and P. R. Chari (New Delhi: Manohar, 2001), 212–17.

69. "India World's 4th Largest Economy," *Hindustan Times,* 30 April 2001, quotes a World Bank report that puts India behind the United States, China, and Japan.

70. See the *Asian Wall Street Journal* report by Robert S. Greenberger and Matt Forney, "China Tests Weapons Limits With Pakistan," reprinted in *Peace Initiatives* (New Delhi), Omnibus Issue on "Sino-Pakistani Strategic Cooperation," V, nos. III-IV (May–December 1999): 89.

71. Evan S. Medeiros, "Rebuilding Bilateral Consensus: Assessing the U.S.–China Arms Control and Nonproliferation Achievements," *The Nonproliferation Review* 8, no. 1 (Spring 2001): 137–38.

8

Regional Conflict Management in Europe

John S. Duffield

This chapter assesses the prospects for the successful management of conflict in Europe during the next decade and possibly beyond.[1] It concludes that these prospects are, on the whole, relatively bright, for two complementary reasons. First, the potential for militarized conflict in Europe is relatively low in comparison with other parts of the world and is likely to remain so. Second, the region possesses substantial institutional capabilities for collective conflict management (CCM).[2] Indeed, Europe is arguably the region where such capabilities are best developed and most numerous.

To be sure, this forecast is not entirely sunny, and the situation does not allow for complacency. In the first place, the potential for violent conflict in Europe, although relatively small, is very real. In particular, serious political conflicts continue to smolder in Southeastern Europe and the former Soviet Union (FSU). Nevertheless, more and more of the continent is being steadily transformed into a "zone of peace" in which armed hostilities on any significant scale are highly unlikely and, increasingly, even unimaginable.[3] Consequently, much of the conflict management activity in the region will take the form of ameliorating and even resolving remaining nonviolent intrastate and interstate differences, and such efforts will be greatly abetted by the processes associated with the enlargement of the North Atlantic Treaty Organization (NATO) and the European Union (EU).

A second caveat follows from the fact that the capabilities for CCM are lodged in several international organizations, the most important of which are the Organization for Security and Cooperation in Europe (OSCE), NATO, and the EU/Western European Union (WEU) nexus. This fragmentation of capabilities complicates the task of CCM whenever the coordination of two or more organizations is required. Thus at least as important as developing further institutional capacity is the task of improving the mechanisms for coordinating the activities of the various extant organizations. Nevertheless, the lack of centralization also results in a certain degree of institutional depth that allows decision makers greater flexibility and a wider range of options for conflict management.

The chapter is organized in four sections. The first section specifies the general tasks of conflict management. The second identifies the most likely regional sources of conflict during the next decade. A third section describes the existing institutional capabilities for CCM in the region. A conclusion assesses the adequacy of those capabilities in view of the nature and magnitude of the challenge, emphasizing the role that regional organizations can play in defusing remaining conflicts by promoting the internal transformation of states into stable democracies marked by the rule of law and respect for human rights.

FRAMEWORK OF ANALYSIS

In order to assess the prospects for successful conflict management, one must first identify the types of conflict that are possible and the forms of conflict management that are necessary and appropriate for addressing them.

This chapter takes a broad view of the types of conflict that might be the object of conflict management efforts in Europe. Relevant conflicts may be either intrastate or interstate in nature, although the former have dominated regional conflict managements activities since the end of the Cold War. Moreover, both domestic and international conflict may assume a variety of forms. At the core of any situation that might prompt efforts at conflict management, however, is a political conflict. Political conflicts can occur between two or more groups over any objects, tangible or intangible, to which those groups may assign value, such as geographical territory, economic and financial resources, political standing, identity, religious expression, and so on.

Frequently, political conflicts are dealt with by the groups involved through nonviolent means. Indeed, the essential purpose of many political structures and processes, both domestically and internationally, is the expression and reconciliation of political differences. Where such political institutions are absent, weak, or lack legitimacy, or where the nature of the political conflict is especially acute, however, the potential exists for the conflict to become violent. One side may choose to resort to the use of armed force to achieve its goals, or an event may occur that may convince one side that it has been—or will soon be—the target of an armed attack and must react accordingly.

Consequently, the focus of this analysis is situations of political conflict in which the potential for physical violence is high, if not yet realized. Such conflicts may remain peaceful yet potentially violent, they may be ameliorated to the point where the potential for violence is low or nonexistent, or they may intensify to the point where violence seems imminent, or what I shall term a "crisis situation." Once a crisis situation is reached, two outcomes are most likely: either a de-escalation of the crisis or the eruption of armed conflict. Militarized political conflict may proceed at various levels of violence and destruction and for varying lengths of time. Should hostilities cease and the conflict reenter a nonviolent phase, the principal possibilities are a renewal of hostilities, a continuation of tensions just short of organized violence, or a further reduction of tension to the point where a more normal situation of political conflict is arrived at (see figure 8.1).

Using this typology of conflict situations, one can identify a number of potential goals and corresponding activities for conflict management. These activities span a wide spectrum ranging from the use of various forms of diplomacy through the employment of economic instruments to the direct application of military force (see table 8.1).

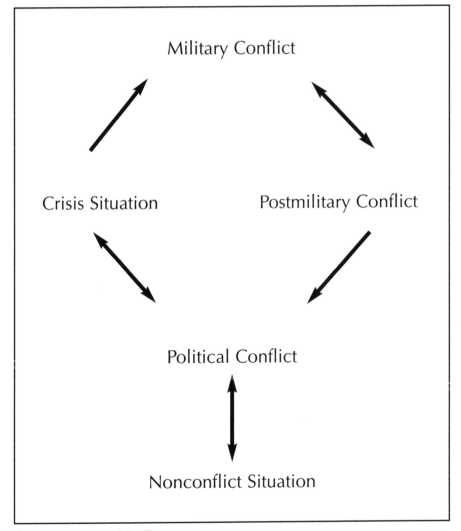

Figure 8.1. Forms of Conflict

Table 8.1.   Conflict Management Goals and Activities

Stage of Conflict	Conflict Management Goals	Conflict Management Activities
Political Conflict (with significant potential for armed hostilities)	Escalation Prevention Amelioration/Tension Reduction Settlement/Resolution	Early Warning: Monitoring, Observation Preventive Diplomacy: Negotiation, Mediation, Arbitration, Conciliation Adjudication Material Assistance CSBMs
Crisis: Acute Political Conflict	Crisis Management Prevention of Hostilities De-escalation/Tension Reduction	Preventive Diplomacy Preventive Deployment Coercion: Political and Economic Sanctions, Embargoes, Threats of Force
Military Conflict	Containment Suppression Alteration of Status Quo	Diplomacy Coercion Use of Force: Sanctions Enforcement, Direct Intervention
Postmilitary Conflict	Escalation Prevention Stabilization/Tension Reduction Rehabilitation/Reconstruction Settlement/Resolution	Diplomacy Coercion Arms Control/CSBMs Monitoring Peacekeeping Material Assistance Administration/Policing Political/Legal Institution Building

In the case of political conflict situations involving a significant potential for armed violence, the goals of conflict management are to prevent the conflict from escalating to a crisis situation and becoming militarized and, ideally, to lower the level of tension if not resolve the conflict altogether. To this end, relevant conflict management activities may consist of early warning; preventive diplomacy, including such approaches to conflict resolution as mediation, arbitration, and conciliation; and adjudication. Concerned outside parties might also employ a range of material and nonmaterial inducements to promote restraint in the short term and, ultimately, to lay a foundation for more peaceful relations among the local adversaries.

Should a crisis situation in which military hostilities seem imminent occur, the goals of conflict management become the prevention of the outbreak of open violence and the de-escalation of the crisis. Associated activities may consist of renewed efforts at preventive diplomacy, preventive military deployments, and coercive actions involving political and economic sanctions, the imposition of embargoes, and the threat of force.

In the face of actual armed hostilities, conflict management goals become the containment of the fighting, its suppression, and, in some cases, bringing about changes in the status quo on the ground. Relevant conflict management activities may include not only diplomacy and the various forms of coercion described above but also the actual use of military force for the purpose of enforcing sanctions and direct intervention.

Finally, once the fighting has come to a halt, the goals of conflict management shift back to preventing a renewal of hostilities, stabilizing the situation and further reducing the level of tension, and possibly rehabilitating damaged areas. At such points, an especially wide range of activities may be appropriate. Diplomacy and coercion continue to be relevant. In addition, the establishment of arms control regimes and confidence- and security-building measures (CSBMs) may help to limit the potential for violence and rebuild trust. Peacekeeping operations can be used to separate warring parties and to monitor and ensure their compliance with any cease-fire agreements. And reconstruction efforts may require the provision of various forms of assistance and even the assumption of administrative and other tasks by third parties.

THE NEED FOR CONFLICT MANAGEMENT:
REGIONAL CONFLICTS IN EUROPE

The next step in assessing the prospects for successful conflict management involves identifying actual and potential regional conflicts. To do this, one must first establish the boundaries of the region in question. Regions are contested concepts, and Europe is no exception. To avoid an extended discussion, this chapter will simply define Europe as consisting of the those territories located east of the Atlantic Ocean, north of the Mediterranean Sea, and west of the Ural Mountains and Caspian Sea.[4] In addition, the United States and Canada are regarded as regional actors, if not European states, in view of their long-standing membership in postwar European security organizations.

Within this area, one finds that a high percentage of the actual or potential military conflicts are located either in the Balkans or on the territory of the former Soviet Union (see table 8.2). The remainder of Europe, especially the territory of those states belonging to NATO or the EU, is virtually free of interstate and intrastate political conflicts that could acquire a military dimension in the foreseeable future. This skewed geographical distribution has implications for actual utility of the institutional capabilities for CCM in the region, as will be discussed below.

In addition, many of the conflicts of relevance to this study, whether internal or international in nature, have a significant ethnic basis. They stem from the presence within the territory of individual states of two or more distinct

Table 8.2.   Conflicts in Europe

Primary Basis of Conflict	Internal	International
Ethnic		
Outside FSU	Bosnia	Albania-Yugoslavia (Kosovo)
	Croatia	Albania-Macedonia
	Yugoslavia (Kosovo, Vojvodina)	Bosnia-Yugoslavia
	Macedonia	Croatia-Yugoslavia
	Turkey	Slovenia-Yugoslavia
		Hungary-Romania
		Hungary-Slovakia
		Hungary-Ukraine
		Turkey-Bulgaria
Within FSU	Moldova	Russia-Estonia
	Georgia (Abkhazia, South Ossetia)	Russia-Latvia
	Azerbaijan	Russia-Ukraine
	Russia (Chechnya, etc.)	Armenia-Azerbaijan
Non-Ethnic	Yugoslavia (Montenegro)	Yugoslavia-Macedonia
	Albania	Macedonia-Greece
		Greece-Turkey

and sizable ethnic groups and the existence of some substantial grievance on the part of at least one of the groups vis-à-vis the other(s). The precise nature of the grievance(s) can vary, but as a result of such grievances, ethnic groups may seek greater political autonomy, outright independence, or unification with neighboring countries dominated by members of the same nationality.

The following summary description distinguishes between those conflicts that are located in the FSU and those elsewhere. As Philip Roeder has noted, "the space previously within the Soviet Union now constitutes a distinct international region." It also differentiates between those conflicts that have a significant ethnic basis and those with other underlying causes.[5]

Outside the Former Soviet Union

Outside of the former Soviet Union, the most acute ethnic conflicts tend to be found on the territory of the former Yugoslavia. The recent bloody struggles between Kosovars (of Albanian ethnicity) and Serbs in Serbia, Croats and Serbs in Croatia, and Serbs, Croats, and Muslim Bosniaks in Bosnia are well known. In addition, tensions exist between the Hungarian minority and the Serb majority in the northern Serbian province of Vojvodina, while those between the Albanian minority (approximately 30 percent of the population) and the Macedonian majority in Macedonia were exacerbated by the influx of refugees from Kosovo. Outside of the Balkans, violence has long been a common feature of relations between Turkey and its Kurdish minority.

Most of these ethnic conflicts also have a significant external dimension. The treatment of the Albanian minorities in Serbia and Macedonia has been at the center of disputes between Albania and those two countries, respectively.[6] During the early 1990s, forces from Serbia were involved in fighting in both Croatia and Bosnia. Hungary has expressed concern about the treatment of ethnic Hungarians in not only Serbia but also Romania, Slovakia, and Ukraine. Likewise, Turkey has criticized Bulgaria's treatment of the Turkish minority (eight hundred thousand) in that country.[7]

Not all of the potential domestic and interstate conflicts outside the FSU can be said to have primarily ethnic foundations, however. In Albania, the potential for violence has been exacerbated by the lack of strong political institutions and a weak economy. Montenegro has been rent by a power struggle between those who would maintain close ties to Serbia and those favoring an opening to the West. On the international side of the ledger, Greece and Turkey have occasionally come close to blows over competing territorial claims in the Aegean, and tensions have at times been high between Greece and Macedonia because of feared revanchist designs associated with the disputed appropriation of various cultural symbols.[8] Finally, the Bulgarians have never recognized the existence of a distinct Macedonian nationality, raising the specter of at least an implicit claim to Macedonian territory.[9]

Before moving on to consider the situation in the FSU, it is important to note those once-feared conflicts that have dissipated or that appear to have been exaggerated in some accounts. Perhaps most notable in this regard are the improvements in relations that occurred between united Germany and its immediate eastern neighbors, Poland and the Czech Republic, during the 1990s. Although not all outstanding issues have been resolved and some bitter feelings remain, armed conflict between these states is unimaginable today. Likewise, significant progress has been made toward a resolution of the problems created by the Hungarian diaspora, especially the Hungarian minority in Romania (Transylvania).[10] And even parts of the former Yugoslavia, Slovenia and increasingly Croatia, have become remarkably stable over the course of the last decade.

Within the Former Soviet Union

A comparable number of violent and potentially violent political conflicts can be found on the territory of the former Soviet Union. This state of affairs should come as no surprise, given that the Soviet Union employed repressive measures to weld together a plethora of nationalities and afforded them few opportunities for meaningful self-expression or self-determination for more than half a century, notwithstanding pretenses to the contrary. These conflicts can be roughly grouped into four subregional categories.

The first concerns relations between Russia and the Baltic states, especially Estonia and Latvia. Russia has been at odds with its much smaller northwestern neighbors to varying degrees over borders, military basing rights, and, most importantly, the treatment and status of ethnic Russians, who have constituted roughly 30 percent of the populations of Estonia and Latvia.[11]

The situation of ethnic Russian minorities has also burdened Russian relations with several other former Soviet republics, most notably Ukraine and Moldova. In the former, the problems created by the presence of some eleven million Russians have been compounded by the concentration of many of them in industrial regions that border Russian territory and Russian claims to the Crimea, which was transferred by Russia to Ukraine in the 1950s and contains a substantial presence of ethnic Russians. In Moldova, the geographically concentrated Russian minority has even attempted to establish an independent republic, which has nevertheless failed thus far to garner international recognition.[12]

Most of the violent conflicts on the territory of the FSU have taken place in the Caucasus region. The territorial integrity of Georgia has been forcibly challenged by armed, ethnically based secessionist movements in Abkhazia and South Ossetia. Nearby, Azerbaijan has been engaged in a violent struggle with separatist ethnic Armenians in the province of Nagorno-Karabakh, which has in turn strained relations between Azerbaijan and neighboring Armenia.

Finally, Russia faces severe internal ethnic troubles of its own. The most prominent of these are also to be found in the Caucasus, where Russia has already waged two expensive wars in Chechnya in less than a decade. Nevertheless, a real potential for violent, ethnic conflict exists in a number of other parts of the country as well, such as Tartarstan, where long-suppressed national minorities strive for greater autonomy if not outright political independence.[13]

INCENTIVES FOR CONFLICT MANAGEMENT

What incentives might other states in the region possess for seeking to manage these conflicts? After all, even if potentially violent conflicts exist, those not directly involved will be disinclined to engage in conflict management efforts if they have no compelling interest to do so, in view of the risks and costs. And as Richard Ullman convincingly argued a decade ago, the stakes that the more stable countries of western and central Europe have in other parts of the region are lower than ever.[14]

Nevertheless, the incentives for conflict management in Europe are not negligible and, indeed, have been sufficient to prompt numerous efforts at CCM, including military operations of substantial magnitude, since the end of the Cold War. The strength of these incentives will vary, however, depending upon the precise nature and location of the conflict. As Joseph Lepgold has noted, moreover, even where significant incentives exist, states may be inhibited from taking strong action because of the collective action problems associated with peace operations.[15]

In the case of conflicts outside the FSU, especially in southeastern Europe, one important incentive is the danger that a violent conflict, if unaddressed, will spread to adjoining territories through a process of spillover, the uncoordinated intervention of outside parties, or both. A second incentive follows from the belief that the illegitimate resort to arms should not go unpunished, as it may otherwise encourage disgruntled groups located elsewhere to use violence if they believe that it promises success and that they can act with impunity. A somewhat more self-interested consideration is that large-scale violence can generate equally large-scale outflows of refugees. In the early 1990s, for example, over eight hundred thousand Bosnians alone sought refuge in other European states, including more than four hundred thousand in Germany,[16] while at the end of the decade, nearly a quarter million Kosovars fled to neighboring Macedonia. Nor, as Western governments have learned in Bosnia and Kosovo, do the material costs stop mounting when the fighting comes to an end. Outside parties interested in preventing a renewal of violent conflict may have to consider making substantial financial contributions to the process of reconstruction over a prolonged period.

At the same time, one should not discount the significance of purely humanitarian motives to protect the innocent and to minimize the suffering of peoples affected by conflict. In an age when the various media provide a steady stream of stories about and images of the consequences of violence, most citizens in the advanced industrial countries of Europe no longer have the luxury of being able to remain ignorant of military depredations taking place on their continent. Thus even where the material stakes have appeared to be low, Western governments have come under considerable public pressure to do something to stem the violence.

As a general rule, the incentives that the states of western and central Europe, not to mention those of North America, have to take action are not as great when it comes to conflicts within the FSU. The level of humanitarian concern may be equally high. But because such conflicts are further removed geographically, these states are much less likely to be affected directly or indirectly, except where a conflict threatens to destabilize Russia or to reverse the hard-won democratic advances that have been made there. Conversely, the costs and risks of involvement are likely to be higher, especially where it might put them at odds with Russia.

The risk of serious tensions over conflict management strategies is not negligible, given that Russia is itself a party to many of the conflicts in the FSU and that, even where it is not, Russian incentives for intervention are arguably broader and potentially inconsistent. Beyond those incentives shared with the other states in the region, such as preventing spillover effects, they include Russia's determination to remain a major player in all aspects of European security affairs, notwithstanding its current economic and political weaknesses. And in those areas that were formerly part of the Soviet Union, such as the Transcaucasus, Russia's motives may extend to a desire to retain or reestablish a significant degree of hegemonic influence.[17] Needless to say, such goals may at times result in Russian actions that run counter to traditional conflict management prescriptions.[18] They also complicate Western calculations of how to proceed, given the understandable desire to maintain good working relations with Russia on a range of other important issues.

In sum, both outside and within the FSU, the precise nature and strength of the incentives to engage in CCM will vary from state to state and from conflict to conflict, but they will rarely be entirely absent. The more practical question concerns the point at which they will be sufficiently strong to prompt action. In particular, will outsiders see fit to intervene early enough or in the most effective manner? The answer to this question depends, in part, on the tools available for CCM, to which I now turn.

INSTITUTIONAL CAPABILITIES FOR
COLLECTIVE CONFLICT MANAGEMENT IN EUROPE

With the partial exception of Russia, the principal actors in the region are likely to engage in conflict management activities only collectively through existing multilateral security institutions. Europe possesses a set of relatively highly developed institutional capabilities of potential use for CCM. Most of these capabilities are lodged in a variety of regional organizations, the most important of which are the OSCE, NATO, and the EU/WEU. In the discussion that follows, I shall refer to such bodies as regional conflict management organizations (RCMO).

Needless to say, given their diverse origins, purposes, and memberships, these organizations differ considerably in terms of their potential CCM capabilities. The OSCE is the only truly pan-regional organization. NATO and the EU/WEU have restricted memberships but are of potentially great relevance to CCM efforts beyond the territory of their members. Yet other RCMOs, like the Commonwealth of Independent States (CIS), are confined in both their membership and activities to particular subregions.

All, however, have evolved considerably during the past decade and will probably continue to do so. Thus the overall picture is very much a work in progress. Nevertheless, the situation has probably stabilized enough that it is possible to provide a description and comparative analysis of these organizational capacities that will not immediately become obsolete. This analysis will consider each of the following relevant organizational characteristics:

1. membership and, where it may differ, geographical area of responsibility (see table 8.3)
2. functional mandate
3. decision-making process
4. organizational capabilities and resources (see table 8.4).

With regard to the fourth characteristic, it should be emphasized that the interest of this study lies in the assets possessed by the organizations themselves

Table 8.3. Membership in European Conflict Management Organizations

NATO	EU — WEU	EU	PFP — CIS	PFP	Other OSCE
Canada	Belgium	Austria	Armenia	Albania	Andorra
Czech Republic	Britain	Finland	Azerbaijan	Bulgaria	Bosnia
Hungary	France	Ireland	Belarus	Estonia	Croatia
Iceland	Germany	Sweden	Georgia	Latvia	Cyprus
Norway	Greece		Moldova	Lithuania	Holy See
Poland	Italy		Russia	Macedonia	Liechtenstein
Turkey	Luxembourg		Ukraine	Romania	Malta
United States	Netherlands			Slovakia	Monaco
	Portugal			Slovenia	San Marino
	Spain			Switzerland	Yugoslavia

Denmark (NATO and EU)

Note: This table excludes the five Central Asian republics.

Table 8.4. Crisis Management Capabilities and Resources by Organization

	OSCE	NATO	EU/WEU	Others
Political conflict	HCNM ODIHR Court of Conciliation and Arbitration Missions Personal representatives CPC FSC (arms control, CSBMs)	PFP EAPC Secretary-General/IS	Satellite Center (early warning) Humanitarian Office Monitoring missions	UN (preventive deployment, preventive diplomacy)
Crisis situation	CPC	IMS (sanctions enforcement)		UN (mediation, sanctions)
Military conflict	Missions (sanctions assistance)	IMS (sanctions, threats of force, use of force)	Military staff (peace making)	UN (mediation, sanctions, mandate to use force)
Postmilitary conflict	Missions (Bosnia, Croatia, Kosovo) CPC (peacekeeping) FSC (arms control, CSBMs)	IMS/PFP (peacekeeping)	Military staff (peacekeeping) Satellite Center (monitoring, verification) Humanitarian Office Agency for Reconstruction Monitoring missions	UN (monitoring, peacekeeping, administration) CIS (peacekeeping)

rather than the national resources of their members. Nevertheless, the two may be closely related insofar as one purpose of the former is to facilitate and ensure the efficient use of the latter.

Organization for Security and Cooperation in Europe (OSCE)

The OSCE is the most comprehensive, both geographically and functionally, of the RCMOs in Europe. All states in the region are eligible for membership, and in fact virtually all European states are members.[19] Correspondingly, the OSCE possesses a standing mandate to address conflicts throughout the region, subject to decision-making constraints. The OSCE is the only RCMO in Europe that is considered a regional arrangement under Chapter VIII of the UN Charter.

At the same time, the OSCE has a very broad mandate with regard to conflict management. Its various decision-making bodies can authorize a wide variety of measures. These include short-term fact-finding and rapporteur missions, long-term in-country missions that may serve several purposes (sanctions assistance, monitoring and verification, etc.), personal representatives of the Chairman-in-Office (CiO), and additional measures for the peaceful settlement of disputes. Furthermore, the OSCE may undertake peacekeeping activities, although this option has not yet been exercised. Nevertheless, the mandate of the OSCE is oriented much more toward the goals of dispute resolution, early warning, escalation prevention, and crisis management rather than dealing with actual military hostilities. In particular, it lacks any explicit authority to call for the employment of coercive measures, such as economic sanctions and the use of military force, by its members.[20]

A further limitation of the OSCE is the cumbersome nature of its decision-making process. In principle, all of its decision-making and negotiating bodies operate by consensus, which "is understood to mean the absence of any objection expressed by a participating State to the taking of the decision in question."[21] This requirement might not be so onerous but for the large and diverse nature of the OSCE membership and the resulting divergence of interests. In addition, decisions of the organization are not legally binding.

Nevertheless, the OSCE has, over the past decade, developed several exceptions to the consensus rule that enhance its abilities to address conflicts in the region. Under the "consensus-minus-one" principle, actions can be taken without the consent of the state concerned in "cases of clear, gross and uncorrected violation" of OSCE commitments. This mechanism was used to suspend Yugoslavia's membership in 1992. Under the "consensus-minus-two" rule, the Ministerial Council can instruct two participating states that are involved in a dispute to seek conciliation, even if the participating states object to the decision, although this option has not yet been made use of. And the Chairman-in-Office may designate personal representatives on his or her own responsibility.

In addition, the OSCE had developed a variety of additional mechanism and procedures that are intended, in cases requiring rapid action, to facilitate prompt and direct contact between the parties involved in a conflict and the mobilization of concerted action by the OSCE. The "Vienna Mechanism" obliges states to respond to requests for information relating to human dimension obligations and to hold bilateral meetings when requested. The "Moscow Mechanism" allows a group of six or more states to initiate the dispatch of a mission of experts to assist a state in the resolution of a particular question or problem relating to the human dimension.[22] The "Mechanism for Consultation and Cooperation as Regards Unusual Military Activities" obliges states to provide information regarding any unusual and unscheduled activities of their military forces when requested. And several other mechanisms were rendered superfluous by the establishment in 1993 of the Permanent Council of national representatives, which can meet on short notice.

To support its various conflict management activities, the OSCE has developed a number of distinct capabilities and resources since the end of the Cold War. Perhaps the most important of these is the Conflict Prevention Centre (CPC), which is responsible for overall support for the implementation of OSCE tasks in the fields of early warning, conflict prevention, crisis management, and postconflict rehabilitation, and for daily follow-up and liaison for the execution of OSCE decisions. Since 1999, the CPC has maintained an Operations Centre to identify potential crisis areas and to plan for future missions and operations. Nevertheless, given the small size of the CPC, the OSCE's ability to prepare and support peacekeeping operations in particular remains highly limited at this point.

Several other structures also merit mention. The High Commissioner on National Minorities (HCNM) functions as an instrument of preventive diplomacy. The HCNM aims to identify—and promote the early resolution of—ethnic tensions that have the potential to endanger peace, stability, or friendly relations between the participating states of the OSCE. The Office of Democratic Institutions and Human Rights (ODIHR) contributes to early warning and conflict prevention, in particular by monitoring the implementation of human dimension commitments. And states may submit disputes to the OSCE-related Court of Conciliation and Arbitration, whose final decisions are legally binding, although not all OSCE states are parties to the convention establishing the Court and the Court has not yet been used.

Somewhere between a decision-making body and an organizational capability is the multipurpose Forum for Security Cooperation (FSC). Its main objectives include conducting negotiations on arms control, disarmament, and confidence- and security-building and holding regular consultations and intensive cooperation on matters relating to security. The FSC is also responsible for the implementation of confidence- and security-building measures (CSBMs), the holding of Annual Implementation Assessment Meetings, the provision of a forum for discussing and clarifying information exchanged under agreed upon CSBMs, and the preparation of seminars on military doctrine. Among its achievements have been the negotiation of a CSBM regime for Bosnia and a subregional arms control agreement for much of the former Yugoslavia.

North Atlantic Treaty Organization (NATO)

NATO, which dates back to 1949, is the oldest of the European organizations with significant CCM capabilities. It is also arguably the one whose security functions have changed the most over the years. In sharp contrast to the OSCE, NATO began as a traditional alliance with a primary focus on the protection of its members against external threats. Only in the 1990s did it acquire explicit conflict management responsibilities. As a result of this rather different life history, many of the areas in which the OSCE is weakest are those in which NATO is strongest, and vice versa.

Unlike the case of the OSCE, membership in NATO is restricted. The existing members may chose to invite other states to join the organization, but there are no explicit criteria for membership. Currently, NATO has nineteen members.[23]

Nevertheless, NATO involves a number of other states in its activities through the Euro-Atlantic Partnership Council (which supplanted the North Atlantic Cooperation Council in 1997) and, especially, its Partnership for Peace (PFP) program. Participation in the PFP is based on agreements negotiated between individual countries and NATO regarding the scope, pace, and level of joint activities in which they would like to engage. Currently, some twenty-seven additional states have established cooperative programs with NATO under the PFP.

The North Atlantic Treaty was carefully worded to ensure that members' obligations to one another did not extend beyond their territories in Europe and North America (with the exception of attacks on member forces located in the Mediterranean and North Atlantic). At the same time, however, the Treaty does not prohibit the members from acting collectively outside this so-called North Atlantic Area, should they wish to do so. In addition, under the terms of the PFP, NATO is obliged to consult with any active participant if that state perceives a direct threat to its security.

One consequence of NATO's restricted membership is that its decisions do not automatically command legitimacy in areas outside those covered by the treaty. As a result, members are typically—but not always, as evidenced in Kosovo—reluctant to act collectively "out of area" in the absence of an explicit mandate from the United Nations or the OSCE. In practical terms, this means that the use of NATO for CCM activities is highly unlikely on the territory of the former Soviet Union and, especially, in Russia proper.

During the Cold War, NATO's formal mandate focused on the closely related tasks of deterring military attacks on its members and defending them should an attack nevertheless occur. Since the end of the Cold War, this mandate has been considerably broadened and now includes explicitly the functions of "conflict prevention and crisis management." The alliance's most recent strategic concept, adopted in 1999, notes the possibility of conducting "crisis response operations" such as those that have been carried out in the Balkans and reiterates NATO's offer to support "peacekeeping and other operations under the authority of the UN Security Council or the responsibility of the OSCE, including by making available Alliance resources and expertise."[24]

Although the strategic concept is less explicit on this point, it also envisages a variety of activities intended to ameliorate or even resolve political conflicts. Through the "active pursuit of partnership, cooperation, and dialogue" with non-members, NATO aims "to overcome divisions and disagreements that could lead to instability and conflict." This task complements the alliance's long-standing (at least since the admission of Germany in 1955), if always implicit, function of defusing political conflict among its members by increasing transparency, promoting military interdependence, and perpetuating U.S. involvement in European security affairs.[25]

Like the OSCE, NATO acts on the basis of consensus. This requirement means that decision making on contentious issues, such as those often associated with conflict management, can be slow and difficult.

For several reasons, however, consensus is generally easier to attain in NATO than in the OSCE. Most obviously, the achievement of consensus is facilitated by NATO's smaller membership. Perhaps even more important is the fact that, as a general rule, the interests of NATO countries are more closely aligned with one another than are those of OSCE members, which is a consequence of the alliance's restricted membership. A third factor is the large number of well-exercised bodies and procedures for timely consultation and the exchange of information. In addition, deliberation within the North Atlantic Council, the alliance's highest-level decision-making body, can be expedited by the presence of a strong secretary-general, who can use his authority to propose and broker compromises in cases where the membership is divided.[26] Finally, in some instances, the existence of a dominant member, the United States, has helped to overcome differences where it has been willing to lead.

NATO's most distinctive organizational asset for carrying out crisis management activities is its integrated military planning and command structure and associated multilateral military assets, such as the NATO Airborne Early Warning Force. When supplemented by PFP-related bodies, especially the Partnership Coordination Cell, the integrated military structure (IMS) greatly facilitates the collective deployment and use of military forces by NATO members and partner countries. Even as it has been considerably streamlined since the end of the Cold War, this structure has developed the ability to orchestrate out-of-area multilateral military operations of substantial size and complexity, as evidenced by the various NATO actions in the Balkans. Consequently, NATO remains the RCMO best positioned to engage in the enforcement of sanctions, peacekeeping, direct intervention, and other types of military operations.

The principal question that has arisen regarding the utility of the IMS concerns possible instances in which one or more members might wish not to participate in a proposed joint military operation outside the NATO area. During the Cold War, the military structure made no provisions for less than unanimous engagement in defense operations by participating states, reflecting the near water-tight obligation to provide assistance contained in Article 5 of the treaty. Many now imaginable out-of-area conflict management activities would carry no such obligation, however. To address this potential problem, the alliance has developed and begun to implement the concept of Combined Joint Task Forces (CJTF), which is intended to allow "coalitions of the willing" to draw upon NATO headquarters and other military assets in order to engage in nondefense actions, as long as no member expresses an objection to them.

In contrast to the OSCE, NATO's organizational capabilities for nonmilitary aspects of conflict management are much less well articulated. Nevertheless, a substantial reservoir of such capabilities is inherent in the large International Staff (IS) maintained by the alliance in Brussels. In particular, the NATO secretary-general possesses the stature and authority to serve as an effective intermediary, as evidenced in Macedonia in 2001.

European Union (EU)/Western European Union (WEU)

The EU and the WEU were originally distinct organizations. During the past decade, however, they have drawn ever closer together, especially with regard to potential activities in the area of crisis management. Consequently, it is necessary to consider them together for the purposes of this chapter.

Currently, the EU and WEU are the least developed of all the major European security institutions as RCMOs. In particular, their dedicated organizational capabilities and resources for engaging in conflict management activities are less substantial than those of either the OSCE or NATO at the moment. Nevertheless, this situation is very much in flux, as the EU has recently launched an unprecedented effort to develop a capacity to conduct military missions in response to international crises. In view of the EU's success in other fields of international cooperation, its potential to become a leading, if not the leading, regional organization in the field of conflict management is considerable, although it is too early to discern clearly how far the EU will actually proceed along this path and the form that it will eventually take.

Like NATO, both the EU and the WEU have restricted memberships. There is much overlap among the three organizations. Of the current fifteen EU members, eleven also belong to NATO and the other four participate in the PFP. All ten present WEU members are in both NATO and the EU.[27]

At the moment, it is arguably more difficult for former Soviet bloc states to join the EU (and, by extension, the WEU) than NATO because of the significant economic ramifications of membership in the former. Nevertheless, beginning in the 1990s, the WEU has sought to work as closely as possible with nonmembers, creating the categories of Associate Member (for European NATO members not in the EU), Associate Partner (for states in neither NATO nor the EU), and Observer. Likewise, the EU has recently indicated its desire to involve nonmembers to "the fullest possible extent" in EU-led crisis management activities, although concrete arrangements have yet to be devised.[28]

Neither the Treaty on European Union (TEU) nor the modified Brussels Treaty on which the WEU is based establishes a clear geographical area of responsibility. Nevertheless, the implications of recent decisions are that both organizations regard a wide range of foreign, security, and defense policy activities beyond the territory of their members as falling within their competence.

Within this broad mandate, what specific types of conflict management activities are envisioned? The original Brussels Treaty of 1948 was concerned with the defense of its signatories against attack, but this function was assumed by NATO in the mid-1950s. In 1987, however, WEU leaders called for concerted policies toward crises outside of Europe, paving the way for the dispatch of a small WEU naval contingent to the Persian Gulf. And in 1992, they articulated a detailed set of military actions, collectively known as the "Petersberg tasks," for which their forces might be used: humanitarian and rescue missions, peacekeeping operations, and the use of combat forces in crisis management, including peacemaking.[29] The following month, the WEU approved the deployment of a naval task force to the Adriatic to monitor the UN arms embargo against former Yugoslavia.

Although its origins date back to the 1950s, the EU did not acquire broad competence in the area of security and defense, as part of a common foreign and security policy, until the formulation and ratification of the TEU (commonly known as the Maastricht Treaty) in the early 1990s. Further amendments, contained in the 1997 Amsterdam Treaty, explicitly identified the Petersberg tasks as part of the EU mandate in this area, setting the stage for a process whereby the EU will assume all WEU functions except that of collective defense. More recently, the European Council, the EU's highest-level decision-making body, has frequently emphasized the importance of the EU's tasks in the field of conflict prevention and crisis management. In fact, the EU has already been very active since the early 1990s in attempting to resolve regional political conflicts, prevent their escalation, and stabilize and reconstruct war-torn areas.

As with NATO, WEU decisions are made on the basis of consensus. Whether consensus is any easier (because of its smaller membership) or difficult (because of the lack of a dominant power) to achieve in the WEU than in NATO on weighty issues is difficult to ascertain, given that the WEU has been used relatively infrequently and in much more limited ways.

The situation in the EU is more complicated. Initially, the TEU required that substantive decisions regarding the common foreign and security policy be made unanimously, except where it had been previously agreed to act on the basis of a qualified majority. The Amsterdam Treaty, however, established a more differentiated process. In principle, the Council would act unanimously when making decisions. However, one or more members could abstain without preventing the adoption of a decision by the others.

Moreover, the Amsterdam Treaty introduced the option of "qualified abstention," involving a formal declaration, whereby the abstaining party would not be obliged to apply the decision even as it accepted that the decision committed the

EU as a whole. Only if the members qualifying their abstention represented more than one third of the weighted votes would a decision not be adopted. Nevertheless, a single country could still block the adoption of a decision by explicitly opposing it, and this novel procedure does not apply to decisions having military or defense implications.

More recently, the EU has created new political and military bodies within the European Council to facilitate effective and timely decision making during the conduct of military crisis management operations. A standing Political and Security Committee (PSC) consisting of national representatives will exercise, under the authority of the Council, the political control and strategic direction of such operations. In addition, a Military Committee (MC) has been established to provide military advice and make recommendations to the PSC.

The principal limitations of the EU and WEU with regard to their potential use for conflict management lie in the area of organizational capabilities and resources. Thus far, the EU has relied primarily on the European Commission, its executive organ, to support nonmilitary crisis management activities. Given its size and resources, the Commission has a great capacity to coordinate diplomatic efforts, observer missions, economic assistance, sanctions, and other measures. Nevertheless, the EU has created few dedicated assets to implement its decisions, and these have tended to be ad hoc bodies with country-specific mandates, such as the European Community Monitor Mission (ECMM) in the former Yugoslavia, the Kosovo Task Force, and the European Agency for Reconstruction.[30]

This situation may see significant change in the near future, however. The EU presidency concluded its work in 1999 with a call for the development of a "rapid reaction capability in the field of crisis management using nonmilitary means." Among the elements envisioned for such a capability were an inventory of relevant national and collective personnel, material, and financial resources, a coordinating mechanism within the Secretariat of the Council of Ministers, and rapid financing mechanisms, such as a Rapid Reaction Fund.[31] In addition, the recently created office of High Representative for the EU in the area of foreign and security policy provides a potentially useful focal point for preventive diplomacy and crisis management activities.[32]

On the military side, the primary crisis management capabilities have resided until recently in the WEU, which established a small planning cell (subsequently renamed the Military Staff) and a satellite data interpretation center in the early to mid-1990s. Nevertheless, the WEU possesses no forces or permanent command structures of its own and relies instead on NATO or individual countries to provide them on a case-by-case basis.

The organizational resources of the EU have been even more limited. It was not until 1999 that the EU made it a priority to acquire a capacity for autonomous action, including the launching and conduct of EU-led military missions, in response to international crises. Particular importance was assigned to the reinforcement of EU capabilities in the fields of intelligence, strategic transport, and command and control. In addition, the EU agreed to create a new Military Staff within the Council that would provide military expertise and support, and perform early warning, situation assessment, and strategic planning for Petersberg tasks. The ultimate goal is to be able to deploy within sixty days and sustain for at least one year military forces of up to fifty to sixty thousand persons.

The principal challenge facing the EU in the development of such a capacity is the expressed need to do so "without unnecessary duplication" of NATO assets. Consequently, emphasis has been placed on developing more effective European military capabilities on the basis of existing "national, binational, and multinational capabilities." The presence of this constraint suggests that the EU will continue to rely heavily on the use of NATO resources and capabilities, should they be available, to mount operations of any significant size for the foreseeable future.

Other Regional Conflict Management Bodies

This survey does not exhaust the list of bodies that have made a contribution to conflict management in the region or could do so in the future. One of these is the Contact Group, which has been used to good effect in Bosnia.[33] In fact, the Contact Group is not a formal organization but rather an informal mechanism for coordinating the policy of a handful of major powers: the United States, Britain, France, Germany, Russia, and Italy. As such, it might be viewed as an emergent regional security council, although it has thus far confined itself to addressing conflicts in the former Yugoslavia.

This arrangement results in both significant advantages and limitations in comparison with other RCMOs. On the one hand, the small size of its membership, the lack of formal procedures, and the possibility of secrecy may facilitate the reaching of agreements in a timely manner, while the identity of its members ensures that any agreements will be backed by significant national resources. On the other hand, the exclusion of other countries may generate hard feelings and cast doubt on the broader legitimacy of any agreed actions, at least until they are considered in other organizational fora. In addition, the Contact Group possesses no capabilities of its own. Consequently, it seems likely that it will be used only sporadically and as a complement to other organizations.

Europe also features several subregional security organizations, the most important of which is the Commonwealth of Independent States (CIS). The CIS was hastily established at the end of 1991 as part of the process by which the USSR was dissolved. Originally consisting of eleven of the fifteen former Soviet republics,[34] it was initially given only a very limited organizational structure and no formal authority in the area of security, reflecting the reluctance of most of its members to create any powerful institutions that could threaten their newfound sovereignty. The highly restricted institutional design was supplemented in 1993 by a Charter that provided for policy coordination and joint consultation in security and defense policy and created a council of foreign ministers and a council of defense ministers. It also established a High Command of the United Armed Forces that could exercise control over groups of military observers and collective peacekeeping forces. Nevertheless, only seven of the eleven original members signed the Charter, greatly limiting its potential application.[35] In fact, the CIS has been employed for the purpose of conflict management only once so far, and then only to give international legitimacy to a Russian peacekeeping operation in Abkhazia. As Neil MacFarlane concludes, "to the extent that [the CIS] serves any purpose, it is as an instrument of Russian foreign policy in the former Soviet space."[36]

THE ROLE OF THE UNITED NATIONS

Before assessing the adequacy of these bodies for regional crisis management, it is necessary to consider the role of the United Nations (UN). Not only is the UN the principal extraregional institution of relevance, but it is also the main vehicle for involvement by potentially interested nonregional powers, notably China by virtue of its status as a permanent member of the Security Council. During the Cold War, the UN was rarely called upon to promote security in Europe. That task fell almost exclusively to the opposing alliance systems and, later, the CSCE. Since 1990, however, the global body has been pressed into service on numerous occasions as a substitute for or complement to regional organizations attempting to deal with conflicts on the continent.

There is no need to review the UN's membership and geographical area of responsibility, functional mandate, decision-making procedures, and organizational capabilities and resources, all of which are well known. For the purposes of this chapter, it will suffice to describe the ways it has been used in Europe during the past decade. These uses fall into four broad categories, reflecting the organization's comprehensive authority.

First, in areas characterized by active hostilities, the UN—or, more accurately, the Security Council—has been the principal author of international sanctions on combatants, most notably in the former Yugoslavia. There, it has variously established an arms embargo, a comprehensive trade embargo, a no-fly zone, safe areas, and heavy weapons exclusion zones. Where the deployment and use of military forces has been deemed necessary to enforce these sanctions, the Security Council has provided mandates to NATO and other regional organizations.

Second, the UN has sponsored peacekeeping operations, preventive military deployments, and observer missions intended to prevent the outbreak or a renewal of hostilities in areas characterized by high levels of tension. In some cases, such as Croatia and Macedonia, these activities have been carried out by traditional "blue helmet" forces. In Bosnia and Kosovo, however, where the military requirements of the mission were expected to be high, the UN has turned responsibility for implementation over to NATO.

Third, the UN has played an important role in postconflict political and economic rehabilitation. In Kosovo, for example, the UN has assumed overall authority as well as day-to-day responsibility for the civilian administration of that war-torn province. Finally, at various stages in several conflicts, the UN has used diplomacy to prevent the escalation of violence and to assist with the search for peaceful solutions.

EVALUATION: THE PROSPECTS FOR
SUCCESSFUL CONFLICT MANAGEMENT

This survey finds that Europe possesses an abundance of institutional capabilities for collective conflict management, many of which reside in three sets of organizations: the OSCE, NATO, and the EU/WEU. Moreover, these capabilities are quite diverse in nature, corresponding to the full range of potentially desirable crisis management activities identified above (table 8.4). Thus, on paper at least, the overall potential for successful conflict management in Europe seems quite high.

Two additional observations lend further credence to this general conclusion. The first is that these capabilities are not simply the result of abstract speculation about what might be desirable. Rather, they have been developed largely in response to the need to address specific recent conflicts in the region, suggesting their relevance to likely future conflicts as well. The second and related observation is that many of these capabilities have been tested in a number of conflict situations during the past decade, to increasingly (although not always) good effect.

The 1990s witnessed multiple cycles in which regional conflicts elicited the development of new organizational capabilities, which were then employed and, where necessary, modified to increase their effectiveness. Through such a process, for example, the ability of the OSCE to plan, deploy, and support long-term missions has been greatly enhanced. Likewise, NATO, in response to external pressures, has made the transition in but a decade from a military organization designed only for deterrence and defense to one that can mount collective enforcement and peacekeeping operations of unprecedented size and intensity. In fact, NATO has supplanted the UN as the principal source of peacekeeping forces in the region. Although the EU has evolved perhaps the most slowly of the major regional organizations, it has departed the furthest from its original purposes, as witnessed by its recent efforts to develop a military capability of its own and to promote stability in Southeastern Europe. And one body, the Contact Group, owes its very existence to post–Cold War regional conflicts, although the limits of its usefulness were also made clear by the deep divisions among its members that arose over the handling of the Kosovo crisis.

To be sure, one can point to numerous instances in which one or more European RCMOs proved ineffective or inadequate for the conflict management task at hand. Indeed, there has probably been no occasion on which a regional organization has performed flawlessly or achieved all of the goals set for it. The more important point, however, is that these CCM capabilities have evolved considerably over time largely in response to their perceived shortcomings and failures. Consequently, the past performance of European RCMOs provides little basis for assessing the future prospects for successful conflict management, although the overall trend—from the EU's unsuccessful diplomacy as Yugoslavia dissolved in 1991 to NATO's forceful intervention in Kosovo at the end of the decade—seems positive.

Within the Former Soviet Union

Nevertheless, the availability and potential effectiveness of these CCM capabilities varies considerably depending on the location of the conflict (see table 8.5). The prospects for successful CCM are dimmest within the FSU, where the involvement of RCMOs is highly dependent upon the approval of Russia. As a result, NATO and the EU/WEU are unlikely to be called upon to address conflict in the region because of Russian mistrust of the Western powers that dominate them. And even though the mandate of the OSCE extends throughout Europe, the nature and degree of that organization's involvement in the FSU also remains hostage to Russian policy.

As a general rule, Russia will probably prefer to act alone, or at least without external constraints, within the former Soviet space and especially on its own

Table 8.5. Organizational Conflict Management Capabilities by Region

Activity	Outside FSU	Inside FSU
Early warning: monitoring, observation	OSCE (HCNM, ODIHR), EU (satellite center, humanitarian office, monitoring missions)	OSCE, UN
Preventive diplomacy and crisis diplomacy	OSCE (HCNM, LT missions), EU (HiRep), Contact Group, UN	OSCE, UN
Adjudication	OSCE	
Preventive deployments	UN, NATO, OSCE	
Coercion: sanctions	UN, OSCE, EU	
Coercion: military threats	UN, NATO (IMS), WEU	
Use of force: sanctions enforcement	NATO (IMS), WEU	
Use of force: direct intervention	NATO (IMS)	
Peacekeeping	UN, NATO (IMS, PFP), EU, OSCE	CIS
Arms control/CSBMs	OSCE (FSC), EU (satellite center)	
Economic and technical assistance	UN, OSCE, EU (Agency for Reconstruction, monitoring missions)	
Civil administration/policing	UN, EU/WEU	
Institution building	EU, UN	OSCE

territory. Russia acted on its own initiative to address the conflicts in Georgia and Moldova, eventually sending forces to both South Ossetia and Abkhazia. (The latter deployment was later authorized as a regional peacekeeping operation by the CIS, although it continued to be manned and financed exclusively by Russia.)[37] And in Chechnya, it has strongly resisted even the most limited proposals by the OSCE and the Council of Europe to dispatch small numbers of observers. To make matters worse, Russia may sometimes have an interest in exploiting ethnic divisions in the former Soviet republics in order to enhance its influence in those states.

In some cases, Russia may be willing to allow the involvement of the OSCE and the UN where doing so appears to advance its own interests. In the Baltics, the OSCE proved useful in ensuring that the interests of Russian minorities were protected. And Russia was able to secure the approval of the UN Security Council for the peacekeeping force that it had already deployed in Abkhazia, thereby legitimating its actions, although it was unsuccessful in obtaining external financing for the operation.

Russia's relationship with these organizations has not been entirely one-sided, however. In several ways, OSCE involvement in the Baltic worked in favor of Estonia and Lithuania, and the resolution of the conflicts there will certainly reduce Russia's influence in the long term.[38] In return for UN and OSCE support in Georgia, moreover, Russia has been required to make accommodations that in turn have limited its freedom of action. International observers in South Ossetia and Abkhazia have increased the level of transparency and to some extent acculturated Russian forces to international norms regarding peacekeeping.[39]

Outside the Former Soviet Union

In contrast, the prospects for successful conflict management in areas lying outside the FSU are relatively bright. There, the full range of CCM capabilities has been employed and is likely to be available for use in the future. Rather than an insufficiency of capabilities, a principal challenge is posed by their dispersal among multiple organizations. No single RCMO can perform all the conflict management activities that might be desirable in a given instance. Each suffers from important limitations in terms of geographical area of responsibility, functional mandate, and organizational capabilities and resources.

This decentralization can result in several different types of problems. First, the existence of multiple organizations may encourage buck-passing, as occurred to some extent in the early stages of the fighting in the former Yugoslavia. At that time, NATO stood on the sidelines while the EU demonstrated the then very limited nature of abilities in the field of conflict management. Second, it creates the potential for interorganizational conflict and the wasteful duplication of assets. Certainly, the initial deployment of separate NATO and WEU naval task forces in the Adriatic to monitor the UN embargo on the former Yugoslavia did not represent the most efficient use of member states' military resources. So far, however, serious problems of this nature have been avoided, although such concerns underlie many of the disagreements over the desirability and feasibility of an EU military force, given the existence of NATO. Thus at least as important as augmenting the conflict management capacity of European RCMOs is the need to ensure that their existing capabilities are well used through careful coordination both during and between crises.

At the same time, it is important to recognize the advantages afforded by this decentralization and perhaps even some organizational redundancy. It broadens the range of options available to decision makers, providing them with fallbacks should an initial approach prove ineffective. Likewise, it enables interested outside parties to bring multiple pressures to bear on conflict situations, as exemplified by the simultaneous NATO and EU diplomatic initiatives in Macedonia in 2001. Alternatively, decentralization may allow for effective task specialization and thus a politically wise distribution of the burdens of conflict management, as long as adequate coordination is attained. Indeed, the functions and capabilities of the OSCE, NATO, and EU might be viewed as increasingly complementary. Certainly, all three of these RCMOs in partnership with the UN have been able to accomplish more working side by side in Kosovo than any one of them might have achieved alone.

A further caveat follows from the enduring dependence of RCMOs on the UN, especially the need for approval by the UN Security Council for the undertaking of coercive sanctions, peacekeeping, and other military actions. With the partial exception of the OSCE, which could, in principle, mount peacekeeping operations without reference to the global body, the security organizations in Europe lack the authority to engage in coercive or forceful activities on their own. Consequently, military actions without a UN mandate will lack legitimacy and, as a result, may want for domestic as well as international support.

To be sure, the recent case of Kosovo, where NATO forces engaged in a large-scale bombing campaign against Serbia over the objections of two permanent members of the Security Council, would seem to contradict this assertion. Nevertheless, Kosovo is much more an exception to the rule than an indication of likely future trends. This aberration was only made possible by an unusual set of circumstances, particularly Serbian leader Slobodan Milosevic's long history of using violence and flouting international efforts to promote peace in the Balkans. Also noteworthy are the limited aims pursued by the NATO allies, which never denied Serbian sovereignty over Kosovo, and the leading UN role in subsequent efforts to restore order in the province. In general, NATO members remain unlikely to take forceful action without the prior approval of the UN.

Notwithstanding such constraints, the most striking feature of the current situation in Europe outside the FSU is the relative abundance of organizational capabilities for CCM in comparison with the potential need to employ them. Even as these capabilities were being built up during the 1990s, a number of regional conflicts were being defused and even resolved. Military conflict within and among the states of Central Eastern Europe now seems no more plausible than in Western Europe, and even parts of the former Yugoslavia—Slovenia and perhaps now Croatia—have become highly stable. As a result, few political conflicts with a significant potential for violence remain outside of the FSU and the Balkans, and in almost every part of the Balkans, the major RCMOs are already heavily involved in activities ranging from the suppression of violence to postconflict rehabilitation.

The Future Importance of Transformational Processes

In view of this situation, one might be tempted to venture that, again with the exception of conflicts in the FSU, the main European RCMOs are in the process of putting themselves out of business. Such a conclusion would betray, however, an inappropriately narrow conception of conflict management. There is still much work to be done, but it is not the type of work, such as air strikes and aggressive peacekeeping, that makes headlines. Rather, the focus will be on transforming potential sites of conflict into stable, prosperous democracies where internal and international differences are consistently addressed through peaceful means. The ultimate goal would be to convert the entire region into a zone of peace in which militarized political conflict is impossible or unimaginable.

Each of the major RCMOs discussed in this chapter has already played a role in this transformational process and can continue to do so. In the case of the OSCE, focal points for such activities are the HCNM and the ODIHR. The mandate of the HCNM describes the position as "an instrument of conflict prevention at the earliest possible stage." As noted above, the High Commissioner's role is to identify and to seek the early resolution of ethnic tensions. Although the HCNM is not intended to act as an advocate for national minorities, the HCNM's recommendations to states often concern the adoption of measures to ensure adequate protection of the rights of persons belonging to minority groups.[40]

The ODIHR, founded in 1990 as the Office for Free Elections, works to transform member states in three principal ways. It promotes democratic elections, particularly by monitoring election processes. It provides practical support, such as training programs, technical assistance, education projects, and the dissemination of information, for the consolidation of democratic institutions and human rights and the strengthening of civil society and the rule of law. And it monitors the compliance of member states with their human rights commitments.[41]

The transformational potentials of NATO and the EU are probably even greater. NATO already works to incorporate potential sites of conflict in Europe into the western zone of peace through two principal, related mechanisms. The first of these is the PFP, which from the beginning has had an explicitly transformational agenda. A central purpose of the PFP has been to promote the commitment to democratic principles. In particular, non-NATO participants pledge themselves to work toward democratic control of their armed forces and transparency in national defense planning and budgeting.[42]

The NATO enlargement process has taken these objectives a step further. The 1995 "Study on NATO Enlargement" set forth the following transformational rationales: encouraging and supporting democratic reforms; promoting good-neighborly relations; increasing transparency in defense planning and military budgets; and reinforcing the tendency toward integration and cooperation in Europe based on shared democratic values. NATO has resisted establishing explicit criteria for membership. Nevertheless, successful applicants almost certainly have to be stable democracies. In addition, the prospect of membership provides aspirants with a powerful incentive to resolve conflicts with their neighbors, as exemplified by the successful conclusion of an agreement in 1996 between Hungary and Romania regarding the Hungarian minority in Transylvania after years of bickering.[43] Although some have questioned whether NATO has in fact done anything to advance democratization,[44] membership in the alliance seems certain to lock in the important democratic gains that have been made in Central and Eastern Europe since the end of the Cold War.

In the long term, however, it may be the EU that does the most to eliminate the potential for military conflict in Europe. The EU disposes of unmatched material resources that can be used to promote economic development, internal reform, and external reconciliation in potential or actual trouble spots. A leading example of such an effort is the EU's Stabilisation and Association Process, which offers substantial economic, financial, and technical assistance to five Balkan states in return for their compliance with a variety of conditions regarding political and economic development and regional cooperation.[45]

Additional resources are being devoted to preparing twelve candidate countries for membership. Although these states are already characterized by stable democratic institutions, substantial progress toward the establishment of market economies, and relatively good human rights records, the process of preparing for EU membership entails undertaking internal changes that go far beyond those required by NATO. Once admitted, moreover, new members will find themselves enmeshed in a set of institutional relationships, involving the sacrifice of some national sovereignty, that largely precludes the possibility of and eliminates the utility of resorting to political violence. A further advantage of the EU is that it is not encumbered like NATO by the baggage of the Cold War, allowing it to include among its current candidate members Estonia, Latvia, and Lithuania, all former Soviet republics.

Thus, it seems quite plausible that, within a decade or two, the zone of peace will have expanded to include most of Europe outside of the FSU and even the Baltic states. Most if not all of these states either will be full members of the EU and NATO or will enjoy very close ties with both organizations. With the exception of the remaining areas of the FSU, traditional conflict management activities—early warning, preventive diplomacy, peacekeeping, and so on—will have been rendered largely irrelevant. It can also be reasonably hoped that substantial and growing ties between the inhabitants of this region and their eastern neighbors, especially Russia and Ukraine, will exert pacifying and stabilizing effects on the latter.

Perhaps the biggest remaining question is whether the members of NATO and the EU will have the political will to see this transformational process through to a desirable conclusion. The costs of EU enlargement, while probably manageable, have nevertheless engendered stiff political opposition from many of the domestic actors who stand to lose. The NATO deployments in Bosnia and Kosovo have frequently been criticized for their open-ended nature and the lack of any well-defined exit strategies. And the new Bush administration took office in 2001 having talked in the presidential campaign about establishing a new "division of labor" within NATO, whereby the United States would no longer participate in Balkan peacekeeping operations, a move that many observers feared would prevent the West from achieving its goals in the region and could even pose a serious threat to the alliance itself.[46]

One should not exaggerate the obstacles, however. Despite the criticism directed at the NATO deployments in the Balkans, they have proven remarkably enduring. Certainly, the experience of Bosnia, where alliance forces have been stationed for more than half a decade, suggests that it may be possible to sustain such missions for an extended period of time. And it did not take long for President Bush to affirm the continuing importance of full U.S. participation.[47] Finally, although enlargement of the EU to include states from the former Soviet bloc is not yet a certainty, the organization took the final steps in the process of preparing itself for the acceptance of new members with the approval of Treaty of Nice in late 2000. The completion of the current negotiations on accession now seems to be just a matter of time.

NOTES

I wish to thank Paul Diehl, William Durch, Joseph Lepgold, Robert Pahre, and the participants in the Workshop on Regional Conflict Management held at the University of Illinois at Urbana-Champaign in May 2001 for helpful comments on previous drafts.

1. As discussed below, I define Europe to include much but not all of the former Soviet Union.

2. A useful discussion of collective conflict management can be found in Joseph Lepgold and Thomas G. Weiss, "Collective Conflict Management and Changing World Politics: An Overview," in *Collective Conflict Management and Changing World Politics,* ed. Lepgold and Weiss (Albany: State University of New York Press, 1998).

3. I borrow the term "zone of peace" from Richard H. Ullman, "Enlarging the Zone of Peace," *Foreign Policy,* no. 80 (Fall 1990).

4. This area includes the Transcaucasian republics but not the Central Asian republics of the FSU.

5. A useful survey is Peace Research Institute Oslo (PRIO), *Conflicts in the OSCE Area* (n.d.); available online at www.prio.no/html/osce-contents.asp [accessed 24 August 2002].

6. Technically, Serbia forms part of Yugoslavia, which also includes Montenegro. Because these conflicts involve the Serbs in particular rather than Yugoslavia as a whole, however, direct reference will frequently be made to Serbia.

7. F. Stephen Larrabee, "Long Memories and Short Fuses: Change and Instability in the Balkans," *International Security* 15 (Winter 1990/91): 78.

8. Writing more than a decade ago, Larrabee noted the existence of an important ethnic dimension to this conflict concerning the rights of the Macedonian minority in Greece (Larrabee, "Long Memories and Short Fuses," 76). More recent reports suggest a significant improvement in Greek-Macedonian relations since the mid-1990s, however.

9. Larrabee, "Long Memories and Short Fuses," 74f.

10. Ronald H. Linden, "Putting on Their Sunday Best: Romania, Hungary, and the Puzzle of Peace," *International Studies Quarterly* 44 (March 2000).

11. Renatas Norkus, "Preventing Conflict in the Baltic States: A Success Story That Will Hold?" in *Preventing Violent Conflict: Issues from the Baltic and the Caucasus,* ed. Gianni Bonvicini, Ettore Greco, Bernard von Plate, and Reinhardt Rummel (Baden-Baden: Nomos, 1998).

12. Stuart J. Kaufman, "Spiraling to Ethnic War: Elites, Masses, and Moscow in Moldava's Civil War," *International Security* 21 (Fall 1996).

13. Jessica Eve Stern, "Moscow Meltdown: Can Russia Survive?" *International Security* 18 (Spring 1994).

14. Richard H. Ullman, *Securing Europe* (Princeton, N.J.: Princeton University Press, 1991), chapter 2.

15. Joseph Lepgold, "NATO's Post–Cold War Collective Action Problem," *International Security* 23 (Summer 1998).

16. *Washington Post,* 14 July 1993, A15.

17. Philip G. Roeder, "From Hierarchy to Hegemony: The Post-Soviet Security Complex," in *Regional Orders: Building Security in a New World,* ed. David A. Lake and Patrick M. Morgan (University Park: Pennsylvania State University Press, 1997), 227–29.

18. Russia has been accused of encouraging and assisting separatist movements in Abkhazia and South Ossetia in Georgia and the Dniestr region of Moldova. For an overview of Russia's involvement in Georgia, see S. Neil MacFarlane, "On the Front Lines in the Near Abroad: The CIS and the OSCE in Georgia's Civil Wars," *Third World Quarterly* 18 (1997).

19. The OSCE currently has fifty-five members, including five Central Asian republics.

20. See also Institute for Foreign Policy Analysis, *European Security Institutions: Ready for the Twenty-First Century?* (Dulles, Va.: Brassey's, 2000), 118.

21. Organization for Security and Cooperation in Europe (OSCE), *OSCE Handbook* (n.d.); available online at www.osce.org/publications/handbook/handbook.pdf [accessed 29 August 2002].

22. The term "human dimension" refers to the commitments made by OSCE participating states to ensure full respect for human rights and fundamental freedoms, to abide by the rule of law, to promote the principles of democracy and, in this regard, to build, strengthen, and protect democratic institutions, as well as to promote tolerance throughout the OSCE area. Organization for Security and Cooperation in Europe (*OSCE Handbook*).

23. Poland, Hungary, and the Czech Republic joined in 1999.

24. The Alliance's Strategic Concept, 24 April 1999, available at www.nato.int/docu /pr/1999/p99-065e.htm [accessed 29 August 2002].

25. For further discussion, see John S. Duffield, "NATO's Functions After the Cold War," *Political Science Quarterly* 109 (Winter 1994/95).

26. A good example is Secretary-General Manfred Wörner's role in facilitating the February 1994 NATO decision to impose a heavy weapons exclusion zone around Sarajevo.

27. The five EU members that do not belong to the WEU are Denmark, which is in NATO, and the traditionally neutral Ireland, Finland, Sweden, and Austria.

28. Cologne European Council, Declaration on Strengthening the Common European Policy on Security and Defense, available at http://europa.eu.int/council/off/conclu /june99/annexe_en.htm [accessed 29 August 2002].

29. Western European Union Council of Ministers, Petersberg Declaration, Bonn, 19 June 1992; a summary is available at http://europa.eu.int/scadplus/leg/en/cig/g4000p .htm [accessed 29 August 2002].

30. A principal exception is the EU's small European Community Humanitarian Office (ECHO).

31. Presidency Conclusions, Helsinki European Council, 10 and 11 December 1999, Annex 2 to Annex IV, Presidency Report on Non-Military Crisis Management of the Europe Union, http://europa.eu.int/council/off/conclu/dec99/dec99_en.htm [accessed 29 August 2002].

32. The High Representative also serves as secretary-general of the intergovernmental European Council.

33. Helen Leigh-Phippard, "The Contact Group on (and in) Bosnia," *International Journal* 53 (Spring 1998).

34. Not participating initially were the three Baltic states and Georgia. In late 1993, however, the latter was pressured into joining in return for Russian help in dealing with its internal conflicts.

35. Sergei A. Voitovich, "The Commonwealth of Independent States: An Emerging Institutional Model," *European Journal of International Law* 14 (1999). Not signing were Ukraine, Moldova, Azerbaijan, and Turkmenistan.

36. MacFarlane, "On the Front Lines in the Near Abroad," 521.

37. MacFarlane, "On the Front Lines in the Near Abroad," 512–14, 521.

38. Norkus, "Preventing Conflict in the Baltic States," 153.

39. MacFarlane, "On the Front Lines in the Near Abroad," 510.

40. Organization for Security and Cooperation in Europe, *OSCE Handbook.*

41. Organization for Security and Cooperation in Europe, *OSCE Handbook.*

42. Partnership for Peace Invitation and Partnership for Peace Framework Document, reproduced in North Atlantic Treaty Organization (NATO), *NATO Handbook* (Brussels: NATO Office of Information and Press, 1995).

43. Linden, "Putting on Their Sunday Best." Valuable discussions of NATO enlargement can be found in Sean Lay, *NATO and the Future of European Security* (Lanham, Md.: Rowman & Littlefield, 1998); and David S. Yost, *NATO Transformed: The Alliance's New Roles in International Security* (Washington, D.C.: U.S. Institute of Peace Press, 1998).

44. Dan Reiter, "Why NATO Enlargement Does Not Spread Democracy," *International Security* 25 (Spring 2001).

45. See "The EU and South Eastern Europe," available at http://europa.eu.int/comm/ external_relations/see/intro/index.htm [accessed 29 August 2002].

46. See, for example, "Bush in Kosovo, Tells U.S. Troops Role Is Essential," *New York Times,* 21 October 2000, and "Bush Would Stop U.S. Peacekeeping in Balkan Fights," *New York Times,* 16 January 2001.

47. "Allies, Questioning Bush Stand, Say U.S. Kosovo Role Is Crucial," *New York Times,* 25 July 2001. For a discussion of some of the theoretical grounds for expecting continued close U.S.–European cooperation in security affairs, see John S. Duffield, "Transatlantic Relations after the Cold War: Theory, Evidence, and the Future," *International Studies Perspectives* 2 (Feb. 2001).

Conclusion

Patterns and Discontinuities in Regional Conflict Management

Paul F. Diehl

What may be evident from a review of the regions covered in the previous six chapters is that there are tremendous contextual differences. The "one size fits all" prescriptions for maintaining peace and security do not take into account this degree of variation. Nevertheless, each regional context is not wholly unique, that is, lacking any commonalities. Indeed, a number of threads exist across the divergent threats, responses, and effectiveness in each region. In this concluding chapter, I attempt to identify both the commonalities and the discontinuities in regional conflict management. Culled from the six case study chapters, the focus is first on the kinds of threats faced in different parts of the world. A second concern is with the different types of conflict management responses to those threats and the types of actors that carry them out. Finally is a brief, comparative assessment of conflict management in different regions and the general conditions associated with its success.

THREATS

During the Cold War, many threats to regional security were indistinct from or subsumed under the superpower competition. Thus, at the global level, nuclear deterrence dominated strategic planning. Concern for regional security was disproportionately focused on Europe and the balance of conventional forces between NATO and the Warsaw Pact. To the extent that other regions were significant, their relation to the superpowers defined their salience. Threats were defined in terms of which regime would support which superpower; much of Africa and Asia became battlegrounds for the configurations of patron-client relationships. Other areas, such as the Middle East, saw greater direct involvement by the superpowers. Threats in those areas involved the potential for violent conflict to spill over to neighboring states and possibly lead to military intervention by the superpowers on opposite sides. The end of the Cold War has led to some significant changes in security threats, yet at the same time, some kinds of challenges seem timeless, transcending different historical eras.

Throughout the Cold War and well before, pairs of states engaged in traditional interstate rivalries. These are characterized by frequent militarized confrontations over a broad period of time. Regional wars and most serious threats to peace seemed to coalesce around these rivalries. For example, Buzan defined the security complex for South Asia as revolving around the India-Pakistan rivalry.[1] We know that such rivalries, often labeled as "enduring rivalries" by the scholarly literature, are the greatest threats to peace.[2] We also know that these rivalries are highly resistant to resolution, and not even easily managed.[3] Perhaps not surprisingly, then, long-standing rivalries persist as significant regional security threats. In South Asia, the India-Pakistan rivalry appears as strong as ever and is the centerpiece of security in that region; as Bajpai points out, however, this is not the only serious conflict in the region and not every one of those conflicts revolves around the India-Pakistan rivalry. Similarly, the multifaceted Arab-Israeli rivalry (in actually, several intertwined rivalries) represents the greatest threat to peace in that region. This rivalry has evolved over time, with Israel coming to various degrees of accommodation with some of her neighbors, including Jordan and Egypt. Nevertheless, the dispute between the Palestinians and the Israelis is at the heart of many regional rivalries. Clearly, however, not every security threat in that region is linked to the Arab-Israeli one; Arab states have clashed repeatedly among themselves. Similarly, the China-Taiwan and North Korea–South Korea rivalries still simmer in the Asian region, more than fifty years since their onset. Although the end of the Cold War has produced many effects, some long-standing rivalries persist and remain the biggest obstacles to regional peace.

Other regions of the world are less defined by one or more central rivalries. Traditionally, Europe revolved around the U.S.–Soviet rivalry, but no longer has its security arrangements organized around that competition. As we note below, security threats in today's Europe are fundamentally different than in the most recent era. Africa and Latin America certainly had traditional rivalries (e.g., Argentina-Chile and South Africa and her neighbors respectively), but these had more limited negative externalities. In most or all cases, such rivalries have largely faded over time in salience (if not completely ended). This is not to say that those regions have no strong security concerns, only that they are not framed in terms of enduring interstate rivalries.

Related to traditional rivalries is the competition for regional dominance or hegemony.[4] In the European theater, this was a major source of war for centuries. Such competition has been largely muted there. Interlocking alliance ties and the evolution of the European Union have lessened desires for regional dominance. To the extent that such competition still exists, it is largely played out in the economic and political institutions of the European Union. In contrast, the East Asian region still has one of the hegemonic competitions from what seems like a bygone era. Japan and China remain competitors, although their quest for regional influence may now be fought on economic grounds rather than purely security ones. Adding to this is the continuing influence of the United States and the rise of Chinese power in the region. With respect to the latter, however, Cha is quick to note that there is no consensus among analysts that China is seeking regional dominance or that its pursuit of hegemony is the major security threat facing that region. Indeed, for some countries, a resurgent and rearmed Japan would be perceived as a greater threat to regional stability. In the Middle East, Arab states (traditionally Iran, Iraq, Egypt, and Syria) may be somewhat united in their support of the Palestinian cause, but still see each other as rivals for pan-Arab influence or leadership.

Another traditional source of conflict has been territorial disputes, in which states fight over the possession of a piece of land, usually geographically contiguous to both sides. Especially dangerous are those disputes that involve territory that is valued for its intangible rather than tangible qualities; that is, religious, ethnic, and historical claims to a territory make it more difficult to find compromise positions than to those territorial disputes over resources or defense concerns.[5] Some boundary disputes persist in Latin America, but most of these are of the less salient variety. One of the reasons that Latin America is alleged to be a "zone of peace" is that it largely settled its borders by the end of the nineteenth century.[6] The same cannot be said for all the other regions of the world. Africa still suffers from the results of the 1885 Berlin Conference in which its colonial borders were drawn without reference to historical delineation or the groups living within various territories. This has been somewhat mitigated, however, by the agreement among African leaders around the time of independence that state borders would not be altered by military force. South Asia also must deal with territorial disputes, most notably the dispute over Kashmir and the problems along the Indian-Chinese border. To the extent that territorial disputes arise, they do so in perhaps the one unifying threat to peace—ethnic or identity conflicts, which appear to transcend regions.

With the end of the Cold War, one might have expected that some of the elements of the superpower competition would be replicated on the regional level.[7] To some extent this is true, but perhaps not as much as might have been predicted. Issues of nuclear deterrence are salient in South Asia.[8] Weapons of mass destruction also appear in the discussion of the Middle Eastern security. Yet surprisingly, the authors of the other case study chapters conspicuously avoid mentioning these strategic concerns. Recall that for more than four decades, European security was intimately related to nuclear issues.

If there are unifying threats to regional peace, with the exception of Latin America, they appear in the form of the interrelated problems of ethnic conflict and "weak states." The rise of ethnic or nationalist conflicts in the post–Cold War era have been much documented and discussed. In the context of regional security, identity crises appear in five of the six regions. In the Middle East chapter, Miller gives the problem of the state-nation disconnect or "imbalance" central attention. This can take many forms. Nations may exist without states. The obvious case is the Palestinians, but this is a similar problem for the Kurds (spread across four different states). Other regions have similar problems. There also exist "states without nations," the inverse of the former. There, states must grapple with ethnic diversity in their midst. Newly independent republics of the former Soviet Union seem plagued by this problem.

In part, the result of identity conflicts, but at the same time exacerbating them, is the presence of weak states in several regions. Most notable is Africa, as Zartman discusses how states, such as Somalia and the Congo (Zaire), are not just weak, but have effectively collapsed. Some states may also be limited in their ability to control peripheral areas, even if they are strong in core regions. For example, Yugoslavian control over Montenegro is somewhat limited, and Moldova has difficulty policing the area surrounding its border with Ukraine. Weak states are breeding grounds for internal instability. Strong governments have the capacity to serve the needs of their peoples. At the same time, even less benign strong governments have the capacity to keep order. In contrast, weak or collapsed states can neither provide basic services nor repress competing groups effectively. In the context of weak states, fragmentation of power occurs, and various groups arise to fill the void at the top. In these conditions, violent competition between these groups (often ethnically based because identity is an effective mobilization tool) occurs.

The reason that ethnic conflicts and weak states are key problems for regional conflict management goes beyond their frequency in the post–Cold War era, although that itself would merit attention.[9] Rather, it is because these conflicts have significant negative externalities, perhaps well beyond those associated with traditional rivalries or competitions for regional hegemony. Historically, internal conflicts were not considered in the purview of the international community, but rather something to be dealt with solely by the state itself. This represented a "hard shell" view of state sovereignty. Not only has that view of sovereignty softened considerably, but ethnic conflicts and weak state fallouts have had direct effects that are not confined to the borders of the affected states. Most obviously, internal fighting can cross state borders, with groups operating out of bases on the other side of national boundaries. Kashmiri rebels use bases in Pakistan, and Palestinian groups have sought sanctuary in southern Lebanon for decades. These are just two of the most prominent examples. In addition, ethnic conflicts and weak states have contributed to greater prospects for intervention by neighboring states. The Congo is the most egregious case of direct intervention into a civil conflict; there a number of neighboring states sent troops to fight for and against various Congolese factions. Even without direct intervention, neighboring states and others may sponsor covert or semicovert actions (e.g., Pakistan in Kashmir, Taliban-dominated Afghanistan in some of its neighbors) as well as funnel arms and supplies to groups in those countries. Thus, what may be an internal conflict has strong implications beyond the borders, and resolving the internal conflict requires some measure of looking beyond just the state involved, but to the region as a whole. Even when regional intervention is not a problem, there exists the possibility of a "demonstration effect"; this occurs when groups in a neighboring state are influenced by the actions or success of groups to begin their attempts at challenging the extant government. Most commonly, this arises with respect to ethnic groups seeking autonomy or their own states, although at least one study questions the pull of this factor in stimulating conflict.[10] Regardless, leaders in neighboring states believe that such a "domino effect" is possible, and accordingly have strong interests in seeing conflicts in their region resolved.

Finally, it is clear that the regional security agenda has several items that represent new problems or those that had previously not been conceptualized as *security* problems worthy of regional attention. As noted by Shaw, this is most evident in Latin America, where issues of democratization and market reform became defined in security terms. The failure of some states to democratize or consolidate their democracies became perceived as a security threat to other states in the region. Also in Latin America, drug enforcement and eradication also became serious security issues as drug warlords acquired military power and threatened the stability of states that opposed their operations. In other areas, such as the Middle East, refugees had security as well as humanitarian implications. In addition, international terrorism, even before the 11 September attacks, appeared as a regional security problem. In the aftermath of those attacks, terrorist networks became a prime concern for several regions. These redefinitions of security threats, beyond traditional concerns, are consistent with a trend toward a broader conceptualization of security that has encompassed "human security" and "environmental security"[11] among other elements.

In summary, regional security threats are a mix of the old and the new. No single configuration of threats fits all regions. Still, there are some common elements across many regions including traditional rivalries and ethnic/weak state induced conflicts. Notably, Latin America and Europe stand out from other regions. The former seems largely insulated from traditional security threats and has been at the forefront of redefining security to include a broader range of issues. Europe has apparently moved away from its hundreds of years of history as being the focal point for security concerns in the world. It is perhaps this region that has been most affected by the end of the Cold War. To the extent that ethnic conflict and other security threats exist there, they are geographically skewed, concentrated mainly in the areas of the former Yugoslavia and former Soviet Union respectively.

CONFLICT MANAGEMENT RESPONSES

As noted above, there is some evidence for convergence in the kinds of threats faced by different regions. With respect to the kinds of conflict management responses, however, there seems to be dramatic variations across different parts of the globe. Even when common mechanisms exist (for example, appeals to international organizations), the salience, operations, and strategies can vary tremendously across regions. The differences in conflict management responses cannot be wholly or even partly explained by reference to the regional variations in threats. The divergence across regions is greater with respect to responses than threats. Furthermore, even when similar threats exist, regions may pursue very different responses.

During the Cold War, a series of interlocking alliances was the mechanism for promoting peace and security. Such alliances relied on traditional deterrence and defense logics, and covered many, but not all parts of the world. U.S.-centered alliances were found in the Pacific, Southeast Asia, North Asia, the Middle East, and Europe. Correspondingly, the Soviet Union not only had alliance partners in Eastern Europe (the Warsaw Pact), but also with other states in various parts of the world as well (e.g., Vietnam, Cuba). Over time, most of these withered away with the primary exception of American ties to Japan and Korea in East Asia and, of course, the NATO alliance. At present, our authors attach varying importance to alliances as a conflict management mechanism. At one extreme, traditional alliances and deterrence are nonexistent in Africa. These were perhaps less significant in the Cold War era anyway, although there were a number of patron-client relationships between the superpowers and local states. At the other extreme, alliance structures are the defining mechanism in East Asia, and those alliances have generally been bilateral ones. In many ways, the various alliance configurations look remarkably similar to those that existed in previous decades. Perhaps this is not surprising given that many of the rivalries and threats to regional peace (e.g., China-Taiwan, South Korea–North Korea) have persisted over long periods. Still, Cha indicates that both Japan and South Korea have incentives to move the East Asian alliance structure from one based on bilateral interests to more of a "multilateral security dialogue." Thus, it is not clear whether some of the last vestiges of the Cold War alliance structure will survive intact for an extended period.[12]

Although Europe traditionally relied on traditional alliances, this has become less so over time and alliance structures have morphed their functions over time. Much has been written about NATO losing its main raison d'être with the demise of the Soviet Union and the Warsaw Pact.[13] Yet the organization persists and has adopted new conflict management functions beyond deterrence. Most notable has been its assumption of peacekeeping duties in Bosnia, and its offensive use of force in Kosovo. NATO has also evolved into a consultative and diplomatic body, often resembling an international organization more than a defensive military alliance.

Alliances play a very different kind of role in the Middle East. One might say that their effect is less as a facilitator of conflict management than as a barrier to it. The alliance between the United States and Israel has certainly contributed to Israeli deterrence, but at the same time has complicated American attempts at diplomacy. On the one hand, the American-Israeli alliance means that Arab states and groups will always view the United States suspiciously; American conflict management initiatives may be quickly dismissed by some of the Arab world. On the other hand, almost paradoxically, that alliance provides the leverage under which the United States can bring Israel to the bargaining table and extract concessions. While criticizing the United States with one hand, some Arab states (and indeed the PLO as well) have welcomed (even demanded) U.S. mediation and intervention as the only vehicle to forge peace with the Israelis. The more informal, and sometimes shifting, alliances between Arab states have constrained individual decision making, with Arab unity becoming a paramount goal relative to peace with Israel.

In the remaining regions, traditional alliances just do not have much significance. Historically, these have been quite limited in Latin America (except for the Rio Pact, which is best understood as being subsumed under the Organization of American States). Africa has similarly not been a region that has depended heavily on military alliances; indeed, the OAU prohibited military alliances as part of its original compact. As Bajpai notes, South Asian alliances have largely broken down with the end of the Cold War; once-strong Indian ties with the Soviet Union no longer exist, and Pakistan has gone through cycles of close relations and hostility with the United States and to a lesser extent with China.

Overall, it is too early to dismiss alliances (and their reliance on deterrence) as mechanisms for regional conflict management in the post–Cold War world. Still they are considerably less important than in previous eras. Furthermore, they appear less well-suited or designed to dealing with many of the threats to regional security outlined in the previous section.

An alternative to traditional alliance configurations (often bilateral) is addressing regional security concerns in the context of international organizations or other formal multilateral arrangements. In half of the regions under examination, regional international organizations were very active in conflict management, although in vastly different ways. In Africa, the overarching regional organization, the Organization of African Unity, is notoriously weak. Indeed, its members deliberately designed the organization that way, giving it little autonomous leadership, few formal institutional components, and limited resources under which to have an impact. Instead, subregional organizations, such as the Economic Community of West African States (ECOWAS), have filled some of the void. Some of these are economically oriented organizations that have assumed security roles.[14] In contrast, the OAS has played an increasingly central role in conflict management efforts in the Western Hemisphere. Its early efforts were perhaps not impressive, but the organization was actually much more involved and ultimately successful than typically given credit for.[15] More recently, the organization has become the primary forum for hemispheric initiatives in the area of peace and security. The OAS has generally operated on the basis of consensus, and there the organization has been more involved with diplomatic effects at conflict management than with more coercive mechanisms (e.g., sanctions, military actions).

The European region is perhaps the most notable for the involvement of international organizations. Conflict management there is a product of multiple and overlapping (although not fully duplicative) regional organizations; Duffield nicely illustrates the different organizations and functions in table 8.4. Clearly NATO has been a bulwark of regional security for five decades, but there are other organizations taking on important security roles as well. Most notably, the Organization for Security and Cooperation in Europe (OSCE), which previously served as a bridge between East and West, has expanded beyond human rights concerns to encompass special efforts at ethnic conflict management and the like.

The remaining regions are similar generally in their lack of reliance on organizations for conflict management. Because East Asia has so heavily relied on traditional alliances, there is no real multipurpose or security-centered organization to perform conflict management functions. Only APEC is an organization that ties together all the states in the region. Yet this organization is still loosely constructed, has concentrated on economic matters (and not yet morphed to security concerns), and indeed includes a very broad membership, extending well beyond the East Asian region.

Similarly, in South Asia, regional organizations play little role in conflict management. The most prominent organization dedicated to regional matters, the South Asian Association for Regional Cooperation (SAARC), has an explicit provision in its charter prohibiting its involvement in bilateral and "contentious" issues. Until that is altered or new structures are created, it is hard to envision any important role for regional organizations there any time soon. Finally, the Middle East has the League of Arab States, an organization that includes collective security provisions in its charter. Yet the composition and orientation of this organization has precluded any meaningful role for it in the Arab-Israeli conflict; the exclusion of Iran and Turkey is important in this regard, but clearly not as important as the exclusion of Israel from membership. The endorsement in 2002 of a Saudi Arabian peace plan was perhaps its first and only effort at seeking to moderate that conflict. Unfortunately, the organization has been equally marginalized in mediating inter-Arab disputes.[16] It did not play a leading role in the Iran-Iraq war or several other serious clashes, largely because its membership was so divided over which sides to support and what actions to take. Similar problems are evident with the Gulf Cooperation Council (GCC). Miller correctly notes that neither Middle East organization has a "full" membership of key players, and therefore is unable to play an important conflict management role.

With the relative weakness of regional organizations in some regions, one might have expected the United Nations to fill the institutional void. Certainly, the United Nations remains the primary organizing agency for peacekeeping operations.[17] That organization has sent operations to East Timor, Kosovo, Sierra Leone, and other hot spots in recent years. Despite some prognostications, regional organizations have not replaced the UN in the peacekeeping realm, although regional peacekeeping operations are more common now than they were in previous decades. Beyond peacekeeping, however, states have not frequently resorted to the UN as a forum for regional conflict management. The UN, except through International Atomic Energy Agency (IAEA) inspections in North Korea, has not been a player in East Asia. Much of this may be a legacy of the UN central role in the Korean War, which complicates its involvement in any security concern involving the Korean peninsula. The recognition of Taiwan for China's permanent Security Council seat until 1971 also raises China's suspicions about impartiality of the organization. In the Middle East, UN resolutions are frequent, but carry little beyond normative weight (if that). Although the UN and its network may be critical in humanitarian assistance, it does not play a central conflict managing role in Africa (despite diplomatic efforts in the Congo and elsewhere), and its presence is minimal in Latin America and most of Europe, the latter two of which have their own well-developed institutional mechanisms.

The most common regional conflict management approaches fell into the category of peacemaking or diplomacy. Yet even with this shared framework, there was significant variation across regions. Multilateral diplomacy, outside of the context of regional organizations, is still possible. Africa has attempted this strategy in the Congo and elsewhere. This seems particularly appropriate for dealing with conflict that involves a great number of neighboring states. Even well-developed international organizations may have difficulty when members fall on opposite sides of the conflict; less formal or ad hoc multilateral diplomatic mechanisms may be needed.

The absence of strong international organizations has led to more bilateral diplomacy in East Asia, the Middle East, and South Asia. A modified form of bilateralism is evident in North Asia. There, North Korea and South Korea have only recently had direct relations with one another. Historically, diplomacy has been triangular, with the United States playing a central role in the negotiations. Virtually all the diplomatic breakthroughs in the Arab-Israeli conflict have been done bilaterally. Israel has made peace with some of her neighbors (Egypt, Jordan) through largely bilateral efforts (although clearly mediated by third parties). Similarly, diplomacy in South Asia has bypassed international forums and has instead concentrated on direct dealings between states, even between hostile rivals such as India and Pakistan. Interestingly, South Asia has the scene of Track II diplomacy, indicating that state-to-state contacts are not the only mechanisms for conflict management. Still, this remains largely an exception rather than a significant occurrence across regions.

Other peacemaking approaches include the resort to legal mechanisms and institutions. This was not frequent in most regions. In Latin America, however, states have often resorted to international arbitration in order to solve territorial disputes.[18] Yet in most cases, international legal structures do not exist in other regions; Europe may be an exception with its developed European Union system. Even when mechanisms exist, however, states have been reluctant to use them and unwilling to create ad hoc legal tribunals. Latin America has also been the region in which economic sanctions have been adopted (and in some cases only threatened) in order to promote conflict management. This has not been the case in other areas, except as symbolic actions against a given state in the region (e.g., Arab states boycott of Israel or further back in history, OAU sanctions against apartheid in South Africa).

Finally, diplomatic efforts have sometimes involved third parties from outside the region. Most notably, the United States has been a central player in the Middle East. It is widely acknowledged that only the United States can play a viable mediator role in the conflict between the Israelis and the Palestinians. Nevertheless, this ignores that the Oslo Accords were actually facilitated by the intervention of the Norwegian foreign ministry. The United States has played similar diplomatic roles in Europe, the latter most evident by the American role in facilitating the Dayton Accords ending the war in Bosnia and its central role in the Good Friday Accords between disputing parties in Northern Ireland.

Regardless of the kind of conflict management response, regional stability may be dependent on the behavior of leading states or hegemons. Either through direct military actions, leading peacekeeping missions, or playing central diplomatic roles, hegemons may be the linchpins upon which regional conflict management hinges. Of course, the influence of hegemons can be either positive or negative in the occurrence and management of conflict. Snyder identifies two different types of hegemony that may contribute to regional order.[19] Unilateral hegemony, as the label implies, involves a single leading state exercising decisive influence over a region. Multilateral hegemony involves several leading states who share common outlooks and strategies, with the Concert of Europe being the most frequently cited example. The latter is not evident in our case study chapters, but there is significant evidence for the importance of the former.

When one thinks of hegemons, generally global powers come to mind. China has attempted to assert itself as a peace broker in South Asia, although its claims to the Spratley Islands and its formerly closer relationship with Pakistan have complicated these efforts. Russia has been a leading player in the area of the former Soviet Union and the surrounding areas. It is difficult to think of any regional order in that part of the world without a significant military and political role by Russia.[20] In Latin America, one might have expected to draw similar conclusions about regional conflict management efforts and hegemony, given the U.S. predominance in the area. Yet, the United States has historically undergone active and passive periods in the organization's handling of crises in the region. Most importantly, it is evident that the United States, while certainly influential, cannot dominate or dictate policy in the OAS.[21] Although the United States plays a significant role in European conflict management, that influence has been increasingly challenged through extant organizations as those institutions have become more autonomous (and divorced from American strategic concerns) over time. Hegemons can also exist on a subregional level as well. Zartman notes that several African management initiatives have been the tools of regional hegemonic states (e.g., Nigeria) more often that not. This is especially the case with respect to peace enforcement activities.

EFFECTIVENESS

The ultimate test of conflict management responses is how well they actually work. In attempting to generalize across regions, one encounters the inherent problem that different regions face different magnitudes of threats. Indeed, the success of Europe in regional conflict management is attributed by Duffield partly to the lower levels of threat present in that region. Nevertheless, the explanation that limited threats lead to success begs the question of why some regions have such limited threats to begin with. Certainly, part of the answer is the success of previous conflict management efforts, and then we have come full circle in our explanations. Despite the problem of circularity in logic, there are some common elements in regional conflict management success and failure.

One of the ways to consider the conditions for successful regional conflict management is through the theoretical lenses of a "security community," a concept first put forward by Karl Deutsch almost half a century ago.[22] A pluralistic security community is a group of states that shares fundamental values and conforms their behaviors to certain principles. Such a community is dedicated to peaceful relations, such that war between them is largely unthinkable. No region has probably reached the level of a true pluralistic security community.[23] Even the geographic area defined by the European Union may fall short of the ideal security community, as there are some disagreements over security policies (illustrated by disagreements over the breakup of the former Yugoslavia). Nevertheless, the chapters here point out the conditions that are associated with the development of security communities and successful conflict management, even if not all are present in every region.[24]

Across all regions, strong commitment to collective goods and the political will to action are associated with conflict management success. This again runs the risk of tautology, but there are several dimensions of this commitment and will. The first is a shared sense of norms among the states in the region. This is generally the basis for security communities cited by constructivists.[25] Within both Latin America and Europe, and to a lesser extent Asia, there are fundamental agreements on the rules of the game. Perhaps the strongest illustration of this is in with respect to the norm of democracy in Latin America.[26] When President Chavez was briefly removed from office in 2002 by the Venezuelan military, it was pressure from members of the Organization of American States that helped restored his democratically elected government. In Europe, there is a similar consensus on democratic governance as well as a shared sense of human rights standards; indeed, democratic government and observance of certain human rights are prerequisites for European Union membership. Of course, the emphasis on democracy means that the "democratic peace" may be operative between members of the region or community, and therefore some significant threats of interstate war are obviated. In the context of shared consensus over values and principles, it is perhaps not surprising that diplomatic initiatives are most effective in conflict management.

Perhaps also reflecting normative consensus, developed institutional mechanisms are necessary to coordinate regional behavior and facilitate conflict management. Developed institutions not only coordinate action, they often also provide resources to conflict management efforts. The failure of regional conflict management in Africa can be traced, in part, to the limited institutional development there and the lack of resources (money, troops, etc.) for conflict management. Similarly, South Asia and the Middle East's problems with conflict are associated with weak or nonexistent institutions, although it is less clear there how much explanatory power follows from this observation. In contrast, Europe has an abundance of resources and many different structures. Of course, Europe's strengths are not without drawbacks; the region does suffer from some duplication and buck-passing among its institutions. Combined with democracy and some trade interdependence, international institutions are vital in creating "virtuous circles" around which community members can interact and resolve differences peacefully.[27]

Beyond norms and institutions, the third element of commitment and will is the support of key regional or extraregional states. This is similar to realist formulations[28] that point to American hegemony for the creation of security communities, although our findings suggest a much broader conception. For the area of the former Soviet Union, it is Russia that will largely define the success of conflict management efforts there. In the Western Hemisphere, the United States still plays a vital role. Chinese designs on East Asia, benign or hostile, will also significantly affect relations in that region. When these states contribute to regional action and promote conflict management, it is much more likely to be successful.

There are certainly other elements of regional security communities that are not addressed here, including the impact of economic interdependence. Nevertheless, it is clear that we are far from the ideal of a pluralist security community on a worldwide or even regional basis. One might expect that the variation in threats, responses, and success that exists across regions will continue to a large degree in the future. In that sense, any attempts to generalize about conflict management must take into account the essential contextual elements that are largely defined by region.

NOTES

1. Barry Buzan, *People, States, and Fear* (Boulder, Colo.: Lynne Rienner, 1983).

2. See Paul F. Diehl and Gary Goertz, *War and Peace in International Rivalry* (Ann Arbor: University of Michigan Press, 2000).

3. Jacob Bercovitch and Paul F. Diehl, "Conflict Management of Enduring Rivalries: Frequency, Timing, and Short Term Impact of Mediation." *International Interactions* 22 (1997): 299–320.

4. Indeed, such competition is defined as a type of rivalry by William Thompson, "Principal Rivalries," *Journal of Conflict Resolution* 39 (1995): 195–223.

5. Paul Hensel, "Territory: Theory and Evidence on Geography and Conflict," in *What Do We Know About War?* ed. John Vasquez (Lanham, Md.: Rowman and Littlefield, 2000), 57–84.

6. Arie Kacowicz, *Zones of Peace in the Third World: South America and West Africa in Comparative Perspective* (Albany: SUNY Press, 1998).

7. For example, see the application of power transition theory to regional conflicts in Douglas Lemke, *Regions of War and Peace* (Cambridge: Cambridge University Press, 2002).

8. Devin Hagerty, *The Consequences of Nuclear Proliferation: Lessons from South Asia* (Cambridge: MIT Press, 1998).

9. Peter Wallensteen and Margareta Sollenberg, "Armed Conflict, 1989–2000," *Journal of Peace Research* 38 (2001): 629–48.

10. Stephen Saideman, "Is Pandora's Box Half Empty or Half Full? The Limited Virulence of Secessionism and the Domestic Sources of Disintegration," in *The International Spread of Ethnic Conflict: Fear, Diffusion and Escalation*, ed. David Lake and Donald Rothchild (Princeton, N.J.: Princeton University Press, 1998), 127–50.

11. For example, see Thomas Homer-Dixon, *Environment, Scarcity, and Violence* (Princeton, N.J.: Princeton University Press, 1999).

12. This is not to say that the East Asian alliances will completely disintegrate. Rather, they may be subject to modification. For a strong argument for the continuing importance of such alliances, see Joint Working Group, *New Frontiers for U.S.–Japan Security Relations*, Policy Paper (Washington, D.C.: Atlantic Council, 2002).

13. For an analysis of changes in NATO, see Joseph Lepgold, "NATO's Post–Cold War Collective Action Problem," *International Security* 23 (1998): 78–106.

14. Katherine Powers, "International Institutions, Trade, and Conflict: African Regional Trade Agreements from 1950–1992" (Ph.D. dissertation, Ohio State University, 2001).

15. Carolyn Shaw, "Institutional Limitations on Hegemonic Influence in International Organizations: Conflict Resolution in the Organization of American States, 1948–1989" (Ph.D. dissertation, University of Texas, 2000).

16. For its role in inter-Arab conflicts, see Ahmed Ali Salem, "Contending IR Theories over Regional Organizations: Roles of the League of Arab States in Inter-Arab Security Crisis," paper presented at the annual meeting of the International Studies Association-Midwest, St. Louis, 2001.

17. For a list of past and present UN peacekeeping operations, see www.un.org/Depts/dpko/dpko/ops.htm [accessed 29 August 2002].

18. An analysis of resort to legal and quasi-legal mechanisms to resolve territorial disputes in Latin America is provided in Beth Simmons, "See You in Court? The Appeal to Quasi-Judicial Legal Processes in the Settlement of Territorial Disputes," in *A Road Map to War: Territorial Dimensions of International Conflict*, ed. Paul F. Diehl (Nashville, Tenn.: Vanderbilt University Press, 1999), 205–37.

19. Jack Snyder, "Military Force and Regional Order," in *Coping with Conflict After the Cold War*, ed. Edward Kolodziej and Roger Kanet (Baltimore: Johns Hopkins University Press, 1996), 291–308.

20. Alexander Kozemiakin and Roger Kanet, "Russia as a Regional Peacekeeper," in *Resolving Regional Conflicts,* ed. Roger Kanet (Urbana: University of Illinois Press, 1998), 225–39.

21. Shaw, "Institutional Limitations on Hegemonic Influence in International Organizations."

22. Karl Deutsch et al., *Political Community and the North Atlantic Area* (Princeton, N.J.: Princeton University Press, 1957). See also Emmanuel Adler and Michael Barnett, eds., *Security Communities* (Cambridge: Cambridge University Press, 1998).

23. There are some lesser forms of a security community. The hierarchy of these forms, with security community, at the top of the ladder are discussed in Edward Kolodziej, "Modelling International Security," in *Resolving Regional Conflicts,* ed. Kanet, 11–40.

24. For an excellent review of the different theoretical approaches as they relate to the conditions for a security community, as well as the author's own reformulation, see Robert Jervis, "Theories of War in an Era of Leading Power Peace," *American Political Science Review* 96 (2002): 1–14.

25. Jervis, "Theories of War in an Era of Leading Power Peace," 1–14.

26. Dexter Boniface, "Is There a Democratic Norm in the Americas? An Analysis of the Organization of American States," *Global Governance* 8 (2002).

27. Bruce Russett and John Oneal, *Triangulating Peace* (New York: W.W. Norton, 2001).

28. Jervis, "Theories of War in an Era of Leading Power Peace."

Index

About the Contributors

Kanti Bajpai is professor of international politics in the School of International Studies, Jawaharlal Nehru University.

Victor D. Cha is associate professor of government and holds the D. S. Song–Korea Foundation endowed chair in the School of Foreign Service at Georgetown University.

Paul F. Diehl is professor of political science and University "Distinguished Teacher/Scholar" at the University of Illinois at Urbana-Champaign.

John S. Duffield is associate professor of political science at Georgia State University.

Joseph Lepgold was associate professor of government at Georgetown University at the time of his death in December 2001.

Benjamin Miller is a faculty member at Haifa University, Israel. He was a visiting professor of international relations in the Department of Political Science at Duke University from 2000–2002.

Carolyn M. Shaw is assistant professor of political science at Wichita State University.

I. William Zartman is the Jacob Blaustein Professor of International Organizations and Conflict Resolution, and director of conflict management studies at the Paul H. Nitze School of Advanced International Studies of Johns Hopkins University in Baltimore, Maryland.